korean
war
almanac

korean war almanac

HARRY G. SUMMERS, JR.
Colonel of Infantry

Facts On File
New York • Oxford • Sydney

KOREAN WAR ALMANAC

Facts On File, Inc.	Facts On File Limited	Facts On File Pty Ltd
460 Park Avenue South	Collins Street	Talavera & Khartoum Rds
New York NY 10016	Oxford OX4 1XJ	North Ryde NSW 2113
USA	United Kingdom	Australia

Text design by Ron Monteleone
Jacket design by Catherine Hyman
Composition by Facts On File, Inc.
Printed in the United States of America

Quality Printing and Binding by:
R.R. Donnelley & Sons Company
1009 Sloan Street
Crawfordsville, IN 47933 U.S.A.

In Honor of

General Matthew B. Ridgway

By his will and strength of character alone he transformed an entire Army

It is the impact of the ebbing of moral and physical strength, of the heart-rendering spectacle of the dead and wounded, that the commander has to withstand—first in himself, and then in all those who, directly or indirectly, have entrusted him with their thoughts and feelings, hopes and fears. As each man's strength gives out, as it no longer responds to his will, the inertia of the whole gradually comes to rest on the commander's will alone. The ardor of his spirit must rekindle the flame of purpose in all others; his inward fire must revive their hope …

Such are the burdens in battle that the commander's courage and strength of will must overcome if he hopes to achieve outstanding success. The burdens increase with the number of men in his command, and therefore the higher the position, the greater the strength of character he needs to bear the mounting load.

Carl von Clausewitz, *On War*

CONTENTS

MAPS

MAP SYMBOLS

Symbols within a rectangle—an oval "tank tread" for armor; a "cannon ball" for field artillery; crossed "pack straps" for infantry etc.—show unit type. Symbols above the rectangle—lines for company, battalion and regiment; x's for brigade, division, corps and army—indicate unit size.

Company, troop or battery
("A" Company, 78th Tank Battalion shown) . . . A ⬭ 78

Battalion or squadron
(52d Field Artillery Battalion shown) . . . . ▪ 52

Regiment or group
(21st Infantry Regiment shown) . . . . ⊠ 21

Brigade
(Turkish Brigade shown) . . . . ⊠ TURKEY

Division
(24th Infantry Division shown) . . . . ⊠ 24

Corps
(IX Corps shown) IX

Army
(Eighth U.S. Army shown) . . . . EIGHT

ACKNOWLEDGMENTS

Many people contributed to the writing of this almanac. First among them are those with whom I served in the 24th Infantry Division during the war, including Norbert Abraham, J.C. Bridges, Chuck Starring and all the other tankers of "A" Company, 78th Heavy Tank Battalion (later Heavy Tank Company, 21st Infantry Regiment), especially our company commander, Lieutenant Leonard Gewin, who was killed in action in the opening days of the war and our first sergeant, the late Robert W. Stephenson of Turtle Creek, Pennsylvania. Then there are the "Gimlets" of "L" Company, 21st Infantry Regiment, including my company commander, Lieutenant Elmer Gainok, platoon leaders Volney Warner and Task Force Smith veteran Carl F. Bernard, platoon Sergeant (later Colonel) Mike Thiel, and infantrymen Hugh Brown, Frank Ivy, Roy Powers and others who still gather each year to keep fresh the bonds that got us through the war alive.

Writing almost four decades after the fact, to accurately portray what the Korean War was all about would be impossible without enormous help. The advice and support of those responsible for the official histories of the war was particularly invaluable. Much thanks goes to Colonel Rod Paschall and his staff at the Army Military History Institute at Carlisle Barracks for the loan of reference material and for assistance in obtaining Korean War photographs with which to illustrate this work. And much thanks as well to Colonel John Cash and others in the Army's Center of Military History in Washington, including Sandy Cochran and Morris MacGregor, who also helped with reference material, facts and figures.

The chief of Air Force history, Dr. Richard H. Kohn, and Sheldon A. Goldberg of his staff helped make the Air Force role in the Korea War more understandable, as did Dr. Ronald Spector, then Director of the Naval Historical Center, when it came to naval matters. Mrs. Ariana Jacob of his staff went out of her way to obtain biographical information on Korean War naval commanders. As always, Brigadier General Edwin H. Simmons, director of Marine Corps History, was quick to provide encouragement and support.

Others who lent a helping hand include retired Colonel Dwight (Hooper) Adams, a fellow Korean War "Gimlet," who provided material from the Army War College course he teaches on the Korean War; retired Colonel William P. Snyder (a Vietnam War "Gimlet" who commanded the Third Battalion, 21st Infantry there) who provided material from the Air War College class he teaches on the Korean War; Kristine Wilcox, assistant editor of the *Naval Institute Proceedings*, who helped sort out what warships were deployed in Korean waters; and William Jayne at the Veterans Administration for the statistical data on Korean War veterans.

Theodore P. Zeigler, my first sergeant during a postwar tour in Korea with the 7th Infantry Division, provided material on the Rakkasans of the 187th Airborne RCT, with whom he served during the war, and Kenwood Ross of the 24th Infantry Division Association provided help, advice and encouragement. Thanks also to my daughter-in-law, Army Chief Warrant Officer Kathy Summers, who provided background material on military intelligence operations during the Korean War.

Particularly helpful was retired Army Captain Shelby Stanton, who provided order of battle information on Army units in Korea. Now working on a detailed *Korean War Order of Battle* for the Army's Center for Military History (publication anticipated in 1990), Stanton is also completing a book on General Almond and the X Corps (*America's Tenth Legion: X Corps in Korea, 1950*) that will be published later this year by Presidio Press.

Special thanks to Gary A. Yarrington, Curator of the Museum, Lyndon Baines Johnson Library and Museum, Austin, Texas, not only for his outstanding May 1988-January 1989 exhibition, "Korea: America's First Limited War," which honored Korean War veterans, but especially for his generosity in providing pictures from that exhibit for reproduction in this almanac.

A final word of thanks to James Warren, senior editor at Facts On File, who provided the original inspiration for this book; to Helen Flynn, assistant editor, for her efficiency in carrying out myriad additional tasks; to Eleanora Schoenebaum, editor, who provided background information on Korean War-era political personalities; and to my wife, Eloise, and our two sons, Major Harry Glenn Summers, III and Major David Cosgrove Summers, United States Army.

In expressing my thanks to those who provide comments and advice, I must add that the conclusions and such errors as this book may contain are solely my responsibility.

H.G.S.
Bowie, Maryland

INTRODUCTION

The Korean War has rightly been described as the "forgotten war." This book—really the first authoritative reference book on the war— attempts to remedy this situation and provide readers with a better understanding of how and why the conflict was fought. There are many reasons why Americans should focus their attention on the battlefields of Korea, not the least of which is that the Korean War is the most likely model for future conflicts, and we ignore its lessons at our peril.

This work is designed primarily for an American audience. Accordingly, U.S. units and organizations and battles in which American forces figured prominently are discussed in greater detail than are those of other nations who participated in the fighting. Nevertheless, every effort has been made to provide objective coverage of all participants.

Korea is an ancient country. As outlined in Part I (Historical Realities), its recorded history goes back two centuries before the birth of Christ. Under Chinese domination for much of its existence, beginning in the 16th century its geographic location between the Chinese and Japanese empires led to its becoming a Great Power battleground. This battleground intensified in the early 20th century when China, Japan and Russia vied for control of the Korean peninsula. Japan prevailed, and in 1911 Korea became a Japanese colony, a status it would retain until the end of World War II.

In the closing days of the war the Allies agreed that Korea would be liberated from Japanese control and that the United States would disarm the Japanese occupiers south of the 38th parallel and the Soviet Union would do likewise north of that line. This temporary arrangement soon hardened to the point where Korea was divided into a communist north and a democratic south (see Part I: The Two Koreas). United Nations efforts to resolve this division through free elections failed when North Korea refused to participate. In 1948, the Republic of Korea (ROK) was established in South Korea and the Democratic People's Republic of Korea (DPRK) was proclaimed in North Korea, and U.S. and Soviet occupation troops were withdrawn.

With the withdrawal of Chiang Kai-shek's Nationalist forces from China to the island of Taiwan (then known as Formosa), the United States disengaged from the East Asian mainland and in January 1950 it publicly omitted Korea from its zone of security in Asia. The only U.S. force present in Korea was a small detachment of U.S. military advisors.

This was the situation when on June 25, 1950 the North Korean Army, under cover of a massive artillery barrage, launched its cross-border invasion of South Korea (see Part II: Chronology and Part III: Invasion of the ROK). The Korean War had begun.

At the time it was assumed that "monolithic world communism," controlled and directed by Soviet Premier Joseph Stalin in Moscow, was spreading by force of arms and that Korea was merely the first step in a communist plan for world conquest. It was this assumption, not the invasion of Korea itself, that triggered the strong reaction to North Korea's aggression. Applying the "lessons of Munich" (where appeasement of Hitler's seizure of Czechoslovakia led to even further Nazi aggression), the United Nations Security Council (which the Soviet Union was then boycotting) called upon all member nations to aid South Korea in resisting aggression.

It can be argued that this reaction was based on a false premise. But so too was the invasion. Recent scholarship holds that it was North Korean Premier Kim Il-sung who masterminded the invasion, after receiving the acquiescence of the Soviet Union and the newly established People's Republic of China. All three evidently felt that the conquest could be achieved quickly before anyone had time to react. They were wrong.

"In war," the Prussian strategist Baron von Moltke had warned, "no plan survives contact with the enemy," and the North Korean plan for the blitzkrieg conquest of South Korea was no exception.

For one thing the South Korean military forces did not collapse as expected, but put up a stiff resistance as they withdrew, buying time for the outside world to react. The United States, which was then still involved in the post-World War II occupation of nearby Japan, was the first to respond to the UN call to arms. U.S. air and naval forces were ordered into action on June 27, 1950 and on June 30, 1950 U.S. ground forces were committed. British naval forces in Asian waters and Australian Air Forces based in Japan were also called into action, and other UN forces soon followed.

The war itself can be divided into four broad stages. First was the three-month UN defensive stage, which began with the North Korean invasion in June 1950 and lasted through the allied invasion of Inchon the following September. The aim during this period was to check the North Korean advance and prevent conquest of the entire peninsula. For a while, allied forces were hard pressed to hold the line. Among the major battles, covered in detail in the individual listings in Part III, were the exploits of Task Force Smith, the fight for Taejon, the battle at Yaechon and the struggle for the Naktong Perimeter.

The second stage of the war was the two-month UN offensive that began with the Inchon invasion in September 1950, included the advance of the U.S. Eighth Army and the X Corps into North Korea and ended with the intervention of Chinese Communist Forces (CCF) in November 1950 and the subsequent UN withdrawal south of the 38th parallel.

The aim during this stage was the liberation of North Korea and the rollback of communism, but after the CCF intervention the aim reverted to the defense of South Korea. The major events of this stage are chronicled in Part III: the Inchon invasion, the Wonsan landings, the Chosin Reservoir battles, the travail of Task Force MacLean/Faith, the evacuation of Hungnam, the battles of Unsan and Kunu-ri and the withdrawal of UN forces from North Korea.

Most significant during this period was the U.S. adoption of containment as a wartime national policy and the resulting shift of American military strategy from the strategic offensive to the strategic defensive. As discussed in the article on U.S. strategy in Part III, this was to have a determining influence on the ability of the United States to wage war in Korea and, later, other areas of the world.

The third stage, covering the period from December 1950 through June 1951, encompassed both the 1951 CCF spring offensive and the UN counteroffensive, which effectively ended the maneuver phase of the war, stalemated the battle lines and set the stage for the subsequent armistice negotiations. Noteworthy during this period was Operation Killer, the battle of Chipyong-ni and the battle for Glouchester Hill.

The final stage of the war, from the beginning of the truce talks in July 1951 through the Korean armistice in July 1953, was characterized by position warfare much like that of World War I. The outpost battles and the battles for Heartbreak Ridge, Porkchop Hill and the Punchbowl are detailed in Part III.

In addition to descriptions of the battles that comprised the war, the key leaders are profiled as well, including U.S. Commanders-in-Chief Harry S Truman and Dwight D. Eisenhower, UN Commanders Douglas MacArthur, Matthew Ridgway and Maxwell Taylor, as well as the subordinate Army, Navy, Air Force and Marine Corps battle captains and such Chinese and North Korean leaders as Kim Il-sung and Peng Teh-Huai.

The U.S. organization for combat is also described in detail, with individual listings for the U.S. I, IX and X corps, the nine Army and Marine combat divisions and three regimental combat teams as well as the various air and naval components of the Far East Air Force and Naval Forces Far East.

The British Commonwealth Division, the Turkish Brigade and the other UN combat battalions are covered as well, as are the armed forces of the ROK. Entries also include the combat forces of North Korea and China.

As the famed military theorist Clausewitz put it, one of the reasons military history is so important is that it allows future generations to "learn about war from books." The Korean War in particular has many lessons to teach. It provided warnings on the limits of American power, offered cautions on the American patience for drawn-out conflicts, warned of the dangers of fighting on the Asian mainland, and evidenced the hazards and difficulties of coalition warfare.

America's idea of what war should be is the model provided by World War II, where the issues were clearly drawn and the ultimate victory complete. But it is the Korean War, not World War II, that remains the paradigm for war in the nuclear age—all the more reason why its lessons must be learned. That's what this Almanac is all about.

Part I

---

the setting

Before the war broke out in 1950, most Americans were probably unaware that a country named Korea existed. And even if they had heard of it, they would have been hard pressed to locate it on a map. Korea had come back into existence as an independent nation only five years before after a generation of Japanese rule, and most maps still showed the area as part of the Imperial Japanese Empire. Instead of *Korea*, the country was labeled *Chosen*, the ancient name preferred by the Japanese occupiers. Indeed many of the maps used in the war still used Japanese place names. The famous *Chosin* Reservoir, for example, site of the First Marine Division's epic fighting withdrawal in November 1950, was actually (in Korean) the *Changjin* Reservoir.

To Americans the difference was moot—all the place names sounded strange and foreign whether they were in Korean or Japanese. The Air Force solved the problem by giving the Korean airfields numbers: K-1 was Pusan West, K-14 was Kimpo, K-24 was Pyongyang and so on. And it wasn't only the language that was foreign. So was everything else about Korea—the terrain, the weather and the entire historical setting.

Although the term was not then in general use, the *environmental impact* of Korea had a major influence on the way the war was fought. This section of the almanac details these geographic and historical realities and then analyzes their significance in shaping U.S. military and political operations.

GEOGRAPHIC REALITIES

"You know," a friend once remarked as he looked out across the frozen Korean rice paddies, "there's a lot of difference between Korea and Kansas." He had a point. Korea was different from Kansas. But they also shared some similarities. Both are located in the northern temperate zone, and both have great extremes in temperature from summer to winter. In Korea the temperature sometimes rises to over 100 degrees in the summer and plunges to 30 or 40 below zero in the winter. Such temperatures are not unknown in Kansas.

And Korea and Kansas are relatively the same size. Kansas occupies 82,227 square miles of territory while Korea occupies 85,246 square miles—38,175 square miles in South Korea and 47,071 square miles in North Korea.

The difference is the mountains. Although most of Kansas consists of plains and prairie, only about 15% of Korea can be considered plains. The plains that do exist, mostly in the south, are coastal, small in area and isolated from one another. From the watershed divide close to the east coast the land slopes sharply and abruptly to the narrow and discontinuous

1

coastal lowland on the east. The slope toward the west is much more gradual. As a result the rivers are relatively longer and the flood plains more extensive along the western and southern coasts.

A natural depression of military significance structurally separates the northern and southern parts of Korea across the narrowest part of the peninsula. Running south from Wonsan on the eastern coast through the Pyonggang-Chorwon area in central Korea, this depression then turns southwest and crosses the 38th parallel (and the current demarcation line some 30 miles north of Seoul).

The mountainous nature of Korea makes the lowlands quite important, for they are the main areas of human settlement. Major transportation routes traditionally ran along the east and west coasts and through the Wonsan-Seoul corridor. Important too are the river valleys, both for transportation and for settlement, including the Chongchon and Taedong Rivers in North Korea and the Imjin, Han, Pukhan, Kum and Naktong Rivers in South Korea.

Also militarily and strategically significant is the shape of the peninsula itself. Separating the Yellow Sea on the west and the Sea of Japan on the east, the Korean peninsula pushes southward some 600 miles from the Northeast Asian mainland to within 120 sea miles of the Japanese islands of Honshu and Kyushu on the southeast. On the north it shares a 850-mile border, much of it along the Yalu River, with two of China's Manchurian provinces. About 75 miles south of the Soviet port city of Vladivostok, Korea also shares an 11-mile border with the Soviet Union along the Tumen River.

Korea's 5,400 miles of coastline include the ports of Nampo (known as Chinnampo during the Korean War) and Inchon on the shallow (140 feet) Yellow Sea. These ports must contend with a tidal variance of 20 to 40 feet. On the east coast along the Sea of Japan, where depths plunge to over 5,500 feet, ports include Nanjin (known as Rashin during the war), Hungnam, Wonsan and Pohang. On the Korea Strait is the major port of Pusan.

Geographic Realities and the Conduct of the War

Korea's geographic realities affected the conduct of the war at the strategic, the operational and the tactical level. At the strategic level, Korea's location had for centuries made it a collision point for the competing interests of major powers. For hundreds of years Korea had been caught between the Chinese Empire on one flank and the Japanese Empire on the other. Then, as Imperial Russia expanded into the maritime provinces, she too became a contender for influence in Korea. Not to be outdone, the United States also was involved with Korea in the mid-19th century.

These strategic rivalries had become quiescent during the 35-year Japanese occupation of Korea, but when that occupation came to an end after World War II, Korea once more became the scene of great power competition. Secretary of State Dean Acheson expressed the desire of the United States to bow out in a speech to the National Press Club on January 20, 1950: He revealed that Korea had been excluded from the U.S. defense perimeter in East Asia. But this only encouraged the Soviet Union and China to give their blessing to North Korea's attempt to bring South Korea into the Communist camp by force of arms. Despite its assurances to the contrary, when that invasion occurred the United States realized it could not stand by and permit its interests in East Asia, and particularly its interests in Japan, which was then under U.S. occupation, to be placed in jeopardy. It was not the nation of Korea per se but Korea's important geographic location that prompted America to intervene in the war.

KOREAN PENINSULA

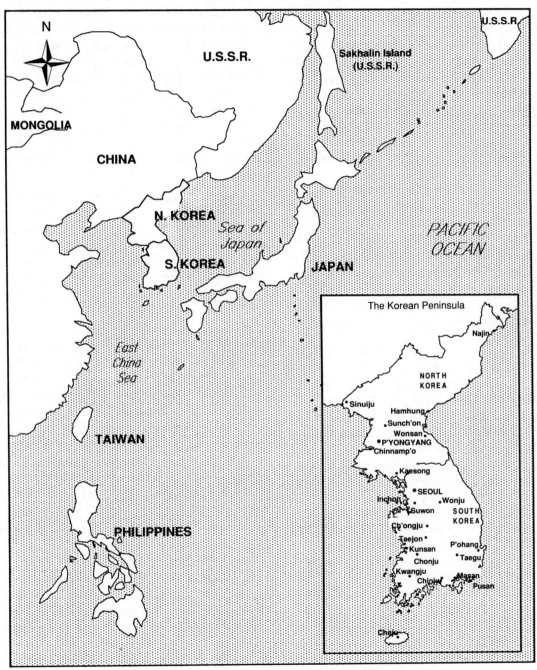

And this key location keeps the United States involved there to this day.

At the operational level, the realities of Korean geography had a major impact on Allied naval operations. Korea's more than 5,000 miles of coastline and the fact that major transportation routes followed the coast made the peninsula exceptionally vulnerable to naval interdiction and blockade. While smaller warships operated in the shallow Yellow Sea, larger naval vessels and fast carriers operated in the Sea of Japan. The Inchon invasion and the evacuation of the port of Hungnam were among the major operations facilitated by use of the seas.

On the ground geography also played a role at the operational level. At first it was a negative one, for in October 1950 geographic considerations prompted the United States to make the cardinal military error of splitting its forces in the face of the enemy. Because of the mountains in North Korea, which made east-west ground coordination almost impossible, the push into North Korea after the September 1950 Inchon invasion was made by two independent forces, neither of which was capable of rendering support to the other. The Eighth U.S. Army followed the west coastal road through Pyongyang and across the Taedong and Chongchon rivers enroute to the Yalu River. On the other side of the mountains X Corps moved up the east coastal roads, also driving for the Manchurian border. In the center, unbeknownst to either, sat two Chinese Communist Forces (CCF) Army groups. The Eighth U.S. Army and the X Corps barely avoided annihilation when the CCF slammed into their exposed flanks at Kunu-ri and the Chosin Reservoir in November 1950.

But after the U.S. withdrew from North Korea and the tactical decision was finally made to get off the roads and move into the mountains (see below), terrain had a positive operational effect. Because Korea was a peninsula, because the Allied navies had almost total sea control and because Korea was only 200 miles across from east to west at its widest part, it was possible to isolate the battlefield. In November 1951, the decision was made to go on the defensive, prepare a series of strong points and entrenchments from one coast to the other, and bring the enormous Allied advantage in firepower to bear. For the final years of the war, terrain worked to the Allied advantage.

Another operational influence of geography was the importance of the so-called Iron Triangle, where the Wonsan-Seoul depression crossed into South Korea. Geography made this area *key terrain* (i.e., possession of this terrain provides a major advantage), and this area was the site of bitter fighting throughout the entire war.

At the tactical level, geography at first worked to the advantage of the enemy. In the opening months of the war the United States tended to be road-bound, conceding the mountains to the enemy. This led to a series of major disasters: the ambush and destruction of much of the 24th Infantry Division at a roadblock east of Taejon; the virtual annihilation of the Second Infantry Division at a roadblock south of Kunu-ri; and the massacre of Task Force Mac-Lean/Faith at roadblocks east of the Chosin Reservoir.

Perhaps this policy was followed because the Eighth U.S. Army at the time was led by General Walton H. Walker, who had been one of General George Patton's corps commanders in World War II and had made his reputation by sending armored columns crashing through enemy lines. Be that as it may, it was not until command passed to a succession of consummate infantrymen, first General Matthew Ridgway and then General James Van Fleet,

POPULATION

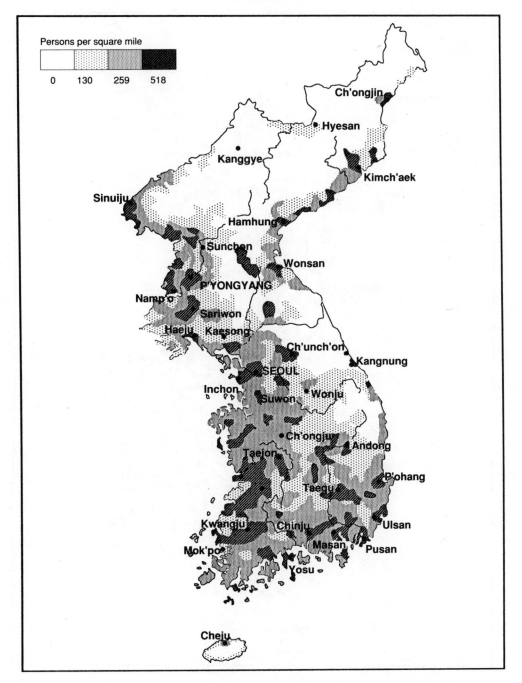

LAND UTILIZATION

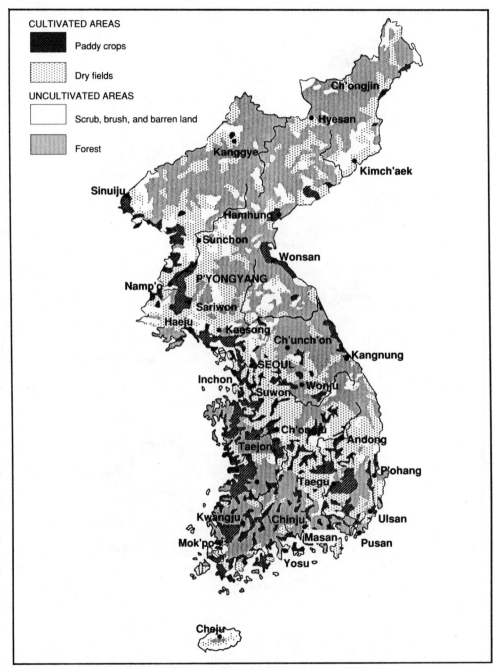

that the Eighth Army left the roads and took to the hills, defeating the enemy at his own game. *See* BLOCKADE AND ESCORT FORCE (TASK FORCE 95); INCHON INVASION (OPERATION CHROMITE); IRON TRIANGLE; KUNU-RI, BATTLE OF; NAVAL FORCES FAR EAST (NAVFE); SEA OF JAPAN; SEVENTH FLEET STRIKING FORCE (TASK FORCE 77); TAEJON, BATTLE OF; TASK FORCE MACLEAN/TASK FORCE FAITH; WITHDRAWAL FROM NORTH KOREA; YELLOW SEA.

Suggestions for further reading: The most complete description of Korea's geography can be found in the area handbooks prepared for the U.S. Army by researchers at the American University in Washington, D.C. See Kenneth G. Clare et al, *Area Handbook for the Republic of Korea*, 1969, and Rinn-Supp Shinn et al, *Area Handbook for North Korea*, 1969 (Washington, D.C.: GPO).

HISTORICAL REALITIES

Korea is one of the world's oldest nations. According to legend, it was founded in 2333 B.C. by Tan'gun, the offspring of a divine creator, and a maiden transformed from a bear. Myths aside, it is known that Tungusic and Mongoloid peoples from Mongolia and Manchuria, whose language was related to Ural-Altaic, moved down the Korean peninsula in the third millennium B.C. (Anthropologists have found evidence that relatives of these early Korean peoples crossed over the land bridge from Asia to America to become the ancestors of American Indians.)

The recorded history of Korea dates from the second century B.C., when the Chinese Han Dynasty destroyed the tribal kingdom of a General Wiman (*Wei-man* in Chinese) and established Chinese colonies in the northern parts of Korea. The colony of Nangnang (*Lolang* in Chinese) flourished for over 400 years, trans-mitting Chinese culture to both Korea and Japan. The other colonies were not so fortunate, however, and by 75 B.C. all had been destroyed by the Koreans, who resented this foreign presence in their country.

From the second century B.C. to the mid-A.D. 600s, Korea was divided into what is known as the Three Kingdoms. *Koguryo* in the north along the Yalu River basin wiped out the Chinese at Nangnang in A.D. 313 and ruled much of the area north of the Han River in Korea, as well as portions of southern Manchuria. *Paekche* was in the Han River basin, and *Silla* was in the southeastern corner of the peninsula. With the aid of the Chinese T'ang Dynasty, Silla overthrew Paekche in 660 and Koguryo in 668, unifying the country under its rule. This unification lasted some 1,290 years, until Korea was again divided in 1945.

With the help of *hwarang* recruited from the nobility (literally "flower boys" but actually more analogous to the knights that flourished in Europe in about the same period), Silla fought off its erstwhile Chinese ally. However, much of the former Koguryo territory in southern Manchuria was lost, as well as areas north of the Taedong River. Korea accepted *suzerain* status as a "tributary but autonomous state" to the Chinese Empire, a position it retained until the 20th century. Among the lasting Chinese legacies were Confucianism and Mahayana Buddhism, which was introduced into Korea in about A.D. 372 and officially sanctioned in 682.

In 935 Silla was overthrown by Wang Kon, who founded the Koryo Dynasty, from which Korea derived its present name. A Chinese-style civil service based on merit was adopted, but because of Korea's rigid land-based class structure, it drew most of its members from the nobility (*yangban* in Korean). Koryo was later plagued by a series of military coups, but its greatest problems came from outside its borders. Koryo's protector, the once powerful Chinese T'ang Dynasty, had come apart and was replaced by the Northern Sung Dynasty. But the Sung were not able to resist the invasions of the Mongols, who under Kublai Khan not only conquered China but in 1259 conquered Korea as well.

As a vassal state under the Mongol's Yuan Dynasty, much of northern Korea was lost, and through intermarriage the Koryo royal line was incorporated into the Mongol ruling family. The Korean crown princes were forced to reside in Peking, the capital the Mongols had established in China. It was not until after the Chinese Ming Dynasty overthrew the Mongols in 1356 that a Korean general, Yi Song-gye, led a revolt against the pro-Mongol Koryo king and seized control of the Korean government.

In 1392 General Yi ascended the throne and established the Yi Dynasty, which ruled Korea until 1910. Shortly afterward the Korean capital was moved from Songdo (present Kaesong) to Seoul (then called Hanyang). Reaffirming its suzerain ties to China, the Yi Dynasty adopted Confucianism as the official state doctrine. The northern portions of Korea that had been lost since the latter half of the seventh century were regained, and Korea assumed its present boundaries. After General Yi's death his successors were beset by factionalism and were virtually helpless to resist the Japanese invasions of General Toyotomi Hideyoshi in 1592 and 1598. The intent of these invasions was to seize Korean bases on the Asian mainland from which to conquer China, and so they led to major battles between Japanese and Chinese armies on Korean soil, devastating much of the country. During this period the Korean admiral Yi Sun-sin invented the iron-clad "turtle ships." They were used to destroy much of the Japanese fleet in 1592 in an attempt to cut Japanese supply lines.

Weakened by its war with Japan, the Chinese Ming Dynasty fell to invaders from Manchuria who established the Manchu or "Chi'ing" Dynasty in 1644. This dynasty ruled China until 1911. Korea, which had been overrun by the Manchus in 1627, again became a suzerain state to the Manchu government in Peking. With foreign relations in the hands of the Manchus, Korea became known as the "Hermit Kingdom" because it resisted attempts by foreigners to open the country to foreign trade and influence.

In the 1840s, for example, a resolution had been introduced in the U.S. Congress to open trade with Korea, but it was not until 1866 that an American merchantman, the *General Sherman*, anchored in the Taedong River below Pyongyang. The Koreans response was to attack the ship and massacre its crew. Attempts by Commander Robert W. Shufeldt of the USS *Wachusett* to investigate the affair and communicate with the king of Korea proved fruitless; on May 30, 1871, an American naval squadron with five ships of war, totaling 85 guns, dropped anchor off the mouth of the Han River. On June 10, 1871, after a prolonged bombardment, the first assault wave of U.S. Marines established a beachhead ashore, and the forts guarding the sea approaches to Seoul were soon overrun. Six Marines and nine sailors of the U.S. Navy's Asiatic Squadron were awarded Medals of Honor for this action. American honor having been satisfied, the squadron withdrew on July 3, 1871.

It was not until May 22, 1882, acting with the help of the good offices of Chinese viceroy Li Hung-chang in Tientsin (who wanted American help in building up the Chinese navy), that by-now Commodore Shufeldt signed an agreement with the Korean Kingdom providing trading rights, extraterritoriality and most-favored nation treatment for the United States. The United States was the first Western power to make a treaty with Korea and for some time was the only such power to send a minister to the Korean court. In 1897 the Korean king, anxious to get some leverage from the United States (a power far enough away not to pose a territorial threat) to use on the Chinese, Japanese and Russians, which were then pressuring him, remarked, "We feel that America is to us as our Elder Brother." But America had neither the interest nor the power to serve as an Elder Brother and stem the tide that was by then engulfing Korea.

In 1894, unable to cope with an antiforeign internal uprising, the Korean government requested help from China. Japan immediately countered by sending a large detachment of soldiers to Seoul to "protect Japanese interests." The result was the Sino-Japanese War of 1894 to 1895, which resulted in an easy victory for Japan.

Meanwhile, Imperial Russia, which had become a Pacific power in 1860 when it wrested the Manchurian coastal area known as the Maritime Province from China, also became involved with Korea, with which it shared an 11-mile border. Between 1896 and 1904 Russia secured valuable timber and mining rights in Korea and attempted to obtain anchorages at Mokpo and Masan on the Korea Straits for its Far Eastern fleet. In 1903 Russia unsuccessfully tried to divide Korea at the 39th parallel, offering to recognize Japanese preeminence in the southern part of Korea in exchange for a Russian "buffer" in the northern portion. This rivalry contributed to the outbreak of the Russo-Japanese War of 1904, which ended with Russia's defeat in 1905. The Treaty of Portsmouth (New Hampshire), negotiated with the help of U.S. President Theodore Roosevelt, obliged Russia to accept Japanese interests in Korea as paramount and opened the way to the Japanese annexation of Korea as a colony in 1910.

It was to be a brutal 35-year occupation. Japan established a colonial governor in Seoul and began a systematic exploitation of the country, turning Koreans into "haulers of water and hewers of wood." In 1918 Koreans were encouraged by U.S. President Woodrow Wilson's call for self-determination, but when those promises proved hollow, a massive revolt involving 370,000 people was staged in 1919 (a similar 1919 revolt in China, the May Fourth Movement, was the precursor of the Chinese Communist Party). According to a Korean source, the Japanese killed 6,670 of the demonstrators, wounded 16,000 and jailed an additional 19,515. During this period many Korean nationalists were forced to flee for their lives. A Korean Provisional Government was established in Shanghai in April 1919 with Syngman Rhee, then in exile in the United States, as president. A Korean Communist Party was formed in Seoul in 1925 but was disbanded on Moscow's orders in 1928 because of factionalism. In 1929 a five-month-long student demonstration against Japanese rule showed that Korea had not become assimilated and still deeply resented its foreign occupiers.

As it had attempted 400 years earlier, Japan used Korea as a base from which to conquer China. Manchuria was seized in 1931 and turned into the puppet state of Manchukuo, and in July 1937 Japan crossed the Great Wall of China and began the invasion of China proper. On December 7, 1941, in order to protect its flanks and rear, Japan launched a preemptory sneak attack on the United States fleet at Pearl Harbor in Hawaii. Not only would this bring the United States into World War II and ultimately lead to Japan's own defeat, it would lead to their loss of Korea as well.

The issue of Korean independence, formally closed by the Japanese annexation in 1911, was reopened by the Cairo Declaration in December 1943. The Allied powers, the United States,

Great Britain and China, affirmed that after Japan's defeat it would be forced to return to the limits that existed prior to the Sino-Japanese War of 1894 to 1895. The declaration went on to say that "mindful of the enslavement of the people of Korea, who are determined that in due course Korea shall become free and independent." These declarations were reaffirmed at the Potsdam Conference of July 1945 and were agreed to by the Soviet Union when it declared war on Japan on August 8, 1945.

In that same month the United States and the Soviet Union agreed to use the 38th parallel as the arbitrary dividing line for the disarming of Japanese troops in Korea. Unfortunately, the line would become much more than that.

Historical Realities and the Conduct of the War

As clearly seen in this historical overview, great power rivalries over Korea have a history that far precedes the Korean War. Almost 200 years before the United States was founded, China and Japan were fighting over Korea. While in June 1950 the United States saw the "spread of Communism" as being responsible for the war in Korea, an argument can be made that ancient rivalries, cloaked in new terms, were the real causes of the clash there.

Another strategic influence of these historical realities is the strength of Korean nationalism. This nationalism worked to America's advantage. South Korean President Syngman Rhee personified that nationalism, while North Korean leader Kim Il-sung was seen by many Koreans and observers on the scene as a pretentious upstart groomed by the Soviet Union to serve its interests in Korea. When, after the defeat of his own military forces, Kim Il-sung invited the Chinese Communist "volunteers" into Korea, it further eroded his credibility, for every Korean knew the 2,000-year history of Chinese domination of their country.

Suggestions for further reading: *James A. Field's History of United States Naval Operations in Korea* (Washington, D.C.: 1962) has an excellent account of U.S. Navy operations in Korea in the mid-19th century. The *Area Handbook for the Republic of Korea* by Kenneth G. Clare et al. (Washington, D.C.: USGPO, 1969) contains a short summary of Korean history. Pearl Buck's *The Living Reed* (New York: John Day, 1963) is a powerful fictionalized account of the struggle for Korean independence. Among detailed histories of Korea are Andred J. Grajdanzev's *Modern Korea* (New York: John Day, 1944); Lee Ki-baik's *A New History of Korea* (Cambridge: Harvard University Press, 1984); and M. Frederick Nelson's *Korea and the Old Order in East Asia* (Baton Rouge: Louisiana State University, 1945).

THE TWO KOREAS

On September 2, 1945, following the surrender ceremonies on the USS *Missouri* in Tokyo Bay, General of the Army Douglas MacArthur, the Supreme Commander of Allied Powers (SCAP), issued General Order One, which among other things detailed the procedures for accepting the surrender of the armed forces of Imperial Japan scattered throughout East Asia.

This was more than just a simple military directive. It had been drafted in Washington by the Army Staff's Strategy and Policy Group; coordinated with the State-War-Navy Coordinating Committee, the Joint Chiefs of Staff and the Secretaries of State, War and Navy; and personally approved by President Harry S Truman. At his direction the document had been coordinated with the British and Soviet leaders, and both had given their concurrence.

In the case of Korea, General Order One specified that Japanese forces north of the 38th parallel would surrender to Soviet forces; those south of the parallel would surrender to

Left to right: Japanese commanders in Korea, General Yashio Sezuki, Governor Genera Nosuzuko Abe and Vice Admiral Yamagushia, await the arrival of U.S. Lieutenant General John R. Hodge, XXIV Corps Commander, in surrender ceremonies in Seoul, September 1945.
(Courtesy U.S. Army Military History Institute.)

American forces. This procedure was not unique. It was used in Indochina as well. At the Potsdam Conference in July 1945 it was agreed that Chinese Nationalist forces would accept the surrender of Japanese forces in Indochina north of the 16th parallel, while British forces would accept their surrender south of that point. Both nations quickly completed their task and withdrew their forces. But it did not prove to be that simple in Korea.

For one thing, when General MacArthur issued the directive, the Soviets had already been on the 38th parallel for several days. Declaring war on Japan on August 8, 1945, the Soviet Union (which shared an 11-mile border with Korea on its eastern coast) invaded Korea on August 11th and 12th. After landing at Rashin, a Korean port on the Sea of Japan just south of Vladavostok, Soviet troops poured out of their maritime provinces and moved down the peninsula against negligible Japanese resistance. V-J Day, August 14, 1945, found them nearing the Kaesong area on the 38th parallel.

On September 3, 1945, Lieutenant General Yoshio Kozuke, commander of the Japanese 17th Area Army in Korea, radioed the designated American commander, Lieutenant General John R. Hodge, that the Soviet Army had stopped on the 38th parallel and was evidently waiting for the Americans to arrive. Even if the Soviets had decided to overrun the entire peninsula, there was little the United States could have done to oppose such a move. General Hodge was still 600 miles away on Okinawa, and his XXIV Corps (the Sixth, Seventh and 40th Infantry divisions) were still in the process of loading for movement to Korea. It was not until September ninth that General Hodge was able to accept the surrender of the Japanese forces in South Korea.

Although the United States saw the 38th parallel dividing line as a temporary expedient, the Soviets seemed quite content that Korea should be partitioned—not surprising, since, as was discussed earlier, they had attempted to do just that 40 years earlier, an attempt that had sparked the Russo-Japanese War of 1904. In December 1945, the same month that a Joint American Soviet Commission on Korea was meeting in Moscow, General Hodge noted that the Soviets were erecting field fortifications along the parallel. Three months before Winston Churchill gave his famous Iron Curtain speech at Fulton, Missouri, the curtain had already descended across Korea.

The United States and the Emergence of the Republic of Korea

The United States was singularly unprepared for the task of nurturing a new government in Korea. Its attention was focused on General MacArthur's democratization of Japan, and there was little time or patience for the anarchy developing in South Korea. General Hodge, the United States Armed Forces in Korea (USAFIK) commander, was a field soldier little suited to the political tasks of military government. When assigned there he received no political guidance on what he was expected to accomplish, and no military government teams were available to provide advice and support.

With a multitude of political parties creating not government but bedlam, with a country in economic collapse and with relief expenses skyrocketing, the main thing the United States wanted in Korea was out. In September 1947 a Joint Chiefs of Staff study concluded that Korea was of little strategic importance to the United States and that the two divisions remaining there ought to be withdrawn. The State Department agreed, and the decision was made to unload the problem on the United Nations (UN).

On September 17, 1947, the United States placed the question of Korean independence on the agenda of the UN General Assembly. A UN commission to supervise the organization of an all-Korea united government was proposed, and a Temporary Commission on Korea was established. The commission reached Seoul in January 1948. Although it got an enthusiastic reception in the south, the north refused to give the commission access to its part of the country. (Of Korea's population of 30 million in 1950, only 9 million lived in the North; this rather than Communism may explain their unwillingness to submit to free elections.) Notwithstanding this lack of cooperation from North Korea, elections were held in May 1948, and following a popular election, the National Assembly elected long-time Korean nationalist Syngman Rhee as the president of the Republic of Korea. On August 15, 1948, the U.S. occupation of Korea came to an end, and the Republic of Korea became a sovereign nation.

In September 1948 the United States began withdrawing its military forces. Of the three original U.S. Army divisions sent to Korea in 1945, the 40th Infantry Division had long since left active duty and returned to the California National Guard; the Sixth Infantry Division at Pusan was deactivated in December 1948; and in early 1949 the Seventh Infantry Division north of Seoul was sent to Japan to replace the 11th Airborne Division, which then returned to the United States. At President Rhee's request, a small American force (the newly formed Fifth Infantry Regimental Combat Team) remained in Korea until June 1949, when it departed for its new duty station in Hawaii. When the Korean War began in June 1950, the only American military unit in the country was a small Korean Military Advisory Group.

Not only had the United States failed to prepare the Republic of Korea for the trials that lay ahead, in January 1950 Secretary of State Dean Acheson publicly excluded it from his discussion of the American defense perimeter in East Asia, thereby making it plain that the United States had abandoned it altogether. From start to finish the tutelage of the Republic of Korea was a sorry performance, and America would pay dearly for that dereliction.

The U.S.S.R. and the Emergence of the Democratic Republic of Korea

The difference between the Soviet and the American approach could not have been more stark. For one thing, unlike the United States, the Soviet Union knew precisely what it wanted. It wanted what Imperial Russia had wanted in 1903—a friendly "buffer state" on its Far Eastern border. And this time it had the means to achieve its goals. Japan, its old Asian nemesis, was in ruins. Not only that, since the Japanese occupation of Korea had begun, some one million Koreans had gone into exile in Soviet or Chinese territory. These refugees were now well indoctrinated in Marxism-Leninism, and many were combat-hardened through service in the Red Armies of China and the Soviet Union; they were the perfect cadre to establish a new government in Pyongyang.

The Soviets knew just what kind of a new government they wanted—a state socialist Marxist-Leninist government patterned on their own. On October 3, 1945, without "wasting time" on popular elections, they unveiled North Korea's new leader, Kim Il-sung. The Soviet-sponsored North Korean government proceeded to eliminate all of its domestic political opposition. Russian-trained Koreans soon held all the key positions, and on February 12, 1946, an Interim People's Committee was formed.

On September 9, 1948, the Democratic People's Republic of Korea was announced. With their cadres now in place, the Soviet Union withdrew all of its forces north of the Korean–Soviet border by December 26, 1948. Colonel General Terenti Shtykov, who had been chief of the Russian delegation to the Joint United States–U.S.S.R. Commission, was named as the first Soviet ambassador to the DPRK (Democratic People's Republic of Korea).

By June 1950, with its political power base secure at home and with assurances of Soviet and Chinese support, North Korea turned its attention to the south. The stage was set for the Korean War.

See KIM IL-SUNG; KOREA MILITARY ADVISORY GROUP (KMAG); NORTH KOREAN PEOPLE'S ARMY (NKPA); REPUBLIC OF KOREA ARMY (ROKA); RHEE, SYNGMAN; 38TH PARALLEL; UNITED NATIONS.

Suggestions for further reading: Richard C. Allen, *Korea's Syngman Rhee: An Unauthorized Portrait* (Rutland, VT: Tuttle, 1960); Max Beloff, *Soviet Policy in the Far East 1944–1951* (New York: Oxford University Press, 1953); Bruce Cummings, *The Origins of the Korean War: Liberation and the Emergence of Separate Regimes* (Princeton: Princeton University Press, 1981); Edward G. Meade, *American Military Government in Korea* (New York: King's Crown, 1951); Robert T. Oliver, *Syngman Rhee: The Man Behind the Myth* (New York: Dodd, 1955); Robert K. Sawyer, Major, USA, *Military Advisors in Korea: KMAG in Peace and War* (Washington, D.C.: GPO, 1962); James F. Schnabel, *U.S. Army in the Korean War: Policy and Direction: The First Year* (Washington, D.C.: GPO, 1972); Robert R. Simmons, *The Strained Alliance: Peking, Pyongyang, Moscow and the Politics of the Korean War* (New York: Free Press, 1975).

Part II

the korean war: chronology 1950–1953

1950

June 25

North Korea launches cross-border invasion of South Korea*.

North Korean People's Army (NKPA) and border constabulary numbers about 135,000 men in seven assault infantry divisions, a tank brigade, an independent infantry regiment, a motorcycle regiment, three reserve divisions and five border constabulary brigades.

Republic of Korea (ROK) Army numbers 98,000 men in eight infantry divisions.

United Nations (UN) Security Council calls for end of aggression and withdrawal of NKPA troops.

June 26

United States Ambassador to Korea John J. Muccio orders all nonessential American Embassy personnel and all U.S. dependents in Korea evacuated to Japan.

June 27

President Truman authorizes U.S. air and naval operations south of the 38th parallel to support ROK forces.

Fifth Air Force Lieutenant William F. Hudson, flying a F-82 Twin Mustang, shoots down a North Korean YAK fighter.

---

* Korean time ("I" Time Zone) is ten hours earlier than Washington, D.C. Eastern Standard Time ("R" Time Zone) and eleven hours earlier than Eastern Daylight Time. For example, the North Korean invasion began at 0400 hours (4 AM), 25 June 1950 local time; but this was 1500 hours (3 PM), 25 June 1950 in Washington. This makes for some confusion in recording events, since in many cases the time difference results in a date difference as well. In this chronology events will be recorded in the time and date where they took place.

Brigadier General John H. Church arrives in Suwan from Japan with General Headquarters, Advance Command and Liaison Group (GHQ ADCOM) team.

UN Security Council adopts U.S. resolution proclaiming NKPA attack a breach of world peace. Asks member nations to assist ROK in repelling aggression.

United States Seventh Fleet ordered to neutralize Straits of Formosa.

Senate Armed Services Committee initiates action on a call-up of reserve components.

June 28

ROK engineers blow Han River bridges in Seoul, trapping much of ROK Army north of the river.

Seoul falls to the NKPA.

United Kingdom Defense Committee places British naval forces in Japanese waters: one light fleet carrier, two cruisers, five destroyer and frigate escort ships under control of U.S. Far East Command (FECOM).

June 29

President Truman authorizes sea blockade of the Korean coast.

Naval Forces Far East's light cruiser USS *Juneau* fires first U.S. naval shore bombardment of the war at Mukho on Korea's eastern coast.

President Truman authorizes bombing of North Korea.

Fifth Air Force's Third Bombardment Group sends 18 B-26 Invader light bombers against Heijo Airfield at North Korean capital of Pyongyang. Twenty-five enemy aircraft destroyed on the ground, one YAK fighter shot down.

President Truman authorizes the sending of U.S. ground troops to Korea for maintaining communications and guarding the port of Pusan.

Actual strength of ground troops in Eighth U.S. Army (EUSA) in Japan is 48.8% of normal authorization for combat troops and 25.9% for service troops.

British Royal Navy ships join FECOM and are attached to U.S. Naval Forces Far East (NAVFE).

Australia places Japan-based destroyer and frigate and 77th Squadron, Royal Australian Air Force, at Iwakuni Air Base under FECOM control; units are attached to NAVFE and Far East Air Force (FEAF) respectively.

June 30

President Truman authorizes commitment of U.S. ground troops to combat in Korea.

Congress authorizes call to active duty for any or all reserve components of the Armed Forces for up to 21 months.

President Truman signs Public Law 599, which extends Selective Service (i.e., the draft) until July 9, 1951, and authorizes the call-up of Reserves and National Guard for up to 21 months active federal service.

July 1

Arrival of first U.S. ground combat troops in Korea: First Battalion, 21st Infantry Regiment, 24th Infantry Division, commanded by Lieutenant Colonel Charles B. Smith (Task Force Smith).

Ongoing transfer of ocean shipping from the Army to the Navy's Military Sea Transportation Service (MSTS) is completed.

July 3

Major General William F. Dean, Commanding General, 24th Infantry Division, lands at Taejon airstrip. Remainder of the division is enroute.

First UN carrier-based air strike of the war when planes from the USS *Valley Forge* and the HMS *Triumph* strike airfields in the Pyongyang-Chinnampo area in North Korea.

Inchon falls to the NKPA.

July 4

United States Army Forces in Korea (USAFIK) headquarters activated to control all U.S. Army troops in Korea.

General Dean assumes command of USAFIK in addition to command of 24th Infantry Division.

United States Korea Military Advisory Group (KMAG) comes under USAFIK control.

Pusan Base Command is organized to support port activities there.

July 5

In first U.S. ground action of the war, 24th Infantry Division's Task Force Smith (First Battalion, 21st Infantry Regiment) engages and delays advancing NKPA forces at Osan.

July 6–8

The 24th Infantry Division's 34th Infantry Regiment delays advancing NKPA at Pyongtaek and Chonan.

July 7

United Nations Security Council asks United States to serve as its Korean War executive agent and to organize a United Nations Command for the prosecution of the war.

July 8

President Truman names General MacArthur to head United Nations Command.

July 8–12
The 24th Infantry Division's 21st Infantry Regiment delays advancing NKPA at Chochiwon.

July 10–18
The 25th Infantry Division moves to Korea from bases in Japan.

July 12
The First Cavalry Division begins loading in the Yokohama area for movement to Korea.

July 13
Lieutenant General Walton H. Walker arrives from Japan and establishes Headquarters Eighth U.S. Army (Forward) (EUSA) at Taegu.

EUSA assumes command of all U.S. ground forces in Korea.

Allied forces total 75,000 men: approximately 18,000 Americans and 58,000 ROK.

Pusan Logistical Command replaces Pusan Base Command.

July 13–16
The 24th Infantry Division's 19th and 34th Infantry regiments delay advancing NKPA at Kum River line.

July 14
President Syngman Rhee of the Republic of Korea assigns control of his nation's armed forces to General MacArthur, the commander in chief, United Nations Command (CINC-UNC).

July 15
The 29th Regimental Combat Team sails from Okinawa for Korea.

July 17
CINCUNC delegates command of all Republic of Korea (ROK) ground forces to General Walker, Commanding General, Eighth U.S. Army.

First elements of U.S. Second Infantry Division sail from Seattle for Korea.

July 18
Lead elements of First Cavalry Division make unopposed landing at Pohang on Korea's eastern coast.

General Walker asks 24th Infantry Division to hold Taejon for two days while First Cavalry Division gets into position.

July 19
The 24th Infantry Division begins defense of Taejon.

President Truman gives secretary of defense authority to mobilize the Organized Reserve and National Guard.

Organized Marine Corps Reserve ordered to report to active duty immediately. Volunteer Marine Corps Reserve ordered to report on August 15, 1950.

July 20
The 24th Infantry Regiment, 25th Infantry Division, launches counterattack at Yechon.

Taejon falls to NKPA.

Major General William F. Dean, 24th Infantry Division commander, reported missing in action.

July 22
Department of the Army issues a call for reserve officers to volunteer for active duty.

July 24
Fifth Air Force relocates headquarters from Japan to Korea.

United Nations Command (UNC) headquarters established in Tokyo collocated with (and essentially identical to) General Headquarters, Far East Command.

July 25
Chief of naval operations orders aircraft carrier USS *Princeton* to be removed from mothball status and manned by a chiefly Navy Reserve crew.

Fifth Regimental Combat Team sails for Korea from Hawaii.

The 29th Regimental Combat Team committed to combat near Chinju.

July 27
President Truman signs Public Law 624, which extends enlistments in the armed forces involuntarily for a period of 12 months.

Draft call issued for 50,000 inductees to report for training in September.

July 29
General Walker tells EUSA to "stand or die."

July 31
Fifth Regimental Combat Team arrives in Korea.

August 1
Lead elements of U.S. Second Infantry Division arrive in Korea from Fort Lewis, Washington.

Yakov Malik, Soviet delegate to the United Nations, ends Moscow's boycott and takes over the presidency of the Security Council.

August 2
U.S. First Provisional Marine Brigade arrives in Korea from Camp Pendleton, California.

I Corps activated at Fort Bragg, North Carolina, and ordered to Korea.

August 3
First airstrike by Marine aircraft launched by VMF-214.

Thirty thousand members of Army Volunteer and Inactive Reserve are recalled and ordered to report involuntarily for active duty in September 1950.

One hundred thirty-four Army National Guard units receive orders to report for active duty.

Congress removes existing limitations on the size of the Army.

August 4
Naktong Perimeter established.

First aeromedical evacuation of casualties by Marine VMO-6 helicopters.

August 7
The First Provisional Marine Brigade committed to combat at Chinju.

August 8–18
First Battle of the Naktong Bulge. The 24th Infantry Division, reinforced by First Provisional Marine Brigade and elements of the Second and 25th Infantry divisions, contains and repels NKPA Fourth Division penetration of Naktong Perimeter.

August 10
Lead elements of First Marine Division sail from San Diego, California, for Korea.

U.S. Army IX Corps activated at Fort Sheridan, Illinois, and ordered to Korea.

Air Force orders Air Force Reserve's 452d Light Bombardment Wing and 437th Troop Carrier Wing to active duty.

The president approves call to active duty of four National Guard divisions (the 28th, 40th,

43d and 45th) and two regimental combat teams (the 196th and 278th).

The president approves increase of authorized Army strength to 1,081,000.

U.S. Army reserve captains and lieutenants (7,862) are recalled and ordered to report involuntarily for active duty in September.

August 10–20
Battle for Pohang on east coast. NKPA Fifth and 12th divisions surround ROK Third Division and capture port of Pohang in northeast corner of Naktong Perimeters. Republic of Korea Eighth and Capital divisions counterattack, joined by ROK Third Division, which had been evacuated by sea by the U.S. Navy from their encirclement and relanded south of enemy penetration. Pohang recaptured and NKPA 12th Division destroyed.

August 12
Pusan Quartermaster Base Depot organized to operate depot operations there.

August 15
The 27th British Brigade (First Battalion, the Middlesex Regiment, and the First Battalion, Argyll and Sutherland Highland Light Infantry) sails from Hong Kong for Korea.

August 15–20
Battle of the Bowling Alley west of Taegu on Naktong Perimeter. Republic of Korea First Division and U.S. 23d and 27th Infantry regiments badly maul NKPA First and 13th divisions.

August 16
United States X (Tenth) Corps activated in Japan to control Inchon invasion force.

The Third Battalion, Seventh Marines (formerly Fleet Marine Force Atlantic's Third Battalion, Sixth Marines, embarked with the Sixth U.S. Fleet in the Mediterranean), sails from Suda Bay, Crete, for Korea via the Suez Canal.

August 17
The remainder of Seventh Marine Regiment activated at Camp Pendleton, California.

August 20
Last elements of U.S. Second Infantry Division close in Korea.

August 23
In a second levy, 77,000 members of the Army Organized Reserve Corps are recalled involuntarily to active duty.

August 25
Japan Logistical Command organized to provide supplies and equipment necessary to support the war in Korea and to assume occupation duties of EUSA.

Major General William F. Dean, former commander 24th Infantry Division, taken prisoner by NKPA after wandering for 46 days after fall of Taejon.

August 26
The Fifth Regimental Combat Team (Fifth Infantry Regiment and 555th Artillery Battalion) assigned to 24th Infantry Division, replacing the 34th Infantry Regiment and 63d Field Artillery Battalion, which are reduced to paper strength and transferred to Japan to be rebuilt.

August 26–27
The 65th Infantry Regiment, Third Infantry Division, sails from Puerto Rico through Panama Canal for Korea.

August 29
British 27th Brigade arrives from Hong Kong.

August 30

The Third Infantry Division (minus 65th Infantry Regiment) sails from San Francisco for Japan.

August 31–September 19

Second Battle of the Naktong Bulge.

September 1

The Seventh Marine Regiment sails from San Diego for Korea.

Army National Guard's 40th and 45th Infantry divisions enter federal service.

Last elements of First Marine Aircraft Wing at El Toro, California, sail for Korea.

September 5

Army National Guard's 28th and 43d Infantry divisions enter federal service.

September 6

The 187th Airborne Regimental Combat Team (187th Airborne Infantry Regiment and the 674th Field Artillery Battalion) sails from San Francisco, California, for Korea.

September 7

The First Provisional Marine Brigade withdrawn from combat in Naktong Perimeter and reassembled at Pusan to embark for Inchon invasion.

September 13

The I Corps becomes operational at Taegu.

The First Provisional Marine Brigade disestablished and reabsorbed by First Marine Division.

September 15

D-day for Inchon invasion by Joint Task Force Seven.

The First Marine Division establishes beachhead ashore.

September 16

The Third Infantry Division (minus 65th Infantry Regiment) closes in Japan as Far East Command reserve.

September 16–22

Eighth U.S. Army (EUSA) breaks out of Naktong Perimeter.

September 17

Kimpo air base liberated by Fifth Marine Regiment. First Marine Aircraft Wing F4U Corsairs land and begin combat operations ashore.

The Seventh Marine Regiment lands at Inchon and rejoins First Marine Division.

September 18

The 32d Infantry Regiment, 7th Infantry Division, lands at Inchon, with rest of division to follow.

September 19

Filipino Battalion arrives in Korea.

The Second Logistical Command replaces Pusan Logistical Command. Mission is to provide logistical support to Eight U.S. Army (EUSA).

The Third Logistical Command activated to provide logistical support to X Corps.

Louis Johnson resigns as secretary of defense.

September 20

The First Marine Division crosses Han River.

September 21

X Corps assumes command of all forces ashore in Inchon-Seoul area from Joint Task Force Seven.

George C. Marshall becomes secretary of defense.

September 23

IX Corps becomes operational at Miryang.

September 24–25

The 187th Airborne Regimental Combat Team (RCT) airlanded at Kimpo air base near Seoul after arrival by sea from Japan on September 20.

September 26

Elements from EUSA's Seventh Cavalry Regiment, First Cavalry Division, pushing north from Naktong Perimeter link up with elements of X Corps' 31st Infantry Regiment, Seventh Infantry Division, moving inland from Inchon.

September 27

Seoul liberated by First Marine Division and Army Seventh Infantry Division.

On Joint Chiefs of Staff recommendation, and with concurrence of State and Defense Departments, President Truman authorizes military operations north of the 38th parallel.

September 28

The Third Battalion, Royal Australian Regiment, arrives in Korea.

September 29

Seoul officially returned to ROK President Syngman Rhee by General MacArthur and reestablished as capital of the Republic of Korea.

September 30

The Republic of Korea Third Division crosses 38th parallel in pursuit of fleeing North Korean People's Army (NKPA).

October 1

The 65th Infantry Regiment, Third Infantry Division, completes movement to Korea.

October 3

With arrival of the Third Battalion, the Royal Australian Regiment, the British 27th Brigade is renamed the 27th British *Commonwealth* Brigade.

Advance party of Thailand Battalion arrives in Korea.

October 4

Chinese Premier Mao Tse-tung makes final decision to intervene in Korean War.

October 6

The Third Logistical Command assumes responsibility for Inchon port operations.

October 6–7

Republic of Korea Sixth and Eighth divisions cross 38th parallel in central Korea.

October 7

United Nations General Assembly passes resolution authorizing use of UN troops anywhere north of 38th parallel to establish unified and democratic Korea.

October 8

United Nations Reception Center established at Taegu University to provide familiarization training for arriving UN units.

October 9

Eighth U.S. Army's (EUSA) I Corps, led by First Cavalry Division, crosses 38th parallel north of Kaesong and attacks northward toward North Korean capital of Pyongyang.

October 9–17

X Corps' First Marine Division, embarks at Inchon for sea movement to Wonsan.

October 10

Republic of Korea Third and Capital divisions capture port city of Wonsan, 110 air miles north of 38th parallel on Korean east coast.

October 14–17

After 350-mile road march from Seoul area, X Corps' Seventh Infantry Division embarks at Pusan for sea movement to Korea's eastern coast.

October 14–20

Chinese Communist Forces (CCF) begin to infiltrate large units into North Korea secretly. By October 20, the CCF commander, Peng Teh-huai, and four 30,000-man field armies had crossed the Yalu; three were positioned opposite EUSA units in western Korea, and one was positioned opposite X Corps units in eastern Korea. By the end of October two additional field armies would cross over to confront EUSA.

October 15

President Truman meets with General MacArthur at Wake Island Conference.

October 17

Republic of Korea Capital Division captures Hamhung and its port city of Hungnam 50 air miles north of Wonsan, and continues drive to seize Iwon 100 miles farther north.

October 18

The First Turkish Armed Forces Command (Turkish Brigade) arrives in Korea.

October 19

North Korean capital of Pyongyang captured by First ROK Division and U.S. First Cavalry Division.

X Corps ordered to move north along east coast toward Yalu River.

October 02

The 187th Airborne Regimental Combat Team makes parachute assault on Sukchon and Sunchon north of Pyongyang.

X Corps headquarters on USS *Missouri* moved ashore and established at Wonsan.

October 21

North Korean Premier Kim Il-sung establishes new capital at Sinuiju on Yalu River opposite Chinese city of Antung.

Advance party of the Netherlands Battalion arrives in Korea.

Advance party of the British 29th Brigade arrives in Korea.

October 25

Chinese Communist Forces (CCF) launch first phase offensive.

The Second Regiment, ROK Sixth Division, attacked by elements of CCF 50th Field Army north of Unsan. First indication China has entered the war.

Elements of ROK I Corps (part of the U.S. X Corps) near Chosin (Changjin) Reservoir capture Chinese soldier who states large numbers of CCF in area.

October 26

Reconnaissance Platoon, Seventh Regiment, ROK Sixth Division, reaches Yalu River at Chosan in western part of Korea, the only

EUSA element to reach the Korean-Chinese border during course of the war.

October 26-28
The First Marine Division lands at Wonsan.

October 29–November 9
The Seventh Infantry Division lands at Iwon on Korea's eastern coast, 150 miles north of Wonsan.

October 30
X Corps orders First Marine Division to replace ROK I Corps in Chosin Reservoir area. Division begins move from Wonsan by road to assembly point near Hamhung.

October 31
Republic of Korea (ROK) II Corps under heavy CCF contact north and east of Kunu-ri.

November 1
The 21st Infantry Regiment, 24th Infantry Division, reaches EUSA "highwater mark" when it captures the village of Chong-go-do, 18 air miles from Sinuiju and the Yalu River.

The Seventh Marine Regiment begins move from Hamhung to Chosin Reservoir, which is 56 miles to northeast.

November 1–2
First U.S. battle with CCF as Eighth Cavalry Regiment, First Cavalry Division, comes under attack from 116th Division, CCF 39th Army, near village of Unsan in western Korea. After the battle the CCF disappear into the hills.

November 2–7
The Seventh Marine Regiment relieves ROK I Corps elements at Sudong south of Chosin Reservoir then runs into heavy resistance from the CCF 124th Division. After stiff fighting, enemy disappears.

November 5–17
The Third Infantry Division lands at Wonsan.

November 7
Advance party of Canadian Second Battalion, Princess Patricia's Canadian Light Infantry Regiment, arrives in Korea.'

November 8
With approval of President Truman, seventy-nine B-29 Superfortress bombers strike the Yalu River bridges at Sinuiju.

First aerial battle between jet aircraft when U.S. Air Force Lieutenant Russell Brown, flying fighter-escort for the bombers in an F-80 Shooting Star, shoots down a MIG-15 fighter near Sinuiju.

November 11
Corporal Harry G. Summers Jr., 21st Infantry Regiment, 24th Infantry Division, promoted to sergeant.

November 21
The 17th Infantry Regiment, U.S. Seventh Infantry Division, reaches Yalu River near its source at Hyesanjin in eastern Korea.

November 24
Eighth U.S. Army (EUSA) begins major offensive.

Seventh U.S. Army activated in Europe.

November 25
Chinese Communist Forces (CCF) XIII Army Group launches second phase offensive on EUSA front.

November 27
X Corps launches attack to relieve pressure on EUSA to the west.

Chinese Communist Forces (CCF) IX Army Group launches second phase offensive on X Corps front.

November 27–December 1
East of Chosin Reservoir, the U.S. Seventh Infantry Division's Task Force MacLean/Faith (named after Colonel Allan D. MacLean and his successor, Lieutenant Colonel Don C. Faith), consisting of Colonel MacLean's 31st Infantry Regiment (minus its First Battalion but with Lieutenant Colonel Faith's First Battalion, 32d Infantry Regiment, in its stead) is annihilated in the CCF attack. Only 385 soldiers of its 3,200-man force survive.

November 27–December 1
Encircled First Marine Division fights its way southward from Chosin Reservoir to Hungnam Perimeter in Battle of the Chosin Reservoir.

November 28
Task Force Kingston (named for its commander, Lieutenant Robert C. Kingston) composed of elements of the Seventh Infantry Division's 32d Infantry Regiment, reaches Yalu River at Sin'galpa'jin to the west of 17th Infantry Regiment position.

November 29
General Walker, EUSA commander, orders a general withdrawal of the Eighth U.S. Army from the Chongchon River line to new defensive line at Pyongyang.

November 29–December 1
Battle of Kunu-ri in western Korea. CCF virtually destroys U.S. Second Infantry Division, which is acting as rearguard for EUSA withdrawal.

November 30
General Almond, X Corps commander, orders withdrawal of X Corps (ROK I Corps, First Marine Division and U.S. Army Third and Seventh Infantry divisions) to Hungnam Perimeter.

December 2
Eighth U.S. Army (EUSA) evacuation of Chongchon River line completed. New defensive line established at Pyongyang.

December 3
Pyongyang defensive line ordered to be abandoned.

Supply depots in Pyongyang area put to the torch.

December 3–7
Elements of Task Force 90, Amphibious Force Far East, evacuate Wonsan. Some 3,834 military personnel, 1,146 vehicles, 10,013 tons of bulk cargo and 7,009 Korean civilian refugees outloaded.

December 5
Pyongyang falls to the enemy.

Evacuation of 1,800 U.S. Army and Navy personnel and 5,900 ROK soldiers from Chinnampo by elements of Task Force 90, Amphibious Force Far East, completed.

December 7, 1950–January 5, 1951
Elements of Task Force 90, Amphibious Force Far East, begin evacuation of Inchon. By January 5, 1951, when the port is abandoned to the enemy, 68,913 personnel, 1,404 vehicles and 54,741 tons of cargo have been outloaded.

December 9
Far East Command (FEC) orders evacuation of X Corps from Hungnam.

Task Force 90, Amphibious Force Far East, ordered to conduct evacuation.

December 14
United Nations passes resolution seeking cease-fire.

December 15
The First Marine Division sails from Hungnam for sea movement to Pusan.

Eighth U.S. Army (EUSA) establishes Imjin River defense line north of Seoul.

December 16
President Truman declares state of national emergency.

December 17
Republic of Korea (ROK) I Corps sails from Hungnam for Pusan.

December 20
Press censorship imposed by United Nations Command over all Allied journalists in Korea.

December 21
U.S. Army Seventh Infantry Division sails from Hungnam for Pusan.

December 22
Chinese reject UN cease-fire proposal.

Army issues third involuntary recall: 7,585 reserve officers to report for active duty in March 1951.

December 23
General Walton H. Walker, Commanding General Eighth U.S. Army, killed in a vehicle accident.

Lieutenant General Matthew B. Ridgway named as successor.

December 24
U.S. Army Third Infantry Division sails from Hungnam for Pusan.

Hungnam evacuation complete. Some 3,600 men, 196 vehicles and 1,300 tons of cargo had been airlifted from the perimeter. Another 105,000 U.S. and ROK military personnel, 91,000 civilian refugees, 17,500 vehicles and 350,000 measurement tons of cargo had been evacuated by sea.

December 26
General Ridgway arrives in Korea and physically assumes command of EUSA.

December 31 1950–January 5, 1951
Chinese Communist Forces (CCF) launch their third-phase offensive.

1951
January 1
Upon evacuation of Inchon, Third Logistical Command, moves to Pusan and becomes subordinate element of Second Logistical Command.

January 4
Seoul abandoned.

January 5
Inchon abandoned.

January 7–15
Enemy offensive halted. New defense line along 38th parallel.

January 16
The 31st and 47th Army National Guard divisions enter federal service.

January 25

Eighth U.S. Army (EUSA) launches counterattack, Operation THUNDERBOLT, to push CCF north of Han River.

February 1

Battle of Twin Tunnels.

February 5

X Corps begins Operation ROUNDUP on eastern front.

February 11–17

Chinese Communist Forces (CCF) launch fourth-phase offensive in central Korea.

February 13–15

Battle of Chipyong-ni. CCF offensive contained.

February 16, 1951–July 27, 1953

Task Force 95, UN Blockade and Escort Force, blockades Wonsan harbor.

February 19

The First Marine Division transferred from X Corps to IX Corps.

February 21

Eighth U.S. Army (EUSA) launches counterattack by IX and X Corps to drive CCF north of Han River (Operation KILLER).

After two-month detachment to ROK Army, First Korean Marine Regiment, rejoins U.S. First Marine Division as its fourth regiment.

February 28

Last enemy resistance south of Han River collapses.

March 7

Operation RIPPER begins with advance across Han River by IX and X Corps.

March 14

Seoul recaptured from the enemy.

March 23

The 187th Airborne Regimental Combat Team makes air assault at Munsan-ni.

March 27–31

Eighth U.S. Army (EUSA) elements reach 38th parallel.

April 5

Operation RUGGED, an advance to Line Kansas, begins. (Line Kansas ran northeast from the Imjin River to Chorwon, the southwestern edge of Iron Triangle then east to the Hwachon Reservoir to the Sea of Japan at Yangyang.)

Letter from General MacArthur to Congressman Joseph W. Martin, House Minority leader, critical of U.S. war policy is made public.

April 11

President Truman relieves General MacArthur of U.S. Far East Command/United Nations Command and from his position as supreme commander Allied powers.

General Matthew B. Ridgway named as successor.

April 14

Lieutenant General James A. Van Fleet assumes command of EUSA.

All forces reach Line Kansas.

April 22

U.S. Far East Command initiates its rotation plan: Service personnel will return to the United States individually (rather than with their units, as is the case with other UN forces) after a specified number of months in Korea.

April 22–30
Chinese Communist Forces (CCF) launch spring offensive with 250,000 men in 27 divisions (first step, fifth-phase offensive) along a forty-mile front north of Seoul, leading to the biggest battle of the Korean War.

April 25
After three-day fight, the First Battalion, the Gloucestershire Regiment, annihilated on "Gloucester Hill."

April 30
Chinese Communist Forces (CCF) offensive contained north of Seoul and north of Han River.

May 1
The First Marine Division reassigned from IX Corps to X Corps.

May 3–May 31
The Senate holds "Great Debate" on U.S. Korean War policy.

May 9
The U.S. Far East Air Force launches 300-plane strike on Sinuiju on Yalu River. Largest raid of war to date.

May 16
Chinese Communist Forces (CCF) launch second step, fifth-phase offensive. Initially gain up to 20 miles of territory.

May 20
Advance of CCF halted.

Far East Air Force launches Operation STRANGLE air interdiction campaign.

U.S. Air Force Captain James Jabara, flying an F-86 Saberjet, becomes first jet air ace in history.

May 21
Eighth U.S. Army (EUSA) counterattacks to drive enemy out of South Korea.

May 30
Eighth U.S. Army (EUSA) returns to Line Kansas.

June 1–16
I and IX corps advance toward Line Wyoming in Iron Triangle.

The First Marine Division advances from Hwachon Reservoir to Punchbowl area.

June 19
President Truman signs Universal Military Training and Service Act, which extends Selective Service until July 1, 1955, lowers draft age to 18 and increases term of service from 21 to 24 months.

June 23
Soviet UN delegate Jacob Malik proposes cease-fire discussions.

June 30
On orders from Washington, General Ridgway broadcasts that United Nations is willing to discuss armistice.

Since June 1950 Army has expanded from 590,000 to over 1,530,000: approximately 172,000 personnel are from the Army Reserve and 34,000 are from the National Guard, having been recalled to active duty; 550,000 inductees have been furnished by the Selective Service system.

Since June 1950 Marine Corps has expanded from 74,279 to 192,620 active duty personnel. Fifty percent of Marines in Korea are reservists.

United Nations Command (UNC) ground forces stand at 554,577, including 253,250 U.S.;

273,266 ROK; and 28,061 ground forces from other UN nations.

July 1
Marshal Kim Il-sung, commander of North Korean People's Army (NKPA), and Peng Teh-huai, CCF commander, agree to begin armistice talks.

July 10
Armistice talks between UN Command and CCF/NKPA begin at Kaesong. UN delegation headed by Admiral C. Turner Joy.

July 14
Republic of Korea (ROK) organizes Korean Service Corps (KSC).

July 22
Admiral William F. Fechteler becomes chief of naval operations, replacing Admiral Forrest P. Sherman, who died in office.

August 5
United Nations Command (UNC) suspends armistice talks because armed troops present in neutral area.

August 10
Armistice talks resume.

August 22
Communists halt truce talks because of violation of neutral area by UN aircraft.

August 31–September 3
The First Marine Division seizes Bloody Ridge at cost of 2,700 casualties.

September 8
Japanese Peace Treaty signed at San Francisco.

September 13–October 15
The Second Infantry Division seizes Heartbreak Ridge at cost of 3,700 casualties.

September 17
Robert A. Lovett replaces George C. Marshall as secretary of defense.

October 1
Eighth U.S. Army (EUSA) either disbands all-black units or infuses them with white personnel, ending segregation of its units.

The 24th Infantry Regiment and 159th Field Artillery Battalion, 25th Infantry Division, disbanded and replaced by 14th Infantry Regiment and 69th Field Artillery Battalion.

October 3–19
Five I Corps divisions (First Cavalry Division, First ROK Division, British Commonwealth Division, Third Infantry Division and 25th Infantry Division) advance to Jamestown line in Old Baldy area at cost of 4,000 casualties.

October 7
Negotiators agree to move armistice talks from Kaesong to Panmunjom.

October 25
Armistice talks resume at Panmunjom.

November 12
Eighth U.S. Army (EUSA) ordered to cease offensive operations and begin active defense.

December 2, 1951–March 15, 1952
Task Force Paik (after its commander, ROK Lieutenant General Paik Sun Yup) conducts Operation RATCATCHER in southwest Korea to eliminate guerrillas operating there.

December 5–December 29
The 45th Infantry Division, arriving from Japan, replaces First Cavalry Division on front line in Korea. First Cavalry Division moves to Japan.

1952

January
The 40th Infantry Division, arriving from Japan, replaces 24th Infantry Division on the front line in Korea. The 24th Infantry Division (minus the Fifth Infantry Regiment and 555th Field Artillery Battalion, which remain as the independent Fifth Regimental Combat Team) moves to Japan.

January 1
General Lemanuel Shepherd replaces General Clifton Cates as commandant of the Marine Corps.

January 2
United Nations Command (UNC) proposes voluntary repatriation of prisoners of war (POWs).

January 8
Communists reject voluntary repatriation.

February 22
North Koreans charge UN with germ warfare.

March 17
First Marine Division reassigned from X Corps, located in eastern Korea, to I Corps, located in far west.

April 17
President Truman signs Executive Order 10345, which extends enlistments involuntarily for nine months.

April 20
United Nations Command (UNC) announces only 70,000 of 132,000 POWs desire repatriation.

April 28
Occupation of Japan officially ends.

U.S.-Japan Mutual Security Treaty comes into effect.

May 2
Communists again reject concept of voluntary repatriation. Both sides announce stalemate on POW issue.

May 7–11
Communist POWs at Koje-do riot then capture camp commandant, Brigadier General Francis T. Dodd, and extract concessions.

May 12
General Mark Clark replaces General Ridgway as commander in chief, United Nations Command/Far East Command.

May 22
Army Major General William K. Harrison replaces Admiral C. Turner Joy as chief of UN delegation at Panmunjom.

June 23
Far East Air Force bombs power plants on Yalu River.

June 30
United Nations Command (UNC) ground forces stand at 678,051 personnel, including 265,864 U.S.; 376,418 ROK; and 35,769 from other UN countries.

August 21
Korean Communications Zone established.

August 29
Far East Air Force bombs Pyongyang in 1,403 plane raid, the largest air raid of the war.

October 1
Army Forces Far East established as Army component of Far East Command.

Japan Logistical Command disestablished.

October 8
Final POW offer rejected by Communists.

United Nations Command (UNC) adjourns armistice talks "indefinitely."

October 16
Second Logistical Command transferred to Korean Communications Zone and disestablished.

October 24
Presidential candidate Dwight D. Eisenhower announces that if elected, he will go to Korea.

November 4
Eisenhower elected president of the United States.

November 10
Eighth U.S. Army (EUSA) announces mobilization of two new Republic of Korea (ROK) divisions.

November 15
Ambassador Ellis O. Briggs replaces John J. Muccio as U.S. ambassador to the Republic of Korea.

December 5–8
Eisenhower visits Korea.

1953

January 20
Dwight D. Eisenhower replaces Harry S Truman as commander in chief.

John Foster Dulles replaces Dean Acheson as secretary of state.

Charles Wilson replaces Robert Lovett as secretary of defense.

February 10
General Maxwell D. Taylor replaces General James Van Fleet as EUSA commander.

March 5
Soviet Premier Joseph Stalin dies in Moscow.

April 20–26
Operation LITTLE SWITCH exchanges sick and wounded prisoners of war.

April 26
Armistice talks resume at Panmunjom.

June 4
Communists accept UN proposals in all major respects.

June 10–16
ROK II Corps at Kumson pushed back 4,000 yards to new positions.

June 18
ROK President Syngman Rhee releases Korean nonrepatriate POWs.

June 30
General Nathan F. Twining replaces General Hoyt Vandenberg as Air Force chief of staff.

July 2–12

The 24th Infantry Division moves from Japan to Korea to bolster rear area defenses and the security of POW camps.

July 6–10

U.S. Seventh Infantry Division dislodged from defensive positions on Pork Chop Hill.

July 13–20

CCF launches six-division attack on ROK II Corps and U.S. IX Corps. Attack contained at Kumsong River line.

July 14

187th Airborne Regimental Combat Team moves from Japan to Korea and is attached to U.S. Second Infantry Division in Kumsong area.

July 27

Korean armistice agreement signed.

Cease-fire goes into effect at 2200 hours (11 PM).

July 31

UNC ground force strength stands at 932,539, including 302,483 U.S. forces, 590,911 ROK forces and 39,145 ground forces from other UN countries.

August 5–September 6

Final exchange of prisoners of war (Operation BIG SWITCH).

Part III

---

the
korean war
a to z

ACES

In aerial warfare downing five enemy aircraft qualifies a fighter pilot for the unofficial designation of *ace*. There were 40 American air aces from action during the Korean War alone. Thir-

ty-eight were from the Air Force, and one each was from the Navy and Marine Corps.

Five of the Air Force fighter pilots (some already aces from World War II) either added to their totals or qualified as aces when their World War II and Korean War kills were combined. Except for the Navy ace all were pilots of F-86 Sabrejets. Navy Lieutenant Guy Bordelon, on detached duty from the USS *Princeton*, shot down five "Bedcheck Charlies"—three YAK-18s and two LA-9s or LA-11s—while flying a propeller-driven F4U-5N Corsair, thus becoming the only Navy ace of the war. While not qualifying as aces, three other Navy pilots (including future astronaut Walter Schirra), flying F-86 Sabrejets while on detached duty with the Air Force, shot down a total of four MiGs; an additional 12 MiGs were downed by carrier-based Navy pilots flying other types of aircraft.

Marine Corps Major John F. Bolt, also flying an F-86 Sabrejet while on detached duty with the Air Force, shot down his fifth and sixth MiG on July 11, 1953, thus becoming the only Marine ace of the Korean War. Nine other Marine pilots, also on detached duty with the Air Force, shot down some 15 MiGs. Among them was John H. Glenn, future astronaut and U.S. senator, then a Marine major. He shot down three MiGs in nine days while flying an Air Force F-86 emblazoned with the words "MiG

F-86 Sabrejets were the MiG killers of the war.
(Courtesy U.S. Army Center of Military History.)

Mad Marine." In addition, land-based and carrier-based Marine pilots flying other types of aircraft shot down 20 enemy planes.

The Korean War marked the first time that jet-propelled aircraft were used extensively in aerial combat; on May 20, 1951, Air Force Captain James Jabara, flying an F-86 Sabrejet, became the first jet air ace in aviation history when he shot down his fifth and sixth enemy MiGs. He went on to shoot down an additional nine enemy aircraft, becoming the world's second triple jet ace, runner-up to Air Force Captain Joseph C. McConnell Jr. (the war's ranking jet air ace), who had 16 MiG kills to his credit.

At age 37, the oldest ace was Air Force Colonel Vermont Garrison, who had shot down 11 German planes in World War II. The youngest was Air Force Lieutenant Henry Buttelmann, who at age 24 shot down five enemy aircraft in just 12 days. The 39th and last jet air ace of the war was Air Force Major Stephen L. Bettinger, whose status was not confirmed until after the armistice was signed. After shooting down his fifth MiG on July 20, 1953, Bettinger was shot down and taken prisoner; his statement as the second confirming witness of the MiG shoot-down could not be obtained until after his release from a North Korean prisoner of war camp in October 1953.

Information on enemy air aces is sparse. According to Hallion (see below), during 1951 to 1952 Colonel Ivan N. Kozhedub, the Soviet Union's leading air ace in World War II, allegedly commanded a Soviet MiG division in Korea. Three Chinese air aces are also mentioned—Li Han, Chang Chi-wei and Wang Hai—but no further information is available.

See also AERIAL COMBAT; BEDCHECK CHARLIES; CHINESE COMMUNIST AIR FORCE; FIRST MARINE AIRCRAFT WING; NORTH KOREA AIR FORCES.

Suggestions for further reading: For a by-name listing of Korean War Air Force aces see *Air Force* magazine, May 1985, pages 202–203. Appendix VII of *The Sea War in Korea* by Commander Malcolm W. Cagle, USN, and Commander Frank A. Manson, USN (Annapolis, Md: United States Naval Institute Press, 1957) has a complete listing of all Navy and Marine Corps aviators who downed enemy aircraft during the Korean War. See also Robert F. Futrell, *The United States Air Force in Korea: 1950–1953*, revised edition (Washington, D.C.: GPO, 1983); Richard P. Hallion, *The Naval Air War in Korea* (Baltimore: The Nautical & Aviation Publishing Company of America, 1986).

ACHESON, DEAN G(OODERHAM) (1893–1971)

Born April 11, 1893, in Middletown, Connecticut, Acheson graduated from Yale University in 1915. After serving in the Navy during World War I, he received a law degree from Harvard in 1918. A member of the law firm of Covington and Burling, during World War II Acheson took a leave of absence to serve as assistant secretary of state for economic affairs from 1941 to 1944; he served as undersecretary of state from 1945 to 1947. Returning to his law practice in the summer of 1947, he succeeded the ailing George C. Marshall as secretary of state in January 1949 and was serving in that capacity when the Korean War began.

In January 1950, in an address to the National Press Club, Acheson defined American defense interests in Asia. Reiterating the official government position agreed upon by the Defense Department and the Joint Chiefs of Staff, he excluded Korea from the Asian defense perimeter. Already under fire for losing China (which had fallen to the Communists in 1949), he was accused of precipitating the June 1950 North Korean invasion. America's withdrawing of all U.S. military forces from Korea in 1949 and its failure to provide an adequate level of military support thereafter probably spoke louder than Acheson's words.

"Acheson held Moscow accountable for the Korean War," notes one biographer. "He argued that the United States must save South Korea not for the Koreans but for the West European nations still skeptical of the American resolve to defend them. Intervention in Korea ... would be in the eyes of the NATO allies the final American atonement for its pre-1941 isolationist policy [and] recommended that the United States commit itself to a war in Korea." This explanation does much to explain why those NATO allies had such a powerful voice—a voice all out of proportion to their military commitment—in the prosecution of that war.

A powerful secretary of state, Acheson defined America's political goal in the Korean War. In the beginning the goal was the restoration of the status quo anti bellum (i.e., the restoration of prewar political boundaries). After the successful Inchon invasion the goal was changed to the liberation of North Korea, but after the Chinese intervention in November 1950 the goal reverted to the original one.

Hampered in his public and congressional relations by his aristocratic demeanor and his haughty disregard for those he considered his intellectual inferiors, Acheson nevertheless served his country well. West Europe was assured of U.S. military support if attacked, and the line of Communist advance was drawn in Asia. Acheson left the Truman administration in January 1953 and was replaced as secretary of state by John Foster Dulles. He later served as an adviser to presidents Kennedy and Johnson and was one of the "wise men" who advised Johnson to deescalate the Vietnam War after the Tet Offensive of 1968. Acheson died on October 12, 1971.

See STATE DEPARTMENT.

Suggestions for further reading: See Dean Acheson, *Present at the Creation: My Years at the State Department*, 1969 and Acheson's *The Korean War*, 1971 (New York: W.W. Norton. See also David S. McLellan, *Dean Acheson: The State Department Years* (New York: Dodd, 1976) and biographic entry in *Political Profiles: The Truman Years*. Eleanora W. Schoenebaum, editor (New York: Facts On File, 1978).

ADVISERS

See KOREA MILITARY ADVISORY GROUP; SOVIET UNION (UNION OF SOVIET SOCIALIST REPUBLICS).

AERIAL COMBAT

Because the United Nations (UN) forces enjoyed air superiority over the majority of the Korean peninsula, aerial combat took place almost exclusively in the skies over North Korea; enemy aircraft flew from airbases north of the Yalu River in Manchuria, which were immune from attack. Principally the battles took place between U.S. Air Force F-86 Sabrejets on the UN side and Soviet-supplied MiG-15 Fagot jet fighters on the Chinese/North Korean side.

The MiG-15 was a light aircraft with a powerful engine, and the F-86 was a heavy airplane with a powerful engine. The MiG-15 constantly outclimbed the F-86, but the F-86 had a slight speed advantage. Standard MiG armament consisted of 23-mm and 37-mm cannon with mechanical sights; the F-86s were armed with six .50-caliber machine-guns having both mechanical and electronic sights.

During the course of the war more than 950 enemy aircraft—including some 792 MiG-15 fighters—were downed in aerial combat. Air Force pilots claimed 900 of these, the Marines 35 and the Navy 16. Meteor-8 jet pilots from the Royal Australian Air Force's 77th Squadron shot down two MiG-15s, and British Royal Navy Lieutenant Peter Carmichael of the HMS *Ocean* shot down a MiG-15 while flying a propeller-driven Seafury. One Air Force Sabrejet pilot, Major Raymond G. Davis, won the Medal of Honor for his actions during a dogfight with 12 enemy MiGs.

The United States lost 147 aircraft in air-to-air combat, including 78 F-86 Sabrejets. The Sabre pilots thus maintained a 10-to-one margin of victory over the Communist Forces MiG-15 jet fighters.

See also ACES; AIRCRAFT CARRIERS; AIR FORCE, U.S.; BEDCHECK CHARLIES; CHINESE COMMUNIST AIR FORCE; FIGHTER AND FIGHTER-BOMBER AIRCRAFT; NORTH KOREAN AIR FORCES; UNITED NATIONS AIR FORCES.

Suggestions for further reading: Robert F. Futrell, *The United States Air Force in Korea: 1950–1953*, revised edition (Washington, D.C.: GPO, 1983); Richard P. Hallion, *The Naval Air War in Korea* (Baltimore: The Nautical & Aviation Publishing Company of America, 1986).

AEROMEDICAL BATTLEFIELD EVACUATION

One of the major innovations of the Korean War was the use of helicopters for evacuating the wounded from the battlefield. Usually the helicopters moved the wounded from battalion aid stations near the front lines to MASH (Mobile Army Surgical Hospital) and evacuation hospitals farther to the rear, but in some cases they were transported to hospital ships anchored offshore.

Because of the mountainous terrain, which made flying difficult and often impossible, the scarcity of helicopters and the technical limitations of the helicopters that were available—in the H-5 model most frequently used, for example, the wounded had to be transported in

external litters—only about one in seven American casualties was evacuated by helicopter. But even with these shortcomings, helicopters made a difference. In World War II, when no tactical aircraft were free to fly American casualties from the battlefield, 4.5% of wounded U.S. soldiers died after finally reaching a medical facility. In the Korean War the rate dropped to 2.5%.

See also HELICOPTERS; HOSPITAL SHIPS; MEDICAL CARE AND EVACUATION.

A-FRAME

Symbolic of Korea to many American veterans of the war there, the *A-frame* is a load-carrying device peculiar to Korea. It consists of a simple wooden backpack frame built roughly in the shape of the capital letter *A* with shoulder straps of woven straw. Using this pack frame, Koreans could carry unbelievably large loads over the most rugged terrain.

AIDMEN, MEDICAL

See COMBAT MEDICAL AIDMEN; COMBAT MEDICAL BADGE; MEDICAL CARE AND EVACUATION.

AIRBORNE OPERATIONS

Airborne operations pioneered in World War II continued to be perfected during the war in Korea. Although gliders were no longer employed, parachutes continued to be widely used, both for aerial assault and for aerial resupply. For example, the 187th Airborne Regimental Combat Team launched two parachute-borne aerial assaults during the Korean War—one at Sukchon-Sunchon on October 20, 1950 and one at Munsan-ni on March 23, 1951. In addition, special operations person-

187th Airborne practices for the Munsan jump.
(Courtesy U.S. Army Military History Institute.)

nel were dropped behind enemy lines by parachute.

Aerial resupply using parachutes to deliver ammunition and other supplies to troops on the ground was even more extensive than aerial assault. Now an Air Force responsibility, at that time aerial resupply was a joint Army–Air Force effort. The Air Force's Combat Cargo Command (315th Air Division) provided the aircraft; the Army's 2348th Quartermaster Airborne Supply and Packaging Company (later the 8081st Army Unit) at Ashiya Air Base in Japan packaged, loaded and lashed the sup-

plies, then provided the "kicker," who ejected the cargo over drop zones in Korea. From July 1950 until June 1951, while the battlefield was in constant motion, the greatest airdrop resupply in history was conducted for troops isolated from the main supply routes or cut off by enemy action. Of all the tonnage dropped, only some 3% of the supplies were lost because they landed outside the drop zones.

See COMBAT CARGO COMMAND; HELICOPTERS; 187TH AIRBORNE REGIMENTAL COMBAT TEAM; RANGER COMPANIES; SPECIAL OPERATIONS.

AIRCRAFT CARRIERS

When the war began the United States Navy had a total of 15 carriers: seven large attack carriers (CVA), four light carriers (CVL), and four escort carriers (CVE). Because World War II carriers were withdrawn from mothball status, strength had increased by 1953 to 34 carriers: 17 CVA's, 5 CVL's and 12 CVE's.

Eleven CVA fleet carriers, many on repetitive tours, served with Task Force 77, the Seventh Fleet Striking Force, which operated chiefly off the east coast of Korea in the Sea of Japan. These included the USS *Antietam* (CVA 36), *Boxer* (CVA 21), *Bon Homme Richard* (CVA 31), *Essex* (CVA 9), *Kearsarge* (CVA 33), *Lake Champlain* (CVA 39) *Leyte* (CVA 32), *Oriskany* (CVA 34), *Philippine Sea* (CVA 47), *Princeton* (CVA 37) and *Valley Forge* (CVA 45). While in Korean waters these CVAs had 24 CAG's (Carrier Air Groups) embarked, with a total of 100 squadrons, including 22 Naval Reserve squadrons. This total included 38 F4U Corsair squadrons, 35 F9F Panther squadrons, 23 AD Skyraider squadrons and 4 F2H Banshee squadrons.

In addition, a number of CVL light carriers and CVE escort carriers with Marine air squadrons embarked served with Task Force 95, the *United Nations Blockading and Escort Force*, which operated chiefly off the west coast of Korea in the Yellow Sea. These included USS *Bairoko* (CVE-115), *Badoeng Strait* (CVE-116), *Bataan* (CVL-29), *Rendova* (CVE-114) and *Sicily* (CVE-118). The Australian aircraft carrier HMAS *Sydney* and the British aircraft carriers HMS *Glory, Ocean, Theseus* and *Triumph* also served with Task Force 95.

Eight of these carriers—the *Badoeng Strait, Bon Homme Richard, Essex, Leyte, Philippine Sea, Princeton, Sicily* and *Valley Force*—won Navy Unit Commendations for their action there. One carrier pilot, the USS *Leyte*'s Lieutenant (junior grade) Thomas J. Hudner Jr., won the Medal of Honor in an attempt to rescue a downed squadron mate.

During the course of the war, U.S. naval air (including land-based Marine air) flew some 275,912 sorties (compared to 392,139 Air Force sorties); flew 40% of the interdiction missions, 53% of the close air support missions, 36% of the counter-air sorties, 30% of the reconnaissance missions and 100% of the antisubmarine patrols.

Five Navy and Marine aircraft were lost in aerial combat: 559 to antiaircraft fire and 684 to other causes not involving enemy action, for a total of 1,248 aircraft lost during the war. Fighter aircraft comprised 400 of the combat losses, followed by 140 attack aircraft, 12 observation aircraft, 8 helicopters, 2 patrol planes and 1 patrol and 1 transport version of the TBM Avengers. On average, a carrier air group sent to Korea could expect to lose 10% of its aircrew to combat and operational losses.

See also AUSTRALIA; BLOCKADE AND ESCORT FORCE; FIGHTER AND FIGHTER-BOMBER AIRCRAFT; FIRST MARINE AIRCRAFT WING; NAVY, U.S.; SEVENTH FLEET STRIKING FORCE; UNITED KINGDOM.

Suggestions for further reading: James A. Field, *History of United States Naval Operations: Korea* (Washington, D.C: GPO, 1962). See also Commanders Malcolm W. Cagle and Frank A. Manson, USN, *The Sea War in Korea* (Annapolis, Md: United States Naval Institute, 1957); Richard P. Hallion, *The Naval Air War in Korea* (Baltimore: The Nautical & Aviation Publishing Company of America, 1986).

AIRFIELDS

During the Korean War the UN Far East Air Force (FEAF) used some 15 air bases in Japan to support combat operations in Korea. These included Chitose air base on the northernmost

Japanese island of Kokkaido; 10 air bases on the main island of Honshu—Misawa in the north, Matsushima (near Sendai) also in the north; Johnson, Yokota and Tachikawa (near Tokyo), Komaki (near Nagoya), and Itami (near Kobe) in the center; and Miho (on the southwest coast) and Bofu and Iwakuni air bases on the southeast coast; as well as four more on the southernmost island of Kyushu—Ashiya, Itazuki, Tsuiku and Brady air bases. Kadena and Naha air bases on Okinawa were also used.

In Korea the Air Force either improved or constructed some 55 airfields, some of which, like K-24 in Pyongyang, were later abandoned to the enemy. These air bases were all numbered, and some became better known by their number than by their name. The more important of these airfields included:

K-1	Pusan West
K-2	Taegu
K-3	Pohang
K-5	Taejon
K-6	Pyongtaek
K-8	Kumsan
K-9	Pusan East
K-10	Chinhae
K-13	Suwan
K-14	Kimpo
K-16	Seoul
K-40	Cheju-do Island
K-46	Hoengsong
K-47	Chunchon
K-55	Osan

See also ENGINEERS; FAR EAST AIR FORCE; FIFTH AIR FORCE; KIMPO AIRFIELD.

Suggestions for further reading: See Robert F. Futrell, *The United States Air Force in Korea: 1950–1953*, revised edition (Washington, D.C.: GPO, 1983).

AIR FORCES, CHINESE COMMUNIST

See CHINESE COMMUNIST AIR FORCE.

AIR FORCE CROSS

See DISTINGUISHED SERVICE CROSS.

AIR FORCE, REPUBLIC OF KOREA

See UNITED NATIONS AIR FORCES.

AIR FORCES, NORTH KOREAN

See NORTH KOREAN AIR FORCE.

AIR FORCES, UNITED NATIONS

See UNITED NATIONS AIR FORCES.

AIR FORCE, U.S.

Less than three years old when the war began—until July 1947 the United States Air Force (USAF) had been the United States Army Air Force (USAAF)—the Air Force played a major part in the Korean War. Air operations fell into four major categories. First was the air war, principally over South Korea, which supported the Republic of Korea Army and United Nations ground operations. This included the close air support of ground troops and interdiction of enemy lines of supply and communication by the Fifth Air Force; aeromedical evacuation and tactical (i.e., intratheater) airlift operations by Combat Cargo Command, a division of the Far East Air Force (FEAF); and intertheater movement of troops, equipment and supplies by Military Air Transport Command.

The second category of operations was the air campaign over North Korea. The purpose was to gain air superiority over (i.e., to neutralize) the North Korean and Chinese Communist air forces and eliminate the threat posed by their high-performance MiG-15 jet fighters and Il-28 jet bombers to Allied ground, air and sea operations in Korea. Third, there was the deep interdiction bombing campaign by the Fifth Air Force's B-26 light bombers and FEAF Bomber Command's B-29 medium bombers against North Korean military and industrial targets, including bridges and hydroelectric plants along the Yalu River between Korea and Manchuria.

Finally there was the coordination of U.S. Naval and Marine Corps air operations, the coordination and support of Allied air operations, the conduction of search and rescue operations, and the air defense of the Republic of Korea and of Japan, which for much of the war was still under U.S. occupation. Command and control of air operations in Korea was relatively straightforward. FEAF headquarters nearby in Japan (in coordination with the commander, Naval Forces Far East) controlled all air operations in Korea and the air defense of Japan through its four principal subordinate commands: the Fifth Air Force, Bomber Command, the 314th Air Division (Japan Air Defense Force) and the 315th Air Division (Combat Cargo Command).

In addition to other combat awards and decorations won by Air Force personnel in Korea, Air Force pilots won four Medals of Honor: one by an F-86 Sabrejet pilot in a dogfight with MiGs, one by an F-80 Shooting Star pilot on a close air support mission, one by an F-51 Mustang pilot also on a close air support mission and one by a B-26 Invader pilot on an aerial interdiction mission. Of the 5,720,000 Americans on active duty in the armed services from June 25, 1950 to July 27, 1953, 1,285,000 were Air Force personnel, second only to the Army in the total who served. During the war 1,466 FEAF aircraft were lost, almost one-half to enemy action and the other half to mechanical and other causes. During air and ground operations 1,180 Air Force personnel were killed in action and 368 wounded in action. An additional 5,884 died of illness, injury or disease; many of the 8,177 personnel still missing in action and unaccounted for are Air Force pilots and aircrews.

See also ACES; AERIAL COMBAT; BOMBER AIRCRAFT; BOMBER COMMAND; CLOSE AIR SUPPORT; COMBAT CARGO COMMAND; FAR EAST AIR FORCE; FIFTH AIR FORCE; FIGHTER AND FIGHTER-BOMBER AIRCRAFT; MEDICAL CARE AND EVACUATION; MOBILIZATION; MATS (MILITARY AIR TRANSPORT SERVICE); SEARCH AND RESCUE OPERATIONS.

Suggestions for further reading: Robert F. Futrell, *The United States Air Force in Korea: 1950–1953*, revised edition (Washington, D.C.: GPO, 1983).

AIRLIFT

See COMBAT CARGO COMMAND; MATS (MILITARY AIR TRANSPORT SERVICE).

AIR MEDAL

First authorized in World War II, the Air Medal was awarded during the Korean War in the name of the president of the United States, recognizing single acts of merit or heroism or meritorious service while participating in aerial flight. Awards were given for acts of heroism during military operations against an armed enemy; the acts were of a lesser degree than those required for award of the Distinguished Flying Cross. Awards were also made for single acts of meritorious achievement involving superior airmanship of a lesser degree than that required for award of the Distinguished Flying Cross; nevertheless, the act was accomplished with distinction beyond that normally expected.

Further, awards for meritorious service were provided for sustained distinction in the performance of duties involving regular and frequent participation in aerial flight. Such awards were intended to recognize those whose duties required them to participate in aerial flight on a regular and frequent basis. After the first award an oak leaf cluster (gold star in the case of Navy and Marine Corps personnel) is worn on the ribbon, denoting subsequent awards.

ALMOND, EDWARD M(ALLORY) (1892–1979)

Born December 12, 1892 in Luray, Virginia, Almond graduated from the Virginia Military Institute in 1915 and was commissioned as a second lieutenant of infantry on November 30, 1916. He commanded the 12th Machine Gun Battalion, Fourth Infantry Division, in World War I during the Aisne-Marne and Meuse-Argonne campaigns; he was wounded in action and awarded the Silver Star Medal for gallantry.

During the interwar years he attended the Infantry School, the Command & General Staff School and the Army War College, as well as the Air Corps Tactical School and the Naval War College. He served on the Army General Staff, commanded a battalion in the Philippines and was serving as a staff officer with VI Corps when the United States entered World War II. During World War II Almond commanded the 92d Infantry Division in the Italian campaign. The only "black" division in the United States Army that saw active combat, the 92d Infantry Division, composed of black soldiers and principally white officers, had a controversial combat record.

When the Korean War broke out, Almond was serving as chief of staff to General of the Army Douglas MacArthur at General Headquarters, Far East Command (FECOM), in Tokyo. In September 1950 (while still retaining his position as Chief of Staff) he was named to command X Corps for the Inchon landing. Separate from Eighth U.S. Army (EUSA) and reporting directly to MacArthur, Almond remained in independent command of X Corps (which then included the First Marine Division and the Army's Third and Seventh Infantry divisions) through the subsequent east coast advance into North Korea, the operations in the Chosin Reservoir area and the retreat to and evacuation from Hungnam.

After that evacuation Almond relinquished both his assignment as FECOM Chief of Staff and his independent status. He commanded X Corps in the eastern sector of EUSA's defensive line across the Korean peninsula until July 1951, when he returned to the United States to serve as commandant of the Army War College. He retired from active duty on January 1, 1953, and died on June 11, 1979.

One of the most controversial officers of the Korean War, Almond was especially detested by the Marine officers who served under his

General Almond receives flowers for liberation of Hamhung, North Korea, in October 1950.
(Courtesy U.S. Army Military History Institute.)

command. Denounced as a toady and sycophant (and as a blatant racist in Clay Blair's recent Korean War history), Almond nevertheless successfully executed the Inchon landings in September 1950 and did avoid annihilation when X Corps was attacked by the vastly superior 120,000-man Chinese Communist Force's Ninth Army Group in November to December 1950.

See X CORPS.

Suggestions for further reading: See Shelby L. Stanton, *X Corps: America's Tenth Legion in Korea* (Novato, CA: Presidio Press, 1989). See also David Childress's biographical sketch in *Dictionary of American Military Biography*, edited by Roger J. Spiller (Westport, Conn.: Greenwood Press, 1984) and Clay Blair's *The Forgotten War: America in Korea 1950–1953* (New York: Times Books, 1987).

AMBASSADOR TO THE REPUBLIC OF KOREA, U.S.

Ambassadors of the United States have authority over all U.S. government personnel—except those under military commands—within their country of assignment. On August 12, 1948, John J. Muccio was appointed as President Harry S Truman's special representative to South Korea, which had been under the control of a military government since 1945, when the U.S. XXIV Corps landed there to disarm the Japanese.

Muccio was given authority to negotiate for the withdrawal of U.S. "occupation" forces and to establish a U.S. diplomatic mission in Seoul. On March 21, 1949, he became the first U.S. ambassador to the Republic of Korea. When the U.S. military withdrew from Korea later that year (*see* Part I: The Setting), the Korea Military Advisory Group (KMAG) came under Ambassador Muccio's control. It was under his command at the outbreak of the war and remained

so until it reverted to military control on July 4, 1950.

Accompanying the government of the Republic of Korea when it withdrew to Taegu and Pusan, as well as on its later return to Seoul, Ambassador Muccio's major wartime concern was maintaining political harmony between the United States and its coalition partner, the Republic of Korea, and especially with its mercurial president, Syngman Rhee. In November 1952, Muccio was replaced by Ellis O. Briggs, former ambassador to Czechoslovakia. Briggs served as U.S. ambassador to the Republic of Korea for the remainder of the war.

See also MUCCIO, JOHN J.; SECRETARY OF STATE.

Suggestions for further reading: Harold J. Noble, *Embassy at War* (Seattle: University of Washington Press, 1975).

AMPHIBIOUS CONSTRUCTION BATTALION

See SEABEES.

AMPHIBIOUS FORCE FAR EAST (TASK FORCE 90)

The Amphibious Force Far East (Task Force 90) was one of the major subordinate commands of U.S. Naval Forces Far East (NAVFE). As with all naval task forces, its composition changed because ships were attached or detached to meet the demands of the assigned mission. Among the Amphibious Force's major accomplishments were the landing at Pohang on July 18, 1950, the Inchon invasion on September 15, 1950, the Wonsan landing in October 1950 and the Hungnam redeployment in December 1950.

In addition the task force provided a constant amphibious threat against North

Korean/Chinese Communist Forces rear areas and lines of communication, a threat reinforced by feints and demonstrations. For example, one feint, known as Operation DECOY, took place against Kojo south of Wonsan on Korea's eastern coast, in October 1952. It involved naval gunfire support from the battleship USS *Iowa* and other cruisers and destroyers, a simulated landing by the First Cavalry Division's Eighth Regimental Combat Team and an intense aerial bombardment that caused the enemy to relocate its reserve divisions from the interior to positions along the coastline.

See INCHON INVASION; WONSAN.

Suggestions for further reading: James A. Field, *History of United States Naval Operations: Korea* (Washington, D.C.: GPO, 1962). See also Commanders Malcolm W. Cagle and Frank A. Manson, USN, *The Sea War in Korea* (Annapolis, Md: United States Naval Institute, 1957), which contains a by-ship listing of the composition of the Pohang, Inchon, Wonsan and Hungnam amphibious forces as well as a listing of the wartime commanders of Task Force 90.

ANTIAIRCRAFT ARTILLERY (AAA)

The U.S. Army deployed some eight divisional antiaircraft artillery automatic weapons (AAA/AW) units to Korea as well as separate AAA units and the AW and gun battalions of the 10th AAA Group. A detachment from the 507th AAA-AW Battalion engaged a number of attacking North Korean fighter planes at Suwon air base on June 29, 1950, shooting down at least one and probably destroying another. But the majority of AAA units in Korea were used in direct support of ground forces.

Ninety-MM antiaircraft guns firing as field artillery in support of ROK forces north of Taegu.
(Courtesy U.S. Army Military History Institute.)

The divisional AAA/AW battalions were equipped with half-track mounted quad (i.e., four-barrel) .50-caliber machine-guns ("quad 50" batteries) and vehicle-mounted 37-mm and 40-mm guns. From the beginning they were used as tanks to place direct fire on enemy positions. Because these AAA soldiers were exposed in their open-firing positions, they took heavy casualties. The 90-mm gun battalions of the 10th AAA Group, on the other hand, were used as field artillery to give fire support to the infantry divisions on the line.

Because AAA units were used to support ground operations, there was a continuing shortage of AAA units to protect Air Force airfields. To remedy this situation, Air Force personnel manned quad 50 batteries and searchlight positions at several of the most critical locations.

Although their chief air defense weapon was the MiG-15 jet fighter, the Chinese and North Koreans also had an impressive array of AAA weapons. At their peak in the winter of 1952 to 1953, they possessed 786 AAA guns and 1,672 automatic weapons. The principal heavy gun was the Soviet 85-mm, which could shoot up to 25,000 feet. The principal automatic weapon was the Soviet 37-mm cannon, which could fire 160 rounds per minute ranging up to 4,500 feet.

See also FIELD ARTILLERY; SEARCHLIGHTS.

Suggestions for further reading: For use of AAA units in support of ground operations see *U.S. Army in the Korean War* series: Roy E. Appleman, *South to the Naktong, North to the Yalu*, 1961; Walter G. Hermes, *Truce Tent and Fighting Front*, 1966; and Billy C. Mossman, *Ebb and Flow*, anticipated in 1990 (Washington, D.C. GPO). For order of battle see Shelby Stanton, *Korean War Order of Battle* (Washington, D.C.: GPO, anticipated in 1990). See also Clay Blair, *The Forgotten War: America in Korea 1950–1953*, revised edition (Washington, D.C.: GPO, 1983).

ANTIWAR MOVEMENT

See BRAINWASHING; GERM WARFARE; PUBLIC OPINION.

ARGYLL AND SUTHERLAND HIGHLANDERS REGIMENT

See BRITISH COMMONWEALTH DIVISION; UNITED KINGDOM.

ARMISTICE AGREEMENT

Since there was no declaration of war to begin the Korean War, it is perhaps fitting that there has been no peace agreement to end it. As it now stands, there is still only a "truce" in Korea—a truce brought about by the military armistice agreement between the United Nations Command (UNC) and the military forces of the North Korean People's Army (NKPA) and the Chinese Communist Forces (CCF) that went into effect on July 27, 1953.

Over two years in the making, the armistice talks officially began on July 10, 1951, at Kaesong. On October 25, 1951 the talks were moved to the nearby village of Panmunjom, where they have continued intermittently ever since. Representatives from the UNC (U.S. Navy Vice Admiral C. Turner Joy from July 10, 1951 to May 22, 1952, and U.S. Army Major General, later Lieutenant General, William K. Harrison Jr. from May 23, 1952, through the signing of the armistice on July 27, 1953); from the Republic of Korea Army (ROKA) (major generals Paik Sun Yup from July 1951 to October 1951, Lee Hyung Koon from October 1951 to February 1952, Yu Chae Heung from February 1952 to April 1953 and Choi Duk Shim from April 1953 to the signing of the armistice); and from the NKPA (General Nam Il and the North Korean premier, Marshal Kim Il-sung) and the CCF (Chinese Marshal Peng

Teh-huai) were present. The delegates met to reach agreement on the demarcation line between the opposing sides, the exchange of the prisoners of war (POWs) and the ending of hostilities.

Marked by bitterness and recrimination, the talks often broke down and were frequently boycotted by first one side and then the other. Although some claim it was merely coincidental, real progress did not begin until after the death of Soviet Premier Joseph Stalin on March 5, 1953. On March 28, 1953, the NKPA/CCF agreed to an exchange of sick and wounded POWs (*see* LITTLE SWITCH), which took place during the period April 20 to May 3, 1953. On April 26, 1953, plenary sessions on the armistice negotiations resumed after a six-months' hiatus.

During the final four months of the negotiations, however, the bitterness and recrimination were not so much between the Allies and the Communists as between the United States and the Republic of Korea. President Syngman Rhee of the Republic of Korea was bitterly opposed to any agreement that did not guarantee the reunification of Korea and allowed CCF troops to remain on Korean soil. He went so far as threatening to refuse to abide by any agreement and to continue the war on his own; on June 18, 1953, he attempted to sabotage the talks by allowing some 25,000 North Korean POWs to escape from custody.

Legally the UNC did not need the approval of the ROK government to sign the armistice. It was a military agreement between military commanders, and ROK military forces had been placed under UNC control by President Rhee himself. As a practical matter, however, the acquiescence of the Republic of Korea was essential if the armistice were to succeed. After United States guarantees of a United States-Republic of Korea Mutual Defense Pact and assurances of long-term U.S. economic and military aid, ROK President Rhee assured U.S. President Eisenhower in a letter dated July 12, 1953, that despite his misgivings over the long-term results he "would not obstruct in any way the implementation of the terms of the armistice."

The acceptance by the Republic of Korea of the inevitable cleared the way for final approval of the armistice agreement. It provided for an armed truce to end the hostilities and for a demilitarized zone on either side of that line, fixed the demarcation line between North and South Korea, and set up procedures for the exchange of POWs.

Signed by Marshal Kim Il-sung and General Nam Il of the NKPA, Marshal Peng Teh-huai of the CCF, UNC Commander General Mark W. Clark and senior UNC delegate Lieutenant General William K. Harrison (but not by representatives of the ROKA), the armistice went into effect at 2201 hours, July 27, 1953. It has held for more than 35 years, and military representatives still meet periodically at Panmunjom to discuss alleged violations of its items.
See JOY, C. TURNER; PANMUNJOM; POWs (PRISONERS OF WAR).

Suggestions for further reading: Walter G. Hermes' *U.S. Army in the Korean War: Truce Tent and Fighting Front* (Washington, D.C.: GPO, 1966) has a lengthy discussion of the armistice talks and includes the complete text of the agreement itself. See also C. Turner Joy, *How Communists Negotiate* (New York: Macmillan, 1953) and William H. Vatcher Jr., *Panmunjom: The Story of the Korean Military Negotiations* (New York: Frederick Praeger, 1958).

ARMOR

Shortly before the Korean War began, the U.S. Army reorganized its infantry divisions to include a heavy tank battalion at division level and a tank company at regimental level. For the most part these were merely paper changes like other Army "improvements" during that period. In 1949, for example, the four infantry divisions in Japan were each authorized a heavy tank battalion: the 71st Heavy Tank in the First Cavalry Division, the 77th Heavy Tank in the Seventh Infantry Division, the 78th Heavy Tank in the 24th Infantry Division and the 79th Heavy Tank in the 25th Infantry Division.

But only A Company in each battalion was organized. And each company and the tank sections of the divisional reconnaissance companies were equipped—not with heavy tanks, which were not even in the Army inventory—but with light M-24 Chaffee reconnaissance tanks, which mounted ineffectual 75-mm guns. Except for some World War II vintage M-15A1 half-tracks, these were the only armor vehicles on hand when the war broke. Initially, the Republic of Korea Army had no armor units, but the North Korean People's Army began the war with some 120 Russian-made T-34 tanks in their 6,000-man 105th Armored Brigade (later known as the 105th Armored *Division*) plus another 30 T-34s in other formations. Mounting a high-velocity 85-mm main gun and possessing exceptional cross-country mobility, the T-34 medium tank was one of the best produced during World War II.

Because of this disparity, North Korean armor dominated the opening days of the war. The M-24 Chaffee light tanks of the 24th Infantry Division's A Company 78th Heavy Tank Battalion and 24th Reconnaissance Company (the first tank units to see action in Korea) were outgunned and outranged by the T-34 medium tanks—especially when the American's first ammunition resupply was reduced-charge training ammunition. Their tanks were shot from under them, and "A" Company's commander, First Lieutenant Leonard E. Gewin, was killed in action. The other light tank com-

panies following them into action fared no better.

As a stopgap measure the Army threw together a composite unit, the 8072d Tank Battalion, in Japan. Manned by veteran World War II tankers culled from headquarters units there (some tanks initially had five master sergeants per crew), the unit was equipped with World War II M-4A3E8 Sherman medium tanks that had been hurriedly rebuilt at the Tokyo Ordnance Depot. Rushed into the Pusan Perimeter in Korea in July 1950, this tank's high-velocity 76-mm main gun proved capable of stopping the T-34s. Renamed the 89th Medium Tank Battalion, it ended up being assigned to the 25th Infantry Division.

Meanwhile other tank units were being rushed to Korea. The Second Armored Division's Sixth Tank Battalion, equipped with brand-new M-46 Patton medium tanks (90-mm gun), joined the 24th Infantry Division; the Armor School's 70th Tank Battalion, equipped with M-26 Pershing medium tanks (90-mm gun) and M-4A3E8 Shermans (76-mm gun), joined the First Cavalry Division; the Infantry School's 73d Tank Battalion, equipped with M-26 Pershings (later M-46 Pattons), was initially under Eighth U.S. Army control but later was attached to the Seventh Infantry Division. These battalions, averaging about 69 tanks each, sailed from San Francisco on July 23, 1950, and landed in Pusan, Korea, on August 7, 1950.

Also in August 1950 the First Marine Tank Battalion disembarked in the Pusan Perimeter as did the Second Infantry Division's 72d Medium Tank Battalion. By the end of that month the United States had six medium tank battalions with more than 500 tanks (Five about equally divided between M-26 Pershings and M-4A3E8 Shermans plus the Sixth Tank Battalion's M-46 Pattons) within the Pusan Perimeter as well as four regimental tank companies and about 30 M-24 Chaffee light tanks

Ninth Infantry soldiers ride an M-26 Pershing into battle on the Nakton Perimeter, September 1950.
(Courtesy U.S. Army Military History Institute.)

that had survived the initial North Korean onslaught. By the beginning of September 1950 American tanks outnumbered the enemy's by at least five to one.

When the Third Infantry Division deployed to Korea in the fall of 1950, it was accompanied by its 64th Medium Tank Battalion (initially an all-black unit), which traded in its M-26 Pershings for M-46 Pattons. Later in the war the 140th Medium Tank Battalion of the 40th Infantry Division and the 245th Medium Tank Battalion of the 45th Infantry Division were also committed to action.

In addition to these tank battalions, there were a number of regimental tank companies. These were organic to the infantry regiments of the Second and Third Infantry Divisions and to

the Fifth Regimental Combat Team. For the Inchon invasion the Seventh Infantry Division was similarly organized, and the Eighth U.S. Army attempted to extend that organization to the First Cavalry Division and the 24th and 25th Infantry divisions as well. For example, in the 24th Infantry Division the survivors of A Company, 78th Heavy Tank Battalion, were reorganized as Heavy Tank Company, 21st Infantry Regiment, and reequipped with M-4A3E8 Sherman tanks. But the Department of the Army refused to allow the reorganization and the units were eventually disbanded.

In addition to American armor units, the United Kingdom also dispatched an armor regiment to Korea, the King's Royal Irish Hussars, which was equipped with some 45 British

One M-46 Patton pulls another from the mud on the way to the front, April 1951.
(Courtesy U.S. Army Military History Institute.)

Cromwell and Centurion tanks. In 1952, Republic of Korea divisions were authorized one tank company per division and were equipped with M-24 Chaffee light tanks.

North Korea's 105th Armored Brigade was virtually eliminated in the summer of 1950. Survey teams after the Inchon invasion and the breakout from the Pusan Perimeter found 239 destroyed or abandoned T-34s: 39 by tank fire, 13 by infantry rocket-launcher fire, 102 by air action (mostly by napalm attack), 59 abandoned undamaged and the rest by a combination of causes. By 1952 North Korea was credited with having reconstituted an armored division and a mechanized division that, together with Chinese armored units that had been deployed into Korea, gave the enemy an estimated 520 tanks and self-propelled guns. However, enemy armor was never considered a major threat after the opening months of the war.

After the tank battles in July and August 1950, most armor operations in Korea were in support of the infantry. One tanker, Master Sergeant Ernest R. Kouma of the Second Infantry Division's 72d Tank Battalion, won the Medal of Honor for his actions in stopping an enemy attack and killing some 250 enemy soldiers.

See also ARTILLERY; CAVALRY; INFANTRY; RECONNAISSANCE.

Suggestions for further reading: For accounts of tank actions in Korea see Captain Russell A. Gugeler, *Combat Actions in Korea* (Washington,

D.C.: Combat Forces Press, 1954). See also Jim Mesko's *Armor in Korea: A Pictorial History* (Carrollton, Texas: Squadron/Signal Publications, 1984); *This Kind of War: A Study in Unpreparedness* (New York: Macmillan, 1963) by T.R. Fehrenbach (who served as a captain in a tank battalion in Korea) is an outstanding history of the war, as is the more recent *The Forgotten War: America in Korea 1950-1953* (New York: Times Books, 1987) by Clay Blair.

ARMORED VESTS

One of the tactical innovations of the Korean War was the development and use of body armor—more commonly known as "armored vests." During World War I France led the way in issuing steel helmets to protect troops from head injuries; by 1915 their use was standard. The United States changed the design of their steel helmets early in World War II from the flat, British-type "wash bowls" it had used in World War I to a more protective design that was used throughout that war and in the Korean War as well.

Because the steel helmet was successful in reducing head wounds, research was conducted to develop body armor that could reduce other wounds. Statistics from 57 U.S. divisions in the European Theater of Operations during World War II indicated that foot soldiers (who comprised 68.5% of the total U.S. strength) suffered 94.5% of the casualties, 61.3% to 80.4% being caused by shell or mortar fragments.

In 1947 the Navy and Marine Corps organized a ballistics center for the development and evaluation of body armor. By the summer of 1951 the center's Lieutenant Commander Frederick J. Lewis, Medical Service Corps, and his researchers developed a Marine Corps armored vest weighing about eight and one-half pounds. The vest combined flexible pads of basket-weave nylon with curved overlapping *doron* plates—plastic armor plates made of laminated layers of glass cloth filaments bonded under heavy pressure to form a thin, rigid slab. The doron plates was named in honor of Army Colonel George F. Doriot, a World War II body-armor researcher.

This garment was capable of stopping a .45-caliber bullet, all the fragments of a U.S. hand grenade at three feet, 75% of the fragments of a U.S. 81-mm mortar and the full thrust of an American bayonet. Forty vests were rotated among front-line troops, beginning in the spring of 1951 to test the armor in the field; the armored vests, although hot and somewhat unwieldy, gained widespread troop acceptance. Standardized as the M-1951 armored vest, it was put into full production in late 1951, and by the spring of 1952 these vests and an inferior Army model, made only of layers of basket-weave nylon, were widely available for issue to both Army and Marine combat troops.

Suggestions for further reading: A discussion of the development of armored vests is contained in *U.S. Marine Operations in Korea: 1950–1953*, Volume IV, *The East-Central Front* by Lynn Montross, Major Hubard D. Kuokka, USMA, and Major Norman W. Hicks, USMC (Washington, D.C.: GPO, 1962).

ARMY

In the military the term *army* has both a general and a specific meaning. In its general sense it is synonymous with ground forces—that is, "a large, organized body of soldiers for waging war, especially on land." The specific meaning in the United States military is an organizational entity commanded by a lieutenant general or general and composed of two or more corps. The Eighth U.S. Army was the only army-level headquarters on the Allied side during the Korean War.

The North Korean People's Army (NKPA), following the then-Soviet model, had a "front" headquarters directly under the NKPA General Headquarters. The Chinese Communist Forces' "army" was actually comparable to a U.S. corps. Their equivalent of a U.S. field army was the CCF Army Group. Two such organizations, the Ninth and the Thirteenth Army Groups (sometimes designated as the IX and XIII Army Groups), were deployed in Korea.

This latter designation was unusual, for to avoid confusion between different-sized units, in U.S. military terminology armies are normally spelled out in full (i.e., Eighth U.S. Army); roman numerals are used for corps (i.e., X Corps for Tenth Corps); arabic numerals used for divisions and smaller units (i.e., 24th Infantry Division, 21st Infantry Regiment, etc.); and alphabetical letters used to designate companies, batteries or troops (i.e., Company A, 78th Heavy Tank Battalion). The map symbol for an army headquarters is a rectangular box superimposed by four *x*'s ▭ (reputedly to denote the number of stars worn by its commander).

See also CORPS; DIVISION.

ARMY, CHINESE COMMUNIST FORCES

See CHINESE COMMUNIST FORCES.

ARMY, NORTH KOREA

See NORTH KOREAN PEOPLE'S ARMY.

ARMY, REPUBLIC OF KOREA

See REPUBLIC OF KOREA ARMY.

ARMY, UNITED NATIONS

See UNITED NATIONS GROUND FORCES.

ARMY, U.S.

The war in Korea was principally a ground war; therefore the U.S. Army furnished the majority of the American combat units and suffered the majority of the casualties. The commander in chief, United Nations Command, in overall command of the war (who was at the same time the commander in chief of the U.S. Far East Command) was an Army general as were the commanding generals of the Eighth U.S. Army and the I, IX and X corps.

During the war the Army deployed eight infantry divisions and three separate regimental combat teams to Korea: the First Cavalry Division, Second, Third, Seventh, 24th, 25th, 40th and 45th Infantry divisions (the latter two from the California and Oklahoma National Guards respectively); and the Fifth, 29th and 187th Regimental Combat teams. These combat forces comprised some 80 infantry battalions, 54 artillery battalions and 8 battalions of armor.

Among other decorations and awards, 78 Medals of Honor were awarded to U.S. Army soldiers for conspicuous bravery in action in Korea. Of the 5,720,000 Americans who served between June 25, 1950, and July 27, 1953, 2,834,000 were Army personnel. Twenty-seven thousand, seven hundred and four of the 33,629 Americans killed in action; 9,429 of the 20,617 who died of illness, injury or disease; and 77,596 of the 103,284 Americans wounded in action were Army personnel, as are the majority of the 8,177 personnel still missing in action and unaccounted for.

See particularly EIGHTH U.S. ARMY. *See also* ANTIAIRCRAFT ARTILLERY; ARMOR; CAVALRY; FIELD ARTILLERY; INFANTRY.

ARTILLERY

See ANTIAIRCRAFT ARTILLERY; FIELD ARTILLERY; ROCKET ARTILLERY; SEARCHLIGHTS.

Army personnel, such as this BAR man and rifleman, comprised 85% of the American combat infantrymen in the war.
(Courtesy Lyndon Baines Johnson Library & Museum.)

ATOMIC WEAPONS

In 1950 there was no nuclear threshhold isolating atomic weapons from other military weaponry. Many saw these weapons as representing only a quantitative rather than a qualitative difference in methods of destruction. According to U.S. military doctrine at the time, atomic weapons merely provided the commander additional firepower of a large magnitude. Such attitudes were no doubt influenced by two facts: Only five years earlier atomic weapons had been used to bring the war with Japan to a close and, until the Soviet Union exploded its own nuclear device in September 1949, the United States had had a total monopo-

ly on such weaponry and thus had no fear of a reprisal in kind.

The main constraints on the use of atomic weapons during the Korean War were not moral—they were practical and political. Atomic weapons were not readily available when the war began, and the Air Force had no planes and no crews capable of mounting an atomic attack. Suitable atomic targets were lacking. And Allied governments, particularly that of Great Britain, opposed them.

Although never authorized, the use of atomic weapons was seriously considered several times during the war. From the start General Douglas MacArthur and the Joint

Chiefs of Staff advocated use of such weapons against enemy lines of communication. After the Chinese intervention in November 1950, using atomic bombs to stop their advance was greatly deliberated, as evidenced by President Harry S. Truman's public statements during a news conference on November 30, 1950. When the Eighth U.S. Army successfully blocked the Chinese advance in January 1951 the issue became moot, but atomic weapons may well have been used if the Eighth Army had been unable to stem the tide and U.S. forces had been in danger of annihilation. Atomic weapons were also carefully thought about as a possible alternative when the Eisenhower administration came into power in January 1953. Both President Dwight D. Eisenhower and Secretary of State John Foster Dulles saw atomic weapons as usable instruments of war and talked publicly of using nuclear weapons in Korea and China. This was more than a bluff. According

An American POW from the 21st Infantry Regiment executed by North Korean forces, July 1950.
(Courtesy Shelby Stanton collection.)

to a 1985 Cornell University analysis, "there is now extensive documentary evidence to show that the use of atomic weapons became an integral part of the planning designed to force a military solution in Korea. The standard explanation for the Communist capitulation in early June [1953]," the study notes, "is that the Chinese and North Koreans were intimidated by the threatened use of atomic weapons ..."

Suggestions for further reading: See Rosemary Foot, *The Wrong War: American Policy and the Dimensions of the Korean Conflict, 1950–1953* (Ithaca, NY: Cornell University Press, 1985); Roger Dingman, "Atomic Diplomacy During the Korean War"; and Rosemary Foot, "Nuclear Coercion and the Ending of the Korean Conflict," *International Security*, Winter 1988/89, volume 13, number 3, pages 50–112.

ATROCITIES

Atrocities are not unknown in war, but usually they are the work of individuals or small groups gone amok in the heat of battle. The atrocities committed by the North Korean People's Army (NKPA) however were so common that they could only have been a matter of official government policy. Beginning in July 1950, the NKPA routinely murdered American prisoners of war (POWs), binding their hands behind their backs and then shooting them in the head. Those that survived the North Korean POW camps testified to cruelty there as well.

North Korean treatment of South Korean civilians was equally harsh. At Taejon, for example, they perpetrated one of the greatest mass killings of the war. When Taejon was recaptured in September 1950, a frightful number of killings and burials were uncovered in the city. Five thousand to 7,000 South Korean civilians, 17 Republic of Korea (ROK) soldiers and 42 American soldiers had been shot in cold blood and their bodies thrown into shallow trenches before the NKPA abandoned the city. It was a pattern they repeated at every opportunity.

See also POWs (PRISONERS OF WAR); POW (PRISONER OF WAR) CAMPS.

Suggestions for further reading: For the Taejon massacre see Roy A. Appleman, *South to the Naktong, North to the Yalu* (Washington, D.C.: GPO, 1961.)

AUSTRALIA

After the vote in the United Nations Security Council on June 29, 1950, to provide military assistance to the Republic of Korea, Australia supplied sea, air and ground forces to the Korean War. First to be committed was the Royal Australian Air Force's 77th Squadron, which was stationed at Iwakuni air base in Japan. Flying first out of its base in Japan and

then from advanced air bases in Korea, the 77th Squadron operated with elements of the Fifth U.S. Air Force. Equipped first with F-51 Mustang fighters and later with Meteor-8 jets, the 77th Squadron usually flew interdiction and close air support missions. However, the Meteor-8 jets did provide bomber escort on occasion and engaged in several dogfights with Chinese MiG-15s.

The Royal Australian Navy was there from the beginning also. Operating with a British fleet in Pacific waters when the war began, the destroyer HMAS *Bataan* and the frigate HMAS *Shoalhaven* were placed at the disposal of the commander, U.S. Naval Forces Far East, on June 29, 1950. These warships were later joined by the destroyer HMAS *Warramunga* and four R.A.N. frigates. On September 28, 1950, the Third Battalion, Royal Australian Regiment (RAR), joined the 27th British Commonwealth

Australian forces cross the 38th parallel, April 1951.
(Courtesy U.S. Army Military History Institute, 1951.)

Brigade in Korea. During the course of the war several other battalions of the RAR deployed to Korea, replacing sister battalions that then returned to Australia; at their peak strength some 2,282 Australian soldiers were serving there.

Although casualty figures for Australia alone are not available, during the course of the war British Commonwealth Forces—Australia, Britain, Canada and New Zealand—suffered casualties of 1,262 killed in action and another 4,817 wounded in action. Twenty-six Australians were repatriated during the exchanges of prisoners of war after the armistice. *See* BRITISH COMMONWEALTH DIVISION; UNITED NATIONS AIR FORCES; UNITED NATIONS NAVAL FORCES.

Suggestions for further reading: Norman Bartlett, editor, *With the Australians in Korea* (Canberra: Australian War Memorial, 1954); Robert O'-Neil, *Australia in the Korean War 1950–1953* (Canberra: Australian Government Press, 1981).

B

BATTALION

The *battalion*, normally consisting of two or more companies or batteries under the command of a lieutenant colonel, is a basic military organizational element. While the information below pertains to U.S. battalions, those of other armies are roughly analogous. One important caveat obtains in all cases: The authorized strength of a battalion and its actual battlefield strength were more often than not two entirely different things.

During the Korean War artillery and tank battalions were usually separate, although artillery battalions were sometimes part of an artillery group or, in the Marine Corps, an artillery regiment. But infantry battalions were integral parts of a regiment. Battalions varied considerably in size depending on their type. A light artillery battalion, for example, consisted of about 500 personnel organized into a headquarters and a service battery, or company, plus three firing batteries, each with six 105-mm howitzers. A tank battalion, roughly the same size as a light artillery battalion, also had a headquarters company and three tank companies, each with 17 tanks.

But an infantry battalion, with some 40 officers and 935 enlisted men, was considerably larger. It consisted of a headquarters company; three rifle companies (each about 200 strong); and a weapons company with an 81-mm mortar section, a 75-mm recoilless-rifle section and a machine-gun section, with both light air-cooled and heavy water-cooled .30-caliber machine-guns.

The three infantry battalions in the standard Army and Marine Corps regiments of the day all followed the same system for letter designating their companies. Companies A, B and C in First Battalion were rifle companies; D was a weapons company. In Second Battalion, E, F and G were rifle companies; H was a weapons company. Likewise in Third Battalion, I, K and L were rifle companies (there was no J Company) and M was a weapons company.

The map symbol for a battalion is a rectangular box superimposed by a two vertical lines. Within the box appropriate symbols denote what type of battalion is involved—a tank tread for an armor battalion, a cannonball for an artillery battalion, crossed rifles for an infantry battalion and so on. Thus the Third Battalion, 21st Infantry Regiment, would be portrayed as 3 ⊠ 21.

See ORGANIZATION FOR COMBAT; REGIMENT.

Suggestions for further reading: Shelby L. Stanton, *Korean War Order of Battle* (Washington, D.C.: GPO, forthcoming 1990).

BATTERY

In the U.S. military, *battery* is the designation for a company-sized unit of artillery. Commanded by a captain, it is composed of just over 100 officers and men and is equipped with differing numbers of guns, howitzers, rocket launchers, searchlights, and so on. While normally part of an antiaircraft (AA) or field artillery (FA) battalion, a number of separate specialized artillery batteries existed in Korea, including antiaircraft automatic weapons batteries, rocket artillery batteries and searchlight batteries.

The map symbol for a battery is a rectangular box superimposed by a single vertical line. Within the box is a cannonball indicating it is an artillery unit. Thus A Battery, 11th Field Artillery Battalion, would be shown as A 🔲 11. *See* BATTALION; ORGANIZATION FOR COMBAT.

Suggestions for further reading: Shelby L. Stanton, *Korean War Order of Battle* (Washington, D.C.: GPO, forthcoming 1990).

BATTLE FATIGUE

Called *shell shock* in the First World War and *PTSD* (post-traumatic stress disorder) later in Vietnam, *battle fatigue* was the term used in World War II and Korea.

During the Korean War specific actions were taken to reduce battle fatigue casualties. The first and perhaps most important step was the realization that the farther to the rear the patient was evacuated for treatment, the sicker he became. Evacuation reinforced in his mind the notion he was mentally ill rather than suffering from an overload of stress. Thus the treatment for battle fatigue in the Korean War was removal to the battalion or regimental aid station for several days of bed rest, then return to the line. The casualty rate plummeted dramatically.

Another prophylactic was the institution of the R&R (Rest and Recuperation) program: Front-line soldiers were removed from combat in midtour and sent to Japan for a short rest break. Yet another means of prevention was the rotation policy that changed the tour of duty from the infinite "duration of the conflict" as in World War II to a finite tour of approximately one year on the front line. While disastrous to combat efficiency, it did make front line service more bearable for those who had to endure its hardships.
See MEDICAL CARE AND EVACUATION; REST AND RECUPERATION.

BAYONET

The Korean War witnessed what may well prove to be the last bayonet charges in military history. One of the most dramatic was the bayonet charge of the Turkish Brigade on January 26, 1951, which overran Chinese positions northeast of Suwon. Initial reports were that the Turks killed 400 enemy, most by bayonet. Although closer examination proved those figures to be exaggerated, Eighth U.S. Army Commander General Matthew B. Ridgway, impressed by the awe the story had inspired, issued an order that all Eighth U.S. Army troops were to fix bayonets.

As one Army historian reported, "The command greatly needed something to symbolize the birth of a new spirit. Restoration of the bayonet, and a dramatizing of that action, was at one with the simple message given to the troops: 'The job is to kill Chinese.'" Medal of Honor citations for the Korean War prove that the order to fix bayonets had the desired effect. For example, "Sergeant Stanley T. Adams ... 19th Infantry Regiment ... leaped to his feet, urged his men to fix bayonets ... and charged ... Corporal Hiroshi H. Miyamura ... Seventh Infantry Regiment ... leaped from his shelter wielding his bayonet in close hand-to-hand combat killing approximately 10 of the enemy."

Usually credited with leading the last deliberate unit bayonet charge in American military history, on February 1951, Medal of Honor winner Captain Lewis L. Millett of the 27th Infantry "while personally leading his company in an attack against a strongly held position ... placed himself at the head ... and, with fixed bayonet, led the assault up the fire-swept hill. In the fierce charge Captain Millett bayoneted two enemy soldiers and boldly continued on, throwing grenades, clubbing and bayoneting the enemy, while urging his men forward ... [his] personal courage so inspired his men that they stormed into the hostile position and used their bayonets with such lethal effect that the enemy fled in wild disorder."

While some Chinese and North Korean rifles were equipped with bayonets, their battle doctrine called for use of assault rifles (such as the "Burp" gun, which had no bayonet) and grenades in close-in fighting.

See also SMALL ARMS.

Suggestions for further reading: The account of the Turkish bayonet charge and General Ridgway's order to fix bayonets is in Clay Blair, *The Forgotten War: America in Korea 1950–1953* (New York Times Books, 1987). Medal of Honor citations are in U.S. Congress. Senate. Committee on Veteran's Affairs. *Medal of Honor Recipients 1863–1973.* 93d Congress, 1st session, 1973.

BAZOOKA

See ROCKET LAUNCHERS.

BEDCHECK CHARLIES

Although Allied air forces exercised almost total control of the air during the Korean War, the enemy did use aircraft, nicknamed "Bedcheck Charlies," to harass Allied positions. These consisted of two types of antique aircraft—Soviet-built Yakovlev YAK-18 training planes and Polikarpov PO-2 wood and fabric biplanes, both with a cruising speed of about 100 knots. Each was capable of carrying one or two small bombs. Flying on dark nights from grass fields in North Korea, these planes stayed as low as possible to avoid radar detection. The damage they were able to do was usually insignificant, but their harassment and nuisance value was high.

Although these raids began in the fall of 1950 and continued intermittently thereafter, they intensified in the closing days of the war. In May 1953, a flight of six PO-2s punctured the gas pipeline at K-14 airfield near Inchon, and on June 8, 1953, an eight-plane raid on Seoul dropped bombs within 1,000 feet of President Syngman Rhee's residence. On the night of June 16, 1953, a 16-plane raid hit a petroleum, oil and lubricants (POL) dump near Inchon, torching some 52,000 gallons of fuel.

Air Force's air defense jet interceptors were too fast to deal with these slow-flying planes, so the Navy volunteered to use their carrier-based F4U-5N propeller-driven Corsair night fighters. Temporarily flying from land bases in the Seoul area, they proved to be the answer to the problem. During the period June 29 to July 17, 1953, Navy Lieutenant Guy P. Bordelon from the USS *Princeton* shot down five Bedcheck Charlies and effectively put an end to these night raids. Awarded the Navy Cross for his actions, Bordelon became the only Navy ace of the war.

See also ACES; NORTH KOREAN AIR FORCE; CHINESE COMMUNIST AIR FORCE.

Suggestions for further reading: See Robert F. Futrell, *The United States Air Force in Korea: 1950–1953*, revised edition (Washington, D.C.: GPO, 1983). See also commanders Malcolm W. Cagle and Frank A. Manson, USN, *The Sea War in Korea* (Annapolis, Md: United States Naval Institute, 1957); Richard P. Hallion, *The Naval Air*

War in Korea (Baltimore: The Nautical & Aviation Publishing Company of America, 1986).

BELGIUM

In addition to several DC-4 air transports, Belgium provided a volunteer infantry battalion (including a 44-man detachment from Luxembourg) to the war in Korea. At their peak strength they numbered some 944 personnel. Commanded initially by B.E.M. Crahay, the battalion normally operated as an attached unit to a U.S. or British Commonwealth regiment or brigade.

Their most noteworthy action took place in April 1951 while attached to the 29th British Brigade. The brigade's positions along the Imjin River came under heavy attack from the three division of the Chinese 63d Field Army. Forced eventually to give ground, the British and Belgian units managed to contain the Chinese attack, although at the cost of one of the British battalions (*see* GLOUCESTER HILL).

Casualty figures for Belgian forces alone are not available, but during the course of the war the United Nations ground forces, including Belgium, Colombia, Ethiopia, France, Greece, the Netherlands, the Philippines, Thailand and Turkey, lost a total of 1,800 soldiers killed in action and another 7,000 wounded in action. One Belgian was repatriated during the prisoner of war exchanges at the end of the war. *See* UNITED NATIONS AIR FORCES; UNITED NATIONS GROUND FORCES.

BIG SWITCH

LITTLE SWITCH was the name for the exchange of sick and wounded prisoners of war (POWs) that took place on April 20 to 26, 1953; BIG SWITCH was the name for the main POW exchange that followed the signing of the Korean armistice agreement on July 27, 1953.

Between August 5 and September 6, 1953, the United Nations Command (UNC) transferred 75,823 POWs directly to the Communists in the demilitarized zone (DMZ) and received 12,773 Allied POWs in return. On September 23, 1953, the UNC turned over 22,604 nonrepatriates (i.e., enemy POWs who had refused repatriation) to the Neutral Nations Repatriation Commission and the Communists delivered 359 UNC nonrepatriates the next day (see discussion of the nonrepatriation issue at POWs [PRISONERS OF WAR]).

Of the 75,823 enemy POWs, 70,183 were North Koreans and 5,640 were Chinese; of the 22,604 nonrepatriates 14,704 were Chinese and 7,900 were Koreans. Of the 12,773 Allied POWs returned 7,862 were from the Republic of Korea (ROK) Armed Forces; 3,597 were from the United States; 945 were British; 229 were Turks; 40 were Filipinos; 30 were Canadians; 22 were Colombians; 21 were Australians; 12 were Frenchmen; 8 were South Africans; 2 were Greeks; 2 were Netherlanders; and there was one each from Belgium, New Zealand and Japan. Of the Allied nonrepatriates 335 were from the ROK, 23 were Americans and one was from the United Kingdom.

See LITTLE SWITCH; POWs (PRISONERS OF WAR); POW (PRISONER OF WAR) CAMPS.

Suggestions for further reading: For official statistics on BIG SWITCH see Appendix B, *U.S. Army in the Korean War: Truce Tent and Fighting Front* by Walter G. Hermes' (Washington, D.C.: GPO, 1966).

BIOLOGICAL WARFARE

See GERM WARFARE.

BLACK SOLDIERS IN KOREA

Although in 1948 President Harry S Truman signed an executive order that he intended to lead to the desegregation of the armed forces, when the Korean War began in June 1950 black service personnel in the Army were still assigned to racially segregated units. In such units all of the soldiers and all of the noncommissioned officers (i.e., corporals and sergeants) were black, as were some of the lieutenants and captains. Almost all of the senior officers, however, were white. (Note that in those days the descriptive term was *Negro* or *colored*. The term *black* is of fairly recent usage, and at the time of the Korean War was considered insulting by all concerned.)

The largest all-black unit was the 25th Infantry Division's 24th Infantry Regiment, including its attached 129th Field Artillery Battalion and 77th Engineer Company, which was stationed at Gifu in Japan when the war began. Landing in Korea on July 13, 1950, the 24th Infantry Regiment and its attached units launched the first successful counterattack of the war at Yechon on July 20, 1950.

In August 1950 other all-black units—the Second Infantry Division's 503d Artillery Battalion and the Third Battalion, Ninth Infantry—arrived in Korea. Later that year more all-black combat units came ashore: the Third Infantry Division's Third Battalion, 15th Infantry Regiment, and 64th Tank Battalion, as well as the separate corps-level 58th Armored Field Artillery Battalion and the 999th Field Artillery Battalion with its self-propelled 155-mm howitzers. In addition all-black combat support and combat service support organizations—port units, transportation truck companies, quartermaster companies and the like—were assigned to Korea.

This segregation policy resulted in a backlog of thousands of qualified black replacements in Japan while white units were starving for man-

Soldiers of the Third Battalion, 24th Infantry Regiment, advance on Chinese Communist positions near the 38th parallel, April 1951.

power. Pragmatism and the need for a more efficient organization finally won out over prejudice, and in early 1951 black soldiers began to be assigned to previously all-white units (BAR man Frank Ivy, an L Company, 21st Infantry Regiment, veteran, was among the first). These battlefield pressures led Commander in Chief Far East Command General Matthew B. Ridgway to totally integrate the fighting units in Korea. On October 1, 1951, the 24th Infantry Regiment was disbanded and its personnel were distributed throughout the Eighth U.S. Army. During the summer and fall of 1951, other black units were either disbanded or infused with white personnel, thus losing their all-black identification. By the end of the war in July 1953, over 90% of black personnel in the Army were serving in integrated units.

Statistics of any kind are hard to come by for the Korean War, but it is known that black military strength in Army Forces Far East (which included both Japan and Korea) increased fourfold during the war. From 201 officers (including 24 female Army nurses) and 12,427 enlisted men on June 30, 1950, black strength grew to 955 officers (including 35 Army nurses and 1 Woman's Army Corps officer); 146 warrant officers; and 50,646 enlisted personnel (including 199 black enlisted women) by June 30, 1953.

This same pragmatism had resulted in the Air Force being almost totally integrated before the Korean War began. Because of the pressure to build the First Marine Division practically from the ground up in a matter of weeks for the Inchon invasion, the Marine Corps was integrated as well. As its official history states, "The war ... witnessed a sizable increase in the number of Negro Marines on active duty. This figure grew from 2 officers and 1,965 enlisted personnel in 1950 to 19 officers and 24,468 enlisted by 1953."

Only the Navy continued to drag its feet, with most of its black personnel assigned to the messman's branch and other such occupations. There was some token integration of the combat forces however, such as the Navy's first black aviator, Ensign Jesse L. Brown of the USS *Leyte*. But Brown, who was killed in action in December 1950, was the exception. A decade after the Korean War the Navy finally caught up with the other armed services.

Although Medal of Honor recipients are not categorized by race, it is known that two members of the 24th Infantry Regiment—Sergeant Cornelius H. Charlton and Private First Class William Thompson—won the Medal of Honor for their actions in Korea. Of the 33,629 Americans killed in action in Korea, 3,223, or 9.3% were black.

See also YECHON, BATTLE OF.

Suggestions for further reading: Morris J. MacGregor, *The Integration of the Armed Forces 1940–1965* (Washington, D.C.: GPO, 1985). For a recent discussion of black combat performance in Korea that takes exception to earlier negative accounts see Clay Blair, *The Forgotten War: America in Korea 1950–1953* (New York Times Books, 1987). See also *U.S. Army in the Korean War* series: Roy E. Appleman, *South to the Naktong, North to the Yalu* (Washington, D.C. GPO, 1961.); Walter G. Hermes, *Truce Tent and Fighting Front*, 1966; and Billy C. Mossman, *Ebb and Flow*, anticipated in 1990 (Washington, D.C.: GPO). For Marine integration see *U.S. Marine Operations in Korea: 1950–1953*: *Operations in West Korea*, Lieutenant Colonel Pat Meid, USMCR, and Major James M. Yingling, USMC (Washington, D.C.: GPO, 1972).

BLOCKADE AND ESCORT FORCE (TASK FORCE 95)

Organized on September 12, 1950, the UN Blockade and Escort Force (Task Force 95) was one of the major subordinate commands of U.S. Naval Forces, Far East (NAVFE). As with all naval task forces, its composition varied as ships were attached or detached to meet the demands of the assigned mission.

The task force was composed of a West Coast Group (Task Group 95.1), which included most of the Allied navies as well as a number of U.S. and Allied light carriers and escort carriers; an East Coast Group (Task Group 95.2); and the Minesweeping Group (Task Group 95.6) as well as the Republic of Korea (ROK) Navy (Task Group 95.7). From time to time the battleships *Iowa*, *Missouri*, *New Jersey* and *Wisconsin* were on the task force's gun line, as were a number of cruisers and destroyers.

A minesweeper hits a Russian-type contact mine in Wonsan harbor, October 1950.
(Courtesy U.S. Army Military History Institute.)

Among the Blockade and Escort Force's major accomplishments were the control of the seas surrounding the Korean peninsula, thus denying the enemy the use of the seas and allowing the free flow of seaborne supplies, equipment and material to support the Allied war effort; the blockade of Wonsan harbor, which denied its use to the enemy; and the interdiction of enemy road and rail lines of communication through aerial attack by fighters and fighter-bombers from the task force's carriers, through shore bombardment by the task force's battleships, cruisers and destroyers, and through the launching of commando raids along the coastline to destroy bridges, tunnels and other critical transportation choke points.

Along with other elements of NAVFE, the UN Blockade and Escort Force fired over four million rounds of ammunition (from 16-inch to small arms) at the enemy, destroying 3,334 buildings, 824 vessels and small craft, 14 locomotives, 214 trucks, 15 tanks, 108 bridges and 93 supply dumps and inflicting 28,566 enemy casualties. In return, 82 ships were damaged by counterbattery fire from enemy shore emplacements.

Clearing enemy minefields was a particularly dangerous part of the task force's operations, especially the extensive minefields at Wonsan and Chinnampo. During the course of the war, 1,535 mines were destroyed at a cost of four U.S. Navy minesweepers and one tug sunk and five ships damaged.

See AIRCRAFT CARRIERS; UNITED NATIONS NAVAL FORCES; WONSAN.

Suggestions for further reading: James A. Field, *History of United States Naval Operations: Korea* (Washington, D.C.: GPO, 1962). See particularly Commanders Malcolm W. Cagle and Frank A. Manson, USN, *The Sea War in Korea* (Annapolis, Md: United States Naval Institute, 1957), which contains a listing of the wartime commanders of Task Force 95 as well as a listing of all U.S. Navy ships sunk or damaged during the Korean War. For minesweeping operations see Arnold S. Lott's *Most Dangerous Seas* (Annapolis, Md: Naval Institute Press, 1959). For naval aviation see Richard P. Hallion, *The Naval Air War in Korea* (Baltimore: The Nautical & Aviation Publishing Company of America, 1986).

BLOODY RIDGE, BATTLE FOR

See HEARTBREAK RIDGE, BATTLE OF.

BOMBER AIRCRAFT

Like fighter and fighter-bomber aircraft, bomber aircraft were in transition during the Korean War from the propeller-driven aircraft of World War II to newer and faster jet-propelled planes. Unlike the fighters and fighter-bomb-

B-29 Superfortresses from Far East Air Force's Bomber Command on a bomb run over North Korea.
(Courtesy U.S. Army Military History Institute.)

ers, however, which became an all-jet force by the end of the war, the bomber war in Korea was fought with older and increasingly obsolete World War II light and medium bombers.

When the war began, the Fifth U.S. Air Force had available in Japan its Third Bombardment Group (later Third Bombardment Wing) with two squadrons of propeller-driven B-26 Intruder light bombers. These were ordered into action over Korea on June 28, 1950. On August 10, 1950, the Air Force Reserve's 452d Bombardment Wing was called to active duty at Long Beach, California. Seventy-seven days later, on October 27, 1950, they flew their first combat mission over Korea. Later redesignated

the 17th Bombardment Wing, their four squadrons were authorized 16 B-26 light bombers each.

Meanwhile on Guam was the Twentieth Air Force's 19th Bombardment Group (later 19th Bombardment Wing), equipped with propeller-driven B-29 Superfortresses. Although it had been classified as a heavy bomber during World War II, with the advent of the B-36 the B-29 was redesignated a medium bomber. Ordered into action over Korea on June 29, 1950, after their move to Kadena Air Base on Okinawa, these aircraft, with their six-ton bomb load, came under the control of the newly formed Far East Air Force Bomber Command. On July 3, 1950, the Strategic Air

Command's (SAC) Fifteenth Air Force was ordered to send the B-29s of their 22d and 92d Bombardment groups to the Far East on temporary duty. In October 1950 they were replaced by the B-29 squadrons of SAC's 98th and 307th Bombardment groups (later Bombardment Wings), which remained attached to the Far East Air Force Bomber Command for the rest of the war.

Bomber aircraft strength changed during the course of the war, but by July 1953 the two light bombardment wings of the Fifth Air Force had 128 B-26 Invader light bombers on hand and the three medium bombardment wings of the Far East Air Force Bomber Command were up to their authorized strength of 31 B-29 Superfortresses each.

The enemy also had a bomber capability, but except for the harassment of the "Bedcheck Charlies" they never committed it to combat. In the winter of 1952 to 1953 it was estimated that at their bases in Manchuria the Chinese Communist Air Force had some 65 conventional light bombers and 100 Ilyushin Il-28 twin-jet medium bombers, which could deliver a two-ton bomb load to a range of 690 miles (i.e., to anywhere in Japan or Korea). Although never sent into action, these bombers caused much concern for Allied air defenses.

See BEDCHECK CHARLIES; BOMBER COMMAND; FAR EAST AIR FORCE; FIFTH AIR FORCE; FIGHTER AND FIGHTER-BOMBER AIRCRAFT.

Suggestions for further reading: See Robert F. Futrell, *The United States Air Force in Korea: 1950–1953*, revised edition (Washington, D.C.: GPO, 1983).

BOMBER COMMAND

A major subordinate command of Far East Air Force (FEAF), Bomber Command (Provisional) was established on July 8, 1950, with headquarters at Yokota Air Base in Japan, to deal with a very specific problem: the lack of an appropriate headquarters for controlling the strategic bombers FEAF intended to use to prosecute the air war in Korea.

The bombers themselves were available. At Andersen Air Base on Guam, under FEAF's Twentieth Air Force, were the B-29 Superfortress medium bombers of the 19th Bombardment Group. Moved to Kadena Air Base on Okinawa, they commenced air operations over Korea on June 29, 1950. But the Twentieth Air Force, with headquarters at Naha Air Base on Okinawa, was responsible for the air defense of Okinawa and the Marianas; they could not devote full attention to the bombing campaign and to the control of the two additional B-29 groups that were then enroute from SAC's (Strategic Air Command) Fifteenth Air Force in the United States.

To correct this situation, FEAF organized Bomber Command. With Washington's approval SAC's Fifteenth Air Force commander, Major General Emmett "Rosie" O'Donnell Jr. was named to head it. He would control the 22d and 92d Bombardment groups on temporary loan from his old command as well as FEAF's own 19th Bombardment Group. When the 22d and 92d Bombardment groups returned to their home station in October 1950, they were replaced by the B-29s of SAC's 98th and 307th Bombardment wings. They along with the Twentieth Air Force's 19th Bombardment Group (later 19th Bombardment Wing), would remain on permanent loan to FEAF Bomber Command for the rest of the war.

Although their strength varied depending on operational circumstances, each of these wings were authorized 31 B-29s each, with a two-spare maintenance overage, giving Bomber Command a total authorized strength of 99 B-29 Superfortresses.

Used initially as tactical bombers and in close support of troops (a role that B-52 Stratofortress strategic bombers would perform a decade and a half later in Vietnam), the B-29s soon began a strategic daylight bombing campaign against North Korean military facilities, war-related industries and road and rail lines of communication. The campaign ended with the September 26, 1950, raid by eight B-29s on the North Korean hydroelectric plants at Fusen, located inland from the North Korean port of Hungnam. With the collapse of the North Korean army after the Inchon invasion, it appeared that the war was coming to an end.

On November 3, 1950, however, when the Chinese Communist Forces (CCF) came into the war, the bombing campaign came back to life. In conjunction with the fighter-bombers and B-26 Invader light bombers of the Fifth Air Force and the carrier-based fighters and fighter-bombers of the Navy's Task Force 77, Bomber Command's medium B-29 bombers launched raids against enemy arsenals in North Korea as well as on the "Korean end" of all international bridges across the Yalu River separating Korea from Manchuria. On November 8, 1950, for example, 70 B-29s dropped 585.5 tons of 500-pound incendiary clusters on the city of Sinuiju at the mouth of the Yalu, one of the major crossing points for CCF "volunteers," nine other B-29s dropped 1,000-pound bombs—unsuccessfully, as it turned out—on the abutments and approaches of the two bridges spanning the river. Although earlier bombing raids had been harassed from time to time by propeller-driven fighters of the North Korean Air Forces, these latest raids drew fire from Chinese Communist Air Force MiG-15 jet fighters flying from air bases across the river in Manchuria that were off limits to Allied attack.

This increased MiG threat was initially overcome by providing the bombers with fighter escorts, chiefly F-84 Thunderjets and the Australian Meteor-8 jets, as well as F-86 Sabrejets when they could be spared from air superiority (i.e. neutralizing enemy air power) missions. This tactic came to a head on October 23, 1951, when some 100 MiG-15s boxed in the F-86s screening the bombing attack while another 50 MiGs engaged the F-84 escorts and attacked the eight Superfortresses taking part in the raid. Two B-29s were lost in the operation, and all the aircraft received major damage. The next day eight B-29s were again attacked by some 40 to 70 MiGs, and one B-29 was lost. On October 28, 1951, the last daylight B-29 attack was conducted. From then on Bomber Command would operate only at night. Thus they pioneered the radar-controlled bombing that would be used extensively in bombing operations in Vietnam 15 years later.

In June 1952, with the approval of President Harry S Truman, Bomber Command—again in coordination with the Fifth Air Force and the Navy's Task Force 77—launched attacks on North Korean hydroelectric plants at Sui-ho, Fusen, Chosen and Kyosen, knocking out 90% of North Korea's electric power potential. The last major bombing operation of the war, launched in May 1953, was another combined attack, this time on North Korea's irrigation dams in order to disrupt their food supplies and force them back to the negotiating table.

On the night of July 20, 1953, a week before the armistice ending the Korean War went into effect, Bomber Command (after three years, still labeled "Provisional") closed out the war in what its commander, Brigadier General Richard H. Charmichael, called a "blaze of glory." Employing 500-pound bombs, its medium bombers attacked the runways at Uiju, Sinuiju, Namsi, Taechon, Pyong-ni, Pyongyang and Saamcham. On the night of July 21, 1953, eighteen B-29s blanketed Uiju's dispersal area with fragmentation bombs and incendiary clusters. When the war ended, every airfield in

North Korea was unserviceable for jet aircraft landings. The obsolete piston-driven B-29s of Bomber Command had exacted their final revenge.

See FAR EAST AIR FORCE; FIGHTER AND FIGHTER-BOMBER AIRCRAFT; FIFTH AIR FORCE; SANCTUARIES.

Suggestions for further reading: See Robert F. Futrell, *The United States Air Force in Korea: 1950–1953*, revised edition (Washington, D.C.: GPO, 1983).

BRADLEY, OMAR N(ELSON) (1893–1981)

Born February 12, 1893, in Clark, Missouri, Bradley graduated from the United States Military Academy in 1915. Initially assigned to the 14th Infantry, which for a time was stationed on the Mexican border, Bradley saw no combat service in World War I. During the interwar years he served in a variety of assignments, including a tour at the Infantry School at Fort Benning, Georgia. There he came to the attention of General George C. Marshall, who was to become the Army's World War II chief of staff. When the United States entered the Second World War, Bradley, then a brigadier general, was serving as commandant of the Infantry School.

Appointed by General Marshal to command the 82d Infantry Division (later to become the 82d Airborne Division) and then the Pennsylvania National Guard's 28th Infantry Division, which was also preparing for overseas service, Bradley was ordered to North Africa in February 1943. There he commanded II Corps during the North African campaign and the invasion of Sicily. Named to command the First Army for the D-day invasion, he later commanded the 12th Army Group during the liberation of Europe.

Following the war, after a tour as director of the Veteran's Administration, Bradley became Army chief of staff on February 7, 1948, and on January 16, 1949, he became the first chairman of the Joint Chiefs of Staff (JCS). Promoted to general of the army (i.e., five stars) in September 1950, he served as JCS chairman throughout the Korean War. A weak chief of staff and vacillating JCS chairman, Bradley supported the ruinous "economy" defense budgets in 1949 and 1950 that doomed many soldiers to their deaths in the early days of the Korean War. Although its audacity almost unnerved him, he reluctantly approved the Inchon invasion. He later agreed to President Truman's dismissal of General Douglas MacArthur as commander in chief of the Far East Command.

Although five-star generals are never officially retired, General Bradley left active military service on August 15, 1953. He died on April 8, 1981.

See JOINT CHIEFS OF STAFF.

Suggestions for further reading: See particularly the posthumous autobiography/biography, Omar Bradley and Clay Blair's *A General's Life* (New York: Simon & Schuster, 1983), which refutes much of the "nice guy" image Bradley carefully cultivated over the years and tells more about his character than he must have intended. See also Charles Whiting's *Bradley* (New York: Ballentine Books, 1971) and Joseph C. Hobbs' biographical sketch in *Dictionary of American Military Biography*, Roger J. Spiller, editor (Westport, Conn: Greenwood Press, 1984).

BRAINWASHING

A peculiar phenomenon to emerge from the Korean War was the notion of *brainwashing*, officially defined as "a prolonged psychological process designed to erase an individual's past beliefs and concepts and to substitute new ones."

Anti-American propaganda statements made by captured American prisoners of war

(POWs), the reported collapse of American will in the North Korean and Chinese POW camps, and the fact that 21 of these POWs refused repatriation and chose to stay with their Communist captors all fueled the idea that there was some kind of insidious Communist brainwashing involved. Movies like *The Manchurian Candidate* helped inflame public sentiments, and for a time there was much public concern, but common sense ultimately prevailed.

According to a 1956 Department of Defense study,

> Several celebrated cases of authentic "brainwashing" have been reported during the last decade in Communist Europe and recently [i.e., 1956] in China. However, it is obvious that such a time-consuming, conditioning process could not be employed against any sizable group, such as a prisoner of war group, because of the excessive time and personnel required.
>
> In Korea, American prisoners of war were subjected to group indoctrination, not "brainwashing" ... The exhaustive efforts of several Government agencies failed to reveal even one conclusively documented case of the actual "brainwashing" of an American prisoner of war in Korea.

One of the results of the brainwashing scare was a six-point "Code of Conduct" for American POWs promulgated by President Dwight D. Eisenhower on August 17, 1955, that remained in effect through the Vietnam War. *See* POWs (PRISONERS OF WAR); POW (PRISONER OF WAR) CAMPS.

Suggestions for further reading: U.S. Department of the Army. Pamphlet 30-101, *Communist Interrogation, Indoctrination and Exploitation of Prisoners of War* (Washington, D.C.: GPO). See also Eugene Kinkead's *In Every War But One* (New York: Norton, 1959) and the rebuttal in Albert D. Biderman's *March to Calumny* (New York: Macmillan, 1963) as well as the discussion in James L. Stokesbury's *A Short History of the Korean War* (New York: Morrow, 1988).

BRIGADE

During the Korean War, *brigade* was an organizational structure used by the British, the Canadians and the Turks. Consisting of a headquarters and two or more battalions, it was roughly analogous to an American regiment.

Interestingly, before and after the Korean War, brigades were an important part of American Army organization. During the Civil War the brigade—commanded by a *brigadier*, hence the present American military rank of brigadier (i.e., one-star) general—was the basic fighting unit of the Army. When divisions became the chief fighting unit in the First World War, they were organized into two brigades, each of which had two regiments. This *square division* was reorganized at the beginning of World War II into a *triangular* division of three regiments each, and the two-brigade headquarters were eliminated.

After the Korean War, the American Army once again reorganized; this time it was the regiment that was done away with, except as a ceremonial title. During the Vietnam War, for example, an American Army division consisted of three brigades, each with three infantry battalions. The Marine Corps, on the other hand, continued to retain the regimental structure.

The map symbol for a brigade is a rectangular box superimposed by a single *x* (supposedly to denote the number of stars worn by its commander). Within the box appropriate symbols denote what type brigade is involved: a tank tread for an armor brigade, a cannonball for an artillery brigade, crossed rifles for an infantry brigade. Thus the Turkish infantry brigade would be portrayed as ⊠ TURKEY .

See also BATTALION; ORGANIZATION FOR COMBAT; REGIMENT.

BRISCOE, ROBERT P(EARCE) (1897–1968)

Born February 19, 1897, in Centerville, Missouri, Briscoe graduated from the United States Naval Academy in 1918. During the First World War he served with the Atlantic Fleet on the battleship USS *Alabama*. During the interwar years he served as an instructor at the Naval Academy in electrical engineering, with the Yangtze River Patrol in China, and again at the Naval Academy as the head of the department of chemistry. Known as one of the pioneers of modern naval electronic development, he was serving as assistant director of the U.S. Naval Research Laboratory when World War II began.

Joining the Third Fleet in the Pacific in May 1942 as commander of the repair ship USS *Prometheus*, he was given command of Destroyer Squadron Five. In July 1943 he took command of the cruiser USS *Denver* and won the Navy Cross for his actions in the Northern Solomons: His ship assisted in the sinking of five Japanese warships and the damaging of four others.

Named commander of the Seventh U.S. Fleet in January 1952, he succeeded Admiral C. Turner Joy as commander Naval Forces Far East in June 1952 and served in that capacity for the remainder of the Korean War. After subsequent service as deputy chief of naval operations and as commander in chief, Allied Forces Southern Europe, Admiral Briscoe retired from active duty on January 1, 1959, and died on October 14, 1968.

See also NAVAL FORCES FAR EAST; SEVENTH FLEET STRIKING FORCE.

Suggestions for further reading: James A. Field, *History of United States Naval Operations: Korea* (Washington, D.C.: GPO, 1962). See also Commanders Malcolm W. Cagle and Frank A. Manson, USN, *The Sea War in Korea* (Annapolis, Md: United States Naval Institute, 1957); Richard P. Hallion, *The Naval Air War in Korea* (Baltimore: The Nautical & Aviation Publishing Company of America, 1986).

BRITISH COMMONWEALTH DIVISION

British Commonwealth Forces—Britain, Canada, Australia and New Zealand—played a major part in the Korean War. First to arrive was the British 27th Brigade from Hong Kong, which disembarked on August 29, 1950. Composed of the First Battalion of the Middlesex Regiment and the First Battalion of the Argyll and Sutherland Highlanders Regiment, the British 27th Brigade formed part of the Naktong Perimeter defense line.

On September 28, 1950, they were joined by the Third Battalion, Royal Australian Regiment, and the British 27th Brigade was officially renamed the 27th *Commonwealth* Brigade. By January 1951 the brigade was reinforced by the Second Battalion of Princess Patricia's Canadian Light Infantry; the 16th New Zealand Field Artillery; and by the Cromwell and Centurion tanks of the King's Royal Irish Hussars. In April 1951, upon the rotation of the brigade commander and his staff, the 27th Commonwealth Brigade was renamed the 28th Commonwealth Brigade.

Meanwhile, on October 24, 1950, the 29th British Brigade had arrived in Korea. It consisted of three infantry battalions—the Fifth Northumberland Fusiliers, the First Battalion of the Gloucestershire Regiment and a battalion of the Royal Ulster Rifles—plus the gunners of the 45th Royal Artillery. In July 1951, these two brigades were combined to form the First British Commonwealth Division.

From 1950 to 1953, Australia provided two infantry battalions; Canada provided a three-battalion infantry brigade; New Zealand provided an artillery battalion; and Great Britain furnished two infantry brigades, an armored regiment and supporting artillery and engineers. Unlike the American Army, which adopted an individual rotation system in Korea, the British Commonwealth forces rotated entire units. Thus the regimental designations of the forces making up the Commonwealth Division changed over the course of the war (see individual nation entries for a complete listing).

At their peak strength in 1953, British Commonwealth ground forces totaled 24,015 (compared with a peak of 302,483 U.S. ground forces and 590,911 Republic of Korea forces), with 14,198 from the United Kingdom, 2,282 from Australia, 6,146 from Canada and 1,389 from New Zealand. During the course of the war 1,263 British Commonwealth soldiers, sailors, airmen and marines were killed in action, and another 4,817 were wounded in action.
See also AUSTRALIA; CANADA; GLOUCESTER HILL, BATTLE OF; NEW ZEALAND; UNITED KINGDOM; UNITED NATIONS AIR FORCES, GROUND FORCES AND NAVAL FORCES.

Suggestions for further reading: *The First Commonwealth Division: The Story of British Commonwealth Land Forces in Korea, 1950–1953* (Aldershot: Gale, Polden, 1954); Tim Carew, *Korea: The Commonwealth at War* (London: Cassell, 1967); James L. Stokesbury, *A Short History of the Korean War* (New York: Morrow, 1988); Max Hastings, *The Korean War* (New York: Simon & Schuster, 1987).

BRONZE STAR MEDAL

First authorized in World War II, the Bronze Star Medal was awarded in the name of the president of the United States for heroic or meritorious achievement or service in connection with military operations against an armed enemy not involving participation in aerial flight. Awards, denoted by a metallic V device worn on the medal ribbon, were made for heroism performed under circumstances of a lesser degree than those required for award of the Silver Star Medal. Awards were also made for combat zone acts of meritorious achievement or for sustained meritorious service over a period of time. Subsequent awards were denoted by an oak leaf cluster (gold star for Navy and Marine Corps personnel) worn on the medal ribbon.

BROWNING AUTOMATIC RIFLE (BAR)

The Browning Automatic Rifle M-1918A2 or "BAR" was the standard squad automatic weapon for both U.S. Army and Marine Corps infantry units during World War II and the Korean War. Designed by John Browning for use in the First World War, it was equipped with a detachable bipod. Forty-eight inches long with an empty weight of 16 pounds, the BAR fired a .30-caliber bullet and was fed from a 20-round magazine. Its cyclic rate of fire could be set at either 350 or 550 rounds per minute. *See* SMALL ARMS.

Suggestions for further reading: Ian V. Hogg and John Weeks, *Military Small Arms of the 20th Century* (Northfield, Ill: DBI Books, 1985).

BURP GUN (PPSH41 7.62-MM SUBMACHINE-GUN)

The most distinctive small arm of the Korean War was the "burp gun": the Soviet Pistolet-Pulemyot Shpagina obr 1941G (PPSh41) submachine-gun and its Chinese-manufactured counterpart. Firing a 7.62-mm bullet from either a 35-round magazine or (more common-

ly) a 75-round drum, its 900 round-per-minute cyclic rate of fire gave it a very distinctive sound, from which its nickname was derived.

Designed for the Red Army by Georgii Shpagin at the beginning of the Second World War, it was a cheap and crudely made weapon, but also a most effective one. One drawback was the poor quality of the ammunition available; this drastically affected the burp gun's accuracy.

Suggestions for further reading: Ian V. Hogg and John Weeks, *Military Small Arms of the 20th Century* (Northfield, Ill: DBI Books, 1985).

North Korean guards at Kaesong armistice talks site armed with "burp guns," July 1951.
(Courtesy U.S. Army Military History Institute.)

CAMPAIGN MEDALS

See SERVICE MEDALS, U.S.

CAMPAIGNS, U.S. MILITARY

The U.S. military categorizes each war it has been involved in in terms of a series of campaigns, defined as a connected series of military operations forming a distinct phase of a war. For units involved in these operations, a streamer embroidered with the name of the particular campaign is displayed along with the unit's colors (its official flag). Those individuals who have participated are authorized to wear a bronze *battle star* for each campaign (or a silver *battle star* to denote participation in five campaigns) on their service ribbon. Ten campaigns were authorized for the Korean War.

Campaign	Inclusive Dates
UN defensive	June 27–September 15, 1950
UN offensive	September 16–November 2, 1950
CCF intervention	November 3, 1950–January 24, 1951
First UN counteroffensive	January 25–April 21, 1951
CCF spring offensive	April 22–July 8, 1951
UN summer-fall offensive	July 9–November 27
Second Korean winter	November 28, 1951–April 30, 1952
Korea summer-fall 1952	May 1–November 30, 1952
Third Korean winter	December 1, 1952–April 30, 1953
Korea summer-fall 1953	May 1–July 27, 1953

See also SERVICE MEDALS, U.S.

CANADA

Canada furnished land, sea and air forces for the Korean War. The Royal Canadian Air Force (RCAF) provided the 426 (Thunderbird) Transport Squadron for the Pacific Ocean airlift and 22 RCAF pilots flew combat missions while attached to the U.S. Fifth Air Force claiming 20 kills of enemy jet fighters. The Royal Canadian Navy (RCN) maintained a number of destroyers on station in Korean waters as part of the U.S. Naval Forces Far East Task Force 95, the Blockading and Escort Force. These included the HMCS *Athabaskan, Cayuga, Crusader, Haida, Huron, Iroquois, Nootka* and *Sioux*. In September 1952, the *Nootka* had the distinction of capturing a North Korean minelayer near the approaches to the heavily mined Chinnampo harbor on Korea's western coast, the only enemy ship captured at sea during the war.

The major Canadian contribution, however, was in ground forces. The first to arrive on the line in February 1951 was the Second Battalion, Princess Patricia's Canadian Light Infantry (PPLI), which was attached to the 27th British Commonwealth Brigade. Later Canada increased its contribution to a peak strength of 6,146 soldiers organized into the three-battalion 25th Infantry Brigade forming part of the First British Commonwealth Division.

Unlike the United States, which followed an individual rotation system, Canadian forces rotated entire units. Thus in the course of the war battalions from three Canadian infantry regiments served in Korea: The First, Second and Third Battalions, Princess Patricia's Canadian Light Infantry; the First, Second and Third Battalions of the Royal Canadian Regiment; and the First, Second and Third Battalions of the French-speaking "Van Doo's" (i.e., vingt-deux) of the Royal 22d Regiment. In addition to these infantry units, elements of Lord Strathcona's Horse; the Royal Canadian Engineers; the Second Field Regiment, Royal Canadian Horse Artillery; the First Regiment, Royal Canadian Horse Artillery; and the 81st Field Regiment, Royal Canadian Artillery, as well as a number of service and support units also served in Korea.

During the course of the war 26,791 Canadian servicemen served in Korea: 22,066 in the Royal Canadian Army, 3,621 in the Royal Canadian Navy and 1,104 in the Royal Canadian Air Force. Canadian forces suffered some 1,543 casualties, including 516 killed in action. Thirty-two Canadians were repatriated during the prisoner of war exchanges following the end of the war.

See also BRITISH COMMONWEALTH DIVISION.

Suggestions for further reading: Lieutenant Colonel Herbert Fairlie Wood, *Strange Battleground: The Operations in Korea and Their Ef-* *fect on the Defense Policy of Canada* (Ottawa: Queen's Printers, 1966); John Melady, *Korea: Canada's Forgotten War* (Toronto: Macmillan, 1983); Thor Grimsson and E.C. Russell, *Canadian Naval Operations in Korean Waters 1950–1953* (Ottawa: Queen's Printers, 1965). In addition to the U.S. Army, Navy and Air Force official histories, see also James L. Stokesbury, *A Short History of the Korean War* (New York: Morrow, 1988).

CASUALTIES

Casualty is a broad term encompassing those killed in action (KIA) on the battlefield, those wounded in action (WIA), those who died of their wounds after reaching medical care (DOW), those missing in action (MIA) and those taken prisoner by the enemy (POW). But the term also includes nonbattle casualties who were killed in plane crashes, vehicle mishaps and other such accidents in the war zone that had nothing to do with enemy action; it also includes those who died in Korea from illness or disease.

Thus to get a precise answer to the question, "How many Americans died in the Korean War?" it is necessary to define the term. The answer is "33,629" if you include only those who died in battle. If you include the 20,617 who died of other nonbattle causes, the answer is "54,246."

The answer is more straightforward for those 103,284 wounded in action, but even that figure is spongy because it probably does not include those whose wounds did not require hospitalization. (In the Vietnam War, where statistics were more precisely compiled, there were 153,329 hospitalized for wounds and another 150,375 lightly wounded who were treated by their unit medics or at the local aid station and immediately returned to duty.)

Yet another complicating factor is the very definition of the term *Korean War*. The forego-

Marines gather their dead for burial at Koto-ri during the Chosin withdrawal, December 1950.
(Courtesy Lyndon Baines Johnson Library & Museum.)

ing statistics are for those who became casualties during the period June 25, 1950–July 27, 1953 (i.e., from when the North Korean invasion began until the day the armistice agreement went into effect). But not everyone uses those dates, and it is not always clear what dates they are using. For example, in awarding Korean service medals, the Defense Department uses the period June 25, 1950 to July 27, 1954, but for determining eligibility for veteran's benefits the Veteran's Administration uses the period June 25, 1950 to January 31, 1955.

When casualty figures for World Wars I and II, Korea and Vietnam are compared (see table), it is noteworthy that not until World War II did battle casualties exceed nonbattle casualties;

until that time illness and disease killed many more soldiers than did enemy action. Because of better preventive medicine (i.e., immunizations and the like) and improved medical care, the ratio in the Korean War increased to three to two; in Vietnam it was almost five to one.

Number of Deaths in Four Wars: World Wars I and II, Korea and Vietnam

	Battle deaths	Other (accidents, disease, etc)
WWI	53,513	63,195
WWII	292,131	115,185
Korea	33,629	20,617
Vietnam	47,244	10,446

Also revealing is the comparison of the cause of battlefield casualties (see table). In World

War II and in Korea *fragments*—i.e., shrapnel from artillery, rockets, mortars and grenades— were the prime cause of death and disablement. In Vietnam the rise in rapid-fire weapons and the closeness of the jungle terrain changed the principal cause of death to small-arms fire.

Percent of Deaths and Wounds in the U.S. Army in Three Wars: World War II, Korea and Vietnam

	Deaths			Wounds		
Agent	World War II	Korea	Viet-nam[1]	World War II	Korea	Viet-nam
Small arms	32	33	51	20	27	16
Frag-ments	53	59	36	62	61	65
Booby traps, mines	3	4	11	4	4	15
Punji stakes	—	—	—	—	—	2
Other	12	4	2	14	8	2

[1]January 1956–June 1970

Source: *Statistical Data on Army Troops Wounded in Vietnam January 1965–June 1970*, Medical Statistics Agency, Office of the Surgeon General, U.S. Army.

In addition to American casualties, British Commonwealth forces—Britain, Canada, Australia and New Zealand—lost 1,263 killed in action and another 4,817 wounded in action. Belgium, Colombia, Ethiopia, France, Greece, the Netherlands, the Philippines, South Africa, Thailand and Turkey lost 1,800 killed and 7,000 wounded. The lion's share on the Allied side, however, was suffered by the Republic of Korea (ROK) Armed Forces, which lost an estimated 59,000 killed and 291,000 wounded. The figures for civilian casualties will never be known, but they are estimated to run into the millions.

Enemy casualty figures are likewise impossible to come by. Recent researchers in Beijing, for example, have found that almost 40 years later the Chinese still guard the totals as state secrets. Although some estimate that as many as one and one-half million Chinese and North Korean soldiers were killed in action, a more reasonable estimate is one-half million killed and another one million wounded in action. *See also* MIA (MISSING IN ACTION).

Suggestions for further reading: Walter G. Hermes, *Truce Tent and Fighting Front* (Washington, D.C.: GPO, 1966) is the source of official U.S. battle casualties. Max Hastings' *The Korean War* (New York: Simon & Schuster, 1987) has statistics on Allied and enemy casualties. Spurgeon Neel's *Medical Support of the U.S. Army in Vietnam* (Washington, D.C.: GPO, 1973) has useful comparisons on wartime casualties and is the source of the two tables shown above.

CATES, CLIFTON B(LEDSOE) (1893–1970)

Born August 31, 1893, in Tiptonville, Tennessee, Cates graduated from the University of Tennessee in 1916. A second lieutenant in the Marine Corps Reserve, he was called to active duty in June 1917 and sailed for France the following January. As a young lieutenant with the Sixth Marine Regiment (part of the Army's Second Infantry Division) Cates fought at Belleau Woods, Soissons and in the Argonne, where he was twice wounded in action. For bravery under enemy fire Cates won the Navy Cross, two Army Distinguished Service Crosses, and two Silver Star Medals as well as the French Legion of Honor and the French Croix de Guerre with Gilt Star. During the interwar years he served several tours with the Fourth and Sixth Marine regiments, both in the United States and in China.

Graduating from the Army War College in 1940, during World War II Cates commanded the First Marine Regiment at Guadalcanal and later commanded the Fourth Marine Division in the Marianas operation, the Tinian campaign and the seizure of Iwo Jima.

On January 1, 1948, General Cates was promoted to four-star rank and appointed commandant of the Marine Corps. He was serving in that position when the Korean War began in June 1950 and presided over the enormous expansion of the Marine Corps for the war, as well as the fight to gain more autonomy for the Marine Corps within the Department of Defense. After his four-year tour of duty as commandant was completed in January 1952, he reverted to three-star rank and served as head of the Marine Corps Schools until his retirement on June 30, 1954. General Cates died on June 4, 1970.

See COMMANDANT, U.S. MARINE CORPS; MARINE CORPS, U.S.

Suggestions for further reading: See the five-volume official history, *U.S. Marine Operations in Korea: 1950–1953*: Lynn Montross and Captain Nicholas A. Canzona, USMC, *The Pusan Perimeter*, 1954; *The Inchon-Seoul Operation*, 1955; *The Chosin Reservoir Campaign*, 1957; Lynn Montross and Majors Hubard D. Kuokka and Norman W. Hicks, USMC, *The East-Central Front*, 1962; and Lieutenant Colonel Pat Meid, USMCR, and Major James M. Yingling, USMC, *Operations in West Korea*, 1972 (Washington, D.C.: GPO). See also Allan R. Millett, *Semper Fidelis: The History of the United States Marine Corps* (New York: Macmillan, 1980).

CAVALRY

Although it survived in name, by the time of the Korean War *cavalry* had almost disappeared from the U.S. Army. It was still officially one of the Army's combat arms, and armor was still only a temporary detail branch, a condition that would not change until after the Korean War was concluded. Then there was the First Cavalry Division with its Fifth, Seventh and Eighth Cavalry regiments. But these had been converted to infantry units during World War II and only used the cavalry designation as a matter of tradition.

Battlefield cavalry functions—reconnaissance, screening and so on—were performed by divisional reconnaissance companies and by regimental intelligence and reconnaissance (I&R) platoons. Elsewhere in Korea there were not only cavalry but horse cavalry as well. The Republic of Korea Army's (ROKA) Capital Division had a cavalry regiment assigned when the war began, and some of its units were mounted. (The ROKA Cavalry Regiment survives—in fact it fought alongside U.S. forces in the Vietnam War—but today, like the U.S. First Cavalry Division, it is in reality an infantry unit.) When the Chinese Communist Forces (CCF) entered the war in November 1950, they also had some mounted cavalry units. Some of their tough Mongolian ponies were captured and used as pack animals by U.S. forces.

See also RECONNAISSANCE.

CEASE-FIRE

See ARMISTICE AGREEMENT.

CENSORSHIP

See MEDIA.

CHAFFEE TANK (M-24)

See ARMOR.

CHAIRMAN, JOINT CHIEFS OF STAFF

By law the chairman of the Joint Chiefs of Staff (CJCS) is the senior officer of the U.S. armed services. A statutory adviser to the National Security Council, he presides over the Joint

Chiefs of Staff. Although in the 1980s the CJCS's operational control over the armed services was expanded, at the time of the Korean War the chairman of the Joint Chiefs of Staff had no command authority but only transmitted the orders of the president and the secretary of defense.

Army general (later general of the Army) Omar N. Bradley, who became America's first chairman of the Joint Chiefs of Staff on August 16 1949, served in that capacity during the entire Korean War. General Bradley was replaced by Navy Admiral Arthur W. Radford on August 15, 1953.

See BRADLEY, OMAR N.; JOINT CHIEFS OF STAFF.

CHEJU-DO ISLAND

See POW (PRISONER OF WAR) CAMPS.

CHEMICAL MORTARS

Manned by Chemical Corps personnel, in the Korean War the Second Chemical Mortar Battalion consisted of a headquarters, a headquarters company and three mortar companies. At full strength each mortar company had 171 officers and men, 12 M-2 4.2-inch mortars, three 2 1/2-ton trucks, five 3/4-ton trucks, 35 1/4-ton jeeps, and both radio and wire communications equipment. The battalion headquarters maintained a fire direction center, where targets were plotted and orders were given to the guns.

A throwback to the First World War, chemical mortars—in reality basic 4.2-inch heavy mortars—were maintained to provide a toxic gas capability if chemical weapons came into use. The Second Chemical Mortar Battalion had served in Italy in World War II and served in the Korean War as well. Because chemical mortars were not required, the battalion was

Mortars (4.2-inch) such as the one shown here were the standard weapon for Chemical Mortar units.
(Courtesy Lyndon Baines Johnson Library & Museum.)

used as a kind of artillery battalion in direct support of infantry units on the line.

From October 1950 to October 1951 the Second Chemical Mortar Battalion was constantly on the line and saw particularly hard fighting in November to December 1950. It was attached to the Eighth Cavalry Regiment at Unsan and the Ninth Infantry Regiment at Kunu-ri when both of those units were overrun by Chinese Communist Forces (CCF). It then served as a IX Corps artillery unit, firing in support of such units as the 27th British Commonwealth Brigade (which, unlike U.S. infantry regiments, had no heavy mortar companies as part of their organization) and in support of ROK (Republic of Korea) units which also lacked sufficient assigned firepower. When the CCF launched their spring offensive in April 1951, elements of the

Second Chemical Mortar Battalion were supporting the Sixth ROK Division, which fled in panic, leaving the mortarmen to fend for themselves. Most eventually made their way back to friendly lines.

In October 1952, the chemical mortar battalions of the U.S. Army were transferred to the infantry (more than likely to quiet the nonsensical enemy propaganda charges that the U.S. was about to use poison gas in Korea) and the Second Chemical Mortar Battalion was disbanded.
See MORTARS.

Suggestions for further reading: "The 2d Chemical Mortar Battalion," in Captain John G. Westover's *Combat Support in Korea* (Washington, D.C. Combat Forces Press, 1955). See also Clay Blair, *The Forgotten War: America in Korea 1950–1953* (New York Times Books, 1987).

CHIEF OF NAVAL OPERATIONS (CNO)

The chief of naval operations (CNO) is the senior officer of the U.S. Navy and, unlike his other service counterparts, exercises command over the Navy's operating forces. He is also a statutory member of the Joint Chiefs of Staff. When the Korean War began, Admiral Forrest P. Sherman was serving as chief of naval operations. When he died in office on July 22, 1951, he was replaced by Admiral William M. Fechteler, who served for the duration of the war.
See FECHTELER, WILLIAM M.; SHERMAN, FORREST P.

CHIEF OF STAFF, U.S. AIR FORCE (CSAF)

By law, the chief of staff, U.S. Air Force, is the senior officer of the Air Force. He is also a statutory member of the Joint Chiefs of Staff. When the Korean War began the chief of staff, U.S. Air Force, was General Hoyt S. Vandenberg, who had been appointed in 1948. General Vandenberg served in that capacity until the closing days of the war when he was replaced by General Nathan F. Twining on June 30, 1953.
See VANDENBERG, HOYT S.

CHIEF OF STAFF, U.S. ARMY (CSA)

By law, the chief of staff is the senior officer of the U.S. Army. He is also a statutory member of the Joint Chiefs of Staff. General J. Lawton Collins, who was appointed Army chief of staff on August 16, 1949, served in that capacity throughout the Korean War. He was succeeded by General Matthew B. Ridgway, the former commander of the Eighth U.S. Army and the Far East Command, on August 15, 1953.
See COLLINS, J. LAWTON.

CHINA LOBBY

"China Lobby" was the label given to those in and out of government who supported the Nationalist government of Chiang Kai-shek and opposed the communist government of Mao Tse-tung. The China Lobby was extremely influential during the Korean War period. In part because of the pressure they exerted, the Truman administration was forced to take a hard line on Korea despite earlier statements that Korea was beyond the borders of U.S. interests in Asia. Already flayed by the China Lobby for the loss of mainland China to the Communists, the loss of Korea would have been politically catastrophic for President Harry S Truman and the Democratic Party.

The China Lobby's members included *Time* magazine owner Henry Luce; publisher William Randolph Hearst; industrialists like Alfred Kohlberg; and a number of senators, including Styles Bridges of New Hampshire, Robert Taft of Ohio and William Knowland of California. Sometimes allied with Senator

Joseph McCarthy in attacking the Truman administration for "losing" mainland China and being "soft on Communism," the China Lobby supported General Douglas MacArthur in his arguments with President Harry S Truman over U.S. strategy for the conduct of the war. *See also* MCCARTHY, JOSEPH R.

Suggestions for further reading: John Paton Davies Jr., *Dragon By the Tail* (New York: Norton, 1972). See also Clay Blair, *The Forgotten War: America in Korea 1950–1953* (New York Times Books, 1987).

CHINA, PEOPLE'S REPUBLIC OF (PRC)

For over two thousand years, China has played a part in Korean affairs (*see* Part I: The Setting). In 1950, there was a "new" China for Korea to contend with. Better known at the time as "Red China" or "Mainland China," the People's Republic of China (PRC) was less than a year old when the Korean War began. On September 21, 1949, the new government had been proclaimed in Peking (now *Beijing*, literally "northern capital"; during the Korean War it was called *Peiping*, "northern peace," by those who denied PRC legitimacy).

After a long struggle begun in 1927, the Chinese Communist Party (CCP) emerged victorious in its civil war with the Kuomintang (Nationalist) forces of Chiang Kai-shek. On December 9, 1949, the last of the Nationalist forces had withdrawn to the island of Taiwan (more generally known at the time as *Formosa*) 90 miles off the mainland coast; the CCP was busy consolidating its control over the mainland.

Although it had a governmental structure that included, among others, Premier Chou En-lai (*Zhou Enlai* in the new English transliteration of the pictograph characters that make up the written Chinese language), who served as foreign minister, real power was in the hands of the CCP and its "Great Helmsman," Chairman Mao Tse-tung (*Mao Zedong*). Born December 26, 1896, in the village of Shao Shan, Hunan Province, in what was then Imperial China, Mao was a founding member of the Chinese Communist Party in 1921. In January 1935, he seized control of the CCP leadership and led the Red Army in its Long March from south China to a new guerrilla base at Yenan in north China. After Japan surrendered in August 1945, Mao led the CCP in its civil war with the Nationalists.

When the Korean War began, China at first was not involved, but on October 4, 1950, the Chinese Politburo made the decision to enter the war. Evidence is sketchy, but the accepted wisdom today is that it was Soviet Premier Joseph Stalin who acquiesced in North Korea Premier Kim Il-sung's decision to "liberate" South Korea, believing the war would be confined to the two Korean states. When the United Nations intervened and it appeared that North Korea was about to be defeated, Stalin encouraged the PRC to send its troops into Korea, playing on Chinese fears that the United States would use the Korean War as a guise to reopen the Chinese Civil War, whose outcome the United States still had not accepted. In any event, on October 13 to 14, 1950, corps-sized Chinese Communist Forces (CCF) began crossing the Yalu River from Manchuria into Korea. After several skirmishes, they attacked United Nations forces at Unsan on November 1, 1950, thus beginning direct PRC military intervention in the war.

There was a general feeling in later years that China had been "had" by the Soviet Union, which not only conned China into bearing the major burden of the fighting but then, after the enormous casualties China had suffered at least partly on the Soviet's behalf, had the gall to bill China for the arms and equipment provided by the Soviets. Some observers believe this was one of the root causes of the Sino-Soviet split in the early 1960s.

In any event, when Premier Chou En-lai's explicit warning on October 3, 1950, that China would send troops into Korea if United Nations forces crossed the 38th parallel was ignored, the die was cast, and the Chinese People's Volunteers were ordered into the war. Chinese battlefield losses were appalling.

It was reported that Mao Tse-tung's own son, Mao An-ying, was killed in the fighting there; how many others died has never been revealed. Exact figures on Chinese losses are still a state secret, but even the most conservative estimates are that the CCF and the North Korean People's Army (NKPA) combined lost a minimum of one-half million soldiers killed in combat and suffered at least another one million wounded in action.

As terrible as these casualty figures are, the sad fact is that from 1950 to 1953 far more Chinese were murdered at home than were killed in Korea. Using the Korean War as an excuse to eliminate all those who might challenge his newly won power, Mao unleashed his "Resist America and Aid Korea" campaign. During the three years in which it was waged, estimates are that as many as 10 to 15 million victims perished. Even sympathetic observers report that at least two million people were slaughtered in cold blood by the Chinese Communist Party—four times as many as died on the Korean battlefield.

The People's Republic of China was one of the signatories to the Korean Armistice Agreement of 1953, and it withdrew all of its troops from Korea shortly thereafter. Not until almost 20 years later, however, with President Richard Nixon's trip to China in 1971, were relations normalized with the United States. As of this writing, the decision to send athletes to compete in the 1988 summer Olympic Games in Seoul may presage the normalization of relations with South Korea as well.

See also CHINA, REPUBLIC OF; CHINESE COMMUNIST AIR FORCE; CHINESE COMMUNIST FORCES; LIN PIAO; PENG TEH-HUAI; SOVIET UNION.

CHINA, REPUBLIC OF (ROC)

When the Korean War began in June 1950, the "China" recognized by the United States government was the Republic of China, also known as "Nationalist China." Only six months earlier the withdrawal of some two million of its supporters from the mainland had been completed under pressure from the Red Armies of the Chinese Communist Party (CCP). The government established itself on the island of Taiwan (then more commonly known as Formosa), 90 miles off the mainland coast.

Supported by the United States in its struggle against the Japanese during World War II, the Republic of China also received U.S. support in its civil war with the CCP from 1946 to 1949. Its defeat in that war touched off a partisan political debate in the United States over "Who lost China?" (See MCCARTHY, JOSEPH R.) but on the eve of the Korean War U.S. patience with the Nationalist government and its leader, Chiang Kai-shek, had largely been exhausted.

But that changed when North Korea launched its invasion of South Korea in June 1950. At the time the United States saw this aggression as part of a monolithic worldwide Communist effort to expand its "empire" by force of arms. Therefore, at the same time President Harry S Truman ordered U.S. troops into South Korea, he ordered the U.S. Navy to patrol the Straits of Formosa (Straits of Taiwan) to prevent a Chinese Communist invasion of the island.

For its part, on July 3, 1950, the Republic of China volunteered to send three infantry divisions to fight with United Nations forces in Korea. But its offer was never accepted, and the ROC never played an active military role in the Korean War. It is noteworthy, however, that after the Korean armistice in July 1953, some 14,704 Chinese prisoners of war refused repatriation to China and instead opted to be sent to Taiwan.

Twenty-five years after the end of the Korean War, on December 15, 1978, the United States officially recognized the People's Republic of China as the government of the mainland, and broke diplomatic ties with the Republic of China.

See also CHINA, PEOPLE'S REPUBLIC OF; POWs (PRISONERS OF WAR).

CHINESE COMMUNIST AIR FORCE (CCAF)

On November 1, 1950, six Russian-built MiG (Mikoyan and Gurevich) jet fighters, flying from air bases in Manchuria, attacked a formation of U.S. F-51 Mustangs. These MiG-15 Fagot fighters, armed with two 23mm and one 37mm cannons, marked the entrance of the Chinese Communist Air Force (CCAF) into the Korean War.

From an estimated strength of 650 aircraft in November 1950, by June 1951 the CCAF had increased to 1,050 planes, including 445 MiG-15s (as compared to 89 Far F-86 Sabrejets in the Far East Air Force inventory). By June 1952, the CCAF reached its peak strength of 22 air divisions and 1,830 aircraft, including 1,000 jet fighters. While the numbers remained stable, the CCAF continued a vigorous modernization program. In November 1952, for example, the CCAF received 100 IL-28 light jet bombers, which had a maximum operating radius of 690 miles with a two-ton bomb load.

Commanded by General Liu Ya-lou, the CCAF was forced by the relatively short range of the MiG-15 to concentrate its efforts on defense against United Nations bombers and fighters in the skies over the northwestern portion of Korea (the so-called MiG Alley). Aerial interdiction and close air support of ground troops were ignored, prompting Chinese Army General Lin Piao to criticize the CCAF as "too easy going."

Throughout the war, most of the CCAF aircraft were based in Manchuria, especially in the Antung area. For political reasons these bases were "off limits" to attack, and these sanctuaries gave the CCAF a major advantage. When MiG pilots got in trouble all they had to do was make it back across the Yalu River and they were safe from attack.

During the course of the war, 147 United Nations aircraft, including 78 F-86 Sabrejets, were lost in air-to-air combat, the majority to CCAF MiG-15s. Three Chinese air aces have been identified—Li Han, Chang Chi-wei and Wang Hai. But at the same time the CCAF and the North Korean Air Force lost 950 aircraft in dogfights with Allied aircraft, including 792 MiG-15s.

See also ACES; AERIAL COMBAT; AIR FORCE, U.S.; AIRCRAFT CARRIERS; NORTH KOREAN AIR FORCES; SANCTUARIES; UNITED NATIONS AIR FORCES.

Suggestions for further reading: Robert F. Futrell, *The United States Air Force in Korea: 1950–1953*, revised edition (Washington, D.C.: GPO, 1983); James A. Field, *History of United States Naval Operations: Korea* (Washington, D.C.: GPO, 1962). See also Commanders Malcolm W. Cagle and Frank A. Manson, USN, *The Sea War in Korea* (Annapolis, Md: United States Naval Institute, 1957); Richard P. Hallion, *The Naval Air War in Korea* (Baltimore: The Nautical & Aviation Publishing Company of America, 1986).

CHINESE COMMUNIST FORCES (CCF)

On October 4, 1950, Chairman Mao Tse-tung of the People's Republic of China ordered elements of the Chinese People's Liberation Army into Korea to "resist the attacks of United States imperialism." Styled with the fanciful title of *Chinese People's Volunteers* to disguise the fact that China was in direct confrontation with the United States, these units were better known at the time as Chinese Communist Forces, or CCF.

There is some confusion about their original commander (see LIN PIAO), but there is no doubt that their eventual commander was Chinese General (later Marshal) Peng Teh-huai (or *Peng Dehuai* in the new English transliteration of the Chinese characters that make up his name). This initial 380,000-man force was broken down into two main elements, the Ninth and 13th army groups (sometimes referred to as the IX and XIII army groups). Each army group was roughly equivalent to a U.S. field army (see ARMY). These army groups were again divided into some nine field armies, each roughly equivalent to a U.S. corps (see CORPS). The field armies were in turn divided into some 30 infantry divisions (see DIVISION).

During the period October 13 to 25 , 1950, the approximately 130,000 troops of the Thirteenth (XIII) Army Group consisted of four field armies (a Chinese field army was roughly equivalent to a U.S. corps, each with three 10,000-man infantry divisions, a regiment of cavalry and several regiments of artillery. Commanded by General Li Tianyu, the mission of the Thirteenth Army Group was to block the Eighth U.S. Army advance in western Korea, which was then closing in on the Korean–Manchurian border.

Within the next two weeks, farther to the east, the Ninth (IX) Army Group, under the command of General Song Shilun, also crossed into Korea. The mission of his five field armies was to confront the elements of the U.S. X Corps advancing up Korea's eastern coast, including the U.S. First Marine Division and the U.S. Army's Seventh Infantry Division in the Chosin Reservoir area.

In both cases the CCF intervention achieved almost total surprise. Although there had been some contact earlier, on November 1, 1950, two Chinese divisions of the CCF Thirteenth Army Group struck the initial blow at the Republic of Korea (ROK) First Division's 15th Infantry Regiment and the Eighth Cavalry Regiment of the U.S. First Cavalry Division at Unsan in the western sector of Korea. Both units were virtually destroyed. After pausing to regroup, on November 25, 1950, the 18 divisions of the CCF Thirteenth Army Group launched the second phase of their offensive; by the end of the year they had driven the Eighth U.S. Army out of North Korea. On January 4, 1951, the South Korean capital of Seoul once again fell to the enemy.

Part of this second phase was an attack on the U.S. X Corps in the eastern sector of Korea. On November 27, 1950, three Chinese divisions of the CCF's Ninth Army Group struck the initial blow on the First Marine Division at the Chosin Reservoir; another division hit elements of the Army's Seventh Infantry Division there. Ultimately committing some 12 divisions, by December 25, 1950, the 120,000-man CCF Ninth Army Group had pushed the U.S. X Corps out of North Korea. Evacuated by sea from the port of Hungnam, X Corps joined the Eighth U.S. Army south of the 38th parallel.

The next major CCF offensive was in the spring of 1951. On April 22, 1951, General Peng Teh-huai threw nine armies—some 27 divisions composed of about 250,000 men—against the UN lines. Although UN forces gave some ground, the CCF offensive was stopped with terrible losses, most of them from air and artillery: The battlefield became stalemated.

When the truce talks began in July 1951, the front line settled down into positional warfare akin to what occurred during World War I. At that time CCF battlefield strength was estimated at 248,100 strong, with 14 field armies organized into 40 divisions. Another six field armies would be identified in their order of battle before the war ended. Although for the next two years the CCF continued to mount attacks against the UN positions and the UN counterattacked in turn, no appreciable gains were made by either side.

A generation after the end of the war, CCF casualties are still a state secret, but conservative estimates are that they and the North Korean People's Army (NKPA) combined lost some one-half million soldiers killed on the battlefield, with probably another one million wounded in action. Both of the CCF's senior field commanders, Marshals Lin Piao and Peng Teh-huai, survived the rigors of the battlefield only to die at the hands of their Chinese Communist political opponents at home.

See also ARMOR; CHINA, PEOPLE'S REPUBLIC OF; CORPS; DIVISION; FIELD ARTILLERY; INFANTRY; LIN PIAO; PENG TEH-HUAI.

Suggestions for further reading: Juergen Domes, *Peng Te-huai: The Man and the Image* (Stanford, CA: Stanford University Press, 1985); Russell Spurr, *Enter the Dragon: China's Undeclared War Against the U.S. in Korea, 1950–1951* (New York: Newmarket Press, 1988); Peng Dehuai, *Memoirs of a Chinese Marshal* (Beijing: Foreign Languages Publishing House, 1984); and Eliot A. Cohen, "Only Half the Battle: American Intelligence and the Chinese Intervention in Korea, 1950," in Eliot A. Cohen and John Gooch, *Military Misfortunes* (New York: The Free Press, 1989). See also Samuel B. Griffith, *The Chinese People's Liberation Army* (New York: McGraw-Hill, 1967); Alexander George, *The Chinese Communist Army in Action* (New York: Columbia University Press,

1967); Allan S. Whiting, *China Crosses the Yalu* (Stanford, CA: Stanford University Press, 1960); Colonel William W. Whitson, *The Chinese High Command* (New York: Praeger, 1973); and Robert B. Riggs, *Red China's Fighting Hordes* (Harrisburg, PA: Telegraph Press, 1951).

CHIPYONG-NI, BATTLE OF

Northwest of Wonju in central Korea, the village ("ni" in Korean) of Chipyong was the site of a major battle on February 13 to 15, 1951. Occupied 10 days before the battle by the U.S. Second Infantry Division's 23d Infantry Regimental Combat Team (RCT)—the 23d Infantry Regiment, the French battalion, the First Ranger Company, the 105-mm howitzers of the 37th Field Artillery Battalion, a battery of 155-mm howitzers from the 503d Field Artillery Battalion, as well as 14 tanks and 10 antiaircraft artillery vehicles—the village found itself containing the left flank of a major Chinese Communist Force (CCF) attack.

Attempts to reinforce the RCT with the British Commonwealth Brigade and the Third Battalion, Ninth Infantry, and the Second Reconnaissance Company proved unsuccessful when these groups ran into the heavy enemy resistance; on February 13, 1951, Chipyong-ni was surrounded by elements of six CCF divisions. That night some 18,000 CCF troops, supported by mortars and artillery, attempted to overrun the perimeter but were beaten back with heavy losses. Reinforced by airdropped supplies and by close air support sorties by UN fighter aircraft, the RCT continued to hold even though their commander had been wounded and their 155-mm howitzers overrun.

On February 15 the First Cavalry Division's Fifth Cavalry Regiment, reinforced by tanks from the 24th Infantry Division's Sixth Tank Battalion, was ordered to break through to the perimeter. Mounting an operation that is still controversial, the Fifth Cavalry broke through to the besieged defenders by the evening of the 15th; the siege was lifted. The garrison had suffered 52 killed, 259 wounded and 42 missing in action.

By foiling the CCF attack, the stand at Chipyong-ni has been credited with being the decisive element in one of the most important victories of the Korean War, the Eighth U.S. Army's successful stand that halted the CCF drive into South Korea and wrecked the better part of 14 CCF divisions. For their part in that battle the 23d Infantry Regiment and attached units were awarded the Presidential Unit Citation.

Suggestions for further reading: Clay Blair, *The Forgotten War: America in Korea 1950–1953* (New York Times Books, 1987) has a most readable account of the battle of Chipyong-ni. See also Billy C. Mossman, *U.S. Army in the Korean War: Ebb and Flow* (Washington, D.C.: GPO, anticipated in 1990).

CHOSIN RESERVOIR, BATTLE OF

The Chosin Reservoir (Changjin Reservoir in Korean), part of North Korea's Japanese-built hydroelectric system, is located in northeastern Korea. The village of Hagaru at the foot of the reservoir is some 64 road miles north of the port of Hungnam. The Yalu River, which forms the border between Korea and Manchuria, lies some 75 air miles farther north.

During the period November 27, 1950 to December 11, 1950, the Chosin Reservoir would be the site of one of the best-known battles of the Korean War. Known principally for the actions of the U.S. First Marine Division, the battle also involved Army Seventh Infantry

Marines clear the area around the Chosin Reservoir on November 3, 1950, before the weather, and the enemy, close in.
(Courtesy Lyndon Baines Johnson Library & Museum.)

Division units east of the reservoir as well as the U.S. Army's Third Infantry Division, which held the Hungnam Perimeter, into which the Marines withdrew.

On the eve of the battle X Corps, which included the First Marine Division, and the Army's Third and Seventh infantry divisions, and the Republic of Korea (ROK) I Corps, which included the ROK Capital and ROK Third infantry divisions, had deployed northward along Korea's eastern coast by road and rail. After November 15, 1950, when the port of Hungnam was cleared of mines, they traveled by sea as well. While the ROK corps and elements of the Seventh Infantry Division raced for the Yalu River, the First Marine Division's First, Fifth and Seventh Marine regiments and the Army's 32d Regimental Combat Team moved northwest to the Chosin Reservoir with orders to later move north to the Yalu River.

After a bitter fight between the Seventh Marines and the Chinese Communist Force (CCF) 124th Division on November 7, 1950, the CCF withdrew from the reservoir area. On November 27, 1950, X Corps launched an attack to relieve pressure on Eighth U.S. Army (EUSA) elements under CCF attack farther to the west, but that night the CCF counterattacked in force with major elements of their 120,000-man Ninth Army Group; the battle of the Chosin Reservoir began.

On the eastern shore of the reservoir the Army's 31st Infantry Regiment was defeated in detail—that is, defeated one unit at a time—and virtually destroyed as a fighting force (see TASK FORCE MACLEAN/FAITH). To the south, attempts to open the 11 miles of road between the First Marine Regiment's base at Koto-ri and the division headquarters at Hagaru, which had come under enemy attack, came to grief on November 29, 1950. Task Force Drysdale, the 41st Commando Battalion of the

British Royal Marines, was commanded by Lieutenant Colonel Douglas S. Drysdale and reinforced by B Company, First Battalion, 31st Infantry, of the U.S. Army's Seventh Infantry Division and other units. On November 29, 1950, this 900-man force ran into stiff resistance while trying to open the road. Some 300 were captured by the CCF, many were wounded, including Drysdale, and only 300 made it to Hagaru; the remaining survivors fell back to Koto-ri.

Essentially, the First Marine Division held a series of strong points along the main supply route between the reservoir and Hungnam, with the Fifth and Seventh Marine regiments at Yudam-ni west of the reservoir, the First Marine Division command post at Hagaru at the foot of the reservoir and the First Marine Regiment at Koto-ri. The remainder of the MSR (Main Supply Route) was temporarily conceded to the CCF.

The first stage of the First Marine Division withdrawal was the movement of the Fifth and Seventh Marine regiments from Yudam-ni to Hagaru. On November 30, 1950, the breakout began; on December 4, 1950, after hard fighting enroute, the last elements of the Yudam-ni force entered the Hagaru Perimeters. Thanks to the airstrip that had been constructed there, some 4,316 Marine casualties were evacuated from Hagaru by air and 537 replacements were flown in.

On December 6, 1950, the Marine withdrawal from Hagaru to Hungnam began. Over the next 38 hours, some 10,000 troops and 1,000 vehicles moved the 11 miles to the First Marine Regiment's perimeter at Koto-ri at a cost of some 616 casualties, including many from units of the Division Trains (i.e., the division's supply and support units).

On December 8, 1950, the advance continued, with the main choke point being a blown bridge in the Funchilin pass, halfway between Koti-ri and Chinhung-ni 10 miles to the south. While the First Battalion, First Marines, at Chinhung-ni (relieved by elements of the U.S. Army's Third Infantry Division, which continued to hold open the approaches to the Hungnam Perimeter) attacked northward to seize the southern approaches to the bridge site, the First Battalion, Seventh Marines, attacked southward from Koto-ri. This major obstacle was overcome when a treadway bridge was airdropped to span the gap, and on December 9, 1950, the advance resumed.

At 1300 hours, December 11, 1950, the last elements of the First Marine Division passed through the lines of the U.S. Army's perimeter around Hungnam, and the battle of the Chosin Reservoir was at a close. On December 15, 1950, the 22,215 Marines of the First Marine Division sailed from the port of Hungnam for debarkation at Pusan and redeployment as part of the Eighth U.S. Army.

Marine Corps losses during the period October 26 to December 15, 1950, included 604 killed in action, 114 died of wounds, 192 missing in action, 3,508 wounded in action and 7,313 nonbattle casualties, mostly from frostbite. Enemy losses were estimated at 1,500 killed and 7,500 wounded by Marine ground forces; and 10,000 killed and 5,000 wounded by Marines air. It has been claimed that the Marine Corps resistance decimated the 120,000-man CCF Ninth Army Group to the point that it was not able to seriously oppose the Hungnam evacuation or take part in the initial CCF attacks in South Korea.

In any event, the Chosin Reservoir withdrawal, far from being seen as a defeat (as was the case with the simultaneous Eighth U.S. Army [EUSA] withdrawal on the western coast), was and is seen as a major U.S. Marine Corps victory over superior enemy forces. For its heroic actions at the Chosin Reservoir, the

First Marine Division and attached units were awarded a Navy Presidential Unit Citation and the First Marine Aircraft Wing was awarded an Army Presidential Unit Citation.

A veterans organization, *The Chosin Few*, is dedicated to reuniting the Allied survivors of the Chosin Reservoir battles. Its president is Frank Kerr, 33 Holbrook Avenue, Hull, Massachusetts 02045. Telephone (617) 925-1529.
See FIRST MARINE DIVISION; HUNGNAM, EVACUATION OF; TASK FORCE MACLEAN/FAITH; X CORPS.

Suggestions for further reading: While there is an abundance of literature on the Chosin Reservoir, the most detailed account is Lynn Montross and Captain Nicholas A. Candoza's *The Chosin Reservoir Campaign*, Volume 3, in the *U.S. Marine Operations in Korea: 1950–1953* series (Washington, D.C.: GPO, 1957). A first-hand account is contained in William B. Hopkins' *One Bugle No Drums: The Marines at Chosin Reservoir* (Chapel Hill, NC: Algonquin Books, 1986), which includes a hitherto unpublished analysis by Army historian S.L.A. Marshall. Roy E. Appleman's, *East of Chosin: Entrapment and Breakout in Korea 1950* (College Station, TX: Texas A&M Press, 1987) details the travail of Task Force MacLean/Faith. See also Clay Blair's, *The Forgotten War: America in Korea 1950–1953* (New York Times Books, 1987), which puts the battle in a larger perspective.

CHOU EN-LAI (ZHOU ENLAI) (1898–1976)

See CHINA, PEOPLES REPUBLIC OF.

CHROMITE OPERATION

See INCHON INVASION.

CIA (CENTRAL INTELLIGENCE AGENCY)

The Central Intelligence Agency (CIA) in 1950 was a far cry from what it is today. Its forerunner, the World War II Office of Strategic Services (OSS), had been eviscerated after the end of the war, and the CIA itself had only been created three years earlier by the National Security Act of 1947.

Operating out of cramped quarters in downtown Washington with only a tiny staff and a limited number of field agents (it was not until May 1950 that a field station was established in Tokyo) the CIA failed to provide advance warning of the June 1950 North Korean invasion—a failing that cost CIA director Admiral Roscoe H. Hillenkoetter his job. Under its new director, Army General Walter Bedell Smith, the CIA began an uphill battle to establish an intelligence early warning network.

A Korea field station was established under Ben Vandervoort and later under Al Haney, a former FBI agent. Haney's assistant was Army Lieutenant Colonel Jack Singlaub, an OSS veteran of World War II, who had been CIA station chief in Mukden until the Communist takeover there. (Twenty-seven years later, Singlaub, by then a major general, would be fired by President Jimmy Carter for publicly disagreeing with Carter's decision, later reversed, to unilaterally withdraw all U.S. ground troops from Korea.)

Although the CIA had begun to build its intelligence apparatus, they again failed to give early warning of the Chinese Communist Forces (CCF) intervention in the Korean War in the fall of 1950. As a result the United States was once again taken by surprise. The Korean War was not the CIA's finest hour.

See also DIRECTOR, CENTRAL INTELLIGENCE; MILITARY INTELLIGENCE; SMITH, WALTER BEDELL; SPECIAL OPERATIONS.

Suggestions for further reading: Max Hastings, *The Korean War* (New York: Simon & Schuster, 1987) has an excellent account of CIA activities during the Korean War. Ephram Kam's *Surprise*

Attack: The Victim's Perspective (Cambridge, Mass: Harvard University Press, 1988) uses the North Korean invasion and the CCF intervention as two of his examples in explaining the dynamics of surprise attack and why they are so difficult to predict. A recent analysis of the failure to predict the CCF intervention is Eliot A. Cohen's "Only Half the Battle: American Intelligence and the Chinese Intervention in Korea, 1950," in Eliot A. Cohen and John Gooch, *Military Misfortunes* (New York: The Free Press, 1989). See also John Ranelagh, *The Agency: The Rise and Decline of the CIA* (New York: Simon & Schuster, 1987); Ann Karalekas, *History of the Central Intelligence Agency* (Laguna Hills, CA: Aegean Park Press, 1977).

CLARK, MARK W(AYNE) (1896–1984)

Born May 1, 1896, at Madison Barracks, New York, Clark graduated from the United States Military Academy in 1917. Within a year he was in combat, commanding a battalion of the 11th Infantry Regiment, Fifth Infantry Division, in France during World War I. In the interwar years he served as an instructor with the Indiana National Guard and at the Army War College. When the United States entered World War II, Clark was a brigadier general serving as assistant chief of staff for operations on the Army General Staff in Washington.

Sent to Great Britain in June 1942 as commander of Army Ground Forces, in January 1943 he assumed command of the Fifth U.S. Army in Italy. As Fifth Army Commander, and later as 15th Army group commander (where he was promoted to four-star rank), Clark was responsible for the long and bloody campaign to drive the Nazi forces from the Italian peninsula.

In May 1952, General Mark Clark replaced General Matthew B. Ridgway as commander in chief, Far East Command, and commander in chief, United Nations Command. Serving in that capacity until the end of the Korean War, General Clark later complained, "In carrying out the instructions of my government, I gained the unenviable distinction of being the first United States Army commander in history to sign an armistice without victory."

General Clark retired from active duty in October 1953 and later served as president of the Citadel for 11 years. He died on April 17, 1984.

See FAR EAST COMMAND.

Suggestions for further reading: Mark W. Clark, *From the Danube to the Yalu* (New York: Harper, 1954). Martin Blumenson, *Mark Clark* (New York: Jonathan Cape, 1985). For biographical information see David Childress's essay in *Dictionary of American Military Biography*, edited by Roger J. Spiller (Westport, Conn.: Greenwood Press, 1984). See also Walter G. Hermes' *U.S. Army in the Korean War: Truce Tent and Fighting Front*

(Washington, D.C.: GPO, 1966); Clay Blair, *The Forgotten War: America in Korea 1950–1953* (New York Times Books, 1987).

CLOSE AIR SUPPORT

Close air support involves the use of fighter, fighter-bomber and, in rare cases, bomber aircraft to strike enemy targets just in front of the battle lines. The aircraft use machine-gun and rocket fire, bombs and napalm. For the infantryman, especially in the first months of the Korean War, close air support was a mixed blessing. It was very effective when it was on target, but too often—especially when delivered by jet fighters like the F-80 Shooting Star—friendly rather than enemy troops were taken under fire. From July to September 1950 almost every front-line unit in the Naktong Perimeter, at one time or another, came under

Navy and Marine F4U Corsairs, shown here at Kimpo shortly after its recapture in September 1950, were expert in close air support.
(Courtesy U.S. Army Military History Institute.)

attack by friendly aircraft, including the newly arrived Argyll and Sutherland Light Infantry, who were hit by a napalm strike in August 1950. According to one account, seven of the 15 Allied war correspondents who were killed in the Korean War were killed by friendly air strikes.

These problems were not caused by a lack of Air Force concern for the close air support mission. When the war began, Fifth Air Force directed that a U.S. Air Force Tactical Air Control party (TACP) be sent out to each regiment, and higher headquarters engaged in active combat operations. In addition, an Air Liaison Officer (ALO)—the personal representative of the Air Force commander—was assigned to every American division and every Republic of Korea (ROK) and U.S. corps. What was missing was the communications equipment to make the system work.

The result was that instead of using the cumbersome World War II system, a new ad hoc method began to emerge centering on the "Mosquito" forward air controllers (FACs) that hovered over the battlefield flying T-6 Texan propeller-driven aircraft, originally designed to train student pilots. Soon these Mosquitoes began relaying air requests from the ground commander directly to the Tactical Air Control Center (TACC). When this change in procedure was combined with the October 1950 arrival of the 502d Tactical Control Group and the 20th Signal Company Air-Ground Liaison, the close air support system became a much more efficient operation.

During the course of the war Fifth Air Force flew some 57,665 close air support sorties, the First Marine Aircraft Wing flew 32,482 and friendly foreign aircraft (i.e., Australian, South African and ROK) flew an additional 6,063 close air support sorties.

As far as the ground troops were concerned, the overwhelming favorite was the support provided by the gull-winged Corsairs of the First Marine Aircraft Wing. The Marines were proficient in close air support partly because their close air support doctrine called for TACPs at the battalion level, with close air support aircraft often on "air alert" directly overhead. Interestingly, in their official history of the Korean War the Air Force disparages the very same Marine Corps system they would later adopt to so great an advantage in the Vietnam War.

See FIFTH AIR FORCE; FIRST MARINE AIRCRAFT WING.

Suggestions for further reading: See Robert F. Futrell, *The United States Air Force in Korea: 1950–1953*, revised edition (Washington, D.C.: GPO, 1983). See also Callum A. MacDonald's *Korea: The War Before Vietnam* (New York: Free Press, 1986). For a comparison of World War II, Korean and Vietnam war close air support see General William W. Momyer's *Airpower in Three Wars* (Washington, D.C.: GPO, 1978).

COAST GUARD, U.S.

See KOREA MILITARY ADVISORY GROUP; SEARCH AND RESCUE OPERATIONS.

COLLINS, J(OSEPH) LAWTON (1896–1987)

Born May 1, 1896, in New Orleans, Louisiana, Collins graduated from the United States Military Academy in 1917. He commanded a battalion of the 18th Infantry Regiment during the Army of Occupation of Germany following World War I. Collins later served on the Military Academy faculty, did a tour with the Philippine Scouts and served on the faculty of the Army War College. When the United States entered World War II, he was serving as chief of staff of VII Corps.

Left, General Collins confers with Major General Frank Milburn, I Corps commander, December 1950.
(Courtesy U.S. Army Military History Institute.)

On May 6, 1942, Collins assumed command of the 25th Infantry Division in Hawaii, took the division into Guadalcanal to relieve the First Marine Division and won the Silver Star Medal for bravery there. He later commanded the division during the New Guinea campaign, where he got the nickname "Lightning Joe" from the lightning bolt in the 25th Infantry Division patch. The only general officer to command in both the Pacific and European theaters of war, Collins was reassigned to command the VII Corps in England in February 1944 and took the corps ashore on D-day at Normandy. Described by General Omar Bradley as "one of the most outstanding field commanders in Europe," Collins led VII Corps in the breakout from the Normandy beachhead and across Europe to meet up with the Russians on the Elbe.

On August 16, 1949, General Collins was appointed chief of staff, United States Army, and served in that position throughout the entire course of the Korean War. Since the Army was acting as executive agent for the Joint Chiefs of Staff for the prosecution of the war, Collins played a major role both in the military build-up for the war as well as in the formulation of military strategy.

Relinquishing the post of Army chief of staff on August 14, 1953, General Collins later served on the NATO Military Committee and as President Eisenhower's personal representative to Vietnam with the rank of ambassador. He retired from active duty on March 31, 1956, and died on September 12, 1987.
See ARMY, UNITED STATES; EXECUTIVE AGENT; JOINT CHIEFS OF STAFF.

Suggestions for further reading: J. Lawton Collins, *Lightning Joe. An Autobiography* (Baton Rouge, La.: Louisiana State University Press, 1979) and his *War in Peacetime: The History and Lessons of Korea* (Boston: Houghton Mifflin, 1969). For biographical information, see Brooks E. Kleber's essay in *Dictionary of American Military Biography*, edited by Roger J. Spiller (Westport, Conn.: Greenwood Press, 1984).

COLOMBIA

Colombia furnished sea and land forces to the war in Korea, the only Central or South American nation to do so. The Colombian contribution to the naval war was the frigate *Almirante Padilla*, and to the land war it contributed an infantry battalion. At the battalion's peak strength in 1953, 1,068 Colombian soldiers were serving in Korea.

Attached to the U.S. 31st Infantry Regiment, Seventh Infantry Division, during the Old Baldy–Pork Chop Hill operation, the Colombian Battalion saw heavy fighting there. Casualty figures for Colombian forces alone are

Colombian soldiers arrive in Korea, June 1951.
(Courtesy U.S. Army Military History Institute.)

not available, but during the course of the war the United Nations ground forces of Belgium, Colombia, Ethiopia, France, Greece, the Netherlands, the Philippines, Thailand and Turkey combined lost 1,800 soldiers killed in action and another 7,000 wounded in action. Twenty-eight Colombians were repatriated during the prisoner of war exchanges at the end of the war.

See PORK CHOP HILL, BATTLE OF; UNITED NATIONS GROUND FORCES; UNITED NATIONS NAVAL FORCES.

COMBAT CARGO COMMAND (315TH AIR DIVISION [Combat Cargo])

One of Far East Air Force's (FEAF) major shortfalls when the Korean War began was an

adequate intratheater combat cargo capability. To correct that deficiency, on September 10, 1950, the FEAF Combat Cargo Command (Provisional) was formed as a major Far East Command operational command. Initially commanded by U.S. Air Force Major General William H. Tunner, who had commanded the World War II China-Burma-India "Hump" operation and the Berlin Airlift, it was later redesignated the 315th Air Division (Combat Cargo).

Several units were assigned to the 315th Air Division: the 374th Troop Carrier Wing with two squadrons of C-54 Skymasters (later C-124 Globemasters); the 21st "Kyushu Gypsy" Troop Carrier Squadron (with the Royal Hellenic Air Force's Flight 13 and the Royal Thai Air Force troop carriers attached) flying C-47 Skytrains, which was to win a Presidential Unit Citation for its bravery at the Chosin Reservoir; the 61st Troop Carrier Group with three C-54 squadrons; and the 314th Troop Carrier Group with four C-119 Flying Boxcar squadrons, which also was to win a Presidential Unit Citation for its bravery at the Chosin Reservoir. They also dropped the 187th Airborne Regimental Combat Team (RCT) in their parachute assault at Sukchon-Sunchon on October 20, 1950 and at Munsan-ni on March 23, 1951.

In the Munsan-ni drop the 314th Troop Carrier Group was joined by the C-46 Commandos of the Air Force Reserve's 437th Troop Carrier Wing (later redesignated the 315th Troop Carrier Wing), which had been called to active duty at Chicago, Illinois, on August 10, 1950, and flew its first combat cargo mission from Japan to Korea on November 10, 1950. In the spring of 1952 yet another Air Force reserve unit joined the Combat Cargo Command when the 403d Troop Carrier Wing (later redesignated the 483d Troop Carrier Wing), which had been called to active duty at Portland, Oregon, on April 1, 1951, arrived in theater and was equipped with C-119s.

During the course of the war the Combat Cargo Command, with an average of 140 combat-ready aircraft, flew 15,836,400 ton miles and 128,336,700 passenger miles. During 210,343 sorties the Combat Cargo Command lifted 307,804 medical air evacuation patients; 2,605,591 passengers; and 391,773 tons of air freight.

See also AIRBORNE OPERATIONS; FAR EAST AIR FORCE; MEDICAL CARE AND EVACUATION; MATS (MILITARY AIR TRANSPORT SERVICE); 187TH AIRBORNE REGIMENTAL COMBAT TEAM.

Suggestions for further reading: See Robert F. Futrell, *The United States Air Force in Korea: 1950–1953*, revised edition (Washington, D.C.: GPO, 1983).

COMBAT INFANTRY BADGE (CIB)

One of the most-prized U.S. Army awards, since it evidences front-line combat service, the Combat Infantryman's Badge (CIB) was first authorized in World War II to distinguish those Army infantrymen actively engaged in ground combat. In the Korean War, as in World War II, one had to be an infantry officer or an infantry soldier with 30 days service on the front line and be recommended by one's commanding officer in order to qualify. Those who had previously received a CIB for their service in World War II wore a star on the badge to denote a second award.

In World War II and the Korean War there was no similar award for Marine Corps Infantryman, and it was not until 1969 that the secretary of the Navy authorized a Combat Action Ribbon award for Marines who had served under enemy fire.

KATUSA Pvt. Yun Chun-gi, age 15, proudly displays his Combat Infantry Badge, won as a rifleman with K Company, 19th Infantry, during the Naktong Perimeter battles.

COMBAT MEDICAL AIDMEN

Primary battlefield first aid was provided by combat medics (corpsmen in the Marine Corps). They were attached to rifle companies on the front lines, being from the regimental medical that was part of Army infantry regiments; in the case of Marine Corps rifle companies, they were attached from Navy medical units.

One of the infantryman's few heroes, the medical care these combat medical aidmen provided while under enemy fire, often at great risk to their own lives, many times made the difference between life and death. In Korea their job was complicated by the extremes of the weather as well as the mountainous terrain.

Second Infantry Division combat medics administer first aid to wounded soldiers, February 1952.
(Courtesy U.S. Army Military History Institute.)

Sometimes six men were needed for each litter to get a wounded soldier or Marine to the battalion aid station behind the front lines. To recognize their bravery and dedication, the Army authorized the award of the Combat Medical Badge, the medic's equivalent of the infantryman's Combat Infantry badge. However, there was no similar award for Navy corpsmen, who served on the front line with the Marines.

During the course of the war three Army combat medical aidmen won the Medal of Honor for their bravery in Korea: Sergeant David B. Bleak, Medical Company, 223d Infantry Regiment, 40th Infantry Division; PFC Richard G. Wilson, Medical Company, 187th Airborne Infantry Regiment; and PFC Bryant E. Womack, Medical Company, 14th Infantry Regiment, 25th Infantry Division. Five Navy

Medical Corpsmen attached to the First Marine Division also were awarded the Medal of Honor: Hospital Corpsman Third Class Edward C. Benfold, Hospital Corpsman Third Class William R. Charette, Hospitalman Richard D. Dewert, Hospitalman Francis C. Hammond and Hospitalman John E. Kilmer. *See also* COMBAT MEDICAL BADGE; MEDICAL CARE AND EVACUATION.

COMBAT MEDICAL BADGE (CMB)

The combat medic's equivalent of the Combat Infantry Badge (CIB), the Combat Medical Badge (CMB) was first authorized in World War II for distinguishing those U.S. Army Medical Department personnel (and Navy Medical Department and Air Force Medical Service personnel attached to the Army) who performed medical duties in direct support of an infantry unit engaged in active ground combat. Battle participation credit alone was not sufficient; the infantry unit must have been in contact with the enemy.

COMMANDANT, U.S. MARINE CORPS

By law, the commandant is the senior officer of the Marine Corps. During the Korean War era the commandant was not (as he is today) a full member of the Joint Chiefs of Staff. In fact, it was not until the Douglas-Mansfield Act was signed into law on June 30, 1952, that the commandant could sit with the Joint Chiefs of Staff and vote on all issues of direct interest to the Marine Corps. Until that time he was compelled to plead his case through the chief of naval operations.

General Clifton B. Cates was commandant when the Korean War began, and he served in that capacity until January 1, 1952, when his four-year tour of duty expired. He was replaced by the Commanding General, Fleet Marine Force Pacific, General Lemanuel C. Shepherd Jr., who served as commandant of the Marine Corps during the remainder of the war.

See CATES, CLIFTON B.; MARINE CORPS, U.S.; SHEPHERD, LEMANUEL C. JR.

Suggestions for further reading: Allan R. Millett, *Semper Fidelis: The History of the United States Marine Corps* (New York: Macmillan, 1980).

COMPANY

In the U.S. Army and Marine Corps—and in most other military organizations as well—a company (*battery* in the artillery, *troop* in the cavalry) is the basic organizational unit. Commanded by a captain (major in British and Commonwealth units), it consists of two or more platoons. Normally part of a battalion, the personnel strength of a company varies widely depending on the type and the mission. During the Korean War, for example, a U.S. rifle company was authorized six officers and 195 enlisted men. A tank company or artillery battery was about half as large. The U.S. military companies that were part of a battalion had letter designations (i.e., Company L, 21st Infantry), but in other armies many had numerical designations (i.e., Third Company).

The map symbol for a company is a rectangular box superimposed by a single vertical line. Within the box appropriate symbols denote the type of company involved: a tank tread for an armor company, a cannonball for an artillery battery, crossed rifles for an infantry company and so on. Thus L Company, 21st Infantry Regiment, would be portrayed as L ⊠ 21.

See BATTALION; ORGANIZATION FOR COMBAT.

CONGRESS, U.S.

Under the Constitution of the United States, the power to declare war and to raise and maintain the armed forces is specifically restricted to the Congress—that is, the United States Senate and the House of Representatives. President Harry S Truman evaded the Congressional warmaking authority by labeling the Korean War a "police action" and basing his commitment of American armed forces to combat on United Nations resolutions. Thus, he set a dangerous precedent that would bring the nation to grief in the Vietnam War.

The irony is that Truman could have had a declaration of war for the asking: The Congress overwhelmingly supported the war from the beginning. In order to "raise" the military the Congress continued the World War II Selective Service laws (i.e., the draft). By overwhelming margins Congress voted the sums necessary to "maintain" the military on a level necessary for the prosecution of the war. If anything, the Congress was more hawkish than the president.

After Truman's April 1951 relief of Far East Command Commander General Douglas MacArthur, the Senate Armed Services Committee and Foreign Relations Committee held joint sessions to inquire into the administration's conduct of the war. Although critical of some aspects, this so-called Great Debate generally supported the administration's handling of the war.

See CHINA LOBBY; DRAFT; GREAT DEBATE; PUBLIC OPINION.

CORPS

In the military the term *corps* has both a general and specific meaning. In its general sense it means a body of men and women who share similar functions, such as the Marine Corps, the Medical Corps or the Signal Corps.

In its specific sense the word designates an organizational unit subordinate to a field army composed of two or more divisions. Normally commanded by a lieutenant general, a corps is designed chiefly for the conduct of combat operations. While it may have artillery units attached (so-called corps artillery), it usually does not include logistical or support units.

On the Allied side the U.S. deployed the I, IX and X corps to Korea (a XVI Corps headquarters was activated in Japan in 1951 but never saw action in Korea). The Republic of Korea Army (ROKA) also deployed three corps headquarters, the I, II and III ROK corps.

North Korea deployed seven corps headquarters: the I, II, III, IV, V, VI and VII NKPA corps, most with three infantry divisions each.

The Chinese Communist Forces (CCF) did not use the corps organization but instead labeled their corps-size units as *armies*. At full strength a CCF army had between 21,000 and 30,000 men organized into three infantry divisions; an artillery regiment; reconnaissance, engineer and transport battalions; a signal company; and an army hospital.

During the course of the war, elements of 20 CCF armies were identified as serving in Korea: the First, 12th, 15th, 20th, 23d, 24th, 26th, 27th, 28th, 39th, 40th, 42d, 46th, 47th, 60th, 63d, 64th, 65th, 67th and 68th armies. This numerical designation of CCF corps-sized units was unusual. To avoid confusion between different-sized units, in U.S. military usage armies are normally spelled out in full (i.e., Eighth U.S. Army); roman numerals are used for corps (i.e., X Corps for Tenth Corps); arabic numerals used for divisions and smaller units (i.e., 24th Infantry Division, 21st Infantry Regiment, etc.); and alphabetical letters used to designate companies, batteries or troops (i.e., Company A, 78th Heavy Tank Battalion). The map symbol for a corps headquarters is a rectangular box superimposed by three *xs* (reputedly to denote the number of stars worn by its commander).

See also ARMY; DIVISION.

CORPSMEN, MEDICAL

See COMBAT AIDMEN; MEDICAL CARE AND EVACUATION.

CORSAIRS (F4U)

See AIRCRAFT CARRIERS, FIGHTER AND FIGHTER-BOMBER AIRCRAFT.

D

DEAN, WILLIAM F(RISHE) (1899–1981)

Born on August 1, 1899, in Carlyle, Illinois, Dean graduated from the University of California at Berkeley in 1922. Commissioned as a second lieutenant in the Army Reserve in 1921, he was tendered a Regular Army commission on October 18, 1923. Promoted to brigadier

Right, General Dean confers with General Walton Walker, the Eighth U.S. Army commander, near Taejon on July, 8, 1950.
(Courtesy Lyndon Baines Johnson Library & Museum.)

general in 1942 and then to major general in 1943, Dean served first as assistant division commander and later as division commander of the 44th Infantry Division in combat in Europe during World War II. There he won the Distinguished Service Cross for bravery.

In October 1947, he became the military governor of South Korea. He took command of the Seventh Infantry Division in 1948 and moved it from Korea to Japan. After service as Eighth U.S. Army chief of staff, he took command of the 24th Infantry Division, then headquartered at Kokura on the southern Japanese island of Kyushu, in October 1949.

When the Korean War began in June 1950, the 24th Infantry Division was the first American ground combat unit to be committed. General Dean arrived in Korea on July 3, 1950 and established his headquarters at Taejon, having orders to fight a delaying action against the advancing North Korean People's Army. Although he planned to withdraw from Taejon, he was asked by General Walton H. Walker, the Eighth U.S. Army Commander, to hold that city until July 20, 1950, in order to buy time necessary for deploying other American units from Japan. His regiments had been decimated in earlier fighting, and Dean personally led tank-killer teams armed with the newly arrived 3.5-inch rocket launchers to destroy the attacking North Korean T-34 tanks.

On July 20, as his division fell back from Taejon, General Dean became separated from his men. After wandering for over a month, he was captured by the North Koreans on August 25, 1950, and remained a POW until his release on September 4, 1953.

Awarded the Medal of Honor for his actions during the defense of Taejon, General Dean was assigned as the deputy commanding general of the Sixth U.S. Army at the Presidio of San Francisco in California after his return from Korea. When he retired from active duty on October 31, 1955, he was awarded the Combat Infantry Badge for his front-line service in World War II and Korea, an award he particularly cherished. General Dean died on August 25, 1981.

See TAEJON, BATTLE OF; 24TH INFANTRY DIVISION.

Suggestions for further reading: William F. Dean and William L. Worden, *General Dean's Story* (New York: Viking Press, 1954). For biographical information see Karl G. Larew's essay in *Dictionary of American Military Biography*, edited by Roger J. Spiller, editor (Westport, Conn: Greenwood Press, 1984).

DECLARATION OF WAR

Article I, Section 8, of the Constitution of the United States specifically reserves to Congress the power to declare war. The intent, as clearly indicated by Alexander Hamilton in *The Federalist*, was to give war-making power to the people (through their elected representatives in the Congress) rather than following the then British system and give those powers to the chief executive. For over 150 years that intent had been faithfully carried out. Past presidents (under their authority as commander in chief of the armed forces granted by Article II, Section 2, of the Constitution) had often temporarily committed American forces to combat in response to immediate crises (Thomas Jefferson's response to the Barbary pirates in 1801, for example). But any prolonged commitment of American forces to battle had been made under the mantle of a declaration of war by the Congress.

President Harry S Truman broke that tradition on June 27, 1950, when he committed American forces to the war (what he labeled a "police action") in Korea. When pressed, he fell back on the United Nations charter and the fact that the UN Security Council had called on UN member nations to provide armed support for the Republic of Korea. At the time neither he nor the senior members of the armed forces realized the terrible precedent that was being set—a precedent that would bring the nation to grief a quarter century later during the war in Vietnam.

Instead of declaring war, President Truman consulted with congressional leaders and on June 27, 1950, issued what in effect was a "war message" to the American people. "The attack on Korea makes it plain beyond all doubt that Communism has passed beyond the use of subversion to conquer independent nations and will now use armed invasion and war," he said. Seeing the attack on Korea as part of a Moscow-directed plot for monolithic world Communism, he not only committed U.S. troops to Korea but also increased American security assistance elsewhere in Asia (including "acceleration in the furnishing of military assistance to the forces of France and the Associated States of Indo-China and the dispatch of a military mission to provide close working relations with those forces," which was the beginning of America's Vietnam involvement). He also began a military build-up of U.S. forces in Western Europe that would become so massive it would seriously detract from the U.S. ability to wage war in Korea.

See UNITED NATIONS.

Suggestions for further reading: The full text of President Truman's "war message" is in the second volume of his memoirs, *Memoirs: Years of Trial and Hope* (Garden City, NY: Doubleday, 1956). The reaction of senior military leaders to the lack of a declaration of war is in Harry G. Summers Jr., *On Strategy: A Critical Analysis of the Vietnam War* (Novato, CA: Presidio Press, 1982). See also: *The Federalist* (particularly Essays 24 and 69), James E. Cook, editor (Middletown, CT: Wesleyan University Press, 1961); Jacob K. Javits, *Who Makes War: The President Versus the Congress* (New York: Morrow, 1973).

DECORATIONS, U.S.

U.S. wartime military decorations include a series of medals awarded to individuals and units for different degrees of heroism or especially meritorious performance. Decorations are distinct from service medals, which, as the name implies, are awarded to denote service during a particular time period or during a particular campaign.

During the Korean War, three decorations, presented in the name of the president of the United States (or, in the case of the Medal of Honor, in the name of the Congress of the United States), were awarded for battlefield heroism only: the Medal of Honor, the Distinguished Service Cross (The Navy Cross for Navy and Marine Corps personnel) and the Silver Star Medal.

Five other decorations were awarded in the name of the president for lesser degrees of valor or for exceptional meritorious service: the Distinguished Service Medal, the Legion of Merit (awarded for valor for Navy and Marine Corps personnel only), the Distinguished Flying Cross, the Bronze Star Medal and the Air Medal. Except for the Distinguished Service Medal and Distinguished Flying Cross, a metallic device was authorized for wear on the ribbon when awards were made for valor. The Purple Heart Medal, although classed as a decoration, is awarded exclusively for wounds received in combat.

Decorations for unit battlefield valor and for unit exceptionally meritorious service included the Army and Navy Presidential Unit Citations (equivalent to a Distinguished Service Cross/Navy Cross if awarded to an individual), the Army Meritorious Unit Commendation, the Navy Unit Commendation and the Air Force Outstanding Unit Award. Subsequent awards of the same decoration were denoted for (Army and Air Force personnel) by an oak leaf cluster worn on the medal ribbon or (for Navy and Marine Corps personnel) by a gold star worn on the medal ribbon.
See also SERVICE MEDALS, U.S.; listings for selected awards.

DEFENSE DEPARTMENT

When the Korean War began, the Department of Defense (DOD) was a relatively new organization, having been created three years earlier by the National Security Act of 1947. It had taken its present form only one year earlier with the Defense Reorganization Act of 1949.

Prior to 1947, the secretary of war and the secretary of the Navy were members of the president's cabinet; the Army chief of staff and the chief of naval operations were the senior military officers of the United States presiding over the Army and Army air force, and the Navy and Marine Corps, respectively. During World War II President Franklin D. Roosevelt had made it clear that when it came to military strategy, operations and tactics, he would exercise his authority as commander in chief directly through these uniformed heads of the military and naval services.

The National Security Act of 1947 created a Central Intelligence Agency, a National

Security Council, a separate Department of the Air Force, which incorporated Army (but not Navy and Marine Corps) air forces, and a National Military Establishment, headed by the Secretary of Defense (SECDEF). Lacking a staff and an executive department of his own, however, the Secretary of Defense lacked real power.

To correct this failing, on August 10, 1949, the Congress amended the National Security Act, eliminating the National Military Establishment and creating a Department of Defense. The previously autonomous Departments of the Army, Navy and Air Force were stripped of their cabinet status and subordinated to the Defense Department. The president delegated (some say abdicated) operational command of the military to the Secretary of Defense, who was also given budget authority over the armed forces.

Since only 10 months elapsed between the creation of the Department of Defense in its present form and the outbreak of the Korean War, the bureaucratic layering that later hampered the prosecution of the Vietnam War did not have time to develop; operational decisions were in the main left to the military professionals of the Joint Chiefs of Staff.
See EXECUTIVE AGENT; SECRETARY OF DEFENSE.

Suggestions for further reading: Douglas Kinnard, *The Secretary of Defense* (Lexington, Ky: University of Kentucky Press, 1980).

DEMILITARIZED ZONE (DMZ)

Created by the 1953 Korean armistice agreement, the demilitarized zone (DMZ) consists of a buffer zone two kilometers on either side of a military demarcation line that follows the general trace of the front lines at the close of the war. On the west coast, the DMZ begins south of the 38th parallel on the north bank of the Han River estuary, about five miles due east of Munsan, runs north through the village of Panmunjom, then northeast across the 38th parallel to the center of the Iron Triangle, east to the north side of the Punchbowl, then northeast again to just south of the town of Kosong on the Sea of Japan.

Suggestions for further reading: The text of the Korean armistice agreement, which contains the official description of the DMZ, is in Walter G. Hermes, *U.S. Army in the Korean War: Truce Tent and Fighting Front* (Washington, D.C.: GPO, 1966).

DEMOCRATIC PEOPLE'S REPUBLIC OF KOREA (DPRK)

See PART I: THE SETTING; KIM IL-SUNG; NORTH KOREAN PEOPLE'S ARMY.

DIRECTOR, CENTRAL INTELLIGENCE

The director, central intelligence (DCI) is the chief intelligence officer for the United States. He is the head of the Central Intelligence Agency (CIA) and also has oversight of the intelligence agencies of the Defense and State departments. While not a member of the president's cabinet, the DCI is a statutory adviser to the National Security Council.

When the Korean War began, the Director of Central Intelligence was Navy Admiral Roscoe H. Hillenkoetter. In October 1950 he was replaced by Army General Walter Bedell Smith, who served in the capacity until the end of the Truman administration in January 1953. General Smith was replaced by his deputy, Allen W. Dulles, who served as director of central intelligence during the last seven months of the war.
See CENTRAL INTELLIGENCE AGENCY; SMITH, WALTER BEDELL.

DISTINGUISHED FLYING CROSS

First authorized in 1926, the Distinguished Flying Cross is awarded in the name of the president of the United States for heroism or extraordinary achievement while participating in aerial flight. The performance of the act of heroism must be evidenced by voluntary action above and beyond the call of duty. The extraordinary achievement must be an accomplishment so exceptional and outstanding that it clearly sets the individual apart from his comrades or from other persons in similar circumstances. Subsequent awards are denoted by an oak leaf cluster for the U.S. Army and Air Force and by a star for the Navy and Marine Corps. Both are worn on the ribbon.

DISTINGUISHED SERVICE CROSS

First authorized in World War I, the Distinguished Service Cross (DSC), along with the Navy Cross (and Air Force Cross after 1960), is America's second highest award for bravery. During the Korean War it was awarded in the name of the president of the United States by the U.S. Army and Air Force for extraordinary heroism while engaged in an action against the enemy not justifying the award of the Medal of Honor. The act or acts of heroism had to have been so notable and involved risk of life so extraordinary that they set the individual apart from his comrades. Subsequent awards were denoted by an oak leaf cluster worn on the ribbon.

DISTINGUISHED UNIT CITATION

See PRESIDENTIAL UNIT CITATIONS, U.S.

DIVISION

In most of the world's military organizations the *division* is the basic combined arms organization for waging war. In the U.S. military it is normally commanded by a major general. During the Korean War it consisted of three regiments of infantry; a four-battalion division artillery (three battalions with 105-mm howitzers, one with 155-mm howitzers); an antiaircraft artillery battalion; a tank battalion; a reconnaissance company; an engineer battalion; a medical battalion; and supporting medical, ordnance, quartermaster and signal companies. Authorized strength was around 20,000 depending upon attachments, but actual strength varied widely. In September 1951, for example, the U.S. 24th Infantry Division had 15,591 U.S. personnel assigned and 3,606 KATUSAs (Korean military personnel) attached.

During the war nine divisions from the U.S. Army and U.S. Marine Corps served in Korea: the First Cavalry Division; the Second, Third, Seventh, 24th, 25th, 40th and 45th infantry divisions; and the First Marine Division. In addition the First British Commonwealth Division also served there. By the end of the war 14 Republic of Korea (ROKA) divisions were in combat: the Capital Division and the First, Second, Third, Fifth, Sixth, Seventh, Eighth, Ninth, 11th, 12th, 15th, 20th and 21st Infantry divisions.

By July 1973 the 260,000-man North Korean People's Army (NKPA) deployed some 23 divisions: the First, Second, Third, Sixth, Eighth, 12th, 13th, 15th, 18th, 19th, 23d, 24th, 27th, 32d, 37th, 45th, 46th and 47th Infantry divisions; the Fourth, Fifth and 105th Armored divisions; and the Ninth and 17th Mechanized divisions.

At full strength a Chinese Communist Forces (CCF) infantry division was authorized about 10,000 men (although battlefield strength was often considerably less) organized into three 3,000-man infantry regiments and a three-battalion artillery regiment. Fifty-four CCF divisions were identified as serving in Korea: the Seventh, 29th, 31st, 33d, 34th, 35th, 44th, 45th, 58th, 59th, 60th, 67th, 69th, 70th, 72d, 73d, 74th, 76th, 77th, 78th, 79th, 80th, 81st, 112th, 113th, 114th, 115th, 116th, 117th, 118th, 119th, 120th, 124th, 125th, 126th, 140th, 141st, 148th, 149th, 150th, 179th, 180th, 181st, 187th, 188th, 189th, 190th, 191st, 192d, 193d, 194th, 195th, 203d and 204th Infantry divisions.

The term *division* is also used by the U.S. Air Force to designate a unit smaller than a numbered air force (i.e., Fifth Air Force) but larger than an air wing. As with an Army or Marine Corps division, it is also usually commanded by a major general. Two air divisions were organized for the Korean War: the 314th Air Division at Nagoy, Japan, responsible for the air defense of Japan, and the 315th Air Division, responsible for combat cargo and tactical airlift.

The map symbol for a division is a rectangular box ⊠ superimposed by two *x*'s (reputedly to denote the number of stars worn by its commander).

See ARMY; BRITISH COMMONWEALTH DIVISION; CORPS; ORGANIZATION FOR COMBAT; REGIMENT; listings for individual U.S. divisions.

Suggestions for further reading: Shelby L. Stanton, *Korean War Order of Battle* (Washington, D.C.: GPO, anticipated in 1990).

DRAFT

Congress, which under the Constitution of the United States has the sole authority to raise armies, first legislated involuntary conscription to fill the ranks of the military—a *draft*—in the Civil War. It was used again in World War I and World War II with great success.

After World War II an attempt was made to man the armed forces with an all-volunteer force, but in March 1948 President Harry S Truman asked the Congress for at two-year reinstatement of the draft; on June 24, 1948, he signed the legislation restoring the Selective Service system into law. Although 9.5 million Americans were registered, only 30,000 were inducted in the late months of 1948. The draft was again suspended in January 1949.

There were no inductions in late 1949 and early 1950, and the draft laws were due to expire on July 9, 1950. But when the Korean War began in June 1950, the Congress quickly passed a two-year extension. By September 1950, 50,000 men were being drafted each month, and by 1952 20 to 30 thousand conscripts were being shipped to Korea each month.

See MOBILIZATION.

Suggestions for further reading: George Q. Flynn, *Lewis B. Hershey: Mr. Selective Service* (Chapel Hill: University of North Carolina Press, 1985). Eliot A. Cohen, *Citizens & Soldiers: The Dilemmas of Military Service* (Ithaca, NY: Cornell University Press, 1985).

EIGHTH U.S. ARMY (EUSA)

Constituted in 1944 to command Army combat units in the World War II New Guinea and Leyte Campaigns, the Eighth U.S. Army

General Matthew B. Ridgway transformed the Eighth U.S. Army from a force wallowing in defeat to a deadly fighting machine.
(Courtesy Lyndon Baines Johnson Library & Museum.)

(EUSA), with headquarters in Yokohama, was the major U.S. Army headquarters in Japan when the Korean War began. On July 9, 1950, EUSA established a forward headquarters at Taegu, and on July 13, 1950, the commanding general, EUSA, assumed command of all U.S. Army forces in Korea.

On July 17, 1950, EUSA also assumed command of all Republic of Korea (ROK) ground forces, which had been placed under the control of the Far East Command/United Nations Command (FECOM/UNC) by South Korean president Syngman Rhee on July 14, 1950. Except for those ROK units directly attached to U.S. units, EUSA directed the ROK Army corps and divisions in the field directly through the ROK Army chief of staff. Other UN ground forces, upon arrival in Korea, came under the operational control of EUSA.

From July to September 1950, during the battles of the Naktong Perimeter, EUSA exercised direct command of combat operations. After the arrival of I Corps on September 13, 1950, and IX Corps on September 23, 1950, however, EUSA exercised command through its corps commanders. Initially independent of EUSA, X Corps was activated in Japan on August 26, 1950 to conduct the Inchon invasion in September 1950 and from September through December 1950 reported directly to FECOM/UNC. After Inchon, while EUSA fought its way up

Korea's western coast, X Corps operated independently on Korea's eastern coast. After the Chosin Reservoir debacle, however, and X Corps's evacuation from Hungnam to Pusan, X Corps reverted to EUSA control on December 24, 1950, and remained so for the rest of the war.

EISENHOWER, DWIGHT D(AVID) (1890–1969)

Born October 14, 1890, in Denison, Texas, Eisenhower graduated from the United States Military Academy in 1915. He saw no combat service in World War I and during the interwar years served in a variety of assignments, including tours as an aide for Army Chief of Staff General Douglas MacArthur.

At the beginning of World War II Eisenhower served in the War Plans Directorate of the Army General Staff and was sent to England in May 1942 to take command of the U.S. Army in the European Theater of Operations (ETO). He commanded the North African invasion in November 1942 and then was named to command the D-day invasion in June 1944.

After service as Army chief of staff after World War II, Eisenhower retired from active military duty in February 1948 to serve as president of Columbia University. In 1951 he returned to active duty serving as supreme commander of the North Atlantic Treaty Organization (NATO). A year later he resigned that post to run for the presidency. In November 1952 Eisenhower was elected as the 34th president of the United States. Reelected in 1956, he returned to private life in 1960 and died on March 28, 1969.

In 1952, Eisenhower campaigned on a pledge that if elected, he would go to Korea and bring that conflict to an end. After his election he made good on his campaign promise and did visit Korea prior to his inauguration. It was

President-elect Eisenhower talks with a soldier in Korea during his visit there in December 1952.
(Courtesy Lyndon Baines Johnson Library & Museum.)

primarily a public relations event that had no connection with military strategy. His subsequent threats to resort to nuclear weapons arguably did help bring that conflict to a close. *See* ATOMIC WEAPONS.

Suggestions for further reading: Dwight D. Eisenhower, *The White House Years: Mandate for Change* (Garden City, NY: Doubleday, 1963). Stephen E. Ambrose, *Eisenhower: A Life*, 2 volumes (New York: Simon & Schuster, 1983, 1984). See also Stephen E. Ambrose's biographical sketch in *Dictionary of American Military Biography*, Roger J. Spiller, editor (Westport, Conn.: Greenwood Press, 1984). For Eisenhower's threat to use nuclear weapons see Roger Dingman's "Atomic Diplomacy During the Korean War" and Rosemary J. Foot's "Nuclear Coercion and the Ending of the Korean Conflict" in *International Security* Winter 1988/89, volume 13, number 3, pages 50–112.

Army SCARWAF engineers supervise laying PSP (pierced-steel planking) to improve an airstrip in Korea, July 1950.
(Courtesy U.S. Army Military History Institute.)

ENGINEERS

When the war began, Korea's lines of communication and supply—that is, its roads, railroads, ports and airfields—were primitive at best. Thus U.S. Army engineers had their work cut out for them from the start. These engineers included the pioneers (i.e., soldiers assigned engineering duties) assigned to infantry battalions and regiments; the combat engineer battalions part of the infantry divisions; the separate companies, battalions, groups and brigades at corps and army level; as well as the Army engineers assigned to Air Force aviation engineer units.

Normal battlefield duties included mine laying, obstacle construction, obstacle demoli-tion, assault river crossings, bridge building, road construction and the like. In addition combat engineers also had the secondary mission of fighting as infantry, and in Korea they were frequently called upon do do so. In August 1950, for example, on the Naktong River line, the 24th Infantry Division reinforced its 21st Infantry Regiment by detailing the attached 14th Engineer Combat Battalion to fight as infantry. The division also formed *Task Force Hyzer* around its own Third Engineer Combat Battalion and then committed it to the line. Named after Lieutenant Colonel Peter C. Hyzer, the Third Engineer Combat Battalion commander, the task force included not only engineers but the 24th Reconnaissance Company and Company A, 78th Heavy Tank Battalion (without tanks); elements of the division headquarters company; and everyone else in the rear area who could be mustered into duty. Task Force Hyzer still stands as the most recent example in Army history of the reconstitution of a division reserve on the battlefield.

The eight combat engineer battalions assigned to the infantry divisions—the Second, Third, Eighth, 10th, 13th, 65th, 120th and 578th Engineer Combat battalions—were reinforced by, among others, the 14th, 74th and 185th Combat Engineer battalions, the 19th Engineer Combat Group, the 1,400-man Second Engineer Special Brigade, as well as a host of special engineer units such as topographical and petroleum engineers, and light and heavy engineer construction battalions.

A unique feature of the Korean War was that the Air Force aviation engineers were all Army personnel. These SCARWAF—Special Category Army With Air Force—aviation engineer personnel were recruited, trained and assigned to units by the Army; once formed, however these engineer aviation units worked for the Air Force. When the war began, Fifth Air Force had only the 930th Engineer Aviation Group assigned, but aviation engineer strength increased: in June 1952 Fifth Air Force had the 417th Engineer Aviation Brigade to supervise airfield construction by its three engineer aviation groups, with the 930th Engineer Aviation Group working on airfields in the southern portion of Korea. The 931st Engineer Aviation Group worked on airfields in the central and northern regions, and the newly arrived 934th Engineer Aviation Group constructing on a new jet-capable airfield, K-55, at Osan in the Seoul area. Even with all these units, there was a chronic shortage of qualified aviation engineers. To correct that deficiency, after the war the Air Force assumed total responsibility for its engineers and the SCARWAF program came to an end.

During the course of the war three Army engineers won the Medal of Honor for conspicuous battlefield bravery: PFC Melvin L. Brown of the Eighth Combat Engineer Battalion, First Cavalry Division; Sergeant George D. Libby, Third Combat Engineer Battalion, 24th Infantry Division; and Corporal Dan D. Schoonover, 13th Combat Engineer Battalion, Seventh Infantry Division.

Suggestions for further reading: For accounts of Army combat engineers and aviation engineers in action see Captain John G. Westover's *Combat Support in Korea* (Washington, D.C.: Combat Forces Press, 1955). See also for Army engineers the *U.S. Army in the Korean War* series: Roy A. Appleman, *South to the Naktong, North to the Yalu*, 1961; Walter G. Hermes' *U.S. Army in the Korean War: Truce Tent and Fighting Front*, 1966; and Billy C. Mossman, *Ebb and Flow*, anticipated in 1990). See also Clay Blair, *The Forgotten War: America in Korea 1950–1953* (New York Times Books, 1987). For Army Engineer units serving with the Air Force see Robert F. Futrell, *The United States Air Force in Korea: 1950–1953*, revised edition (Washington, D.C.: GPO, 1983).

ENLISTED RANKS

In the U.S. Army (and to a lesser degree in the other armed services as well) the enlisted rank structure during the Korean War was quite different from what it had been in World War II and from what it would be in the Vietnam War.

The major change from World War II was the inversion of the numbering of pay grades. In World War II the highest enlisted rank was an E-1; by the time of the Korean War the pay grades had been renumbered so that an E-1 was the lowest enlisted grade. Another major change was the elimination of the T/3, T/4 and T/5 *technical* ratings (see table below). Now all E-4s and above were considered noncommis-

U.S. ARMY ENLISTED RANKS

World War II	Korean War	Vietnam War
		Sergeant Major (E-9)
		Master Sergeant (E-8) First Sergeant
Master Sergeant (E-1) First Sergeant	Master Sergeant (E-7) First Sergeant	Sergeant First Class Platoon Sergeant Specialist 7th Class
Technical Sergeant (E-2)	Sergeant First Class (E-6)	Staff Sergeant Specialist 6th Class
Staff Sergeant (E-3) Technician 3rd Class (T/3)	Sergeant (E-5)	Sergeant Specialist 5th Class
Sergeant (E-4) Technician 4th Class (T/4)	Corporal (E-4)	Corporal Specialist 4th Class
Corporal (E-5) Technician 5th class (T/5)	Private First Class (E-3)	Private First Class
Private First Class (E-6)	Private (E-2)	Private E-2
Private (E-7)	Recruit (E-1)	Private E-1

sioned officers (NCOs) and half-sized colored stripes were used to differentiate between combatants (blue stripes on gold) and noncombatants (gold stripes on blue).

By the time of the Vietnam War a decade and a half later the despised half-sized colored stripes had long since been abandoned and two "supergrades," E-8 and E-9, had been added to the top of the enlisted rank structure. Further, the World War II differentiation between line NCOs and technicians, now called *specialists*, had returned.

ETHIOPIA

Ethiopia furnished the Kagnew Infantry Battalion (so named for Ethiopian King Menelik's war horse in the first Ethiopian-Italian war) to fight in the Korean War, the only African nation to provide ground troops for the conflict. Ar-

riving in Korea in early 1951, the Ethiopian Battalion was attached to the U.S. Seventh Infantry Division for much of the war and fought with that unit in the Old Baldy–Pork Chop Hill area.

Unlike the American system of individual rotation, the Ethiopians favored a unit rotation. In March 1952 the original battalion was replaced by a fresh unit from Ethiopia, and in the spring of 1953 this unit in turn was replaced by yet another fresh battalion. It was this third battalion whose May 1953 "incredible patrol" was extolled by Army historian S.L.A. Marshall in his study of combat operations in the Pork Chop Hill area.

At their peak strength in 1973, 1,271 Ethiopian soldiers were serving in Korea. Casualty figures for Ethiopian forces alone are not available, but during the course of the war the United Nations ground forces of Belgium,

Ethopian officers attend a briefing on air-ground operations before reporting to the front lines.
(MHI)

Colombia, Ethiopia, France, Greece, the Netherlands, the Philippines, Thailand and Turkey combined lost 1,800 soldiers killed in action and another 7,000 wounded in action. *See* UNITED NATIONS GROUND FORCES.

Suggestions for further reading: S.L.A. Marshall, *Pork Chop Hill: The American Fighting Man in Action, Korea, Spring 1953* (New York: Morrow, 1956).

EXECUTIVE AGENT

One of the hallmarks of the Korean War was the use of the *executive agent* system: In a situation where several actors are involved, the one with the heaviest commitment is assigned as *executive agent* to act for the others and is given the chief responsibility for the conduct of necessary operations.

The United Nations Security Council asked the United States to in effect act as their executive agent for the conduct of the Korean War; President Harry S Truman accepted the responsibility of American leadership and in turn named General Douglas MacArthur, the commander in chief of the Far East Command, to serve as his executive agent while MacArthur was fulfilling the position of commander in chief of the United Nations Command (CINC UNC).

General MacArthur and his successors as CINC UNC received their instructions through the Army chief of staff; acting as executive agent for the Joint Chiefs of Staff. The Army Staff, which by training and experience was expert in the conduct of ground warfare, took the lead in formulating plans and strategies for the conduct of the war and ensuring the proper flow of arms, equipment and material, all the while coordinating its activities with the Navy and the Air Force.

Suggestions for further reading: Walter G. Hermes' *U.S. Army in the Korean War: Truce Tent and Fighting Front* (Washington, D.C.: GPO, 1966).

FAR EAST AIR FORCE (FEAF)

Activated at Brisbane, Australia, on June 15, 1944, the Far East Air Force (FEAF) fought its way across the Pacific during World War II as the air force component of General Headquarters Far East Command (GHQ FEC). When the Korean War began, it was part of the postwar occupation of Japan, with headquarters in Tokyo. Its major subordinate units included the Fifth Air Force at Nagoya, Japan, the 13th Air Force at Clark Air Base in the Philippines and the 20th Air Force at Kadena Air Base on Okinawa.

In reorganizing itself for combat, FEAF left the Thirteenth and Twentieth air forces to provide air defense for their geographic areas of responsibility and transferred most of their tactical aircraft to the Fifth Air Force. Soon deployed from Japan to front-line air bases in Korea, the Fifth Air Force became FEAF's tactical fighting element. FEAF then created three new organizations: a strategic fighting element, Bomber Command, which controlled FEAF's long-range B-29 Superfortress medium bombers as well as those on loan from the Strategic Air Command (SAC); a tactical intratheater airlift element, Combat Cargo Command (later the 315th Air Division); and an element for the air defense of Japan, the Japan Air Defense Force (later the 314th Air Division).

The FEAF commander not only served as the principal air adviser to the commander in chief,

Far East Command/United Nations Command, he also coordinated the Military Air Transportation Service (MATS) intertheater airlift between the Zone of Interior (i.e., continental United States) and Japan and had coordination control over the naval and Marine Corps air assets of the Naval Forces Far East (NAVFE) as well.

FEAF was initially commanded by Air Force Lieutenant General George E. Stratemeyer. When he had a serious heart attack in May 1951, he was replaced by Air Force Lieutenant General Otto P. Weyland, who commanded FEAF for the remainder of the war. From 44 squadrons, 657 aircraft and 33,625 officers and airmen in June 1950, FEAF grew to 69 squadrons, 1,536 aircraft and 112,188 officers and airmen by the war's end.

Over the course of the war FEAF flew a total of 720,980 sorties, almost three-quarters of the over one million sorties flown by all United Nations aircraft. These included 66,997 counter-air sorties by Fifth Air Force aircraft, which shot down some 950 enemy planes; 192,581 air interdiction sorties by the bombers and fighter-bombers of Bomber Command and Fifth Air Force, which also flew 57,665 close air support sorties; 181,65 cargo sorties by Combat Cargo Command; and 222,078 miscellaneous reconnaissance air control and training sorties.

In the course of these sorties FEAF delivered 460,000 tons of bombs, 32,357 tons of napalm,

313,600 rockets, 55,797 smoke rockets and 166,853,100 rounds of machine-gun ammunition. Between June 26, 1950 and July 27, 1953, U.S. Air Force, Marine, and friendly foreign aircrews claimed to have destroyed 1,317 tanks, 882,920 vehicles, 967 locomotives, 10,407 railway cars, 1,153 bridges, 118,231 buildings, 65 tunnels, 8,663 gun positions, 8,839 bunkers, 16 oil-storage tanks, and 593 barges and boats, and to have killed 184,808 enemy troops.

During the Korean War FEAF lost 1,446 aircraft. Friendly foreign units operating under FEAF lost another 152, and the First Marine Aircraft Wing, which also often operated under FEAF control, lost 368. Of this total of 1,986 aircraft lost, 945 were lost to nonenemy causes (accidents, air crashes, etc.) and 1,041 to enemy action, including 147 in air-to-air combat, 816 to hostile ground fire and 78 to unknown enemy actions. FEAF sustained 1,729 officer and airmen casualties in air operations, including 1,144 dead, 306 wounded, 30 missing in action (MIA) who returned to U.S. control, 214 prisoners of war (POWs) who were repatriated under the armistice agreement and 35 still believed held in captivity. An additional 112 casualties—36 dead, 62 wounded, 8 MIA who returned to duty and 6 repatriated POWs—were lost to ground action.

In addition to other combat awards and decorations won by FEAF personnel in Korea, four Air Force pilots won Medals of Honor: one by an F-86 Sabrejet pilot in a dogfight with MiGs, one by an F-80 Shooting Star pilot on a close air support mission, one by an F-51 Mustang pilot also on a close air support mission and one by a B-26 Invader pilot on an aerial interdiction mission.

See ACES; AERIAL COMBAT; AIR FORCE, U.S.; BOMBER AIRCRAFT; BOMBER COMMAND; CHINESE COMMUNIST AIR FORCE; COMBAT CARGO COMMAND; FIFTH AIR FORCE; FIGHTER AND FIGHTER-BOMBER AIRCRAFT; MATS (MILITARY AIR TRANSPORT SERVICE); NORTH KOREAN AIR FORCES; STRATEMEYER, GEORGE E; TRANSPORT AIRCRAFT; UNITED NATIONS AIR FORCES; WEYLAND, OTTO P.

Suggestions for further reading: See Robert F. Futrell, *The United States Air Force in Korea: 1950–1953*, revised edition (Washington, D.C.: GPO, 1983).

FAR EAST COMMAND (FECOM)

Officially established effective January 1, 1947, as one of the Joint Chiefs of Staff's newly organized worldwide geographical commands, General Headquarters, Far East Command (GHQ FECOM), was the successor to General of the Army Douglas MacArthur's World War II Southwest Pacific Command. As such it retained much of the old command's structure and many of its wartime personalities and units as well. Thus it was not organized by the book as a *unified command*, with three coequal service component commands and a joint staff of Army, Navy and Air Force officers drawn from these commands. As it was originally structured, the Navy and Air Force felt that their activities within the Far East Command were actually being directed by an Army staff under an Army commander.

There was some truth to their complaints, for the Army was in fact first among equals. Its *service component commander* was General Douglas MacArthur himself, who not only was commander in chief, Far East Command (CINC FECOM), but was at the same time the commanding general, U.S. Army Forces Far East. This put army component forces on a higher plane than naval forces, which were under MacArthur's naval component commander, Vice Admiral C. Turner Joy, the commander, Naval Forces Far East (NAVFE); and air forces, which were under MacArthur's air component commander, Lieutenant General George E. Stratemeyer, the Far East Air Force (FEAF) commander.

Shortly after the Korean War began in June 1950, FECOM was given operational command of the Republic of Korea (ROK) armed forces by ROK President Syngman Rhee. Soon thereafter FECOM was designed as the United Nations Command (UNC), which gave it authority over Allied personnel as well.

The commander in chief of FECOM/CINC UNC exercised direct command over battlefield ground forces: the Eighth U.S. Army (EUSA) and, from August through December 1950, the then independent X Corps. Command over combat air forces—primarily Fifth Air Force and Bomber Command—was exercised indirectly through the FEAF commander. This was true as well of the aircraft carriers and warships of the naval task forces operating in the Yellow Sea and the Sea of Japan; these aircraft carriers and warships were under the direct command of the NAVFE commander.

This command relationship continued during the tenure of General MacArthur and, after his relief by President Harry S Truman on April 12, 1951, through the tenure of his successor, General Matthew B. Ridgway, as well. It was not until after FECOM's final wartime commander, General Mark Clark, assumed command from General Ridgway in May 1952 that action was taken to make GHQ FECOM a true joint command. On October 1, 1952, an Army component headquarters—U.S. Army Forces Far East, which had been established on paper in 1951—was made operational and all three services were placed on an even footing. Further, three deputy chiefs of staff, one from each of the services, were appointed, and a joint staff—J-1 (Personnel), J-2 (Intelligence), J-3 (Operations) and J-4 (Logistics)—was created. Thus FECOM entered the last stages of the war

as a genuine joint command. As the Army official history concluded, however, "whether the change would have a real effect upon the conduct of a static war would be difficult to determine."

Determining its future effectiveness would appear not too difficult if its future operations are taken into account, however.

After the Korean War ended, FECOM headquarters was moved to Honolulu, Hawaii, and renamed U.S. Pacific Command (PACOM). Under the command of a Navy admiral, it was the strategic headquarters for the conduct of the war in Vietnam.

See CLARK, MARK W.; EIGHTH U.S. ARMY; FAR EAST AIR FORCE; MACARTHUR, DOUGLAS; NAVAL FORCES, FAR EAST; RIDGWAY, MATTHEW B.; UNITED NATIONS COMMAND; X CORPS.

Suggestions for further reading: *U.S. Army in the Korean War* series: *South to the Naktong, North to the Yalu*, 1961, by Roy E. Appleman; *Truce Tent and Fighting Front*, 1966, by Walter G. Hermes; and *Policy and Direction: The Early Years*, 1972, by James Schnabel (Washington, D.C.: GPO).

FECHTELER, WILLIAM M(ORROW) (1896–1967)

Born March 6, 1896, in San Rafael, California, the son of a career naval officer who later attained four-star rank, Fechteler graduated from the United States Naval Academy in 1916. During World War I he served on the battleship *Pennsylvania*, an experience that affected his entire naval career. When World War II began, Fechteler was serving as a staff officer with the Pacific battle fleet. In August 1943 he assumed command of the battleship *Indiana* and participated in several campaigns in the Central Pacific. Promoted to Rear Admiral, he ended the war in command of Amphibious Group Eight in the Seventh Fleet.

In January 1946 Fechteler was promoted to vice admiral and given command of the battleships and cruisers of the Atlantic Fleet. After later service on the Navy staff in Washington, he was promoted to full admiral in January 1950 and assigned as commander in chief of the Atlantic Fleet. He was serving in that capacity when the Korean War broke out.

When the Chief of Naval Operations (CNO) Admiral Forrest P. Sherman, had a heart attack and died on July 1951, Fechteler was one of more than six candidates for that position. After personal interviews with President Harry S Truman, Fechteler was appointed as the new chief of naval operations, effective August 16, 1951. The war in Korea had become stalemated before Admiral Fechteler took office, so his main task as CNO, so far as the Korean War was concerned, was to maintain American naval strength at the levels previously agreed upon.

Serving as chief of naval operations for the remainder of the war, he left office in August 1953. After subsequent service with NATO as the commander, Allied forces in Southern Europe, Admiral Fechteler retired from active duty in July 1956. He died at Bethesda Naval Hospital on July 4, 1967.

See CHIEF OF NAVAL OPERATIONS; JOINT CHIEFS OF STAFF; NAVY, U.S.

Suggestions for further reading: For biographical information, see Gerald Kennedy's essay in *The Chief of Naval Operations*, edited by Robert William Love Jr. (Annapolis, Md.: Naval Institute Press, 1980). See also James A. Field, *History of United States Naval Operations: Korea* (Washington, D.C.: GPO, 1962); Commanders Malcolm W. Cagle and Frank A. Manson, USN, *The Sea War in Korea* (Annapolis, Md: United States Naval Institute, 1957); and Richard P. Hallion, *The Naval Air War in Korea* (Baltimore: The Nautical & Aviation Publishing Company of America, 1986).

FIELD ARTILLERY

As befits its nickname, artillery was indeed the "King of Battle" for UN forces in the Korean War. The United States deployed some 54 battalions of field artillery to Korea, including 27 battalions of light towed 105-mm howitzers; two self-propelled 105-mm howitzer battalions; eight medium 155-mm towed howitzer battalions; 11 tractor-drawn and self-propelled medium and heavy 155-mm gun and howitzer battalions; and three heavy tractor-drawn 8-inch howitzer battalions.

Of these battalions, four battalions (one medium 155-mm howitzer battalion and three light 105-mm howitzer battalions) were assigned to each of the eight Army infantry divisions and each separate Regimental Combat Team (RCT) had one assigned light 105-mm battalion. The rest were assigned to I, IX and X corps artillery and were shifted to meet changing tactical situations.

Heavy artillery was increased as the war progressed. In the fall of 1952, the Eighth U.S. Army had 45 heavy eight-inch howitzers and thirty-six 155-mm guns. Originally designed to demolish such fortifications as Nazi Germany's Siegfried line, two 240-mm howitzer battalions were also formed in March 1953.

American artillery in Korea could literally put out a wall of steel. For example, on May 22, 1951, X Corps artillery fired 49,986 rounds on the corps front alone. The logistics effort required to sustain such a rate of fire was prodigious. During a 60-day period in 1951, 158,303 tons of ammunition were delivered to units on the line. This represented 27 Liberty shiploads, or 3,332 rail-car loads, or 39,527 2 ½-ton truckloads of ammunition. Artillery firepower was considerably augmented both by close air support from Air Force, Navy and Marine fighters and bombers and by naval gunfire support from ships lying offshore.

The 937th Field Artillery's self-propelled 155-mm "Long Tom" guns light up the sky with a nighttime shoot.
(Courtesy U.S. Army Military History Institute.)

In addition to Army field artillery, four field artillery battalions of the 11th Marine Regiment were also deployed to Korea. Other UN forces also sent field artillery units to Korea, most notably Great Britain's 45th Royal Artillery, the 16th New Zealand Field Artillery Battalion, the First Canadian Horse Artillery, and the artillery part of the Turkish Brigade. Originally authorized only one 105-mm battalion per division, in May 1952 Republic of Korea (ROK) Army field artillery was increased to three 105-mm and one 155-mm battalions per division.

Initially the North Korean People's Army (NKPA) was well equipped with Soviet-made field artillery. Each division had 12 122-mm howitzers, 24 76-mm guns, and 12 SU-76 self-propelled guns. Each regiment also had four 76-mm howitzers. Most of this artillery was lost, however, during the NKPA's rout after the Inchon invasion. The Chinese entered the war

with little field artillery support, but later deployed some eight artillery divisions to Korea.

In July 1951 the enemy had some 350 field artillery pieces along the front, the majority of which were 75-mm and 76-mm, with some 105-mm, 122-mm, and a few 150-mm guns and howitzers. By the spring of 1952 this had increased to 710 tubes, and by June 1952 to 884 artillery pieces. Their artillery continued to increase so that in July 1953 they fired 375,565 rounds at Allied positions. By comparison, in June 1953 UN forces fired 2,710,248 rounds at the enemy, with an additional 2,000,982 rounds fired in July.

Three field artillerymen, Marine Second Lieutenant Sherrod E. Skinner Jr., a forward observer from the 11th Marines, Army First Lieutenant Lee R. Harsell, a forward observer from the Second Infantry Division's 15th Field

Artillerymen from the 38th Field Artillery fire captured North Korean 76-mm howitzers, September 1950.
(Courtesy U.S. Army Military History Institute.)

Artillery, and Army Lieutenant Colonel John U.D. Page of X Corps Artillery, won the Medal of Honor for their actions in Korea.

See also ANTIAIRCRAFT ARTILLERY; MORTARS; ROCKET ARTILLERY.

Suggestions for further reading: For Army field artillery see *U.S. Army in the Korean War* series: Roy A. Appleman, *South to the Naktong, North to the Yalu*, 1961; Walter G. Hermes' *Truce Tent and Fighting Front*, 1966; Billy C. Mossman, *Ebb and Flow*, anticipated in 1990 (Washington, D.C.: Superintendent of Documents, GPO). For Marine field artillery see the five-volume official history, *U.S. Marine Operations in Korea 1950–1953*: Lynn Montross and Captain Nicholas A. Canzona, USMC, *The Pusan Perimeter*, 1954; *The Inchon-Seoul Operation*, 1955; *The Chosin Reservoir Campaign*, 1957; Lynn Montross and Majors Hubard D. Kuokka and Norman W. Hicks, USMC, *The East-Central Front*, 1962; and Lieutenant Colonel Pat

Meid, USMCR, and Major James M. Yingling, USMC, *Operations in West Korea*, 1972 (Washington, D.C.: GPO). For ROK units see Major Robert K. Sawyer, USA, *Military Advisors in Korea: KMAG in Peace and War* (Washington, D.C.: GPO, 1962). For order of battle see Shelby L. Stanton, *Korean War Order of Battle* (Washington, D.C.: GPO, anticipated 1990). For ammunition resupply see Captain John G. Westover, editor, *Combat Support in Korea* (Washington D.C.: Combat Forces Press, 1955).

FIFTH AIR FORCE

Activated at Brisbane, Australia, on September 3, 1942, the Fifth Air Force fought its way across the Pacific in World War II as one of the principal tactical elements of the U.S. Far East Air Force (FEAF). When the Korean War began, the Fifth Air Force was part of the occupation force in Japan, with headquarters at Nagoya. Equipped with propeller-driven F-51 and F-82 Mustangs and Twin Mustangs and jet-propelled F-80 Shooting Stars, its Eighth Fighter-Bomber Wing was stationed at Ashiya and Itazuke air bases on Kyushu, Japan's southern island. Its 35th Fighter-Interceptor Wing and 49th Fighter-Bomber Wing were stationed at Yokota and Misawa air bases on Honshu, the center island. Also on Honshu were the B-26 Invader light bombers of the 3d Bombardment Wing, at Johnson Air Base north of Tokyo, and the F-51 Mustangs of the 77th Squadron, Royal Australian Air Force (RAAF), at Iwakuni Air Base.

On June 27, 1950, President Harry S Truman authorized the use of U.S. air power in support of the Republic of Korea (ROK), and Fifth Air Force fighters, which had been providing air cover for the Seoul U.S. Embassy evacuation since June 26, were committed to action. On June 27, 1950, a Fifth Air Force F-82 Twin Mustang fighter pilot, Lieutenant William F. Hudson, shot down the first enemy plane of the war, a North Korean Air Force YAK fighter. It was to be the first of many.

Fifth Air Force's first combat missions were flown from its bases in Japan, but on July 24, 1950, Fifth Air Force displaced its headquarters from Japan to Korea. And as bases were prepared, aircraft were deployed forward as well. Meanwhile, reinforcements were on the way. The RAAF's 77th Squadron had been attached on June 29, 1950; 13th Air Force's 18th Fighter-Bomber Wing was reassigned to Fifth Air Force in July 1950, and 20th Air Force's 51st Fighter-Interceptor Wing joined soon thereafter. The F-51 Mustangs of the Second South African Air Force (SAAF) Squadron arrived in November, and in December 1950 they were joined by the F-86 Sabrejets of the Fourth Fighter-Interceptor Wing, formerly of the Continental Air Defense Command, and the F-84 Thunderjets of the 27th Fighter-Escort Wing, on loan from the Strategic Air Command (SAC). In July 1951 and again in July 1952 more F-84s came from the Air National Guard's 116th and 474th fighter bomber wings (later redesignated as the 474th and 58th fighter bomber wings). In addition, the fighters and fighter-bombers of the several wing-size Marine Air Groups (MAGs) of the First Marine Aircraft Wing (First MAW) also often operated under Fifth Air Force control.

Meanwhile, the Fifth Air Force's Third Bombardment Wing (Light) had been joined by the Air Reserve's 452d Bombardment Wing (later redesignated the 17th Bombardment Wing), giving Fifth Air Force six squadrons of B-26 Invader light bombers. Modernization also continued apace. By the spring of 1953, F-51s and F-80s had totally been phased out of the U.S. inventory and replaced by F-84s and F-86s. At the end of the war Fifth Air Force had 128 B-26s, 218 F-84s, 132 F-86 fighter-bombers and 165 F-86 fighter-interceptors.

Lieutenant General Earle E. Partridge commanded the Fifth Air Force until he was replaced on May 21, 1951 by Lieutenant General Frank E. Everest. On May 30, 1952, Everest was replaced by Lieutenant General Glenn O. Barcus, who in turn was succeeded by Lieutenant General Samuel E. Anderson on May 31, 1953. After the Korean War Fifth Air Force returned to Japan, where it has remained until this day.

Over the course of the war Fifth Air Force flew 66,997 counter-air sorties, shooting down some 950 enemy planes; flew (with FEAF's Bomber Command) 192,581 air interdiction sorties and 57,665 close air support sorties; and flew a major portion of FEAF's 222,078 miscellaneous reconnaissance, air control and training sorties. In the course of these sorties Fifth Air Force and Bomber Command combined delivered 460,000 tons of ordnance against the enemy, including 386,037 tons of bombs; 32,357 tons of napalm; 313,600 rockets; 55,797 smoke rockets; and 166,893,100 rounds of machine-gun ammunition.

Between June 26, 1950, and July 27, 1953, Bomber Command and Fifth Air Force aircrews (including those of the First MAW and the RAAF and SAAF) claimed to have destroyed 1,317 tanks, 882,920 vehicles, 967 locomotives, 10,407 railway cars, 1,153 bridges, 118,231 buildings, 65 tunnels, 8,663 gun positions, 8,839 bunkers, 16 oil-storage tanks and 593 barges and boats, and to have killed 184,808 enemy troops.

During the Korean War FEAF lost 1,446 aircraft, the majority from Fifth Air Force. Friendly foreign units operating under Fifth Air Force control lost another 152. The First Marine Aircraft Wing, which also often operated under Fifth Air Force control, lost 368. Of this total of 1,986 aircraft lost, 945 were lost to nonenemy causes (accidents, air crashes, etc.) and 1,041 to enemy action, including 147 in air-to-air combat, 816 to hostile ground fire and 78 to unknown enemy actions. Fifth Air Force sustained the majority of FEAF's 1,729 officer and airmen casualties in air operations, which included 1,144 dead, 306 wounded, 30 missing in action (MIA) who returned to U.S. control, 214 prisoners of war (POWs) who were repatriated under the armistice agreement and 35 still believed held in captivity. Another 112 casualties—36 dead, 62 wounded, 8 MIA who returned to duty and 6 repatriated POWs— were lost to ground action.

In addition to other combat awards and decorations won by Fifth Air Force personnel in Korea, four won posthumous Medals of Honor: Major George A. Davis Jr., an F-86 Sabrejet pilot, in a dogfight with MiGs; Major Charles J. Loring Jr., an F-80 Shooting Star pilot on a close air support mission; Major Louis J. Sebille, an F-51 Mustang pilot also on a close air support mission; and Captain John S. Walmsley, a B-26 Invader pilot on an aerial interdiction mission.

See ACES; AERIAL COMBAT; AIR FORCE, U.S.; BOMBER AIRCRAFT; CHINESE COMMUNIST AIR FORCE; FAR EAST AIR FORCE; FIGHTER AND FIGHTER-BOMBER AIRCRAFT; FIRST MARINE AIRCRAFT WING; NORTH KOREAN AIR FORCES; PARTRIDGE, EARL E; UNITED NATIONS AIR FORCES.

Suggestions for further reading: See Robert F. Futrell, *The United States Air Force in Korea: 1950–1953*, revised edition (Washington, D.C.: GPO, 1983).

FIFTH REGIMENTAL COMBAT TEAM

An old-line infantry regiment dating back to the War of 1812, the Fifth Infantry Regiment formed the core of the Fifth Regimental Combat Team (RCT), which also included the 555th Field Artillery Battalion, a regimental tank company (with M-4A3E8 Sherman medium tanks), and other supporting units.

After service with the 71st Infantry Division during the Rhineland and Central Europe campaigns in World War II, the Fifth Infantry Regiment was deactivated in 1946. It was recalled to active duty on January 15, 1949, at Seoul, Korea, as the Fifth RCT serving as the residual U.S. force presence there. When the decision was later made to withdraw all U.S. forces from Korea, the Fifth RCT sailed from Inchon in four increments from May 28 to June 29, 1949, to Schofield Barracks in Hawaii, where it was stationed when the Korean War began.

Ordered back into action in Korea, the Fifth RCT sailed from Hawaii on July 25, 1950, with 178 officers and 3,129 men, and arrived in Korea on July 31, 1950. At first operating independently under Eighth U.S. Army control and reinforcing the defenses of the Naktong Perimeter on August 26, 1950, the Fifth RCT was assigned to the 24th Infantry Division, replacing the 34th Infantry Regiment and 63d Field Artillery Battalion, which had been reduced to paper strength. The Fifth RCT fought as part of the 24th Infantry Division until January 1952, when that division was replaced on the front lines by the 40th Infantry Division and moved to Japan. From January 1952 until the end of the war, the Fifth RCT again operated as an independent unit under first IX Corps and then X Corps control.

The Fifth RCT as a whole was awarded three Republic of Korea Presidential Unit Citations for its actions in Korea. The Third Battalion won a U.S. Presidential Unit Citation for gallantry in action at Chinu, and Company A, First Battalion, won a U.S. Presidential Unit Citation for bravery at Songnaedong. In addition to other awards won by members of the unit, two Fifth RCT soldiers won the Medal of Honor for bravery above and beyond the call of duty. During its service in Korea the Fifth RCT suffered 4,222 casualties, including 867 killed in action or died of wounds, 3,188 wounded in action, 16 missing in action and 151 prisoners of war.

The Fifth Infantry Regiment Association publishes a regimental newsletter (further information can be obtained from Mr. Robert T. Weston, 26 Park Street, Portland, Maine 04101), and many Fifth RCT veterans are members of the 24th Infantry Division Association headed by Mr. Kenwood Ross, 120 Maple Street, Springfield, Massachusetts 01103.

See also 24TH INFANTRY DIVISION.

Suggestions for further reading: See *U.S. Army in the Korean War* series: Roy A. Appleman, *South to the Naktong, North to the Yalu*, 1961; Walter G. Hermes, *Truce Tent and Fighting Front*, 1966; Billy C. Mossman, *Ebb and Flow*, 1990 (Washington D.C.: GPO). For order of battle see Shelby Stanton, *Korean War Order of Battle* (Washington, D.C.: GPO, anticipated 1990). See also Clay Blair, *The Forgotten War: America in Korea 1950–1953* (New York Times Books, 1987).

FIGHTER AND FIGHTER-BOMBER AIRCRAFT

The Korean War was fought in a time of transition for fighter and fighter-bomber aircraft from propeller-driven models to jet-propelled planes. The U.S. Air Force is a case in point. When the war began, the Fifth U.S. Air Force in Japan had both propeller-driven F-51 Mustang fighters, which had been developed as fighter-escorts in World War II, and its all-weather version, the F-82 Twin Mustang, which was precisely what its name implied, as well as jet-propelled F-80 Shooting Stars. Ironically, at the beginning of the war several F-80 squadrons had to be reequipped with the older F-51s because of the lack of suitable jet-capable airfields in Korea.

Early in the war the F-51 Mustang fighter was the workhorse for the U.S. Air Force and for the Australians, South Africans and South Koreans as well.
(Courtesy U.S. Army Military History Institute.)

While effective at close air support and interdiction, neither the F-51 nor the F-80 were a match for the enemy's Soviet-supplied MiG-15 Fagots. It was not until December 15, 1950, however, that the first F-86 Sabrejets began flying over Korea. These planes, which proved to be the MiG killers of the war (see ACES) shot down their first MiG on December 17, 1950. Arriving in Korea on December 6, 1950, the F-84 Thunderjet eventually replaced both the F-51s (which flew their last mission on January 23, 1953) and the F-80s (whose last mission was on April 30, 1953).

Other ground-based United Nations Air Force fighter units—the Second Squadron, South African Air Force; and the 77th Squadron, Royal Australian Air Force—also flew F-51 Mustangs at the beginning, but the Australians later changed to Meteor-8 jets, and the South Africans to F-86s.

For Navy carrier pilots and for Marine Corps pilots on land or aboard U.S. Navy carriers at sea, the workhorses were the propeller-driven AD skyraiders, F7F Tigercats and the gull-winged F4U Corsairs, as well as the jet-propelled F2H Banshees and F9F Panthers. Australian and British Royal Navy carrier pilots flew propeller-driven Fairey Fireflies, Hawker Seafires and Supermarine Seafuries.

Meanwhile the North Koreans began with Soviet-supplied propeller-driven Yakovlev YAK-3, YAK-7 and YAK-9 fighters; Ilyushin Il-2 and Il-10 Shturmovik ground attack aircraft; and Lavochkin LA-5, LA-7, LA-9 and LA-11 fighters. They were soon swept from the sky, however, by UN fighter aircraft. When the Chinese entered the war in November 1950, the main enemy aircraft became the Mikoyan and Gurevich MiG-15 Fagot jet fighter, which outclassed everything but the F-86 Sabrejet.

See ACES; AERIAL COMBAT; AIRCRAFT CARRIERS; AIR FORCE, U.S.; CHINESE COMMUNIST AIR FORCE; FIFTH AIR FORCE; FIRST MARINE AIRCRAFT WING; NORTH KOREAN AIR FORCE; UNITED NATIONS AIR FORCES.

Suggestions for further reading: See Robert F. Futrell, *The United States Air Force in Korea: 1950–1953*, revised edition (Washington, D.C.: GPO, 1983). Richard P. Hallion, *The Naval Air War in Korea* (Baltimore: The Nautical & Aviation Publishing Company of America, 1986).

FIRST CAVALRY DIVISION

Organized in 1921, The First Cavalry Division brought together several famous horse cavalry regiments that had distinguished themselves during the Indian wars on the Western plains. During World War II, it was reorganized to fight on foot and deployed for combat to the southwestern Pacific. The first American unit to enter Manila, the division was selected by General Douglas MacArthur to be the first American unit to land in Japan. Because of these historic firsts, the division became known as the "First Team." When the Korean War broke out, the First Cavalry Division (actually an infantry division in everything but name) was stationed in Japan as part of the American occupation force there.

The division was composed of the Fifth, Seventh and Eighth Cavalry regiments, which were originally committed to combat at reduced two-battalion strength. It was not until the last week of August 1950 that they received their third battalions: the Third Battalion, Fifth Cavalry (which had been the Third Battalion, 14th Infantry), from Fort Carson, Colorado; the Third Battalion, Seventh Cavalry (which had been a battalion of the 15th Infantry), from Fort Benning, Georgia; and the Third Battalion, Eighth Cavalry (which had been a battalion of the Seventh Infantry), from Fort Devens, Massachusetts. The Battalion was commanded by Lieutenant Colonel Harold K. Johnson who rose to become Army chief of staff from 1964 to 1968.

These infantry regiments were supported by the 105-mm howitzers of the 61st, 77th and 99th field artillery battalions and the 155-mm howitzers of the 82d Field Artillery Battalion. Armor was initially provided by the M-24 Chaffee light tanks of A Company, 71st Heavy (sic) Tank Battalion, which deployed with the division from Japan; these were soon replaced by the M-26 Pershings of the 70th Medium Tank Battalion, which was rushed to Korea from the Armor School at Fort Knox, Kentucky. Other divisional units included the Eighth Engineer Battalion, the 92d Antiaircraft Artillery Battalion (Automatic Weapons) and the 16th Reconnaissance Company.

On July 18 to 22, 1950, the division landed at Pohang-dong on Korea's eastern coast and was immediately committed to battle. The First Cavalry Division took part in the battles of the Naktong Perimeter from July to September 1950 and led the breakout from the perimeter after the September 15, 1950, Inchon invasion. After linking up with X Corps elements on September 26, 1950, near Osan, the division led the drive of the Eighth U.S. Army (EUSA) up Korea's western coast and was the first U.S. unit in the North Korean capital of Pyongyang on October 19, 1950.

On November 1, 1950, the First Cavalry Division scored another historic first when it became the first U.S. unit to clash with Chinese Communist Forces (CCF); its Eighth Cavalry Regiment was decimated by a two-division Chinese Communist Forces (CCF) attack at Unsan, about 50 air miles south of the Yalu River. Falling back into South Korea with the rest of EUSA, the division took part in combat operations along the front, including the February 1951 battle of Chipyong-ni. In December 1951, it was replaced on the line by the 45th Infantry Division and returned to Japan as part of the Far East Command reserve. Except for occasional participation of its units in feints and rear area security operations, the division saw no further combat in the war.

The First Cavalry Division won a Republic of Korea Presidential Unit Citation for its actions at Waegwan and Taegu in the Naktong Perimeter. In addition to other awards won by members of the division, seven First Cavalry Division soldiers won the Medal of Honor for conspicuous bravery on the battlefield. During the fighting in Korea the division suffered 16,498 soldiers killed or wounded in action, over four times as many as the 4,055 casualties it had suffered in World War II.

Remaining in the Far East until 1965, the First Cavalry Division returned to the United States, becoming the first airmobile division in the United States Army. The first U.S. division to be sent to Vietnam, it saw extensive combat service there from September 1965 to April 1970. Now mechanized, the First Cavalry Division is presently stationed at Fort Hood, Texas. It maintains a museum at Fort Hood and has an active division association that schedules periodic reunions for members and former members of the "First Team." Further information can be obtained from Colonel Robert F. Little Jr., 302 North Main, Copperas Cove, Texas 76522-1799.

See UNSAN, BATTLE OF.

Suggestions for further reading: See *U.S. Army in the Korean War* series: Roy A. Appleman, *South to the Naktong, North to the Yalu*, 1961; Walter G. Hermes, *Truce Tent and Fighting Front*, 1966; and Billy C. Mossman, *Ebb and Flow*, anticipated in 1990 (Washington, D.C.: GPO). For order of battle see Shelby L. Stanton, *Korean War Order of Battle* (Washington, D.C.: GPO, anticipated 1990). See also Clay Blair, *The Forgotten War: America in Korea 1950–1953* (New York Times Books, 1987).

FIRST CORPS

See I CORPS.

FIRST MARINE AIRCRAFT WING (1ST MAW)

The First Marine Aircraft Wing (MAW) consisted of two Marine Aircraft Groups (MAGs), MAG-12 and MAG-33, each with a number of aircraft squadrons designated "V" (Aviation), "M" (Marine), and "A" (Attack), "F" (Fighter), "O" (Observation), "J" (Photo), etc. At the beginning of the war these squadrons were rotated in and out of Korea, but in the later years an individual replacement system was used. At its peak strength in 1953, the 1st MAW included some 923 officers and 6,582 enlisted personnel and consisted of six Marine attack squadrons (VMA 121, 212, 251, 312, 323 and 332); two fighter squadrons (VMF 115 and 311); a night-fighter squadron (VMF [N]-513); a photographic squadron (VMJ 1); a helicopter transport squadron (HMR 161); and an observation squadron (VMO 6); and the First 90-mm Antiaircraft Artillery Gun Battalion as well as a variety of support and service units.

Flying from escort aircraft carriers (CVE) and light aircraft carriers (CVL) such as the USS *Baedong Strait, Bairoko* and *Sicily* as well as from air strips ashore, the First MAW's combat aircraft included propeller-driven F4U Corsairs, AD-4 Skyraiders, and F7F Tigercats as well as the jet-propelled F3D-2 Skyknights, F9F Panthers and F2H-2P Banshees. In addition, HO3S-1 observation helicopters and HRS-1 cargo helicopters and other fixed-wing aircraft were part of the MAW.

From October 1950 until the end of the war the First MAW was under the operational control of the Fifth Air Force. While a departure from normal Marine Corps doctrine (which holds that the Marines control their own air assets), this system worked well in Korea. However, it was an issue that would resurface during the Vietnam War.

From its first combat operations on August 3, 1950, until the armistice on July 27, 1953, aircraft of the First MAW flew 127,496 combat sorties, including some 39,500 close air support sorties, flew interdiction sorties against enemy lines of communication, escorted B-29 bombers on their raids over North Korea and downed 35 enemy planes, including the first night kill made by a United Nations aircraft. Major John F. Bolt of VMF 115, flying an F-86 Sabrejet as an exchange officer with the Air Force, shot down six MiG-15s, thus becoming the only Marine Corps air ace of the war, although Major John H. Glenn of VMF 311 came close. Glenn, the future astronaut and United States senator, was also flying an F-86 as an exchange officer with the Air Force when he shot down three MiGs in nine days, the last one on July 22, 1953, five days before the end of the war.

Helicopter transport and resupply operations were pioneered, as was the use of helicopters for battlefield evacuation of wounded. In another facet of First MAW operations, the F2H-2P Banshee jets of VMJ 1 flew 5,025 photo reconnaissance sorties, representing over 50% of all Fifth Air Force photo reconnaissance.

For its combat operations in Korea the First Marine Aircraft Wing was awarded two Korean Presidential Unit Citations and the U.S. Army Presidential Unit Citation. A total of 436 aircraft were lost in combat or operational accidents, 258 Marines were killed (including 65 missing in action and presumed dead) and 174 were wounded in action.

In May 1965, the First MAW (including MAG 12) returned to combat, this time in Vietnam. With headquarters at Da Nang in the northern part of South Vietnam, it saw hard fighting in the skies over North and South Vietnam and over the Ho Chi Minh trail in Laos. The First MAW withdrew from Vietnam in April 1971 and is now headquartered at Marine Corps Air Station Futenma on Okinawa.

The Marine Corps Aviation Association includes among its members veterans of all Marine Corps aviation units, and its director, Colonel S.H. Carpenter, USMC (Retired), is a Korean War First MAW veteran. The association can be reached at PO Box 296, Quantico, Virginia 22134. Telephone (800) 336-0291.

See ACES; HELICOPTERS; FIRST MARINE DIVISION; FIRST PROVISIONAL MARINE BRIGADE.

Suggestions for further reading: See the five-volume official history, *U.S. Marine Operations in Korea 1950–1953*; Lynn Montross and Captain Nicholas A. Canzona, USMC, *The Pusan Perimeter*, 1954; *The Inchon-Seoul Operation*, 1955; *The Chosin Reservoir Campaign*, 1957; Lynn Montross and Majors Hubard D. Kuokka and Norman W. Hicks, USMC, *The East-Central Front*, 1962; and Lieutenant Colonel Pat Meid, USMCR, and Major James M. Yingling, USMC, *Operations in West Korea*, 1972, which has a by-name listing of Marine pilots who downed enemy aircraft during the Korean War (Washington, D.C.: GPO). See also Richard P. Hallion, *The Naval Air War in Korea* (Baltimore: The Nautical & Aviation Publishing Company of America, 1986) and Robert F. Futrell, *The United States Air Force in Korea: 1950–1953*, revised edition (Washington, D.C.: GPO, 1983).

FIRST MARINE DIVISION

The first division in U.S. Marine Corps history, the First Marine Division was organized on February 1, 1941, and took part in the amphibious assault on Guadalcanal, combat operations in New Guinea and New Britain and the assaults on Peleliu and Okinawa during World War II. Stationed at Camp Pendleton, California, when the Korean War began, the division's First and Seventh Marine

Marines head for "Blue Beach" at Inchon as the September 1950 invasion begins.
(Courtesy U.S. Army Military History Institute.)

regiments had been deactivated. Only the Fifth Marine Regiment and the artillery units of the 11th Marine Regiment remained on active duty.

After dispatching the Fifth Marines to Korea as the nucleus of the First Provisional Marine Brigade on July 12 to 14, 1950, the division began to rebuild. With a worldwide influx of personnel from other Marine units and the call to active duty of the Marine Corps Reserve, the First Marine Regiment was reconstituted; two battalions of the Seventh Marine Regiment were formed (a third battalion came from Fleet Marine Forces with the Sixth Fleet in the Mediterranean and sailed through the Suez Canal to join the rest of the regiment in Korea).

The First Marine Division ultimately included the infantry battalions of the First, Fifth and Seventh Marine regiments (and, for most of the war, the battalions of an attached fourth regiment, the 3,000-man First Republic of Korea [ROK] Marine Regiment); the four artillery battalions of the 11th Marine Regiment; the First Tank Battalion; the First Amphibious Tractor Battalion; the Firsts Armored Amphibious Battalion; the First Engineer Battalion; and other service and supply units. When the division sailed from San Diego, California, on August 10 to 22, 1950, however, its units were still scattered across the globe.

Arriving at Kobe, Japan, the division staged for the Inchon invasion (minus the Seventh Marines, which had sailed on September 3, 1950, and were still enroute, and the Fifth Marines, which were still ashore in the Naktong Perimeter). Regaining control of its Fifth Marine Regiment at sea on September 13, 1950, the First Marine Division led X Corps' assault landing at Inchon on September 15, 1950. Joined by the Seventh Marines on September 21, the division moved inland to recapture the South Korean capital of Seoul on September 27, 1950.

Reembarking on October 12, 1950, the division's next operations included the landing at Wonsan, the movement up Korea's eastern coast and the advance and subsequent retreat from the Chosin Reservoir in November to December 1950. Redeployed by sea from Hungnam to Pusan, the division initially formed part of Eighth Army's eastern defensive line in the Hwachon Reservoir and Punchbowl area. In March 1952, the First Marine Division moved to the far western sector of the defensive line, blocking enemy approaches to Seoul. It remained in that area until the end of the war and beyond, not returning to Camp Pendleton until April 1955.

During its service in Korea the First Marine Division (not including the First Marine Aircraft Wing or the attached ROK Marine Regiment) suffered 30,112 casualties, including 4,004 killed in action, 264 nonbattle deaths and 25,864 wounded in action. In addition to other awards won by members of the division, 42 Medals of Honor were won by First Marine Division personnel (and five by attached Navy corpsmen) for conspicuous battlefield bravery. The division won three U.S. Presidential Unit Citations, a Navy Unit Commendation and the Republic of Korea Presidential Unit Citation for its actions in Korea.

In July 1965 the First Marine Division would again take to the battlefield, this time in Vietnam. After hard fighting in the northern provinces of South Vietnam, the division again returned to Camp Pendleton in April 1971, where it remains stationed to this day.

The First Marine Division has an active veteran's association. Further information can be obtained from Sergeant Major George F. Meyer, USMC (Retired), First Marine Division Association, 1704 Florida Avenue, Woodbridge, Virginia 22191.

See CHOSIN RESERVOIR; FIRST MARINE AIRCRAFT WING; FIRST PROVISIONAL

MARINE BRIGADE; INCHON INVASION; MARINE CORPS, REPUBLIC OF KOREA; PUNCHBOWL, BATTLE OF.

Suggestions for further reading: See the five-volume official history, *U.S. Marine Operations in Korea 1950–1953*: Lynn Montross and Captain Nicholas A. Canzona, USMC; *The Pusan Perimeter*, 1954; *The Inchon-Seoul Operation*, 1955; *The Chosin Reservoir Campaign*, 1957; Lynn Montross and Majors Hubard D. Kuokka and Norman W. Hicks, USMC, *The East-Central Front*, 1962; and Lieutenant Colonel Pat Meid, USMCR, and Major James M. Yingling, USMC, *Operations in West Korea*, 1972 (Washington, D.C.: GPO). See also *The First Marine Division and its Regiments* (Washington, D.C.: History and Museums Division, U.S. Marine Corps, November 1981).

FIRST PROVISIONAL MARINE BRIGADE

The first U.S. Marine Corps unit to see combat in Korea was the First Provisional Marine Brigade, drawn from the First Marine Division and the First Marine Aircraft Wing at Camp Pendleton, California. The 6,534-man brigade, commanded by Brigadier General Edward A. Craig (with the First Marine Aircraft Wing's Brigadier General Thomas A. Cushman as his deputy) consisted of the three infantry battalions (each with only two rather than the three authorized rifle companies) of the Fifth Marine Regiment; one 105-mm howitzer battalion of the 11th Marine Regiment; Company A First Tank Battalion with newly issued M-26 Pershing medium tanks; and supporting transport and engineer elements as well as the three Corsair squadrons and one air observation squadron (which included 4 HO3S-1 Sikorsky helicopters) of Marine Air Group (MAG) 33.

Sailing from San Diego, California, on July 12 to 14, 1950, MAG 33 reached Japan on July 31. The air observation squadron continued on to Korea, and the one land-based night-fighter Corsair squadron initially was deployed to Itazuke airfield in Japan, while the remaining two squadrons were embarked on the aircraft carriers *Sicily* and *Baedong Strait*. From August 3, 1950, until September 14, 1950, the fighter aircraft of MAG 33 flew some 1,511 close air support sorties in support of combat operations along the Naktong Perimeter.

Meanwhile, the brigade's ground force elements arrived at Pusan, Korea, on August 2, 1950, and were immediately committed in defense of the Naktong River line; they saw their first combat action on August 7, 1950, in the Masan area. For the next month the brigade saw heavy combat all along the Naktong Perimeter as a key part of the Eighth U.S. Army's "fire brigade," which was used to reinforce threatened portions of the defensive line.

Withdrawn from combat on September 7, 1950, and reassembled at Pusan for embarkation as part of the Inchon invasion force, the brigade was deactivated on September 13, 1950; its units immediately assumed their old designations as part of the First Marine Division and First Marine Aircraft Wing.

During the 67 days of its existence the First Provisional Marine Brigade suffered 148 killed in action, 15 died of wounds, 9 missing in action (7 of whom were later reclassified as killed in action when their bodies were recovered) and 730 wounded in action. It is estimated the brigade inflicted 9,900 casualties on the opposing North Korean People's Army (NKPA) units. For its actions in defense of the Naktong Perimeter the brigade was awarded the Republic of Korea Presidential Unit Citation and the U.S. Navy Presidential Unit Citation and received written commendations from the commanding general, Eighth U.S. Army, and the commanding general, 24th Infantry Division.

See FIRST MARINE AIRCRAFT WING; FIRST MARINE DIVISION; NAKTONG PERIMETER, BATTLE OF.

Suggestions for further reading: See Lynn Montross and Captain Nicholas A. Canzona, USMC, *U.S. Marine Operations in Korea 1950 to 1953*, volume 1: *The Pusan Perimeter* (Washington, D.C.: GPO, 1954).

FORMOSA

At the time of the Korean War, "Formosa" was the name used for the island of Taiwan, to which the Chinese Nationalist forces under Chiang Kai-shek had withdrawn in 1949. Likewise, the Taiwan Straits between Taiwan and mainland China was known as the "Straits of Formosa."
See CHINA, REPUBLIC OF.

40TH INFANTRY DIVISION

Organized in 1917 as part of the National Guard, the 40th "Sunshine" Infantry Division was called to active duty in World War I but saw no action in that conflict. Headquartered in Los Angeles, California, the division was called to active duty in March 1941. It served with the Sixth U.S. Army in the Bismark Archipelago and Southern Philippines campaigns and won a bronze arrowhead for its assault landing on Luzon. In September 1945, as part of the U.S. XXIV Corps, the division moved to Korea to disarm Japanese forces there and remained in Korea until 1946, when it left active federal service and returned to state control as part of the California National Guard.

On September 1, 1950, the 40th Infantry Division was once again called into active

The California National Guard's 40th Infantry Division took part in the 1952 to 1953 outpost battles along the front. Here a soldier fires a 57-mm recoilless rifle at enemy bunker positions.
(Courtesy Lyndon Baines Johnson Library & Museum.)

federal service as part of America's mobilization for the Korean War. It consisted of the 160th, 223d and 224th Infantry regiments; the 105-mm howitzer battalions of the 143d, 980th and 981st Field Artillery battalions; the 40th Reconnaissance Company; and the 578th Engineer Battalion. The division arrived in Japan in April 1951 and began an intensive training program. During this period the division was infused with Regular Army soldiers and draftees, including an infantry platoon leader recently graduated from West Point, Lieutenant Edward C. "Shy" Meyer, who would later rise to become Army chief of staff from 1979 to 1983.

In January 1952 the 40th Infantry Division replaced the 24th Infantry Division on the front line in Korea. From January 1952 until the armistice in July 1953 the division participated in four campaigns. It fought in the Kumsong area in the central sector, helped defend Heartbreak Ridge and fought in the Punchbowl area in the eastern sector.

For its actions in Korea the 40th Infantry Division was awarded the Republic of Korea Presidential Unit Citation. In addition to other awards won by members of the division, three "Sunshine Division" soldiers won the Medal of Honor for conspicuous bravery on the battlefield. During the course of the war the division suffered 1,848 casualties, including 376 soldiers killed in action or died of wounds, 1,447 wounded in action, 10 missing in action and 15 prisoners of war.

Released from federal service on June 30, 1954, the division is once again part of the California National Guard. The 40th Infantry Division Association sponsors periodic reunions for those who served with the division. Further information can be obtained from Mr. Edward Lown, 210 Highland Avenue, Maybrook, New York 12543. Telephone (914) 427-2320.

See MOBILIZATION.

Suggestions for further reading: See *U.S. Army in the Korean War* series: Walter G. Hermes, *Truce Tent and Fighting Front* (Washington, D.C.: GPO, 1966). For order of battle see Shelby L. Stanton, *Korean War Order of Battle* (Washington, D.C.: GPO, anticipated in 1990). See also Clay Blair, *The Forgotten War: America in Korea 1950–1953* (New York Times Books, 1987).

45TH INFANTRY DIVISION

Organized in 1920 as part of the Oklahoma National Guard, the 45th "Thunderbird" Infantry Division was called to active duty in September 1940 as part of America's mobilization for World War II. It served during eight campaigns in the European Theater of Operations, including assault landings at Sicily, Naples-Foggia and Southern France, and the campaign at Anzio. In 1946 it returned to state control as part of the Oklahoma National Guard.

On September 1, 1950, the 45th Infantry Division was once again called into active federal service, this time for the Korean War. It consisted of the 179th, 180th and 279th Infantry regiments; the 105-mm howitzer battalions of the 158th, 160th and 171st Field Artillery battalions and the 155-mm howitzers of the 189th Field Artillery Battalion; the 14th Antiaircraft Artillery Battalion (Automatic Weapons); the 245th Medium Tank Battalion; the 45th Reconnaissance Company; and the 120th Engineer Battalion. The division arrived in Japan in April 1951 and began an intensive training program.

In December 1951 the 45th Infantry Division replaced the First Cavalry Division on the front line in Korea. From December 1951 until the armistice in July 1953 the division participated in four campaigns. It fought in the Chongjamal area east of Chorwon in the central sector, helped defend Heartbreak Ridge and fought in the Punchbowl area in the eastern sector.

For its actions in Korea the 45th Infantry Division was awarded the Republic of Korea Presidential Unit Citation. In addition to other awards won by members of the division, one "Thunderbird Division" soldier won the Medal of Honor for conspicuous bravery on the battlefield. During the course of the war the division suffered 4,038 casualties, including 834 soldiers killed in action or died of wounds, 3,170 wounded in action, 1 missing in action and 33 prisoners of war.

Released from federal service on April 30, 1954, the division (since 1968 the 45th Infantry Brigade) is once again part of the Oklahoma National Guard. The 45th Infantry Division Association publishes a newsletter and conducts periodic reunions for those who served with the division. Further information can be obtained from Mr. Robert A. Wilson, 2145 NE 36th Street, Oklahoma City, Oklahoma 73111. Telephone (405) 946-0417.

FORWARD AIR CONTROLLERS (FAC)

See CLOSE AIR SUPPORT.

FRANCE

Even though at the time engaged in a desperate struggle in her Indochina colonies with Vietminh insurgents led by Ho Chi Minh, France nevertheless sent military and naval forces to assist the United Nations effort in Korea. To some degree it was a quid pro quo. On June 27, 1950, at the same time President Harry S Truman ordered U.S. military forces into the Korean War, he also authorized increased aid and the dispatch of a military assistance team to help France and the "Associated States of Indochina" in their struggle against the Viet-

minh, an act some mark as the beginning of U.S. involvement in the Vietnam War.

In any event, the French contribution to the war at sea was the frigate RFS *La Grendiere*. On land the contribution was a French infantry battalion—the *Battalion de Corée*—commanded by Ralph Monclar, the *nom de guerre* of a French foreign Legionnaire and World War I veteran who had risen to the rank of three-star general; he reverted to the rank of lieutenant colonel in order to lead the French battalion in Korea.

Usually attached to the U.S. Second Infantry Division, the French battalion saw hard fighting at the Twin Tunnels (where it was awarded a U.S. Presidential Unit Citation for bravery), Chipyong-ni (where it was again awarded a U.S. Presidential Unit Citation), Hongchon (where it won a third Presidential Unit Citation) and Heartbreak Ridge. At its peak strength the French battalion had 1,185 soldiers in Korea. While the Americans favored individual rotation, the French rotated the entire original battalion in the winter of 1951, replacing it with a fresh unit from France.

Casualty figures for French forces alone are not available, but during the course of the war the United Nations ground forces of Belgium, Colombia, France, Greece, the Netherlands, the Philippines, Thailand and Turkey combined lost 1,800 soldiers killed in action and another 7,000 wounded in action. Twelve Frenchmen were repatriated during the prisoner of war exchanges at the end of the war.

When the Korean armistice went into effect in July 1953, the *Battalion de Corée* was transferred to Indochina, where the First Indochina War between the French and the Vietminh was nearing its climax. Arriving there on November 19, 1953, still wearing their Second U.S. Infantry Division patches (i.e., cloth shoulder insignia), they were redesignated the Korea Regiment. The Korea Regiment was reinforced with the *Commando Beregol*, the *Bataillon de Marche* of the

43d Colonial Infantry and a Group of the 10th Colonial Artillery to form *Groupement Mobile Nr. 100* (GM 100). In July 1954, on the road between Pleiku and Ban Me Thut in Vietnam, GM 100 was destroyed in a series of Vietminh ambushes, only days before the July 20, 1954, cease-fire ending the First Indochina War went into effect.

See CHIPYONG-NI, BATTLE OF; HEART-BREAK RIDGE, BATTLE OF; UNITED NA-TIONS GROUND FORCES; UNITED NA-TIONS NAVAL FORCES.

Suggestions for further reading: For an account of the French Battalion's actions at the battles of the Twin Tunnels, Chipyong-ni and Heartbreak Ridge see Clay Blair's *The Forgotten War: America in Korea 1950–1953* (New York Times Books, 1987). For an account of the *Bataillon de Corée* in the First Indochina War see Bernand Fall, *Street Without Joy* (Harrisburg, Pa.: The Stackpule Co., 1967).

GERM WARFARE

The enemy in Korea made several attempts to turn public opinion against the United States. Communist Party organizations and Communist-front organizations used their worldwide propaganda apparatus, which had been perfected over the years by the supposedly defunct Moscow-directed Comintern (Communist International). One of the most successful campaigns was the "germ warfare" charges leveled in early 1952.

On February 2, 1952, Soviet Ambassador to the United Nations Jacob Malik accused the U.S. of using bullets filled with "toxic gas" in Korea. This theme was expanded upon by China and North Korea to include charges that U.S. aerial bombs and artillery shells carrying bacterial warfare agents—beetles, lice, ticks, and so on—had been used to spread typhus, bubonic plague and other diseases behind their lines.

Fake exhibits were constructed, and a number of U.S. prisoners of war were coerced and otherwise "brainwashed" into making public statements supporting these charges. Fueled by such journalists as the Australian Communist Wilfred Burchett and investigated by the Moscow-backed World Peace Council (the International Red Cross and the UN World Health Organization were specifically barred by the Communists), the campaign had remarkable initial successes, partly because the United States was so slow to counter the charges.

Suggestions for further reading: Clay Blair's *The Forgotten War: America in Korea 1950–1953* (New York Times Books, 1987) links the germ warfare campaign with the enemy's humiliation over the fact a month before the charges were leveled most of the troops held prisoner by the Allies had refused repatriation. Callum A. MacDonald's *Korea: The War Before Vietnam* (New York: Free Press, 1986) examines the arguments for and against germ warfare and finds the charges unlikely. See also John Clews, *The Communists New Weapon: Germ Warfare* (London: Lincoln Praeger, 1953).

GHQ (GENERAL HEADQUARTERS)

See FAR EAST COMMAND.

GLOUCESTER HILL, BATTLE OF

Named after the British Brigade's First Battalion, the Gloucestershire Regiment, "Gloucester Hill" (actually Hill 235) was part of the Eighth U.S. Army defensive line along the Imjin River north of Seoul. The Gloucesters held the left of 29th British Brigade's nine-mile defensive line, a battalion of the Royal Northumberland Fusiliers was in the center and the Belgian battalion was on the right across the Imjin River. In reserve was a battalion of the

I CORPS DEFENSE OF SEOUL

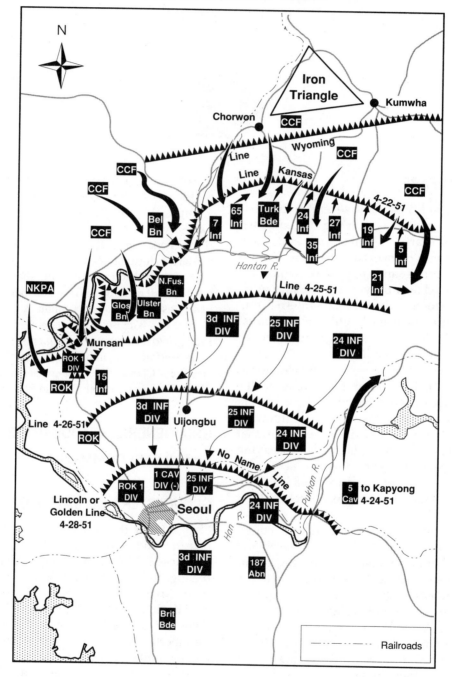

Royal Ulster Rifles and the Centurion tanks of the Eighth Hussars, while the 25-pound guns of the 45th Royal Artillery battalions were in direct support.

On April 22, 1951, the Chinese Communist Forces (CCF) launched their spring offensive, committing some nine armies organized into 27 divisions to the attack. This 250,000-man force struck along a 40-mile front, and the British Brigade found itself faced with the 187th, 188th and 189th divisions of the CCF 63d Army. The Belgians were almost immediately cut off, and the CCF succeeded in driving a wedge between the Gloucesters and the Fusiliers as they withdrew into hilltop perimeters.

After three days of bitter fighting the British Brigade was ordered to withdraw, and survivors of the Fusiliers, Ulsters and the Belgian battalion fell back in good order. The Gloucesters, however, were unable to extricate themselves and remained cut off on Gloucester Hill. Attempts to resupply them by air were unsuccessful, and on April 25, 1951, the Gloucesters were ordered to abandon their position and make for friendly lines.

After the battle, 169 of 850 Gloucesters mustered for roll call. Sixty-three had been killed, three times as many had been wounded and the rest had been captured by the Chinese. For their heroic stand, the First Battalion, the Gloucestershire Regiment, was awarded a U.S. Presidential Unit Citation, which described their action as "the most outstanding example of unit bravery in modern warfare."

See SPRING OFFENSIVE.

Suggestions for further reading: For a first-hand account see Sir Anthony Farrar-Hockley's *The Edge of the Sword* (London: Frederick Muller, 1954). Farrar-Hockley was the Gloucester's adjutant during the battle. Max Hastings, *The Korean War* (New York: Simon & Schuster, 1987) also has an excellent account, as does Clay Blair's *The For-* *gotten War: America in Korea 1950–1953* (New York Times Books, 1987).

GOLD STAR

Marine Corps/Coast Guard equivalent of the Army/Air Force oak leaf cluster, a metallic gold star was worn on a medal ribbon to denote subsequent awards of the same decoration. *Gold Star* (as in *Gold Star mother*) also referred to a small flag with a gold star emblem that was given to the families of servicemen who had died in wartime.

See also OAK LEAF CLUSTER.

GREAT DEBATE

Also known as the "MacArthur Hearings," the so-called Great Debate on the Korean War began in May 1951 with hearings before the 26-man joint Senate Foreign Relations and Armed Services committees. Chaired by the Armed Forces Committee's Senator Richard B. Russell (Democrat, GA), all of the principals were called to testify: Secretary of State Dean Acheson; Defense Secretary George Marshall; General of the Army Omar Bradley, the chairman of the Joint Chiefs of Staff; the uniformed heads of the Army, Navy, Air Force and Marine Corps; as well as General of the Army Douglas MacArthur himself, only the month before fired by President Harry Truman.

Used by those critical of the conduct of the war as an opportunity to publicly air their dissatisfaction and by the Truman administration as a chance to rebut their critics, the proceedings were ostensibly held in closed session. In fact the testimony was released to the public on a daily basis. At first front page news, by mid-June 1951 the story had been relegated to the inside pages as the public lost interest in the complexities of the arguments. The five-part record of the hearings, however, is an invaluable source for those exploring the early years of the Korean War.

Suggestions for further reading: United States Congress. Senate. Joint Committee on Armed Services and Foreign Relations. *Military Situation in the Far East.* 82d Congress. First Session (Washington, D.C.: GPO, 1951).

GREECE

Greece sent Flight 13, Royal Hellenic Air Force, as it was then known, to Korea. After arriving on November 26, 1950, their C-47 Skytrain aircraft were attached to the U.S. Air Force's 21st Troop Carrier Squadron, which won a Presidential Unit Citation for its actions at the Chosin Reservoir.

Earlier, in October 1950, Greece had sent a battalion of infantry to fight in the Korean War. Commanded by Dionyssios G. Arbouzis (who by 1974 would rise to the rank of four-star general and serve as commander in chief of the Greek Armed Forces), the troops were mostly combat veterans of the Greek civil war. On December 19, 1950, they joined the Seventh Cavalry Regiment, First Cavalry Division, and served with that unit for most of the war. At their peak strength in 1953, 1,263 Greek soldiers were serving in Korea.

Casualty figures for Greek forces alone are not available, but during the course of the war the United Nations ground forces of Belgium, Colombia, Ethiopia, France, Greece, the Netherlands, the Philippines, Thailand and Turkey combined lost 1,800 soldiers killed in action and another 7,000 wounded in action. Three Greeks were repatriated during the prisoner of war exchanges at the end of the war. *See* COMBAT CARGO COMMAND; UNITED NATIONS AIR FORCES; UNITED NATIONS GROUND FORCES.

Suggestions for further reading: Clay Blair, *The Forgotten War: America in Korea 1950–1953* (New York Times Books, 1987).

GROUP

Normally commanded by a colonel, in the U.S. Army a *group* is a command structure controlling several battalion-sized elements and is subordinate to a brigade. Groups are used principally by artillery, engineer, quartermaster corps and transportation corps units that have a number of separate battalions under their command. In naval aviation units, a CAG (Carrier Air Group) and a MAG (Marine Air Group), commanded by a Navy captain or Marine Colonel, are control headquarters subordinate to a wing, which commands several aircraft squadrons.
See WING.

GUERRILLAS

Antigovernment guerrilla bands, some sponsored by North Korea, had been a problem in the Republic of Korea (ROK) before the Korean War began, especially in southwestern Korea. These forces were greatly strengthened in September 1950 when large numbers of North Korean troops cut off after the Inchon invasion sought refuge in the countryside. It was estimated in late 1950 that there were some 8,000 guerrillas behind friendly lines, 5,400 of whom were armed. One area of concentration was the Chiri-san region of southwestern Korea.

On December 1, 1951, the ROK government declared martial law in southwestern Korea, and Task Force Paik (named after its commander, ROK Lieutenant General Paik Suh Yup) launched Operation RATKILLER to eliminate the guerrilla forces there. Deploying the ROK Eighth Division and the ROK Capital Division as well as National Police and other security forces, by the 14th of December, 1,612 guerrillas had been killed and another 1,842 captured. Shifting their attention northly to the mountains around Chonju, by December 31 another 4,000 guerrillas had been killed and 4,000 captured. In the final phase of the operation Task Force Paik again swept the Chiri-san area, and by the end of the campaign on March 15, 1951, some 19,000 guerrillas (over twice as many as had originally been estimated) had been killed or captured. The two ROK divisions returned to the front and antiguerrilla operations were turned over to local authorities. *See* SPECIAL OPERATION.

Suggestions for further reading: Details of Operation RATCATCHER are contained in Walter G. Hermes, *U.S. Army in the Korean War: Truce Tent and Fighting Front* (Washington, D.C.: GPO, 1966).

H

HANGUL

The Korean language is one of the oldest in the world. It does not belong to the tonal family of languages, such as Mandarin Chinese and Vietnamese, in which meanings change depending on tonal inflection; instead, it belonged to the Ural-Altaic family, which includes Finnish and Hungarian.

It was written in Chinese ideographs (i.e., characters that represent not sounds but ideas) until the 15th century: In 1443 Emperor Sejong devised a simple phonetic alphabet called *Hangul*. Originally made up of 28 characters, the alphabet in its modern version contains 24 easily learned characters roughly equivalent to the 26-character Western *abc*'s.

ㄱ (k or g), ㄴ (n), ㄷ (t or d), ㄹ (r or l), ㅁ (m), ㅂ (p or b), ㅅ (s), ㅈ (ch or j), ㅊ (ch'), ㅋ (k'), ㅌ (t'), ㅍ (p'), ㅎ (h'), ㅇ (ng), ㅏ (a), ㅑ (ya), ㅓ (ŏ), ㅕ (yŏ), ㅗ (o), ㅛ (yo), ㅜ (u), ㅠ (yu), ㅡ (ŭ), ㅣ (i).

HEARTBREAK RIDGE, BATTLE OF

Named by news correspondents covering the action, "Heartbreak Ridge" was an extension of Bloody Ridge three miles to the south and was located in the eastern sector of the Eighth U.S. Army (EUSA) defensive line in the Punchbowl area. It was a long, narrow ridge running north and south between the Mundung-ni valley on the west and the Sat'ae-ri valley on the east, with spurs running off to the west and west like the skeleton of a fish.

Following the seizure of Bloody Ridge on September 5, 1951, after an almost month-long battle, the U.S. Second Infantry Division was ordered to continue the attack and seize Heartbreak Ridge in order to prevent the enemy from using the adjacent valleys to attack X Corps positions west of the Punchbowl. The 23d Infantry Regiment (later reinforced by the French Battalion) led the assault on September 13; when it ran into heavy resistance, the 9th Infantry Regiment was also committed. Fighting continued until September 27, when the piecemeal frontal assault was called off; a coordinated division attack by the Ninth, 23d and 38th Infantry regiments and attached units was launched on October 5, 1951. Heartbreak Ridge was finally seized on October 13, 1951, by the 23d Infantry Regiment and the French Battalion.

The Second Infantry Division suffered over 3,700 casualties during the September 13 to October 15 period, and these high losses marked the end of major UN offensive operations for the remainder of the war. Artillery support had been so intense that it created a temporary ammunition shortage throughout

Enemy entrenchments, such as the bunker shown here, made battles like Heartbreak Ridge a particularly bloody affair.
(Courtesy Lyndon Baines Johnson Library & Museum.)

EUSA. These guns fired 62,000 rounds of 76-mm ammunition; 401,000 rounds of 105-mm (the 15th Field Artillery Battalion set a record by firing 14,425 rounds in 24 hours); 84,000 rounds of 155-mm; and 13,000 rounds of 8-inch; as well as 119,000 rounds of 60-mm, 82-mm and 4.2-inch mortar ammunition. Fifth Air Force flew 842 sorties over Heartbreak Ridge and loosed 250 tons of bombs. Estimates of enemy losses totaled close to 25,000 men.

Although Heartbreak Ridge (then defended by elements of the 160th Infantry Regiment, 40th Infantry Division) came under attack by the NKPA's 14th Regiment on November 3,

1952, the assault was beaten back, and the ridge remained in friendly hands until the end of the war.

Suggestions for further reading: See *U.S. Army in the Korean War* series: Walter G. Hermes, *Truce Tent and Fighting Front* (Washington, D.C.: GPO, 1966). See also Clay Blair, *The Forgotten War: America in Korea 1950–1953* (New York Times Books, 1987).

HELICOPTERS

Although a few helicopters had been used experimentally in World War II, they did not play

Following the lead of the Marines and Air Force, the Army too sent helicopters to Korea, such as the Bell H-13 observation helicopter, which was also used for casualty evacuation.
(Courtesy Lyndon Baines Johnson Library & Museum.)

a significant role in that conflict. The Korean War was a different matter. One of the major military innovations of that war was the use of helicopters for battlefield observation, evacuation of wounded, air-sea rescue and transport of men and supplies.

In the Air Force the Third Air Rescue Squadron was equipped with the H-5 light observation helicopter and the H-19 and H-21 medium cargo helicopters. These aircraft were intended for air-sea rescue operations, but were also used extensively for evacuation of the wounded from front-line positions to hospitals in the rear areas. During the battles of Chipyong-ni in February 1951, for example, six Air Force H-5s delivered medical supplies to the encircled forces there and evacuated 52 wounded personnel. In March 1951 the small

H-5s, which could only carry a pilot and one passenger internally and two passengers in external litter capsules, were augmented by H-19 cargo helicopters, which could carry eight litter patients or 10 passengers plus a pilot and a medical technician. The larger H-21 cargo helicopters did not reach the war zone until the end of the war and played no significant role there.

By January 1951 the Army had deployed a number of Bell H-13 and Hiller H-23 light helicopters to Korea, and had organized helicopter ambulance detachments, gradually relieving the Air Force of responsibility for battlefield evacuation. But Army–Air Force interservice bickering about who was responsible for battlefield airlift delayed the Army's deployment of cargo helicopters to Korea until the end of the war. In June 1953 the Sixth and Seventh Transportation companies (Helicopter) used H-19 helicopters for the first time to resupply front-line regiments.

But it was the Marine Corps that really pioneered the use of helicopters. When the First Provisional Marine Brigade deployed to Korea in August 1950, part of the First Marine Aircraft Wing's contingent was Marine Observation Squadron' Six (VMO-6). This squadron included four Sikorsky HO3S-1 observation helicopters hastily assigned from the Marine Corps' test unit at Quantico, Virginia. VMO-6 had the distinction of being the first helicopter unit in U.S. military history to be formed for overseas service.

As with their Air Force and Army counterparts, medical evacuation of casualties from the battlefield soon became an important Marine Corps helicopter mission. Throughout the war nearly 10,000 Marines were evacuated by helicopter to rear-area hospitals or to hospital ships lying offshore.

In August 1951 VMO-6 was joined by Marine Helicopter Transport Squadron 161 (HMR-161), with fifteen 10-seat Sikorsky HRS-1 cargo helicopters. On September 13, 1951, HRS-1 helicopters carried out the first aerial resupply operations in history when in two and one-half hours it lifted 18,848 pounds of gear and 74 Marines a distance of seven miles thus providing one day's supplies to the Second Battalion, First Marines, in the Soyang River area on Korea's eastern front. In November 1951 HMR-161 pioneered the battlefield movement of combat forces by helicopter when it lifted 950 troops to the front and brought back an equal number to positions in the rear. The concept of vertical envelopment had been born; it would come to fruition a decade and a half later in Vietnam.

See HOSPITAL SHIPS; MEDICAL CARE AND EVACUATION.

HOSPITALS

See HOSPITAL SHIPS; MASH (MOBILE ARMY SURGICAL HOSPITALS); MEDICAL CARE AND EVACUATION.

HOSPITAL SHIPS

At the close of World War II, the United States Navy had 14 active hospital ships, all in the Pacific Theater of Operations. But the last of these, the USS *Repose* (AH 16), had been decommissioned in January 1950; thus none were immediately available when the Korean War began the following June. Filling the gap was the British Royal Navy's HMS *Maine*, the first hospital ship to arrive in Korean waters. Later a Danish hospital ship, the *Jutlandia*, also served there.

Meanwhile the *Repose*, the USS *Haven* (AH 12) and the USS *Consolation* (AH 15) were brought back into active service. On August 16, 1950, the *Consolation* arrived at Pusan, Korea, followed by the *Repose*. In October 1950 the *Haven* arrived at Inchon to support activities there. In 1951 *Consolation* returned to the United States to be fitted with a helicopter landing platform, and on December 18, 1951, it became the first hospital ship to receive casualties flown by helicopter directly from the battlefield. This innovation was so successful that *Haven* and *Repose* were later also fitted with helicopter flight decks.

Although during World War II hospital ships were used to shuttle wounded personnel from the front to the rear area and to stateside hospitals, by the Korean War this task had been taken over by Air Force medical evacuation flights. Instead of medical transports, hospital ships became the floating equivalent of the land-based MASH and evacuation hospitals.

After the Korean War the hospital ships were once again decommissioned; however, the

Repose was recalled to active duty for the Vietnam War. When it was yet again decommissioned in May 1970, the *Repose* had earned 18 battle stars for service in Korea and Vietnam.

Suggestions for further reading: JO2 David Whitney, "Mercy Afloat ... a Navy Tradition," *All Hands*, March 1968, pages 16–27.

HUMAN WAVE ATTACKS

See TACTICS.

HUNGNAM, EVACUATION OF

A seaport on North Korea's eastern coast, Hungnam was the port from which the five divisions of the U.S. X Corps—the U.S. Marine Corps' First Marine Division, the U.S. Army's Third and Seventh Infantry divisions, the Republic of Korea I Corps (ROK Third and Capitol divisions) and the ROK II Corps—were evacuated following the massive Chinese Communist Forces (CCF) intervention in November 1950 and the subsequent retreat from the Chosin Reservoir.

The chief responsibility for the evacuation was given to NAVFE's Task Force 90, the Amphibious Force Far East, backed up by the aircraft carriers and gunfire support ships of Naval Forces Far East's (NAVFE) Task 77, the Seventh Fleet Striking Force. Task Force 90 was also responsible for the simultaneous evacuation of X Corps forces from Wonsan further south as well the withdrawal of Eighth U.S. Army forces from Chinnampo and Inchon on Korea's western coast.

At Hungnam the evacuation began on December 10, 1950, as elements of the First Marine Division began to board ships in the harbor. On December 15, the Marines sailed for Pusan. The ROK regiments followed on December 17; the Seventh Infantry Division on December 21; and the rear guard, the Third

Infantry Division, sailed on December 24, 1950, bringing the evacuation to a close.

Air cover was provided by four carriers of Task Force 77—the USS *Philippine Sea, Leyte, Princeton* and *Valley Forge*—as well as by three smaller carriers from Task Force 95 (the UN Blockade and Escort Force)—USS *Sicily, Baedong Strait* and *Bataan.* Naval gunfire support was provided by the battleship USS *Missouri*, the heavy cruisers *St. Paul* and *Rochester*, the destroyers *Forrest, Royal, Norris, Borie, English, Lind, Hank* and *Massey* as well as the rocket ships LSMR 401, 403 and 404. From December 15 to 24, 1950, a total of 1,700 air sorties were flown inside the Hungnam Perimeter and from December 7 until December 24, 1950, the gunfire support ships fired a grand total of 162 rounds of 16-inch, 2,932 rounds of 8-inch, 18,637 rounds of 5-inch, 71 rounds of 3-inch, 185 rounds of 40-mm and 1,462 rockets.

Far East Air Force's one hundred twelve C-119 Flying Boxcars and other transport planes and 10 Marine transport aircraft airlifted 3,600 men, 196 vehicles and 1,300 tons of cargo from the Yonpo airfield at Hungnam. But the vast majority of the evacuation was by sea. Over 105,000 U.S. and ROK military personnel and 91,000 civilian refugees were embarked, as well as 17,500 vehicles and 350,000 tons of cargo.

Abandoned to the enemy on December 24, 1950, the port of Hungnam was placed under siege by UN warships on April 26, 1951, a siege that would not lift until the armistice in July 1953.

See CHOSIN RESERVOIR, BATTLE OF.

Suggestions for further reading: The best account of the Hungnam evacuation is in Commanders Malcolm W. Cagle and Frank A. Manson, USN, *The Sea War in Korea* (Annapolis, Md: United States Naval Institute, 1957). See also James A. Field, *History of United States Naval Operations: Korea* (Washington, D.C.: GPO, 1962).

I CORPS

I Corps (in reality *First* Corps but always called "I" Corps from its roman numeral designation) had fought as part of the American Expeditionary Force during World War I. It had fought its way across the Pacific with the Eighth U.S. Army (EUSA) in World War II, and until it was disbanded on March 28, 1950, as an "economy measure," it had controlled the 24th and 25th Infantry divisions from its headquarters at Kyoto as part of the American occupation of Japan.

Reactivated in response to an urgent request from the Far East Command (FECOM), on August 2, 1950, I Corps was formed from what had been V Corps headquarters at Fort Bragg, North Carolina. The corps headquarters, along with the Fourth Signal Battalion, was ordered to Korea. The corps commander and his staff arrived in Tokyo, Japan, by air on August 13, 1950, and I Corps itself arrived by sea on September 6, 1950. On September 13, 1950, at Taegu, I Corps officially became operational. I Corps would hence serve as one of EUSA's chief battlefield control headquarters throughout the remainder of the war. Like all corps organizations, it had no fixed combat structure. Depending on the tactical situation, I Corps might command a number of corps artillery battalions as well as several U.S. and Republic of Korea (ROK) infantry divisions.

I Corps was initially commanded by Lieutenant General John R. Coulter, who brought it to Korea. On September 11, 1950, command of I Corps passed to Lieutenant General Frank W. "Shrimp" Milburn, who had just brought IX Corps to Korea. General Milburn led the corps in the breakout from the Naktong Perimeters, the advance into North Korea and the subsequent retreat, and during the 1951 counteroffensive against the Chinese Communist Forces. In the fall of 1951 he was replaced by Lieutenant General John W. "Iron Mike" O'Daniel, who led the corps until June 29, 1952, when he was succeeded by Lieutenant General Paul W. Kendall. On April 10, 1953, Lieutenant General Bruce C. Clarke assumed command of I Corps and led it through the remainder of the war.

For its service in Korea I Corps was awarded the Republic of Korea Presidential Unit Citation. It remained in Korea for many years after the war and is now stationed at Fort Lewis, Washington.

See IX (NINTH) CORPS; X CORPS: ORGANIZATION FOR COMBAT.

Suggestions for further reading: See *U.S. Army in the Korean War* series: Roy A. Appleman, *South to the Naktong, North to the Yalu*, 1961; Walter G. Hermes, *Truce Tent and Fighting Front*, 1966; James F. Schnabel, *Policy and Direction: The First Year*, 1972; and Billy C. Mossman, *Ebb and Flow*,

THE INCHON LANDING

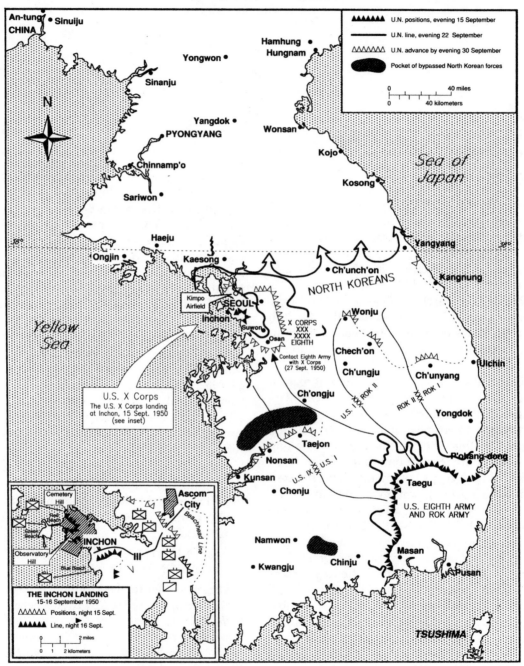

anticipated in 1990 (Washington, D.C.: GPO). For order of battle see Shelby L. Stanton, *Korean War Order of Battle* (Washington, D.C.: GPO, anticipated 1990). See also Clay Blair, *The Forgotten War: America in Korea 1950–1953* (New York Times Books, 1987).

IMJIN RIVER

Following the course of the northeast-southwest Wonsan-Seoul valley, the Imsin River, 157 miles long, begins southwest of the North Korean city of Wonsan and flows south through North Korea until it crosses the 38th parallel, then turns southwest and empties into the Han River Estuary on the Yellow Sea. The last 30 miles of its course lie just south of the 1951–1953 MLR (main line of resistance), which was to become the DMZ (demilitarized zone) between North and South Korea.

Because of its physical location, that portion of the river from its mouth to where it crosses the 38th parallel was known as the "Imjin River line." Called "Line B" in December 1950, it was where the Eighth U.S. Army (EUSA) made its initial stand after withdrawing from North Korea. In March 1950 it was redesignated as the western portion of Line Kansas. The Imjin River line was often the scene of hard fighting, including the last stand of the British Gloucester Battalion in April 1951.
See GLOUCESTER HILL, BATTLE OF; KILLER OPERATION.

INCHON INVASION (OPERATION CHROMITE)

The X (Tenth) U.S. Corps amphibious invasion at Inchon on Korea's western coast on September 15, 1950 (officially designated Operation CHROMITE), ranks as one of the boldest military maneuvers in history. It was General of the Army Douglas MacArthur's finest hour,

for the invasion had been the brainchild of the U.S. Far East Command/United Nations Command (FEC/UNC) commander in chief from almost the beginning of the Korean War.

In one sense it should have been predictable to enemy order-of-battle (OB) specialists, since strategic envelopment had been General MacArthur's World War II trademark. Time and again in island-hopping campaign across the Pacific, MacArthur avoided bloody frontal assaults (and therefore had the lowest casualty rate of any major commander in World War II) by using one portion of his force to keep pressure on the enemy and fix him in place while using another portion of his force to strike deep and sever enemy lines of communication and supply. Thus Japanese forces, without reinforcement or resupply, were cut off and left to wither away.

But for several other compelling reasons it was understandable that the North Korean Order of Battle specialists (who are charged

Its 28-foot tide convinced everybody (except General MacArthur) that an amphibious invasion at Inchon was impossible.
(Courtesy Lyndon Baines Johnson Library & Museum.)

with keeping track of enemy units and personalities and divining their intent) were taken by surprise and failed to give strategic warning to the North Korean People's Army (NKPA). The first reason was geographic. The port of Inchon, which serves the capital city of Seoul, is located not quite half-way up Korea's western coast on the Yellow Sea. The entire Yellow Sea is shallow, and tidal differences range from 20 to 40 feet. At Inchon the tide ranges from 23 feet to 35 feet; at low tide the entire inner harbor is reduced to a vast swamp of mud flats that would strand landing raft high and dry. Besides, two islands, Wolmi-do and Sowolmi-do, linked to each other by a causeway, guard the harbor entrance. The need to reduce those obstacles before the main attack would forfeit tactical surprise.

The other reasons were military. From the beginning of the war in June 1950, NKPA forces had maintained the tactical initiative and Eighth U.S. Army (EUSA) forces had been hard pressed to contain their advance. It was hard to visualize EUSA, backed into the Naktong Perimeter some 180 air miles southeast of Inchon, as the "fixing force" for a strategic envelopment.

Then there was the matter of the enveloping force. Even though the commander of the amphibious phase of the operation, the U.S. Seventh Fleet/Joint Task Force Seven Vice Admiral Dewey Strubble, was experienced, the expeditionary force commander, Major General Edward M. Almond, had only activated his X (Tenth) Corps headquarters on August 26, 1950. The approximately 70,000 men of his two maneuver divisions—the First Marine Division and the Army Seventh Infantry Division, which had been brought up to strength a month earlier by the infusion of 8,652 barely trained South Korean soldiers—his corps artillery (the 155-mm howitzers of the 92d and 96th Field Artillery battalions); and his

other corps troops, such as the 56th Amphibious Tank and Tractor Battalion, the Second Engineer Special Brigade and the 19th Engineer Combat Group, had been hastily assembled over the previous two months and many had never trained or even served together before the invasion.

The assault force, the First Marine Division, was a case in point. When the Korean War began in June 1950 the division had only one active infantry regiment, the Fifth Marines. In August 1950 this regiment had been organized into the First Provisional Marine Brigade and committed to the defense of the Naktong Perimeter; they joined the division at sea on September 13, 1950. The division's First Marine Regiment had been assembled at Camp Pendleton, California, after the outbreak of the war and had had only a few days to stage in Japan before reembarking for Korea. Its Seventh Marine Regiment, also formed since the outbreak of the war, was still enroute (one battalion, constituted from the Sixth Fleet in the Mediterranean, sailed directly for Korea through the Suez Canal) and did not arrive until after the invasion.

The First Marine Division's attached 2,786-man First Korean Marine Regiment had also joined the division at sea, and the 2,760 soldiers of the attached U.S. Army units—the 96th (155-mm) Field Artillery Battalion. The 73d Medium Tank Battalion, the Second Engineer Special Brigade, the 73d Combat Engineer Battalion, the 50th Engineer Port Construction Company, and the 65th Ordnance Ammunition Company—had also never served with the First Marine Division before. These geographic and military realities had caused the Joint Chiefs of Staff in Washington some understandable concern, but in the end they reluctantly approved the plan on August 28, 1950.

On September 15, 1950, the invasion began. Supported by air strikes and by naval gunfire

Aboard Task Force Seven's command ship, the USS *Mount McKinley*, General MacArthur and his commanders and staff watch the amphibious assault on Inchon begin.
(Courtesy Lyndon Baines Johnson Library & Museum.)

(including the 16-inch guns of the USS *Missouri*) the Third Battalion, Fifth Marines, hit the beach at Wolmi-do at 0633 hours, and the island was secured by 0750 hours. At a cost of 17 wounded, the initial assault had killed 108 enemy soldiers and captured 136. Waiting for the next high tide, the First Battalion, Fifth Marines, breasted the sea wall at Inchon's Red Beach at 1733 hours and were soon followed by the Second Battalion, Fifth Marines. Meanwhile, at 1732 hours, elements of the First Marine Regiment began their assault at Blue Beach. By 0130 hours, September 16, 1950, the initial D-day objectives had been achieved. Marine casualties on D-day were 20 men killed, 1 missing in action and 174 wounded in action.

By September 18, 1950, Kimpo airfield had been recaptured, and that afternoon Corsairs of the First Marine Aircraft Wing landed and began operations. On September 21, 1950, command of the operation passed from Admiral Strubble to General Almond, who by that time had 50,000 troops, 250,000 tons of equipment and 6,000 vehicles ashore. On the morning of September 26, 1950, elements of the 31st Infantry Regiment, Seventh Infantry Division, met lead elements of the Seventh Cavalry Regiment, First Cavalry Division, near Osan, and the X-Corps–EUSA linkup was complete.

The recapture of Seoul by the First Marine Division and Seventh Infantry Division was announced on September 27, 1950, but the city was not completely cleared of enemy forces until September 28, 1950. First Marine Division elements continued to drive northward toward Munsan and Uijongbu until they were relieved by EUSA units on October 7, 1950; Operation CHROMITE was at an end.

During the course of the operation X Corps captured some 7,000 NKPA soldiers and another 14,000 were killed in action at a cost of some 3,500 friendly casualties. The Seventh Infantry Division had 572 battle casualties (including 166 KATUSAs) with 106 killed in action, 409 wounded in action and 57 missing in action. The First Marine Division suffered 2,450 casualties, including 366 killed in action, 49 died of wounds, 6 missing in action and 2,029 wounded in action.

The Inchon invasion was a complete operational and tactical success. Given the state of readiness of their forces on the eve of the invasion, great credit must go to all the participating commanders. Except for some scattered guerrilla forces they left behind, the NKPA fell back into North Korea in complete disarray, and for all practical purposes the war in South Korea had been won. At the strategic level it can be argued that the success was so complete that it encouraged the change in political goals from restoration of the prewar status quo (which had been achieved) to the liberation of the entire Korean peninsula. This change in goals would precipitate the Chinese Communist Forces (CCF) intervention in November 1950 and change the nature of the war entirely. See AMPHIBIOUS FORCE FAR EAST; FIRST MARINE AIRCRAFT WING; FIRST MARINE DIVISION; SEVENTH INFANTRY DIVISION; X CORPS.

Suggestions for further reading: *U.S. Army in the Korean War* series: Roy A. Appleman, *South to the Naktong, North to the Yalu*, 1961; James F. Schnabel, *Policy and Direction: The First Year*, 1972; Lynn Montross and Captain Nicholas A. Canzona, USMC, *U.S. Marine Operations in Korea 1950–1953: The Inchon-Seoul Operation*, 1955; James A. Field, *History of United States Naval Operations: Korea*, 1962 (Washington, D.C.: GPO). See also Commanders Malcolm W. Cagle and Frank A. Manson, USN, *The Sea War in Korea* (Annapolis, Md: United States Naval Institute, 1957), which has a ship-by-ship listing of the Inchon invasion force; Clay Blair, *The Forgotten War: America in Korea 1950–1953* (New York Times Books, 1987). Shelby Stanton, *X Corps: America's Tenth Legion in Korea* (Novato, CA: Presidio Press, 1989).

INFANTRY

Korea was an infantryman's war. Although infantry—the "queen of battle"—tends to be the decisive force in most wars, the mountains in Korea made it especially so there. Virtually inaccessible except to the foot soldier, the mountain ridges running southward from the Manchurian border along the entire length of the Korean peninsula proved to be the war's key terrain. By definition *key terrain* is a piece of ground whose possession gives the holder a major advantage, and the North Korean People's Army (NKPA) and the Chinese Communist Forces (CCF) realized that from the beginning.

But it took a while for the United Nations Command to come to the same realization. Commanded by General Walton H. Walker, an armor officer who had led the XX Corps in General George Patton's Third Army in World War II, the Eighth U.S. Army (EUSA) tended to be road-bound in the early days of the war. Criticized during the withdrawal into the Naktong Perimeter in July to August 1950, his armor-type tactics appeared to be vindicated in the breakout after the Inchon invasion and the race—keeping to the roads for quick move-

The 19th Infantry moves forward, September 1950.
(Courtesy Lyndon Baines Johnson Library & Museum.)

ment—for Korea's northern border along the Yalu River.

But disaster struck when the CCF intervened. In November 1950, CCF infantry virtually destroyed the road-bound Second U.S. Infantry Division at Kunu-ri, and the First Marine Division and other X Corps units only narrowly escaped disaster as they withdrew by road from the Chosin Reservoir to the port of Hungnam. Like it or not, U.S. military commanders had to face the fact that Korea was an infantryman's war. Fortunately that was apparent to World War II combat infantryman General Matthew B. Ridgway, who succeeded to EUSA's command after General Walker's death in December 1950. (As the 82d Airborne Division commander, Ridgway had jumped into Normandy on D-day with his 505th Parachute Infantry Regiment.) It was also obvious to General James A. Van Fleet, who suc-

ceeded Ridgway in April 1951 and led EUSA through all but the last five months of the war. (Also a veteran combat infantryman, Van Fleet had won the Silver Star for bravery as commander of an infantry machine-gun battalion in World War I and the Distinguished Service Cross for heroism while commanding the Eighth Infantry Regiment during the World War II assault on Normandy's UTAH beach on D-day.) Under Ridgway and Van Fleet's leadership, EUSA left the roads, went into the mountains and successfully turned back the tide of the CCF and NKPA.

The NKPA began the war in June 1950 with some 31 infantry regiments (at full strength a regiment as about 3,000 personnel). After losing most of them after the September 1950 Inchon invasion, they rebuilt their forces so that by the end of the war in July 1953 they had an estimated 60 infantry regiments in Korea.

On the United Nations side most of the infantry—42 regiments—was provided by the Republic of Korea Army (ROKA). For its part the United States committed 26 Army infantry regiments and three Marine infantry regiments; the battalion-sized contribution of other Allied nations provided the equivalent of another six infantry regiments to the war.

There was a bitter divide during the Korean War between those who fought the war on the front lines under conditions of terrible hardship and those in the "rear echelon" who served in relative comfort behind the lines. For this reason the most prized award in Korea was the Combat Infantry Badge, which honored those Army infantrymen who fought the enemy face-to-face (the Marine Corps would not have a similar award until it authorized the Combat Action Ribbon 15 years later during the war in Vietnam).

Numerous U.S. and ROK Presidential Unit Citations for battlefield bravery were awarded to infantry units. In addition the overwhelming majority of the 132 Medals of Honor awarded for extraordinary heroism during the Korean War went to infantrymen. Ten went to infantrymen in the First Marine Regiment, 10 to infantrymen in the Fifth Marine Regiment and 21 to infantrymen in the Seventh Marine Regiment.

Of the 67 Medals of Honor awarded to Army infantrymen, one went to Major General William F. Dean, the commander of the 24th Infantry Division, three to Fifth Cavalry and two to Eighth Cavalry Regiment infantrymen, two to infantrymen of the Fifth Infantry Regiment,

An infantry skirmish line lays down a base of fire.
(Courtesy Lyndon Baines Johnson Library & Museum.)

eight to the Seventh Infantry Regiment, six to the Ninth Infantry Regiment, two to the 14th Infantry Regiment, three to the 15th Infantry Regiment, six to the 17th Infantry Regiment, three to the 19th Infantry Regiment, two to the 21st Infantry Regiment, six to the 23d Infantry Regiment, two to the 24th Infantry Regiment, five to the 27th Infantry Regiment, four to the 31st Infantry Regiment, one to the 32nd Infantry Regiment, three to the 35th Infantry Regiment, three to the 38th Infantry Regiment, one to the 179th Infantry Regiment, two to the 187th Airborne Infantry Regiment and two to the 223d Infantry Regiment.

See also ARMOR; COMBAT INFANTRY BADGE; FIELD ARTILLERY; REGIMENT.

Suggestions for further reading: See *U.S. Army in the Korean War* series: Roy A. Appleman, *South to the Naktong, North to the Yalu*, 1961; Walter G. Hermes, *Truce Tent and Fighting Front*, 1966; and Billy C. Mossman, *Ebb and Flow*, anticipated in 1990. (Washington, D.C.: GPO). For order of battle see Shelby L. Stanton, *Korean War Order of Battle* (Washington, D.C.: GPO, anticipated 1990). For U.S. Marine Corps infantry (and for the texts of Presidential Unit Citations awarded to Marine units) see the five-volume official history, *U.S. Marine Operations in Korea 1950–1953*: Lynn Montross and Captain Nicholas A. Canzona, USMC; *The Pusan Perimeter*, 1954; *The Inchon-Seoul Operation*, 1955; *The Chosin Reservoir Campaign*, 1957; Lynn Montross and Majors Hubard D. Kuokka and Norman W. Hicks, USMC, *The East-Central Front*, 1962; and Lieutenant Colonel Pat Meid, USMCR, and Major James M. Yingling, USMC, *Operations in West Korea*, 1972 (Washington, D.C.: GPO). See also T.R. Fehrenbach, *This Kind of War: A Study in Unpreparedness* (New York: Macmillan, 1963); Clay Blair, *The Forgotten War: America in Korea 1950–1953* (New York Times Books, 1987). For a listing of the unit awards made to Army infantry regiments and reproductions of regimental crests see *Infantry Regiments of the United States Army*, edited by Kenneth S. Gallagher and Robert L. Pidgeon (New York: Military Press, 1986).

INFILTRATION

A major problem, especially in the opening days of the war, was the infiltration of Allied lines by North Korean People's Army (NKPA) soldiers posing as refugees. Wearing traditional Korean white robes over their uniforms, they easily blended in with the literally millions of South Koreans who had fled their homes to avoid the war. Once behind friendly lines these infiltrators regrouped and attacked Allied positions from the rear.

As this tactic became well known, there was an unfortunate tendency for Allied forces to fire on refugee columns merely on the off chance there might be infiltrators among them. The problem eventually solved itself when the front lines stabilized in the spring of 1951 and the refugee flow was cut to a trickle.
See also GUERRILLAS; MILITARY POLICE.

INTELLIGENCE

While not nearly so sophisticated as they would become in later years, there were several levels of units, staff agencies and organizations devoted to intelligence during the Korean War: the collection, evaluation and dissemination of information on the enemy. They ranged from ground and aerial reconnaissance units (*see* RECONNAISSANCE) to Military Intelligence staffs at every level (*see* MILITARY INTELLIGENCE) to national-level intelligence organizations (*see* CENTRAL INTELLIGENCE AGENCY).

INTELLIGENCE AND RECONNAISSANCE (I&R) PLATOONS

See RECONNAISSANCE.

In the early days of the war, refugee columns served as cover for North Korean infiltrators.
(Courtesy Lyndon Baines Johnson Library & Museum.)

INVASION OF THE REPUBLIC OF KOREA

At 4 AM on Sunday, June 25, 1950 (3 PM, June 25, 1950, Washington time), forces of the Republic of Korea Army (ROKA) First Division along the western end of the 38th parallel dividing North and South Korea came under intense North Korean artillery fire. A half hour later the North Korean People's Army (NKPA) tank-supported First and Sixth Infantry divisions followed up with a ground attack to fix the South Korean defenders in place. The North Korean invasion of South Korea—and the Korean War—had begun.

Supported by the some one hundred fighter aircraft of the North Korean Air Forces, the main NKPA attack by the Third and Fourth divisions and 105th Armored Brigade came shortly thereafter, aimed at the ROK Seventh Division defending the critical Uijongbu Corridor that leads directly to Seoul. Although the ROK Second Division was ordered to reinforce this critical area, their units did not get there until the defenders were forced back, thus uncovering the flanks of the ROK First Division to their west, which was forced to fall back as well.

Meanwhile, supporting NKPA attacks were launched all along the parallel. The ROK 17th Infantry Regiment was forced to abandon the

THE NORTH KOREAN INVASION

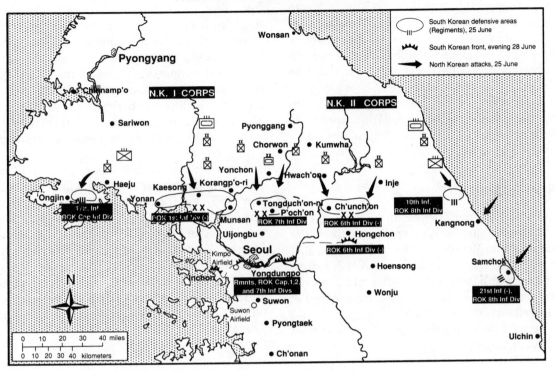

Ongjin peninsula on the far left of the ROK defensive line. In the center, north of Wonju, the NKPA Second and Seventh divisions struck the ROK Sixth Division; on the far right along the east coast the NKPA Fifth Division, supported by a motorcycle regiment, hit the Eighth ROK division with a frontal attack as well as with an amphibious invasion to its rear mounted from armed junks and sampans.

On June 27, 1950 (June 26, 1950, Washington time), General of the Army Douglas MacArthur, the commander U.S. Far East Command (FECOM), advised Washington that ROKA could not hold Seoul and was in imminent danger of collapse. President Harry S Truman authorized MacArthur to use U.S. naval and air forces in support of ROKA to hold

the NKPA invasion. But this was not enough, and Seoul fell to the enemy on June 28, 1950. The next day General MacArthur arrived to personally inspect ROKA's Han River defenses. It was obvious they would be unable to hold the Han River line; unless drastic action was taken the NKPA would reach Pusan within 14 days, and their conquest of South Korea would be complete.

On June 29, 1950 (June 30, 1950, Tokyo time), President Truman authorized General MacArthur to use U.S. service troops in Korea to maintain communications, commit U.S. combat troops to defend the port of Pusan and employ naval and air forces against military targets in North Korea. At 4:47 AM (EST) the next day (6:47 PM, July 1, 1950, Tokyo time), after being briefed on MacArthur's trip to Korea, the president authorized MacArthur to commit to combat in Korea an American infantry regiment to be followed by two U.S. infantry divisions. Although there had been no formal congressional declaration of the fact, the United States was at war.

Suggestions for further reading: Roy A. Appleman, *U.S. Army in the Korean War: South to the Naktong, North to the Yalu* (Washington, D.C.: GPO, 1961).

IRON TRIANGLE

The so-called *Iron Triangle* of the Korean War was a triangularly shaped area of relatively flat terrain about 30 miles north of the 38th parallel in the mountains of east-central North Korea. At its western base was the town of Chorwon, at its eastern base the town of Kumhwa and at its northern apex the town of Pyonggang (not to be confused with the North Korean capital of Pyongyang).

Bisected by the natural depression that runs from Wonsan to Seoul (see PART I: The Setting), the Iron Triangle was an important North Korean rail and road communications center linking east and west coastal areas with each other and connecting them in turn with the communications net leading south. These factors made it attractive to the enemy as a staging area and "key terrain"—that is, terrain the possession of which gives the holder a major advantage.

Part of what EUSA designated as Line Wyoming, it was captured by Allied forces in April 1951, lost during the Chinese Communist Forces (CCF) offensive later that month, then recaptured in May 1951. The Iron Triangle was fought over again and again during the remainder of the war; today it is still divided by the DMZ (demilitarized zone) between North and South Korea. Pyonggang is in North Korea, while Chorwon and Kumhwa are in South Korea.

J

JAPAN

When the Korean War began in June 1950, Japan was not a sovereign country. It was still under the Allied military occupation that followed its defeat in World War II and was administered by the commander in chief, Far East Command, in his capacity as supreme commander Allied powers (SCAP).

U.S. military occupation forces included the Eighth U.S. Army with the 24th Infantry Division on the southern island of Kyushu, the 25th Infantry Division on the southern part of Honshu, the First Cavalry Division in the Tokyo area and the Seventh Infantry Division on the northern island of Hokkaido. In addition, Fifth Air Force bases included Chitose air base on the northernmost Japanese island of Hokkaido; 10 airbases on the main island of Honshu—Misawa in the north, Matsushima (near Sendai) also in the north; Johnson, Yokota and Tachikawa (near Tokyo), Komaki (near Nagoya) and Itami (near Kobe) in the center; and Miho (on the southwest coast) and Bofu and Iwakuni air bases on the northernmost Japanese island of Hokkaido; 10 air bases on the main island of Honshu—Misawa in the north, Matsushima (near Sendai) also in the north; Johnson, Yokota and Tachikawa (near Tokyo), Komaki (near Nagoya) and Itami (near Kobe) in the center; and Miho (on the southwest coast) and Iwakuni and Bofu air bases on the southeast coast; as well as four more on the southernmost island of Kyushu—Ashiya, Itazuki, Tsuiku and Brady air bases. Naval Forces Far East maintained major naval facilities at Sasebo on Kyushu and at Yokuska on Honshu. Australia, the only Allied power with significant military forces stationed in Japan, maintained a fighter squadron at Iwakuni air base on Honshu.

In his capacity as SCAP, General Douglas MacArthur was able to use Japanese bases for the prosecution of the war in Korea without prior approval by the Japanese government. This continued until April 28, 1952, when the provisions of the Japanese Peace Treaty (signed at San Francisco on September 8, 1951) went into effect and Japanese sovereignty was restored. After that date, use of Japanese bases by U.S. forces was provided for by the United States—Japan Mutual Security Treaty, which remains in effect until this day.

After Japan was stripped of combat forces for the war in Korea, there was much concern for the security of Japan, especially since Japan had become a kind of "privileged sanctuary" for United Nations Command's (UNC) prosecution of the war and was vulnerable to Chinese Communist Forces (CCF) and Soviet air attack. In May 1951, the XVI Corps was activated in Japan as a control headquarters for the 40th and 45th Infantry divisions, which had arrived in

Japan in April 1951. When those divisions deployed to Korea in December 1950 to January 1951, they were replaced by the First Cavalry Division and the 24th Infantry, which were withdrawn from Korea to Japan. Later in 1952, the 187th Airborne Regimental Combat Team was also withdrawn from Korea and stationed in Japan as part of the Far East Command General Reserve. The Air Force's 314th Air Division, Japan Air Defense Force, and the Navy's Task Force 96, Naval Forces Japan, were also committed to Japanese security.

With the Korean port of Pusan only some 165 nautical miles away from the Japanese port of Sasebo, the logistic facilities in Japan were especially critical to the prosecution of the war. These included not only depots like the Tokyo Ordnance Depot and Kokura Quartermaster Depot but also a number of hospitals such as Tokyo and Osaka General and smaller facilities such as the 118th Station Hospital at Fukuoka. Important also was Japan's industrial production capacity, which furnished tentage, clothing and other military equipment and supplies. It has been argued that this Korean War industrial production was the beginning of Japan's remarkable economic development.

Japan would later serve as a U.S. base for the prosecution of the war in Vietnam. Today the U.S. Army's IX Corps, the U.S. Fifth Air Force and the U.S. Seventh Fleet are based in Japan; Army and Air Force units as well as the Third Marine Division and First Marine Aircraft Wing are stationed on Okinawa, which reverted to Japanese control on May 15, 1972. *See* JAPAN LOGISTICS COMMAND.

JAPAN LOGISTICS COMMAND

On August 24, 1950, Japan Logistical Command (JLC) was established to relieve Eighth Army Rear Headquarters in Yokohama (which was displacing to Korea). Its mission was to process supply requisitions from the Eighth U.S. Army (EUSA) in Korea, maintain theater stock records and order supplies from the United States for direct shipment to Korea or for the restocking of depots in Japan. The operation of ports, depots and other installations in Japan for logistic support also came under its jurisdiction. In addition, the command retained EUSA's responsibility for occupation duties in Japan.

JLC established a Central Command at Yokohama, a Northern Command at Sapporo, Japan, and a Southwestern Command with headquarters at Osaka. On July 10, 1952, a Korean Communications Zone was established that assumed some of the logistic functions of JLC. On October 1, 1952, a new unit—U.S. Army Forces, Far East—was established to become the principal Army administrative headquarters in Japan, and Japan Logistic Command was discontinued.
See KOREAN COMMUNICATIONS ZONE.

Suggestions for further reading: A comprehensive account of U.S. Army logistics operations in the Korean War has yet to be written. For a start see Terrence J. Gough, *U.S. Army Mobilization and Logistics in the Korean War: A Research Approach* (Washington, D.C.: GPO, 1987).

JOHNSON, LOUIS A(RTHUR) (1891–1966)

Born January 10, 1891, in Roanoke, Virginia, Johnson graduated from the University of Virginia in 1912 and was elected to the West Virginia House of Delegates in 1917. After military service with the American Expeditionary Force in France during World War I, he became active in Democratic Party politics and served as assistant secretary of war from 1937 to 1940.

In March 1949, after personally contributing $250,000.00 to President Harry S Truman's 1948 election campaign, he was appointed secretary of defense. Arguably the worst individual ever to serve in that post, his false economics cut military readiness to the bone, reduced military organizations to skeleton forces and cut supplies and material. These policies led to disaster when the Korean War broke out in June 1950.

Under strong public and congressional pressure for his bungling of the mobilization for Korea, Johnson resigned on September 19, 1950, and was replaced by former Army chief of staff and former secretary of state George C. Marshall. After leaving government service Johnson became a senior partner in the Washington law firm of Steptoe and Johnson and died on April 24, 1966.
See SECRETARY OF DEFENSE.

Suggestions for further reading: See biographic entry in *Political Profiles: The Truman Years*, Eleanora W. Schoenebaum, editor (New York: Facts On File, 1978). See also Douglas Kinnard, *The Secretaries of Defense* (Lexington, Ky: University of Kentucky Press, 1980) and Clay Blair, *The Forgotten War: America in Korea 1950–1953* (New York Times Books, 1987).

JOINT CHIEFS OF STAFF

A continuation of the ad hoc command arrangements by which the United States fought World War II, the organization of the Joint Chiefs of Staff (JCS) was formalized by the National Security Act of 1947. Originally consisting only of the chiefs of staff of the Army and Air Force and the chief of naval operations, a chairman chosen from the different services on a rotating basis was added in 1949 to preside over their deliberations. At that time the commandant of the Marine Corps was not a member, and it was not until June 1952 that he was permitted to sit with the Joint Chiefs of Staff when Marine Corps matters were discussed.

The JCS was an advisory body only and had no command authority. It transmitted the orders of the president (the national commander in chief) and the secretary of defense (in effect, the national general/admiral in chief) to the unified commanders in the field (in the case of Korea, to the commander in chief, Far East Command, in Tokyo). It was a weak body that had little influence on the conduct of the war.

Appointed on January 16, 1949, as the first chairman of the Joint Chiefs of Staff, Army General Omar N. Bradley (promoted to general of the Army—that is, five-star general—in September 1950) served in that position during the entire Korean War. Army Chief of Staff General J. Lawton Collins also served for the whole war, except for the last 27 days) so did Air Force Chief of Staff General Hoyt S. Vandenberg, who was replaced by General Nathan F. Twining on July 1, 1953.

The chief of naval operations when the war began, Admiral Forrest P. Sherman died in office in August 1951 and was replaced by Admiral William M. Fechteler, who served during the remainder of the war. The commandant of the Marine Corps at the beginning of the war, General Clifton B. Cates, completed his four-year tour of duty in December 1951 and was replaced by General Lemanuel C. Shepherd on January 1, 1952. General Shepherd became the first Marine Corps commandant to take part in deliberations of the Joint Chiefs of Staff.
See also EXECUTIVE AGENT; Listings for individual services; Listings for individual members.

Suggestions for further reading: James F. Schnabel and Robert J. Watson, *The History of the Joint Chiefs of Staff: The Joint Chiefs of Staff and National Policy.* Volume 3, *The Korean War* (Wilmington, DE: Michael Glazier, 1979). For a critical analysis of JCS performances see Lawrence J. Korb, *The Joint Chiefs of Staff: The First Twenty-Five Years* (Bloomington, IN: Indiana University Press, 1976); Mark Perry, *Four Stars* (Boston: Houghton Mifflin, 1989); and Richard K. Betts, *Soldiers,*

Sailors and Cold War Crises (Cambridge, Mass.: Harvard University Press, 1976).

JOY, C(HARLES) TURNER (1895–1956)

Born February 17, 1895, at Saint Louis, Missouri, Joy graduated from the United States Naval Academy in 1916. During the First World War he served on the battleship USS *Pennsylvania*, the flagship of the Commander in Chief of the Atlantic Fleet. During the interwar years he served with the Yangtze River patrol in China, commanded the USS *Litchfield* and served as head of the department of ordnance and gunnery at the Naval Academy. When the United States entered World War II, he was serving as the operations officer of the Scouting Force of the U.S. Pacific Fleet.

From September 1942 to June 1943 Joy commanded the cruiser USS *Louisville* in the Aleutians campaign. After service in Washington he returned to sea as commander of the Pacific Fleet's Cruiser Division Six and took part in the assault on Saipan, the first battle of the Philippine Sea, and the amphibious assaults on Guam, Peleliu, Leyte, Iwo Jima and Okinawa.

On August 26, 1949, he was assigned as commander, Naval Forces Far East, and was serving in that position when the Korean War began. He was awarded the Army's Distinguished Service Medal for his organization of naval operations for the war and especially for his part in the planning and execution of the Inchon invasion in September 1950. From July 10, 1951, until May 23, 1952, Admiral Joy also served as the senior United Nations delegate to the Korean Armistice Conference.

Returning to the United States in 1952, he was appointed superintendent of the United States Naval Academy. Admiral Joy retired from active duty on July 1, 1954, and died on June 13, 1956.

A destroyer, the USS *Turner Joy* (DD-951), was subsequently named in his honor. Ironically, although Admiral Joy helped get the United States *out* of the Korean War, his namesake helped get the United States *involved* in the Vietnam War. On August 4, 1964, the USS *Turner Joy* came to national attention when an alleged North Vietnamese attack on it and the USS *Maddox* led to the Gulf of Tonkin Resolution, which provided the initial basis for direct U.S. military involvement in the Vietnam War.

See also ARMISTICE AGREEMENT; FAR EAST COMMAND; NAVAL FORCES FAR EAST.

Suggestions for further reading: C. Turner Joy, *How Communists Negotiate* (New York: Macmillan, 1954). See also James A. Field, *History of United States Naval Operations: Korea* (Washington, D.C.: GPO, 1962). See also Commanders Malcolm W. Cagle and Frank A. Manson, USN, *The Sea War in Korea* (Annapolis, Md: United States Naval Institute, 1957); Richard P. Hallion, *The Naval Air War in Korea* (Baltimore: The Nautical & Aviation Publishing Company of America, 1986).

KAESONG

A city in western Korea just south of the 38th parallel, Kaesong was the ancient capital of Korea. On the "invasion route" to Seoul, it was the first city to fall to the North Koreans on June 25, 1950.

Although still behind enemy lines, beginning on July 10, 1951, Kaesong was the initial site of the truce talks between the United Nations Command (UNC) and the Chinese Communist Forces (CCF)/North Korean People's Army (NKPA). From the first this proved to be an awkward arrangement. The Communists chose this site for propaganda purposes, suggesting that the UNC was coming hat in hand to beg for peace. The Western (but not the Communist) press was barred, and the UNC delegation found themselves constantly harassed. When the CCF/NKPA broke off the talks on August 22, 1951, the UNC decided that they must be moved to a more neutral site. After some haggling, on October 7, 1951, the CCF/NKPA agreed that the senior delegates resume talks at the neutral site of Panmunjom.

When the final armistice agreement was reached in July 1953, Kaesong was among the few areas south of the 38th parallel conceded to the enemy; it is now part of the Democratic Republic of Korea, that is, North Korea.

See ARMISTICE AGREEMENT.

KATUSA (KOREAN AUGMENTATION TO THE U.S. ARMY)

On August 15, 1950, with the concurrence of the government of the Republic of Korea (ROK), the United Nations Command ordered the Eighth U.S. Army (EUSA) to increase the strength of each U.S. company-sized unit by 100 Korean soldiers. In addition, 8,652 KATUSAs were shipped to Japan to join the Seventh Infantry Division, then staging for the Inchon invasion. These soldiers would still legally be part of the ROK Army and would be paid and administered by the ROK government, but they would be fed and equipped by

The KATUSA Platoon of L Company, 21st Infantry Regiment, 24th Infantry Division.
(Courtesy Lyndon Baines Johnson Library & Museum.)

their host unit. They were called KATUSAs (Korean Augmentation to the U.S. Army) or KATCOMs (Koreans Attached to Common-wealth Forces). The initial intent was to have each Korean soldier teamed with a UN soldier in a kind of "buddy system." Some units used this approach, while other kept the Koreans in separate platoons. By June 1951, there were 12,718 KATUSAs serving with U.S. units. Given the cultural and linguistic problems in-volved, KATUSAs were a valuable addition to a unit's combat strength and performed well under enemy fire.

As a result of this experience, in July 1952 authorization was given to increase KATUSA strength to 2,500 per division with an addition-al 7,000 authorized for nondivisional combat support and combat service support units. When the war ended in July 1953, approximate-ly 27,000 KATUSAs were serving with U.S. units.

See REPUBLIC OF KOREA ARMY.

Suggestions for further reading: See *U.S. Army in the Korean War* series: Roy A. Appleman, *South to the Naktong, North to the Yalu*, 1961; Walter G. Hermes, *Truce Tent and Fighting Front*, 1966; and Billy C. Mossman, *Ebb and Flow*, anticipated in 1990 (Washington, D.C. GPO). See also Clay Blair's *The Forgotten War: America in Korea 1950–1953* (New York Times Books, 1987) and Max Hastings, *The Korean War* (New York: Simon & Schuster, 1987).

KILLER OPERATION

Launched February 21, 1951, Operation KILLER (and its extensions, Operations RIP-PER, COURAGEOUS, RUGGED and DAUNT-LESS) marked the beginning of the Allied counteroffensive to drive the Chinese Com-munist Forces (CCF) and the North Korean People's Army (NKPA) out of South Korea. Initially its objectives were to hold the Han River line south of Seoul while mounting an attack to the east so that South Korean territory lost to the advancing CCF earlier that year could be recovered, but not to cross the 38th parallel itself.

Renamed Operation RIPPER on March 7, 1950 (and, at the insistence of the State Depart-ment, who thought code names like KILLER/RIPPER too beastly, soon thereafter rechristened Operation COURAGEOUS), the objective changed: a deliberate river crossing of the Han River to outflank Seoul to the east while continuing to advance to the parallel along a 50-mile front was planned. On March 15, 1950, the enemy abandoned Seoul, and by April 1, 1951, EUSA's 12 front-line divisions had advanced some 70 miles and had reached the 38th parallel.

General Ridgway then ordered a continua-tion of the EUSA advance: first, an advance to Line Kansas (Operation RUGGED), which ran diagonally along the Imjin River northeast above the 38th parallel to the Hantan River then east to the south shore of the Hwachon Reser-voir to the east coast at Yangyang. When these objectives were reached on April 11, 1951, Ridgway ordered a further advance (Operation DAUNTLESS) to Line Wyoming, which bulged northward to take in the southern portion of the Iron Triangle, and to Line Quantico, which ex-tended to the northern shore of the Hwachon Reservoir. They were the lines upon which the war would eventually end more than two years later.

But during this advance Line Wyoming was not to be reached, for on April 22, 1951, the CCF launched their 27-division spring offensive, and Allied forces were once again driven south of the 38th parallel.

See SPRING OFFENSIVE, 1951.

Suggestions for further reading: See especially Clay Blair, *The Forgotten War: America in Korea 1950–1953* (New York Times Books, 1987). See

In a classic infantry-armor-artillery coordinated operation, U.S. forces attack across frozen rice paddies to drive the Chinese out of South Korea.
(Courtesy Lyndon Baines Johnson Library & Museum.).

also *U.S. Army in the Korean War* series: Billy C. Mossman, *Ebb and Flow*, anticipated in 1990 (Washington, D.C.: GPO).

KIM IL-SUNG (1912–)

Born April 15, 1912, as Kim Song Ju in the town of Mangyongdae near the city of Pyongyang (now the capital of the Democratic People's Republic of Korea), Kim's early years are obscured by the fog of deification that now surrounds North Korea's self-proclaimed "Great Leader." According to the legend, soon after Kim was born his father, a schoolteacher and early revolutionary leader, took the family to live in eastern Manchuria to escape the Japanese, who were then occupying Korea. He supposedly joined the Communist Youth League in 1926 and became the league's secretary in Kirin, Manchuria. During this period he is credited with attendance at the Whampoa Military Academy in Canton, China, where several soon-to-be Chinese revolutionary leaders were in training. In any event, when the Japanese invaded Manchuria in 1931, Kim allegedly took to the hills and organized a guerrilla resistance band.

His hagiographers then have him as commander of the Sixth Division of the Chinese Communist First Route Army in 1936 and later as commander or the Route Army itself. During World War II he reportedly traveled to the Soviet Union, studied at a Russian military academy and served in the Soviet Army as commander of one of the two Korean units that fought at Stalingrad in 1942 to 1943. By the end of the war he had risen to the rank of colonel and had been awarded the Order of Lenin by Soviet Premier Joseph Stalin. When Soviet troops entered Korea in August 1945 to disarm the Japanese occupiers, they brought Kim with them to administer the country. By this time he had been promoted to general in recognition of his guerrilla activities in Manchuria.

Taking the name "Kim Il-sung" in honor of his uncle who had disappeared soon after taking part in the 1919 independence uprising, in 1946 he was unanimously elected chairman of the Provisional People's Committee for North Korea and head of the politburo of the Korean Labor Party. On September 9, 1948, Kim Il-sung was appointed Premier of North Korea—officially the Democratic People's Republic of Korea or DPRK. After the Korean War began on June 25, 1950—according to the legend, by a South Korean invasion of North Korea!—Marshal Kim Il-sung was appointed supreme military commander of the North Korean People's Army (NKPA).

But there is another version. According to the area study on North Korea prepared by Asian scholars at the Foreign Area Studies Department, the American University, in Washington, D.C., "Kim Il-sung's military reputation, as claimed and established by his Communist publicists, has been subject to interminable debunking by nearly all non-Communist observers." The Japanese authorities, until 1945, described Kim Il-sung as a bandit chieftain of about 40 to 50 marauders. Evidently in June 1937 Kim's band, as part of a larger force, did attack the Japanese police station in the town of Poch'onbo near the Manchurian border and kill a number of policemen. The "division" he commanded in the Chinese Route Army was only about 300-men strong, and although he probably did serve in the Soviet Army in World War II, he returned to Pyongyang in 1945 not as a colonel but as a Soviet Army major. In any event, he was chosen by the Soviets to be their man in Pyongyang, and as part of the grooming process his past, in the best Orwellian tradition, was carefully redesigned to fit his future.

Although at the time North Korea's invasion of South Korea on June 25, 1950, was attributed to the machinations of Moscow-directed monolithic world Communism, many historians now believe that the invasion was primarily conceived and directed by Kim Il-sung. The argument goes like this: Believing U.S. public pronouncements that South Korea was outside the American defense perimeter, seeing the wretched state of South Korean defenses and noting the parsimonious level of American military aid, Kim concluded that the time was right for the unification of Korea by force of arms. He then evidently convinced Soviet Premier Joseph Stalin that it was a sure thing, a low-risk operation strictly between the two Koreas that could be concluded in a matter of days. Communist China was probably not even consulted before Stalin gave his stamp of approval and the Soviet military was ordered to bring the North Korean People's Army (NKPA) up to 100% combat strength in small arms, mortars, machine-guns, tanks and artillery.

On the morning of June 25, 1950, Marshal Kim Il-sung launched his blitzkrieg. Surprised and overwhelmed, the ill-equipped Republic of Korea Army (ROKA) fell back in confusion, and within 48 hours the NKPA's tank-led columns had overrun and captured the South Korean capital of Seoul. His predictions appeared to be correct, and it looked like only a matter of days before the entire Korean peninsula would be under his control.

But on June 27, 1950, it was Kim Il-sung's turn to be surprised. Reversing its previous policy, the United States intervened in the war. And it did so under the authority of the United Nations, which condemned North Korean aggression and called on member nations to come to the aid of South Korea. At first it seemed that this aid had come too late, as U.S. and ROK forces were pushed back into the Naktong Perimeter in the southeast corner of Korea. Then came the Inchon invasion in September

1950 and the complete collapse of the NKPA. Pyongyang fell on October 19, 1950, to the First ROK Division, and Kim Il-sung, with some 20,000 to 30,000 NKPA soldiers, all that remained of the 200,000 he had sent south, fell back to Kanggye, in the remote mountain region of northwest Korea some 70 miles from the Yalu River. Korea was being reunified, but it was being reunified by the Republic of Korea backed by the forces of the United Nations. Kim Il-sung's *original plan* had failed.

But help was on the way. Fearful of directly confronting the United States itself, Kim's Soviet backers had convinced the Chinese that it was in China's best interest to intervene in the Korean War. Beginning in mid-October 1950, more than 300,000 Chinese People's Volunteers crossed into North Korea and in November 1950 began an offensive that would drive the United Nations forces out of North Korea and restore Kim Il-sung to his throne. Although Kim Il-sung was ostensibly in charge, the remainder of the Korean War would be fought by Chinese Marshal Peng Teh-huai, the CCF (Chinese Communist Forces) commander. On July 27, 1953, Kim Il-sung and Peng Teh-huai would sign the Korean armistice agreement that brought the fighting in Korea to and end.

As of this writing Kim Il-sung still rules North Korea. Proclaiming himself North Korea's "Great Leader" (and his son and chosen successor Kim Jong Il as "Dear Leader"), his cult of personality is unique in the Communist world. In recent years, as he has seen North Korea slip farther and farther behind its South Korean rival, Kim Il-sung has increasingly used terrorism as an instrument of state power. The result is that North Korea and its Great Leader Kim Il-sung have become international pariahs.

See PART I: THE SETTING; NORTH KOREAN PEOPLE'S ARMY.

Suggestions for further reading: Rinn-Sup Shinn et al, *Area Handbook for North Korea* (Washington, D.C.: GPO, 1969). The authorized hagiography is Bong Baik, *Kim Il-sung: Biography*, 4 volumes (Beirut: Dar Al-Talia, 1973).

KIMPO AIRFIELD

Located on the outskirts of Seoul, Kimpo was and is the Republic of Korea's major airport. It was the site of the first clash between U.S. combat forces and those of the enemy. On June 27, 1950, U.S. F-82 Twin Mustangs from the Fifth Air Force shot down three North Korean Air Forces (NKAF) YAK fighters attempting to interfere with aerial evacuation of U.S. civilian personnel and dependents from Seoul. Later that day, in the first aerial victory for U.S. jet fighters, F-80 Shooting Stars shot down four NKAF Il-10 Stormovik fighters.

Lost to the enemy soon thereafter, Kimpo airfield was recaptured in September 1950 as part of the Inchon invasion. On September 19, 1950, Corsairs from VMF 212, Marine Aircraft Group 33, landed there to begin operations in support of X Corps. Designated by the Air Force as "K-14," Kimpo again fell to the enemy on January 5, 1951, as the invading Chinese Communist Forces (CCF) pushed the Eighth U.S. Army south of Seoul. Again recaptured in April 1951, Kimpo became fully operational in May 1951 and continued to support UN forces for the remainder of the war.

See FAR EAST AIR FORCE; FIFTH AIR FORCE.

Suggestions for further reading: Robert F. Futrell, *The United States Air Force in Korea: 1950–1953*, revised edition (Washington, D.C.: GPO, 1983).

KOJE-DO ISLAND

See POW (PRISONER OF WAR) CAMPS.

KOREAN COMMUNICATIONS ZONE (KCOMZ)

According to Korean War era Army doctrine, the *Communications Zone* was a specified area behind the front lines where ports and supply depots could be established. Its purpose was to relieve the front line commander of responsibility for logistics and for rear area control.

The Korean Communications Zone (KCOMZ) had its origins in the establishment of the Pusan Base Command at that southeastern Korean port on July 4, 1950. On July 13, 1950, the unit, which was responsible for providing logistic support to the United Nations forces in Korea, was renamed the Pusan Logistical Command, and on September 19, 1950, was once again redesignated as the Second Logistical Command.

The Second Logistical Command was responsible not only for supporting all UN forces in Korea but also for dealing with refugees, prisoners of war and the operation of subsidiary ports. Among its subordinate units was the Third Logistical Command, which was originally organized to supply X Corps through the port of Inchon. When Inchon was evacuated in December 1950, the Second Logistical Command absorbed most of the Third Logistical Command's units.

In July 1952, the Korean Communications Zone (KCOMZ) was created to relief the commander, Eighth U.S. Army, of his responsibility for logistic and territorial operations, and for political relations with the government of the Republic of Korea. With headquarters at Taegu, this new rear area command extended over the southern two-thirds of the Republic of Korea, sharing a boundary with the Eighth Army that ran roughly along the 37th parallel. In mid-October 1952, the second Logistical Command was officially transferred to KCOMZ and absorbed by that unit.

Commanded by Army Major General Thomas W. Herren, the Korean Communications Zone was designed to have a force of 75,000 to 100,000 personnel and to support a force of approximately 400,000. Because of personnel shortages, the KCOMZ only had about 30,000 troops assigned and had to support 800,000 United Nations and Republic of Korea combat troops in addition to well over 100,000 prisoners of war and civilian internees.
See also JAPAN LOGISTICS COMMAND.

Suggestions for further reading: Since *Theater Logistics*, the fifth volume of the Army's official history of the Korean War, has yet to be completed as of this writing, see Terrence J. Gough, *U.S. Army Mobilization and Logistics in the Korean War: A Research Approach* (Washington, D.C.: GPO, 1987). For excellent vignettes on various logistic units—Transportation Corps, Signal Corps, Ordnance Corps, and Quartermaster Corps—see Captain John G. Westover, *Combat Support in Korea* (Washington, D.C.: Combat Forces Press, 1955). For order of battle see Shelby Stanton, *Korean War Order of Battle* (Washington, D.C.: GPO, anticipated in 1990). In addition to the Army's official histories see also Clay Blair, *The Forgotten War: America in Korea 1950–1953* (New York Times Books, 1987).

KOREA, DEMOCRATIC PEOPLE'S REPUBLIC OF (NORTH KOREA)

See PART I: THE SETTING; KIM IL-SUNG; NORTH KOREAN PEOPLE'S ARMY.

KOREA MILITARY ADVISORY GROUP (KMAG)

Established on July 1, 1949, the Korea Military Advisory Group (KMAG) was the successor to provisional military advisory teams dating back to January 1946. At that time 18 U.S. Army lieutenants from the deactivating 40th Infantry

Division were detailed to organize eight Korean Constabulary Regiments, originally envisioned as police reserves for maintaining public order.

In March 1948 the Constabulary was increased to 50,000 men and training was intensified. Weapons schools set up the U.S. Army's Sixth and Seventh Infantry divisions trained Korean Constabulary troops in the use of machine-guns, mortars, antitank weapons and field artillery. When the Republic of Korea (ROK) declared its independence on August 15, 1948, the nucleus of a national defense force had been created; the Constabulary became the Republic of Korea Army (ROKA) on December 15, 1948. The KMAG worked hard to set up a military schools system, including the Korean Military Academy, and to send selected officers to military service schools in the United States. The beginnings of a professional military were starting to emerge. By June 1950, the ROKA would include eight poorly equipped divisions: the Capital Division and the First, Second, Third, Fifth, Sixth, Seventh and Eighth divisions, with half along the border with North Korea and the remainder in reserve.

Meanwhile, in September 1946, 15 U.S. Coast Guard personnel arrived in the country to organize a Korean Coast Guard, which would become the forerunner of the Republic of Korea Navy. These U.S. Coast Guard personnel remained in Korea until August 1948, when they were withdrawn by the secretary of the treasury and replaced by U.S. civilian technicians. On August 4, 1950, responsibility for ROK Coast Guard/Navy advisory functions was transferred to the commander, U.S. Naval Forces Far East (NAVFE).

On October 10, 1949, over the objections of the United States, the ROK organized their own air force. Although Army advisers helped to train liaison and observation pilots, fighter pilot training did not begin until after the outbreak of the war. Ten F-51 Mustang fighters were given to the fledgling ROK Air Force on July 27, 1950, and "Bout-One," a composite unit of American and South Korean airmen, was organized by the Far East Air Force's (FEAF) Eighth Fighter-Bomber at Taegu on June 30, 1950, to train ROK pilots in combat operations. Later ROK pilot training would be provided by FEAF's 36th Fighter-Bomber Squadron at Itazuki Air Base in Japan.

Likewise, when the war began KMAG became a subordinate command of the Eighth U.S. Army (EUSA), which supervised its advisory operations. From a strength of 175 officers, 5 warrant officers and 290 enlisted men in July 1950, the KMAG grew to a strength of 454 officers, 14 warrant officers and 840 enlisted men. But this did not begin to keep pace with the rapid expansion of the ROK Army.

Theoretically, each ROKA division, regiment and battalion was supposed to have a U.S. adviser attached, but in practice this was never achieved. KMAG advisers were almost always present at division and regimental level on the battlefield, however, and in the early part of the war when much of ROKA fell apart under enemy pressure the assignment was considered so dangerous that cynics said the acronym KMAG stood for "Kiss My Ass Goodbye."

But instead of giving up on ROKA and pushing it to one side (as we would later do with the Republic of Vietnam Armed Force [RVNAF] in Vietnam), the decision was made to continue to train and develop ROKA forces on the battlefield. There was no need for "Vietnamization" in the Korean War because "Koreanization" had been U.S. policy from the beginning. And because of that, KMAG played a crucial role.

ROKA began the war with 115,000 men and eight poorly equipped infantry divisions. Battlefield reverses in the opening days of the war required that most of those divisions be retrained and reconstituted, and a similar reconstruction took place after the intervention of the Chinese Communist Forces (CCF). But each time the ROKA bounced back, thanks in good part to the valiant efforts of their KMAG advisers. When the war ended, the ROK military had 590,911 men under arms and some 16 well-trained and well-equipped battle-hardened divisions in the field, with four more in the planning stages.

See REPUBLIC OF KOREA ARMY.

Suggestions for further reading: See particularly Major Robert K. Sawyer, USA, *Military Advisers in Korea: KMAG in Peace and War* (Washington, D.C.: GPO, 1962). See also *U.S. Army in the Korean War* series: Roy A. Appleman, *South to the Naktong, North to the Yalu*, 1961; Walter G. Hermes, *Truce Tent and Fighting Front*, 1966; and Billy C. Mossman, *Ebb and Flow*, anticipated in 1990 (Washington, D.C.: GPO). For order of battle see Shelby L. Stanton, *Korean War Order of Battle* (Washington, D.C.: GPO, anticipated in 1990). See also Clay Blair, *The Forgotten War: America in Korea 1950–1953* (New York Times Books, 1987).

KOREAN SERVICE CORPS (KSC)

Also known as the "mule train" after a popular song of the era, the Korean Service Corps (KSC) began with the ad hoc recruitment of civilian porters to move military supplies from where

Korean ammunition bearers, led by an armed guard for protection, move toward the front.
(Courtesy U.S. Army Military History Institute.)

the roads ended to the front-line positions. Using A-frames, each carrier was expected to transport 50 pounds of supplies 10 miles daily.

Previously, infantrymen had had to double as porters: Because of the rough terrain food, ammunition and equipment had to be packed in. Since pack animals were virtually nonexistent (and cargo helicopters were in their infancy), human carriers had to be used. These civilian laborers and porters relieved combat soldiers of their supply-carrying responsibilities so that the infantrymen could concentrate on fighting the enemy.

This ad hoc arrangement was replaced by the creation of the Civil Transport Corps under the immediate supervision of ROK Army officers and the control of the Eighth U.S. Army transportation officer. In mid-1951 the Army replaced this civilian organization with the Korean Service Corps, a military entity formed partially from ROK Army units. Carriers, who served for six-month terms, now had military training and labored under full military discipline. Increased in size to 60,000 personnel in November 1951, the KSC grew to 75,000 by September 1952 and to 100,000 by the end of the war.

See also A-FRAMES.

Suggestions for further reading: In addition to the official histories of the war, see Terrence J. Gough, *U.S. Army Mobilization and Logistics in the Korean War: A Research Approach* (Washington, D.C.: GPO, 1987); and Major Robert K. Sawyer, USA, *Military Advisers in Korea: KMAG in Peace and War* (Washington, D.C.: GPO, 1962).

KOREAN SERVICE MEDAL

Beginning with the Civil War, what traditionally have been called "campaign medals" but what officially are "service medals" have been awarded to members of the U.S. armed forces to recognize their wartime service.

The Korean Service Medal was authorized by Presidential Executive Order 110179 to recognize service within the territorial limits of Korea or in waters immediately adjacent thereto for one or more days between June 27, 1950, and July 27, 1954. A service star (commonly called a "battle star") is worn on the ribbon of the service medal to denote each separate campaign in which the wearer participated (*see* CAMPAIGNS, U.S. MILITARY). In addition, an arrowhead is worn on the ribbon of the service medal to denote participation in a combat parachute jump or an amphibious assault landing.

See also CAMPAIGNS, U.S. MILITARY; NATIONAL DEFENSE SERVICE MEDAL; UNITED NATIONS SERVICE MEDAL.

KOREA, REPUBLIC OF (ROK; SOUTH KOREA)

See PART I: THE SETTING; REPUBLIC OF KOREA ARMY; SYNGMAN RHEE.

KUNU-RI, BATTLE OF

The site of one of the major battles of the Korean War, the village ("-ri" in Korean) of Kunu is located in northwestern Korea about 20 miles upstream from the mouth of the Chongchon River and some 75 air miles southeast of the Manchurian border. On November 29, 1950, it marked the right flank of the Eighth U.S. Army (EUSA), which was under heavy pressure from the Chinese Communist Forces (CCF) 130,000-man 13th Army Group. The CCF had just entered the war.

Kunu-ri was the key to the EUSA withdrawal plans. While the remainder of EUSA withdrew down the main Sinanju-Pyongyang highway, the Second Infantry Division and attached units would block at Kuni-ri thus preventing a CCF flank attack on the withdrawing troops;

THE RETREAT OF EIGHTH ARMY

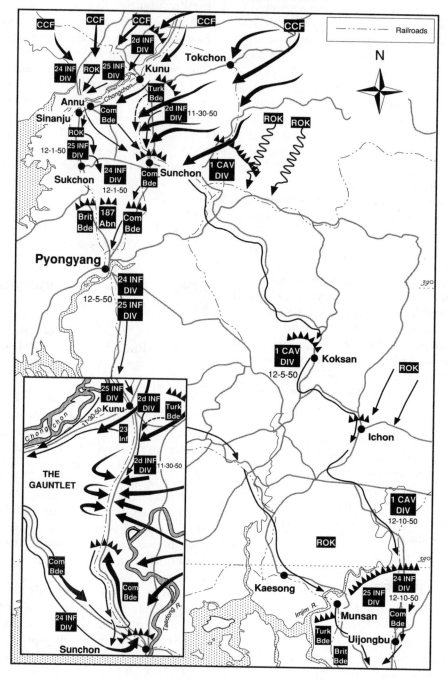

then the Second Infantry Division would itself withdraw down a secondary road leading from Kunu southwest to Sunchon, where it rejoined the main highway.

Already badly battered in earlier fighting, the regiments of the Second Infantry Division were deployed northeast and east of Kunu-ri, with the Ninth and 23d Infantry regiments on the left, the ROK Third Regiment in the center and the 38th Infantry Regiment and the remnants of the Turkish Brigade, which had been routed earlier by the CCF, on the right. In support were the division's 15th 37th and 38th (105-mm howitzer) Field Artillery battalions, its 503d (155-mm howitzer) Field Artillery Battalion and the attached eight-inch howitzers of the 17th Field Artillery Battalion, as well as the 72d Tank Battalion.

On November 29, 1950, the CCF attacked in force. Breaking through the Turkish sector, two regiments of the CCF 113th Division established roadblocks on the division's Kunu-ri–Sunchon withdrawal route. Although attempts to clear these roadblocks by the Second Reconnaissance Company had failed, the division commander, Major General Laurence B. "Dutch" Keiser, rejected advice to withdraw eastward along the south banks of the Chongchon River and then southward along the Sinuiju-Pyongyang road; instead he stuck to the original withdrawal plan.

On November 30, 1950, with the 23d Regimental Combat Team (RCT), made up of the 23d Infantry Regiment and the 15th Field Artillery Battalion, serving as the rear guard, the division began its withdrawal toward Sunchon. Meanwhile, the British Commonwealth Brigade had attacked northward from Sunchon to link up with the Second Infantry Division and assist their withdrawal; however, they had bogged down six miles south of the division's positions. This six-mile gauntlet through mountain passes that separated the two units was to be the killing ground for much of the Second Infantry Division. The Ninth and 38th Infantry regiments were decimated, and most of the division artillery was lost to the CCF.

Seeing this carnage, Colonel Paul F. Freeman, the commander of the rear guard 23d RCT still at Kunu-ri, made the (still controversial) decision to withdraw westward along the Chongchon River and thus escaped the disaster that enveloped the rest of the Second Infantry Division. When the survivors broke through to the British Commonwealth Brigade's lines on December 1, 1950, it was found that the division had suffered 4,940 casualties, almost one-third of its strength. The Ninth Infantry had taken 1,267 casualties; the 38th Infantry 1,075; the division artillery 1,461; the engineers 561; and Freeman's 23d Infantry 485.

General Keiser, the division commander, was relieved of his command and replaced by Major General Robert B. McClure, who a month later would also be relieved of command and replaced by Major General Clark L. "Nick" Ruffner. Under his command the Second Infantry Division was rebuilt and revitalized and went on to win decisive battles at Wongju and Chipyong-ni in February 1951.

Suggestions for further reading: The classic work on the battle of Kunu-ri is Army historian S.L.A. Marshall's *The River and the Gauntlet: Defeat of the Eighth Army by the Chinese Communist Forces, November 1950, in the Battle of the Chongchon River, Korea* (New York: Morrow, 1953). An account of the battle from the CCF perspective is in Russell Spurr's *Enter the Dragon: China's Undeclared War Against the U.S. in Korea, 1950–1951* (New York: Newmarket Press, 1988). An excellent account of the battle in its larger context is in Clay Blair's *The Forgotten War: America in Korea 1950–1953* (New York Times Books, 1987).

LINE

In the Korean War the word *line* had several specific meanings. In the phrase "main *line* of resistance" (MLR) the word meant the trace of the front line separating friend from foe. On one side were the Allied forces of the United Nations (UN), on the other side was the enemy: the North Korean People's Army (NKPA) and the Chinese Communist Forces (CCF).

This clear division of the battlefield facilitated the use of a "bomb line" a line on the battlefield far enough forward of the MLR that bombs could be dropped (and strafing runs conducted) without endangering friendly troops. Those wringing their hands over the "unprecedented barbarity" of "free fire zones" in the later Vietnam War would no doubt be appalled to know that anything forward of the bomb line was a free fire zone in Korea (and in World War II as well).

The linear dimensions of the battlefield in Korea also led to the use of "phase lines," which were extensively used as battlefield control measures. In order to mark the limit of advance, for example, a phase line, such as Line Kansas (which, along with *Line Wyoming*, became the cease-fire line) was designated on a map. United States defensive positions often became known by these code words. Among other phase lines used during the war were Line Jamestown; Line Lincoln, Line Missouri, Line Quantico, Line Utah and the No-Name Line.
See MLR (MAIN LINE OF RESISTANCE); For use of phase lines see IMJIN RIVER; KILLER OPERATION.

LIN PIAO (LIN BIAO) (1907–1971)

Born in 1907 in the village of Liu-chia-wan, Huang-an county, Hupeh Province, in what was then Imperial China, Lin Piao (*Lin Biao* in the new English transliteration of the Chinese characters that make up his name) attended Whampoa Military Academy in Canton from 1925 to 1926. He joined the Chinese Communist Party (CCP) in 1926 and commanded the vanguard of the Long March, which was made by the CCP from south China to new guerrilla bases in north China in 1934 to 1935. In July 1936 he was named president of the Worker-Peasant Red Army University (later the Anti-Japanese Military and Political University) in Yenan. Wounded severely in a battle with the Japanese in 1938, he was evacuated to Moscow for medical treatment. There he reportedly attended the Frunze Military Academy. In 1942 he returned to China. After a brief assignment with the CCP's liaison office with the Nationalist Government in Chungking, he again took up his post with the university.

When the Chinese Civil War began in 1946, Lin Piao commanded the Shantung Military Region and later the Fourth Field Army in the fight to "liberate" Manchuria. After the successful termination of that campaign he moved south into Central China, captured Hankow in his native Hupeh Province and then swept into South China to the Sino–Vietnamese border. When the Korean War began he was serving as First Secretary of the Chinese Communist Party's Central-South Bureau.

Accounts of his service in Korea are sketchy and in some cases totally contradictory. According to some accounts he was the initial commander of all Chinese Communist Forces (CCF) in Korea. Other accounts have it that while troops of his Fourth Field Army were committed there, he himself never served in Korea. Because of his reputed assassination attempt on Mao Tse-tung in 1971 (see below) he has become a "nonperson" in China, and the truth may never be known.

According to the U.S. Army's official military history of the war, in the fall of 1950 during the initial stages of China's intervention Lin Piao commanded the 180,000-man Chinese Communist Forces (CCF) 13th Army Group (which included elements of his Fourth Field Army). This army group directly confronted the Eighth U.S. Army. After early successes his forces were badly mauled in January to February 1951. Incapacitated either by wounds or by illness, Lin Piao was replaced by General Peng Teh-huai (Peng Dehuai), then China's Deputy Minister of Defense, on February 16, 1951.

Promoted to the rank of marshal in the People's Liberation Army in 1955, Lin Piao replaced Peng Teh-huai as China's Minister of Defense in September 1959. His September 3, 1965 article, "Long Live the Victory of People's War," was seen for many years as the Communist's blueprint for the conduct of worldwide guerrilla war. Named as the heir apparent to then CCP leader Mao Tse-tung (Mao Zedong) in April 1969, Lin Piao began to fall out of favor a year later. On September 21, 1971, reportedly in the aftermath of a failed assassination plot against Mao, Lin Piao supposedly died in a plane crash in Mongolia; he was trying to flee to sanctuary in the Soviet Union. Other reports, however, have it that Lin Piao was actually killed by Mao Tse-tung's bodyguards.

See also CHINA, PEOPLES REPUBLIC OF; CHINESE COMMUNIST FORCES; PENG TEH-HUAI.

LITTLE SWITCH

"Little Switch" was the code name for the exchange of sick and wounded prisoners of war (POW) by the United Nations and the Chinese/North Koreans during the period April 20–26, 1953. During the exchange at Panmunjom the United Nations turned over 5,194 North Korean soldiers, 1,030 Chinese soldiers and 446 civilian detainees for a total of 6,670 POWs, including 357 litter cases. The Chinese/North Koreans turned over 684 sick and wounded Allied POWs, including 94 litter cases. Of these, 149 were Americans, 471 were South Koreans, 32 were from the United Kingdom, 15 were Turks, 6 were Colombians, 5 were Australians, 2 were Canadians and there was one POW each from the Philippines, the Union of South Africa, Greece and the Netherlands.

See also BIG SWITCH; POWs (PRISONERS OF WAR); POW (PRISONER OF WAR) CAMPS.

Suggestions for further reading: Walter G. Hermes, *U.S. Army in the Korean War: Truce Tent and Fighting Front* (Washington, D.C.: GPO, 1966).

LOVETT, ROBERT A(BERCROMBIE) (1895–1986)

Born September 14, 1895, in Huntsville, Texas, Lovett left Yale University in 1917 to organize the Yale unit of pilots and commanded the first U.S. Naval Air Squadron in World War I. During the interwar years he worked for his father-in- law's banking firm, specializing in international investments. His recommendations on increasing aircraft production to meet what he saw as the growing German threat led to his appointment as assistant secretary of war in April 1941; he served in that position throughout World War II.

In 1947 he became undersecretary of state, helped oversee the preparation of the Marshall Plan to rebuild war-devastated Europe and was deeply involved in the creation of the North Atlantic Treaty Organization (NATO). When George Marshall resigned as secretary of state in January 1949, Lovett also left government service. In September 1950, when Marshall returned to Washington to serve as secretary of defense, he asked Lovett to serve as his deputy secretary. While Marshall concerned himself with the operational aspects of the Korean War, Lovett concentrated on the Pentagon's internal administration, budgeting and procurement. When Marshall resigned in September 1951 because of ill health, President Harry S Truman nominated Lovett as Marshall's successor.

Lovett served as secretary of defense until the end of the Truman administration in January 1953, when he was replaced by Charles Wilson. As secretary of Defense he continued to concentrate on administrative and logistic matters, and the Chairman of the Joint Chiefs of Staff, General of the Army Omar Bradley (whom Truman had persuaded to serve a second two-year term as JCS Chairman) stepped in to become Truman's closest military adviser.

After leaving government in 1953, Lovett returned to banking. But he continued to serve as a member of the American "establishment" and was a member of several presidential advisory commissions during the 1960s. He died on May 7, 1986.
See also BRADLEY, OMAR N.; MARSHALL, GEORGE C.; SECRETARY OF DEFENSE.

Suggestions for further reading: See biographic entry in *Political Profiles: The Truman Years*, Eleanora W. Schoenebaum, editor (New York: Facts On File, 1978). See also Douglas Kinnard, *The Secretary of Defense* (Lexington, Ky.: University of Kentucky Press, 1980).

LUXEMBOURG

See BELGIUM.

M

M-1 RIFLE

Invented by weapons designer John C. Garand, the "U.S. Rifle, Caliber .30 M-1" was adopted by the U.S. Army in 1932. By 1941 most of the active Army had turned in their bolt-action M-1903 Springfield rifles and had been issued this new self-loading rifle. It was the standard U.S. infantry rifle in both World War II and the Korean War. When production ceased in the 1950s, about 5,500,000 rifles had been produced.

Forty-three and one-half inches long and weighing nine pounds, eight ounces, when empty, the M-1 held an eight-round clip of .30-caliber ammunition. It was a semiautomatic rifle: i.e., a single-shot rifle that self-loaded after every round was fired. Its eight-round clip automatically ejected through the top of the open receiver after the last round was fired.

Equipped with a stud for attachment of a standard bayonet with a 9.75-inch knife-type blade (as opposed to the Soviet/Chinese rod-type bayonet), the M-1 was a rugged and dependable weapon that stood up well to the rigors of the Korean battlefield.

See BAYONET; INFANTRY; SMALL ARMS.

Suggestions for further reading: Ian V. Hogg and John Weeks, *Military Small Arms of the 20th Century* (Northfield, Ill: DBI Books, 1985).

MacARTHUR, DOUGLAS (1880–1964)

Born January 26, 1880, in Little Rock, Arkansas, he was the third son of Arthur MacArthur. Arthur MacArthur had won the Medal of Honor at Missionary Ridge in the Civil War and went on to become a distinguished commander in the Spanish-American War and the Philippine insurrection; he served as the highest ranking officer in the Army from 1906 to 1909. In his day the elder MacArthur was so esteemed that Fort MacArthur, California, and MacArthur Boulevard in Washington, D.C., were named in his honor.

Douglas MacArthur graduated first in his class from the United States Military academy in 1903 and served on the War Department General Staff from 1913 to 1917, including a tour as the Army's first censor. Promoted to colonel upon America's entry into World War I, he was assigned as chief of staff to the 42d (Rainbow) Division and sailed with the division to France. Promoted to brigadier general, he served as a brigade and division commander during the battles of Champagne-Marne and St. Mihiel, and the Meuse-Argonne operations. Twice wounded in action, he won two Distinguished Service Crosses and seven Silver Star Medals for bravery on the battlefield.

During the interwar years MacArthur served as superintendent of the U.S. Military

As the infantryman in the foreground loads a new clip into his M-1 rifle, his companion fires at the enemy, January 1951.
(Courtesy Lyndon Baines Johnson Library & Museum.)

Academy from 1919 to 1922 and as Army chief of staff under Presidents Herbert Hoover and Franklin D. Roosevelt from 1930 to 1935. Becoming field marshal in the Philippine Army after his retirement from the U.S. Army in 1937, MacArthur was recalled to active duty in 1941 on the eve of World War II and when America entered World War II he was serving as commanding General, U.S. Forces Far East, with headquarters in Manila.

After directing the defenses of Bataan and Corregidor against the Japanese invaders, he was evacuated to Australia, where he assumed command of the Southwest Pacific Theater. Directing the Sixth and Eighth U.S. armies as well as the Fifth Air Force and attached Australian units, MacArthur fought a series of campaigns through New Guinea, the Admiralties, New Britain and the Moluccas. Making good on the pledge made when he left the Philippines in 1942 that "I shall return," his forces liberated Leyte and Mindoro and landed on Luzon on January 1945. His use of strategic envelopments to cut off and isolate enemy forces rather than attacking head-on led to his having the lowest casualty rate of any major U.S. commander in World War II.

Awarded (like his father) the Medal of Honor by President Roosevelt and promoted to general of the Army (i.e., five-star rank) in December 1944, MacArthur was named commanding general, U.S. Army Forces Far East

(USAFFE), in April 1945, and supreme commander Allied powers (SCAP) in August 1945 when he accepted the Japanese surrender. In addition to overseeing the Allied occupation of Japan, in 1947 MacArthur was given responsibility as Commander in Chief, Far East Command (FECOM), which was composed of all U.S. forces in Japan, Korea (until 1949 when all U.S. troops were withdrawn), the Ryukyus (including Okinawa), the Philippines, the Marianas and the Bonins. He was serving in that capacity when the Korean War began.

Designated commander in chief of the United Nations Command (UNC) by President Harry S Truman on July 8, 1950, and given command of the Republic of Korea (ROK) Armed Forces by ROK President Syngman Rhee on July 14, 1950, MacArthur had operational command of all Allied land, sea and air forces engaged in the Korean War.

His bold response to the North Korean People's Army (NKPA) cross-border invasion of the Republic of Korea (South Korea) without doubt saved that nation from what would have been certain conquest. His masterstroke, conceived in early July 1950 when U.S. forces were falling back in disarray, was the invasion at Inchon on September 15, 1950, to cut off the enemy's lines of supply and communication. By October 1, 1950, the original war aims of UN forces in Korea—restoration of the prewar status quo—had been achieved. It was MacArthur's finest hour.

Ordered by Washington to cross the 38th parallel into North Korea and take the strategic offensive to liberate that area from Communist control, MacArthur made the classic military error of splitting his forces in the face of the enemy. Under his direction the Eighth U.S. Army (EUSA) drove up Korea's western coast to seize the North Korean capital of Pyongyang with orders to continue to the Manchurian border at the Yalu River. Meanwhile X (Tenth)

General of the Army Douglas MacArthur.
(Courtesy Lyndon Baines Johnson Library & Museum.)

Corps (which under MacArthur's control had independently carried out the Inchon invasion) drove up Korea's eastern coast to the border. The mountainous area between these two forces was left unguarded.

MacArthur's tactics were successful so long as he was moving against the disorganized remnants of the NKPA. But what neither he nor Washington had counted on was the massive intervention of the Chinese Communist Forces (CCF) into that unguarded mountainous area. Brushing aside evidence that the CCF had entered the war, MacArthur was caught by surprise when in late November 1950 the CCF 130,000-man 13th Army Group struck EUSA on the west and the CCF 120,000-man Ninth Army Group struck X Corps on the east. Both Allied forces were forced into retreat. Fighting its way back from the Chosin Reservoir, X Corps withdrew from North Korea through the port of Hungnam on December 24, 1950. On the west EUSA fell back, abandoning first Pyongyang and then Seoul to the enemy. To add to the confusion, Lieutenant General Walton H. Walker, the EUSA commander, was killed in a vehicle accident on December 23, 1950.

Walker was replaced by Lieutenant General Matthew B. Ridgway, to whom MacArthur gave total battlefield control in the face of a rapidly deteriorating situation (some believed EUSA would be unable to even hang on to a foothold on the peninsula). Although Ridgway soon halted the retreat and assumed the tactical and operational offensive, a major and unprecedented change had taken place at the strategic level in Washington: The United States abandoned its national policy of rolling back Communism and liberating North Korea in favor of the policy of containing Communist expansion. In accordance with this change in national policy, military strategy changed from the strategic offensive, which up to that time had always been the American way of war (i.e., taking the war to the enemy and destroying his will to resist), to the strategic defensive (i.e., holding back and containing enemy offensive actions so as to stalemate the battlefield and prepare the way for political negotiations for bringing the war to a close). This change in policy and strategy (a change not well understood either then or now) was the fundamental cause of the clash between General MacArthur and President Truman.

Although never directly refusing a presidential order, MacArthur made it plain that he was not in sympathy with this change in strategy and publicly criticized the administration's conduct of the war. The final straw was MacArthur's attempt to inject partisan political politics into the controversy—a letter from MacArthur to Republican Congressman Joseph Martin of Massachusetts, a former speaker of the House of Representatives, in March 1951, advocating the use of Chinese Nationalist forces in the war. Congressman Martin read the letter on the floor of Congress on April 5, 1951. MacArthur was relieved from command on April 11, 1951.

Returning to a hero's welcome, he addressed a joint session of the Congress on April 19, 1951, and took part in the Great Debate on the war. During those debates, MacArthur was reminded by a hostile senator that in 1932, as Army chief, he had said that the head of state alone should determine a war's objectives and the means of attaining them. MacArthur replied, "As I look back, Senator, on my rather youthful days then, I am surprised and amazed how wise I was."

As he himself had prophesied, MacArthur soon "faded away" from further public political-military involvement, especially after his former amanuensis and aide-de-camp, General Dwight D. Eisenhower (for whom no love was lost), was elected to the presidency. Honored with a gold medal and a Resolution of the thanks and appreciation of the Congress and the American people by the Congress in 1962, General MacArthur died on April 5, 1964.

See GREAT DEBATE; INCHON INVASION; MARTIN, JOSEPH W. JR.; STRATEGY, U.S.; WAKE ISLAND CONFERENCE.

Suggestions for further reading: See D. Clayton James's biographical sketch in Roger J. Spiller, editor, *Dictionary of American Military Biography* (Westport, Conn.: Greenwood Press, 1984). See also Douglas MacArthur, *Reminiscences* (New York: McGraw-Hill, 1964). Although there have been a great many books written on MacArthur, the definitive work is Professor D. Clayton James's three-volume account, *The Years of MacArthur* (Boston: Houghton Mifflin, 1970, 1975, 1985). The third volume, *Triumph and Disaster: 1945–1964*, covers the Korean War period.

MACHINE-GUNS

In the First World War the machine-gun had revolutionized the battlefield; a generation later many of these same weapons were still being used on the battlefield in Korea. At the squad level in U.S. Army and Marine Corps units (and those units equipped by the United States) the M-1918A2 Browning automatic rifle (BAR), with its 20-round magazine, substituted for a light machine-gun. The light machine-gun in the weapons squad of the infantry platoon was the belt-fed Browing .30-caliber air-cooled M-1919A6 machine-gun, which had a shoulder stock and bipod. The machine-gun squads in the infantry battalion weapons company (which, in combat, were attached to the rifle companies) had the M-1919A4 machine-gun, identical to the A6 except that it was tripod-mounted and had no shoulder stock or bipod. The squads also had the extremely accurate belt-fed Browning .30-caliber water-cooled M-1917A1 machine-gun. The U.S. Army's heavy machine-gun at the time was the belt-fed Browning .50-caliber air-cooled M-1921M2HB.

The light machine-gun for British Commonwealth forces in Korea was the British .303-caliber Mark 1 Bren Gun. With its 30-round magazine, it was essentially the equivalent of both the BAR and the A6. Their standard infantry machine-gun was the belt-fed .303-caliber water-cooled Mark I Vickers machine-gun, which had been adopted by the British Army in 1912 (and remained in service until 1965).

For the North Koreans and the Chinese the most common light machine-gun was the Soviet 7.62-mm air-cooled DP (Degtyaryova pakhotnyi) 1928 model. Bipod mounted, it was equipped with a 47-round drum. Their water-cooled machine-gun was the Soviet belt-fed 7.62-mm PM (Pulemyot Maxima) 1910 model, usually mounted on a "Sokolov" wheeled carriage. Their heavy machine-gun was the Soviet belt-fed air-cooled 12.7-mm DShKM (Degtyaryova-Shpagina-Krupnokalibernyi) M1938/46 model, which was equipped with a wheeled mount that converted to an anti-aircraft tripod.

See BROWNING AUTOMATIC RIFLE; BURP GUN; SMALL ARMS.

Suggestions for further reading: Ian V. Hogg and John Weeks, *Military Small Arms of the 20th Century* (Northfield, Ill.: DBI Books, 1985).

MANCHURIA

An area of China north of the Great Wall composed of the provinces of Heilungkiang, Kirin and Liaoning, Manchuria was originally a separate nation ruled by the Manchus, whose culture and Tungusic language differed from that of the Chinese. In 1643 to 1644 the Manchus conquered China and set up the Ch'ing Dynasty, which ruled China until 1911. A quarter century later Manchuria again became a base for the invasion of China. In 1931, attacking from their bases in Korea, the Imperial Japanese Army conquered Manchuria and turned it into the puppet state of Manchukuo. From this Manchurian base, Japan launched a full-scale invasion of China in 1937 and began a conflict that would not end until Japan's surrender in 1945.

Because of this historical experience and Manchuria's location on the traditional invasion route into the north China plain, this was a sensitive region for the Chinese. When advancing United Nations forces approached the Manchuria–Korea border in the fall of 1950, the Chinese evidently felt they had just cause for alarm, one of the factors that may have sparked their October-November 1950 intervention into the Korean War.

From that time on Manchuria became a headquarters and staging area for the Chinese Communist Forces (CCF); a depot area for CCF

resupply; and the site of a number of airfields in Changchun, Mukden and Antung, where more than 1,115 Chinese Communist Air Force (CCAF) aircraft were stationed. Although the CCAF used these bases to launch air attacks on United Nations aircraft over North Korea, political restrictions turned these bases into sanctuaries immune from Allied attack.
See SANCTUARIES.

Suggestions for further reading: For Manchurian air bases see Robert F. Futrell's *The United States Air Force in Korea: 1950–1953*, revised edition (Washington, D.C.: GPO, 1983). For the CCF in Manchuria see Russell Spurr's *Enter the Dragon* (New York: Newmarket Press, 1988).

MAO TSE-TUNG (MAO ZEDONG) (1893–1976)

See CHINA, PEOPLES REPUBLIC OF.

MARINE CORPS, REPUBLIC OF KOREA

Organized in 1949, the 3,000-man First Korean Marine Corps Regiment (KMC/RCT) was attached to the U.S. Fifth Marine Regiment for the Inchon invasion in September 1950 and took part in the subsequent recapture of Seoul, the landing at Wonsan and the Chosin Reservoir operation. Detached to Republic of Korea (ROK) Army control for a time in early 1951, on March 17, 1951, the First Korean Marine Corps Regiment was attached permanently to the U.S. First Marine Division for the remainder of the war.

During the 1952 to 1953 period the KMC/RCT, by then grown to a 4,400-man force that included three infantry battalions, an artillery battalion and a tank company, provided the U.S. First Marine Division with a quarter of its combat strength and became the fourth regiment of the division. The ROK Marine Corps also had a Second Korean Marine Corps Regi-

ment, which served as the defense force for islands lying off Korea's eastern and western coasts; and a Fifth Korean Marine Corps battalion, which was part of the Kimpo peninsula defense force and was also attached to the U.S. First Marine Division in 1952. These attachments continued until the end of the war.

In 1965, ROK Marine Corps forces would again serve with the U.S. Marines when the ROK Marine Corps Second (Blue Dragon) Brigade landed in Vietnam and established a base at Hui An in the III Marine Amphibious Force area.
See FIRST MARINE DIVISION.

Suggestions for further reading: See the five-volume official history, *U.S. Marine Operations in Korea 1950–1953*: Lynn Montross and Captain Nicholas A. Canzona, USMC; *The Pusan Perimeter*, 1954; *The Inchon-Seoul Operation*, 1955; *The Chosin Reservoir Campaign*, 1957; Lynn Montross and Majors Hubard D. Kuokka and Norman W. Hicks, USMC, *The East-Central Front*, 1962; and Lieutenant Colonel Pat Meid, USMCR, and Major James M. Yingling, USMC, *Operations in West Korea*, 1972 (Washington, D.C.: GPO).

MARINE CORPS, U.S.

The U.S. Marine Corps played a major role in the war in Korea. The First Provisional Marine Brigade was instrumental in the defense of the Naktong Perimeter in August–September 1950. The First Marine Division led the way during the Inchon invasion and the recapture of Seoul in September 1950; and its epic withdrawal under enemy pressure from the Chosin Reservoir in November–December 1950 was one of the major engagements of the war. From January 1951 to March 1952 the Marines manned the eastern sector of Eighth Army's defensive line in the Hwachon Reservoir–Punchbowl area, and from March 1952 to the

Marine litter bearers evacuate a wounded comrade during the battle for Seoul, September 1950.
(Courtesy Lyndon Baines Johnson Library & Museum.)

end of the war they manned the western sector and the approaches to Seoul.

Throughout the entire war the First Marine Aircraft Wing not only provided close air support for Army and Marine Corps ground operations, but it also provided escort for Far East Air Force's long-range bombers, provided much of the photo reconnaissance of the battlefield, and pioneered the use of helicopters in medical evacuation and battlefield resupply.

Among other decorations and awards, 42 Medals of Honor were awarded to U.S. Marine Corps personnel (and an additional five to Navy corpsmen attached to Marine Corps units). Of the 5,720,000 Americans who served during the Korean war era between June 25, 1950, and July 27, 1953, 424,000 were Marines. According to the official history, the Marine Corps suffered 30,544 casualties in Korea, in-cluding 4,262 killed in action, 244 nonbattle deaths and 26,038 wounded in action.

See CHOSIN RESERVOIR, BATTLE OF; FIRST MARINE AIRCRAFT WING; FIRST MARINE DIVISION; FIRST PROVISIONAL MARINE BRIGADE; INCHON INVASION; MOBILIZATION; NAKTONG PERIMETER, BATTLE OF; PUNCHBOWL, BATTLE OF.

Suggestions for further reading: See the five-volume official history, *U.S. Marine Operations in Korea 1950–1953*: Lynn Montross and Captain Nicholas A. Canzona, USMC; *The Pusan Perimeter*, 1954; *The Inchon-Seoul Operation*, 1955; *The Chosin Reservoir Campaign*, 1957; Lynn Montross and Majors Hubard D. Kuokka and Norman W. Hicks, USMC, *The East-Central Front*, 1962; and Lieutenant Colonel Pat Meid, USMCR, and Major James M. Yingling, USMC, *Operations in West Korea*, 1972 (Washington, D.C.: GPO).

MARSHALL, GEORGE C(ATLETT) (1880–1959)

Born December 31, 1880, at Uniontown, Pennsylvania, Marshall graduated from the Virginia Military Academy in 1901 and was commissioned a second lieutenant of infantry in 1902. After service in the Philippines and at the Army Staff College at Fort Leavenworth, Kansas, he served as the G-3 (operations officer) of the First Infantry Division on the Western Front in France in World War I and later as chief of operations for the First U.S. Army in the Meuse-Argonne campaign.

In the spring of 1919 Marshall was assigned as aide to General John "Blackjack" Pershing and remained in that position until 1924, when he was posted to the 15th Infantry in Tientsin, China. In 1927 he returned to the United States as an instructor first at the Army War College and then at the Infantry School at Fort Benning, Georgia. After commanding a battalion of the Eighth Infantry in 1932 to 1933, he was promoted to colonel and briefly commanded the Eighth Infantry Regiment. From 1933 to 1936 he was senior instructor of the Illinois National Guard and later commanded the Fifth Infantry Brigade. In the summer of 1938 Marshall was appointed to head the War Plans Division of the Army General Staff, and in 1939 he was named deputy chief of staff of the Army. On September 1, 1939, the day World War II began in Europe, Marshall was appointed Army chief of staff.

Serving in that capacity throughout World War II, Marshall was instrumental in building the Army and Army Air Force to its wartime strength and responsible for overseeing its commitment to combat. The senior military adviser to both Presidents Franklin D. Roosevelt and Harry S Truman, he played a key role in formulating national strategies for the prosecution of the war.

Leaving active military service on November 20, 1945, he was sent to China in an unsuccessful attempt to mediate the civil war between the Nationalist and Communist factions. Nominated as secretary of state by President Truman, Marshall returned from China in January 1947 and was sworn into office later that month. His best-known accomplishment in that position was the European Recovery Act (i.e., the Marshall Plan), for which he won the Nobel prize in 1953. Retiring as secretary of state because of ill health in January 1949, he was replaced by Dean Acheson, who had been his deputy in 1947 and had helped set up the Marshall Plan.

In July 1950 he was asked by President Truman to return to government service as secretary of defense, and Marshall agreed to a one-year posting. Replacing Louis Johnson as secretary of defense on September 21, 1950, he supervised the mobilization for the Korean War, pressed for increased war production and restored morale after the chaotic performance of his predecessor. Involved in the relief of General Douglas MacArthur in April 1951, he later defended his actions with a strong statement in behalf of civilian control of the military.

On September 12, 1951, Marshall again left public service and was succeeded as secretary of defense by Deputy Secretary of Defense Robert A. Lovett. Retiring to his farm in Leesburg, Virginia, General Marshall died on October 16, 1959.

See DEFENSE SECRETARY.

Suggestions for further reading: See Forrest C. Pogue's biographical sketch in Roger J. Spiller, editor *Dictionary of American Military Biography* (Westport, Conn.: Greenwood Press, 1984). Although other books have been written, the definitive work on George C. Marshall is Forrest C. Pogue's four-volume account, *George C. Marshall* (New York: Viking Press, 1963–1987). The last volume in that series, *George C. Marshall: Statesman 1945–1959*, covers the Korean War period. See also Douglas Kinnard, *The Secretary of Defense* (Lexington, Ky.: University of Kentucky Press, 1980).

MARTIN, JOSEPH W(ILLIAM) JR. (1884–1968)

Born November 3, 1884, in North Attleboro, Massachusetts, Martin declined a scholarship to Dartmouth College in 1902 to become a reporter for the North Attleboro *Sun*. He later became editor and publisher of the Attleboro *Evening Chronicle* and still later purchased the Franklin, Massachusetts, *Sentinel*.

Entering Republican Party politics in 1911, he served in the Massachusetts House of Representatives and Massachusetts Senate until his election to the United States House of Representatives in 1924. In 1939 Martin became House minority leader, a position he held from 1939 to 1947, from 1949 to 1953 and from 1955 to 1959. Elected speaker of the House in 1947, Martin served in that position from 1947 to 1949 and from 1953 to 1955.

While serving as House minority leader in 1951, Martin sent General Douglas MacArthur, then commander in chief of the Far East Command/United Nations Command in charge of the war in Korea, a copy of a speech he had made. Martin had proposed releasing Chinese Nationalist leader Chiang Kai-shek to attack the Chinese mainland and solicited MacArthur's views. In a letter to Martin, MacArthur replied that using Chinese Nationalist troops to counter Chinese Communist troops was a logical move; he went on to criticize the Truman administration's emphasis on building up NATO defense in Europe rather than on fighting the war in Asia. He added that "there was no substitute for victory."

Martin read General MacArthur's reply on the floor of the Congress on April 5, 1951, and released copies to the press. This was the last straw for President Harry S Truman, already smarting from other MacArthur criticisms of his war policies. After consultation with Secretary of Defense George C. Marshall and with the Joint Chiefs of Staff and others, President Truman relieved General MacArthur from command on April 11, 1951.

Martin helped arrange MacArthur's address to the joint session of Congress upon his return and helped set up the congressional "Great Debate" on the war, unsuccessfully trying to spark a move to nominate MacArthur for the presidency. Again elected speaker of the House following the 1952 Eisenhower landslide, Martin's influence began to wane, and he failed to gain reelection as minority leader in 1959. In 1966, after 42 years in the Congress, he lost his bid for reelection in his home district. Retiring to Florida, Congressman Martin died on March 6, 1968.

See MACARTHUR, DOUGLAS.

Suggestions for further reading: See biographic entry in *Political Profiles: The Truman Years*, Eleanora W. Schoenebaum, editor (New York: Facts On File, 1978).

MASH (MOBILE ARMY SURGICAL HOSPITALS)

Popularized by the movie *M*A*S*H* and especially by the television series of the same name, the MASH (Mobile Army Surgical Hospital) has become symbolic of the Korean War. For Korean War veterans that is rather ironic, for although the television series was set during the Korean War, the characters frequently expressed antiwar attitudes more like those of the Vietnam War era.

One thing about the TV series was accurate, however: The timely medical care these hospitals provided saved countless lives. As its name indicated, a MASH was a *mobile* hospital

The 8225th Mobile Army Surgical Hospital in Korea, October 1951.
(Courtesy U.S. Army Military History Institute.)

designed to move frequently, thereby keeping pace with combat operations. Their tents were usually located near the front-line infantry division's medical clearing stations so that they could receive and treat patients whose wounds needed immediate surgical care. After this emergency surgery patients were not kept at the MASH to recover but instead were evacuated to hospitals farther to the rear.
See HELICOPTERS; MEDICAL CARE AND EVACUATION.

MATS (MILITARY AIR TRANSPORT SERVICE)

Established as a unified logistic organization by the National Security Act of 1947, the Military Air Transport Service (MATS) operated a global military "scheduled airline." Before the Korean War began, its Pacific Division was operating about 60 multiengine transports across the Pacific. These included propeller-driven C-54 Skymasters, C-97 Stratofreighters, C-118 Liftmasters, C-119 Flying Boxcars, C-121 Super Constellations and C-124 Globemasters.

To meet enormously increased wartime demands, MATS pressed additional planes into service, chartered available civilian aircraft and took advantage of the loan of a Royal Canadian Air Force (RCAF) transport squadron. By the end of July 1950 they had increased their lift to 250 aircraft and were moving 106 tons a day. This was helpful, especially for high-priority items such as the 3.5-inch rocket launchers that were rushed to Korea in the opening days of the war to stop the advancing North Korean armor; strategic airlift, however, was still coming of age during the Korean War.

Because of the lack of jet transports, time-distance factors were greatly inhibiting. The 5,688-mile Great Circle route from McChord Air Base at Tacoma, Washington, to Anchorage, Alaska, to Shemya, in the Aleutians, to Tokyo took 30 to 33 hours. The 6,718-mile Mid-Pacific route from Travis Air Base near San Francisco to Honolulu to Wake Island to Tokyo took 34 hours, and the 8,000-mile Southern route from California to Honolulu to Johnson Island to Kwajalein and Guam to Tokyo took 40 hours. The result was that for every ton moved by MATS, the Navy moved 270 tons by sea.

But there was one area in which MATS came into its own. In earlier wars casualties had been evacuated from the battle area by hospital ship. In the Korean War medical evacuation was taken over by MATS, which during the course of the war moved 43,196 casualties from the battle area to hospitals in the United States. Instead of spending their time transporting patients, hospital ships became hospitals on par with the MASH (Mobile Army Surgical Hospitals) and evacuation hospitals on shore. *See* COMBAT CARGO COMMAND; HOSPITAL SHIPS; MSTS (MILITARY SEA TRANSPORT SERVICE); TRANSPORT AIRCRAFT.

Suggestions for further reading: See Robert F. Futrell, *The United States Air Force in Korea: 1950–1953*, revised edition (Washington, D.C.: GPO, 1983).

McCARTHY, JOSEPH R(AYMOND) (1909–1957)

Born November 14, 1909, in Grand Chute, Wisconsin, McCarthy graduated from Marquette University in 1935 with a degree in law. When World War II began he was serving as a circuit court judge; he waived deferment and joined the Marine Corps, where he served as an intelligence officer in the South Pacific.

In 1944, while still in uniform, he ran unsuccessfully for a seat in the United States Senate. Two years later he succeeded and was elected as Wisconsin's junior senator. Flamboyant, power hungry and bombastic from the start, McCarthy alienated many of his colleagues. In February 1950 he found the issue that would make him infamous: the charge that the United States government, and the State Department in particular, was infiltrated by Communists. A reluctant supporter of the war in Korea, he denounced President Truman in January 1951 for allowing the British government to set foreign policy; in April 1951 he called for Truman's impeachment over the relief of United Nations Commander General Douglas MacArthur.

Throughout the period 1950 to 1952 he concentrated his fire on Secretary of State Dean Acheson and went so far as to accuse Secretary of Defense George C. Marshall of near treason during his mission to China in the late 1940s. His inflammatory charges became so lurid that *McCarthyism* has entered the dictionary, defined as "the use of indiscriminate, often unfounded, accusations, sensationalism, inquisitorial investigative methods, etc., ostensibly in the suppression of communism."

In the short term, McCarthy succeeded in hounding out of government most of the "old China hands"—John Paton Davies, John Steward Service, John Carter Vincent and the like—who could have warned of China's likely intervention in the Korean War. In the long run his tactics actually facilitated rather than suppressed subversion against the United States since charges of "McCarthyism" could be used by genuine subversives to deflect any investigation of their activities.

Miscalculating his strength, McCarthy attacked the Army in 1954 for being soft on Communism. Rather than retreat as had been the case in the past, Secretary of the Army Robert

T. Stevens authorized Army counsel Joseph Welsh's attack on McCarthy's lies and distortions. This proved to be the beginning of the end. Censured by the Senate in December 1954, McCarthy went into decline and died in May 1957.

See CHINA LOBBY.

Suggestions for further reading: Thomas C. Reeves, *The Life and Times of Joe McCarthy* (New York: Stein & Day, 1982). See also biographic entry in *Political Profiles: The Truman Years*, Eleanora W. Schoenebaum, editor (New York: Facts On File, 1978).

MEDAL OF HONOR

First authorized during the Civil War, the Medal of Honor (often incorrectly called the "Congressional" Medal of Honor) is the highest American military award for battlefield bravery. It is awarded by the president, in the name of the Congress, to those members of the armed forces who have distinguished themselves conspicuously by gallantry and intrepidity at the risk of their lives above and beyond the call of duty while engaged in action against the enemy. The deed performed must have been one of personal bravery or self-sacrifice so conspicuous that it clearly distinguishes the individuals above their comrades; the deed must have involved risk of life.

The first Medals of Honor for a Korean campaign were awarded to six Marines and nine sailors of the United States Navy's Asiatic Squadron for an assault on Korean forts guarding the approaches to Seoul on June 9 to 11, 1871. (See Part I: The Setting.)

During the 1950 to 1953 Korean War, 131 Medals of Honor were awarded, 93 of them posthumously. Army soldiers won 78 Medals of Honor: Three were won by combat medical aidmen, three by combat engineers, two by cavalrymen, two by artillerymen (one a forward observer and the other in the retreat from the Chosin Reservoir), one by a tanker and the remaining 67 by infantrymen. Marines won 42 Medals of Honor, one by an artillery forward observer and the remainder by infantrymen. Navy personnel won seven Medals of Honor, five by hospital corpsmen attached to the First Marine Division and two by pilots—one a Corsair pilot from the USS *Leyte* and the other a helicopter pilot—who were attempting to rescue downed comrades. Air Force pilots won four Medals of Honor: one by an F-86 Sabrejet pilot in a dog fight with MiGs, one by an F-80 Shooting Star pilot on a close air support mission, one by an F-51 Mustang pilot, also on a close air support mission, and one by a B-26 Invader bomber pilot on an aerial interdiction mission.

See also DECORATIONS, U.S.

Suggestions for further reading: U.S. Congress. Senate. Committee on Veterans Affairs. *Medal of Honor Recipients 1863–1973.* 93d Congress, 1st session (Washington, D.C.: GPO, 1973) has the citations for all Medal of Honor awards as well as an extensive bibliography. See also *America's Medal of Honor Recipients* (Golden Valley, Minn.: Highland Publishers, 1980); *And Brave Men Too*, by Timothy S. Lowry (NY: Crown, 1985).

MEDIA

Korea was the last war covered almost exclusively by print journalists—newspaper, magazine and wire service reporters from the Associated Press (AP), United Press (UP) and International News Service (INS). Television was in its infancy and instantaneous satellite transmission of news film was still years away. Although there were newsreel cameramen in Korea, their film had to be flown back to the United States; even under the best of conditions that took several days.

When the war began there were only five wire service correspondents in Seoul. By the time the 24th Infantry Division's Task Force Smith went into action on July 5, 1950, there were some 70 reporters in the country. By September 1, 1950, there were 238 American and foreign reporters accredited to Far East Command (FECOM); this total increased to 270 during the course of the war. (By comparison, there were 419 news media representatives accredited to MACV [Military Assistance Command Vietnam] in 1966.)

Among these reporters was the *New York Tribune*'s Marguerite Higgins, who was constantly getting expelled from one battle after another on the grounds it was too dangerous for a woman; through her persistence, however, she pioneered the way for future female war correspondents. Another "first" in the Korean War was the reporting of Allied country war correspondents from the enemy camp, most notably the Australian Communist Wilfred Burchett and the *London Daily Worker*'s Alan Winnington. This would have been considered treason in earlier wars.

Ten American correspondents died during the fighting in Korea, most of them in the chaotic first months of the war. For example, UP's Peter Kalischer just barely escaped capture at Osan on July 5, 1950, while accompanying Task Force Smith, and one photographer, Frank Noel of AP, was captured by Chinese Communist Forces (CCF) on December 1, 1950, and spent the next two and one half years in Communist prison camps.

When the war began the FECOM Commander in chief, General of the Army Douglas MacArthur (who, as a young major, had been the Army's first censor in the early days of the First World War), specifically ruled out censorship, which he called "abhorrent." Contradictory as it may sound, it was the newsmen who pressed for censorship. The competitive pres-

Left, Marguerite Higgins of the *New York Herald Tribune* pioneered the way for female war correspondents.
(Courtesy U.S. Army Military History Institute.)

sure to disclose more information than their rivals was enormous, and serious security leaks were beginning to develop. The Inchon invasion, for example, was reported in American newspapers while the troops were still at sea.

For this and other reasons, press censorship was imposed on December 20, 1950. First administered by Eighth U.S. Army (EUSA) censors, responsibility later shifted to FECOM censors in Japan on June 15, 1951. Press censorship (favored, according to one study, by 90% of the journalists) remained in effect until the end of the war.

Acrimonious as they sometimes were, military-media relations in the Korean War never reached the depths to which they plummeted in the Vietnam War. According to a 1985 analysis by journalist Peter Braestrup (*Washington Post* bureau chief in Saigon during the Vietnam War and a combat Marine officer in the Korean War), "The inconclusive war became unpopular at home—an issue in the 1952 election—but neither [EUSA commander] General James Van Fleet nor other U.S. commanders in Korea later blamed this evolution on the security lapses, mood swings, exaggerations, or forebodings of the press."

Suggestions for further reading: For contemporary accounts by Korean War war correspondents see Keyes Beech, *Tokyo and Points East* (Garden City, NY: Doubleday, 1964); Marguerite Higgins, *War in Korea: The Report of a Woman Combat Correspondent* (Garden City, NY: Doubleday, 1951); and E.J. Kahn Jr., *The Peculiar War: Impressions of a Reporter in Korea* (New York: Random House, 1952). The best account of military-media relations in the Korean War is in Peter Braestrup's *Battle Lines: Report of the Twentieth Century Fund*

Task Force on the Military and the Media (New York: Priority Press Publications, 1985). See also John Hohenberg's *Foreign Correspondence: The Great Reporters and Their Times* (New York: Columbia University Press, 1964). For a critical account of military-media relations see First Lieutenant Martin Blumenson et al., *Monograph: Special Problems in the Korean Conflict*, Headquarters Eighth U.S. Army Korea, February 5, 1952.

MEDICAL CARE AND EVACUATION

Medical care and the evacuation of the wounded during the Korean War were vastly improved since World War II. In World War II, 28% of all wounded American soldiers died. In Korea this was reduced to 22%. The mortality

Rapid evacuation of casualties by helicopter from the battlefield to MASH and Evacuation hospitals behind the lines saved countless lives.
(Courtesy Lyndon Baines Johnson Library & Museum.)

rate of hospitalized wounded dropped from 4.5% to 2.5%.

Because of the pioneering work done during the Korean War in peripheral vascular surgery, the amputation rate for brachial wounds was reduced from 35% to zero, for femoral wounds from 61% to 4.8% and for popliteal wounds from 73% to 18%. Some battlefield killers were eliminated entirely. In World War I, gas gangrene developed in 5% of all wounded with a fatality rate of 28%. In World War II, 0.7% developed gas gangrene, with a fatality rate of 31%. In Korea, 0.08% developed gas gangrene, with no reported fatalities.

Medical innovations during the Korean War included not only peripheral vascular surgery, which was attempted for the first time, but also the use of plastic bags for intravenous solutions, including blood; the recognition of a clotting defect in the seriously wounded; and the documentation of hypertensive shock. Another innovation was the treatment of battle fatigue cases. Instead of evacuating them to the rear, which increased their conviction of being mentally ill, they were treated with bed rest and hot food in regimental clearing stations immediately behind the lines, then returned to duty. The recovery rate was far greater than in World War II.

Perhaps the greatest lifesaver was not a medical innovation at all but a transportation innovation: the use of aircraft for medical evacuation. Studies during World War I had shown that there was a direct relationship between the hours that elapsed between severe wounding and treatment, and the mortality rate. In World War II, when medical evacuation was by hand-carried litter and by vehicle, the evacuation time could run as high as 12 to 15 hours. In Korea, medical evacuation was also by hand-carried litter, especially from mountain positions inaccessible to other transportation. It was also by vehicle and by hospital

train. But for the first time helicopters were used extensively to evacuate wounded from the battlefield. From July 1950 to February 1951, for example, H-5 helicopters from the U.S. Air Force's Third Air Rescue Squadron evacuated 750 critically wounded soldiers. As a result the average evacuation time in Korea was cut to four to six hours.

At first helicopter medical evacuation was almost entirely by Air Force and Marine Corps helicopters, but in January 1951 the Army began to field air ambulance companies. An agreement was worked out so that the Army handled aeromedical evacuation forward of its Mobile Army Surgical Hospitals while Air Force transports provided medical air evacuation rearward to hospitals in Japan and in the continental United States.

During the course of the war the U.S. Air Force (USAF) 801st Medical Air Evacuation Squadron and its successor, the 6481st Medical Air Evacuation Group, provided aeromedical evacuation of 311,673 sick and wounded patients within Korea, between Korea and Japan, and within Japan, where a number of major military hospitals were located. In addition, the USAF's Military Air Transportation Service moved 43,196 casualties to the United States for further medical treatment.

See CASUALTIES: COMBAT MEDICAL AIDMEN; HELICOPTERS; MASH (MOBILE ARMY SURGICAL HOSPITALS); JAPAN.

Suggestions for further reading: The best account of Korean War aeromedical evacuation is contained in Robert F. Futrell, *The United States Air Force in Korea: 1950–1953*, revised edition (Washington, D.C.: GPO, 1983). See also Robert M. Hardaway, M.D., *Care of the Wounded in Vietnam* (Manhattan, Kansas: Sunflower Press, 1988), which has extensive comparisons between medical care in World War II, Korea and Vietnam. The definitive work, however, is Albert E. Cowdrey's *The Medic's War* (Washington, D.C.: GPO, 1987).

MEMORIAL

In October 1986 the Congress approved the construction of a memorial to Americans who had fought in the Korean War, the only war without a monument in Washington, D.C. The Korean War memorial bill designates the American Battle Monuments Commission as the group in charge of selecting the site and design. The construction of the memorial, estimated to cost some $6 million, has been authorized $1 million in federal funds, with the rest to be raised by public donations.

MERITORIOUS UNIT COMMENDATIONS

The Army, Navy and Air Force all awarded Meritorious Unit Commendations during the Korean War. All had different criteria, and each award emblem was distinct.

The Army award required the highest standard of performance, being granted only for the performance of outstanding service for at least six continuous months during a period of military operations against an armed enemy. The degree of achievement required was the same as that needed for award of the Legion of Merit to an individual. The award emblem at the time was a cloth gold wreath (commonly called the "toilet seat") worn on the lower sleeve, but that has since been replaced by a red ribbon encased in a gold frame worn on the right breast.

The Navy Unit Commendation was awarded for service under combat or noncombat conditions, and the character of service required was the same as that needed for award of a Bronze Star Medal to an individual. The award emblem was a green ribbon with blue/gold/red stripes at either end. The Air Force Outstanding Unit Award (a blue ribbon with a white/red/white stripe in the center and a red/white stripe at either end) was also awarded for combat and noncombat service.

In all cases these emblems can be worn permanently by those personnel assigned to the unit at the time of the award.
See UNIT AWARDS.

MIA (MISSING IN ACTION)

Although most were officially written off long ago as "presumed dead," there are some 8,177 Americans still missing in action (MIA) and unaccounted for after the Korean War. Most are truly "missing"—that is, they are airmen who went down at sea or in rugged mountainous terrain, soldiers and Marines who disappeared in the confusion of battle and whose bodies were never recovered. However, there are 2,233 members of the United Nations Command (UNC), including 389 Americans, who were known to have been alive in Chinese Communist Forces (CCF) or North Korean People's Army (NKPA) prisoner of war (POW) camps

Difficulty in casualty recovery and identification contributed to the large number of MIAs in the Korean War. Here the Marines gather their dead after an ambush during the Chosin Reservoir withdrawal.
(Courtesy Lyndon Baines Johnson Library & Museum.)

and who were not repatriated in the POW exchange following the armistice agreement in July 1953.

Although the issue has been raised periodically at meetings of the Armistice Commission at Panmunjom, the CCF and NKPA have denied any knowledge of the whereabouts of these missing Americans for over three decades. A Korean War veteran's organization, The Chosin Few, has led the way in calling national attention to the plight of Korean War MIAs. Their MIA Chairman is Mr. Thomas Gregory, 3500 University Boulevard North, Jacksonville, Florida 32211. Telephone (904) 743-0627.

See POWs (PRISONERS OF WAR).

Suggestions for further reading: The most recent comprehensive examination of the Korean War MIA issue is Daniel Greene's three-part series, "Korean War's POW Mysteries," in the October 13, 20, 27, 1986 *Army Times*.

MILITARY INTELLIGENCE

During the Korean War, Military Intelligence organization and assets were a far cry from what they are today. In today's infantry divisions, for example, there is both a Military Intelligence (MI) Battalion and a battalion-level cavalry squadron for the collection and evaluation of battlefield intelligence; in the Korean War there was an attached 17-man Counter Intelligence Corps (CIC) detachment and a divisional reconnaissance *company*.

Military intelligence did not become one of the Army's formal branches of service (i.e., like the Infantry, Ordnance Corps or Signal Corps) until 10 years after the war ended; many intelligence personnel serving in S-2 or G-2 (chief intelligence officer) positions at battalion, regiment, division, corps and field Army level during the Korean War were untrained amateurs.

One significant intelligence shortfall was the lack of Korean and Chinese linguists within the military. When the war broke out, the G-2 of the Far East Command, Major General Charles Willoughby, had only two Korean linguists on his staff, and the Army had no training programs in these languages before the crisis erupted.

Through an intensive recruitment and training program this deficiency was soon overcome, however, and IPW (Interrogation of Prisoners of War) teams were soon active on the battlefield. POW interrogation became a primary source of battlefield intelligence—for example, the interrogation of North Korean People's Army (NKPA) Colonel Lee Hai Ku, Chief of Staff of the NKPA 13th Division (the highest ranking POW taken during the war), in September 1950. The October 27, 1950, interrogation of two Chinese POWs revealed that Chinese Communist Forces (CCF) had entered the war (unfortunately the revelation was dismissed by General Willoughby in Tokyo and the Eighth U.S. Army G-2, Lieutenant Colonel James C. Tarkenton, in the field).

POW interrogation became so critical that battalion-sized raiding parties were launched to capture enemy soldiers and special R&R (rest and recuperation) leaves to Japan were offered for any soldier capturing an enemy prisoner.

Another important source of tactical and operational intelligence was by ground patrolling and aerial overflight of enemy positions. Every unit along the MLR (main line of resistance) routinely sent out combat patrols to their front to find out what the enemy was up to, and extensive use was made of aerial reconnaissance. Air Force, Navy and Marine aerial photo reconnaissance operations are discussed elsewhere (*see* RECONNAISSANCE), but the Army used L-5 observation aircraft for both visual and photo reconnaissance, and each

POW interrogation was an important source of military intelligence during the Korean War.
(Courtesy Lyndon Baines Johnson Library & Museum.)

division G-2 section had their own photo inter-preters.

A final source of intelligence was communications intelligence. The operations of the Army Security Agency (ASA) (which would become the National Security Agency in 1952) was formed to provide communications security (i.e., provide friendly forces with codes and ciphers) and to oversee interception and monitoring of enemy radio and other electronic transmissions. The ASA did, however, play a significant role in the Korean War. In October 1950, the ASA's 60th Signal Service Company began operations in Korea and was later joined by the 501st Communications Reconnaissance Group, which directed three ASA battalions and five ASA companies. During the course of the war ASA units received 14 Meritorious Unit Citations and 14 Republic of Korea Presidential Unit Citations.

Military Intelligence during the Korean War is remembered chiefly in terms of its strategic intelligence failures—failure to predict the NKPA invasion of South Korea in June 1950 and failure to give warning of the CCF intervention in November 1950. But while Military Intelligence shares a portion of the blame, these were principally national level intelligence failures beyond the scope of Military Intelligence operations. Less well remembered are the operational and tactical successes of Military Intelligence—the warnings of impending enemy attack, the estimates of enemy order of battle, the protection from espionage and sabotage provided by the teams from the 441st CIC Detachment in Japan that were rushed to the battlefield in Korea and the technical intelligence analysis of enemy arms and equipment.

See also CENTRAL INTELLIGENCE AGENCY; DIRECTOR, CENTRAL INTELLIGENCE: RECONNAISSANCE; SMITH, WALTER BEDELL; SPECIAL OPERATIONS.

Suggestions for further reading: For an excellent analysis of strategic surprise, see Ephram Kam's *Surprise Attack: The Victim's Perspective* (Cambridge, Mass: Harvard University Press, 1988), which uses the NKPA invasion and the CCF intervention as cases in point. Another recent analysis of the CCF intervention is Eliot A. Cohen's "Only Half the Battle: American Intelligence and the Chinese Intervention in Korea, 1950," in Eliot A. Cohen and John Gooch, *Military Misfortunes* (New York: The Free Press, 1989). For Military Intelligence activities in the Korean War see John Patrick Finnegan, *Military Intelligence: A Picture History* (Arlington, Va.: History Office, U.S. Army Intelligence and Security Command, 1985). See also Clay Blair, *The Forgotten War: America in Korea 1950–1953* (New York Times Books, 1987).

MILITARY POLICE

Each Army division had an assigned military police (MP) company. In addition several separate MP companies and battalions were sent to Korea. Four MP missions proved especially critical: traffic control, refugee control, POW (prisoner of war) control and rear area security.

Given the inadequate road network in Korea, traffic control was essential for battlefield maneuver, that is, the shifting of combat divisions from one section of the line to another. MP traffic control points were established at road junctions and other critical points to ensure efficient traffic flow; these isolated outposts were often subject to enemy attack.

Another important MP task was refugee control. There were more than three million civilian refugees during the Korean War. Not only did Korean MPs set up checkpoints to screen these refugee columns so that they could not be used as a cover for infiltrating North Korean People's Army (NKPA) soldiers, but they also controlled the refugee flow so that it did not clog the main supply routes and delay essential military traffic. There was also the problem of POW control. In October 1951 the 8137th MP Groups was organized on Koje-Do island, with three assigned battalions and four additional escort guard companies, to control the enemy POWs there. This group was later reinforced by combat infantry units from the mainland.

The final MP mission was rear area security against North Korean infiltrators bent on sabotage and against the guerrilla bands left behind when the NKPA retreated from South Korea after the Inchon invasion in September 1950. This mission included stationary guard posts on key facilities as well as roving patrols armed with machine-guns and other light weapons.

See GUERRILLAS; INFILTRATION; POW (PRISONER OF WAR) CAMPS; RED BALL EXPRESS.

Suggestions for further reading: Captain John G. Westover, *Combat Support in Korea* (Washington, D.C.: Combat Forces Press, 1955).

MINESWEEPING

See BLOCKADE AND ESCORT FORCE, TASK FORCE 95; WONSAN.

A road sign marks the Main Line of Resistance (MLR).
(Courtesy U.S. Army Military History Institute.)

MLR (MAIN LINE OF RESISTANCE)

MLR was the military abbreviation for "main line of resistance"—that is, the location of the main battle lines or front lines. As it did in World War II (but unlike the later war in Vietnam), the MLR defined the battlefield. Everything in front of it was enemy territory (in effect, a free fire zone); everything behind it (except for some pockets of guerrilla resistance) was friendly. Success or failure was measured, not only by the military but by public opinion as well, by whether the MLR advanced or fell back.

During the maneuver warfare of the early days of the war—the withdrawl into the Naktong Perimeter and the later drive into North Korea—the MLR was fluid and changed frequently. But as the battlefield stabilized after

the spring of 1951, the MLR became relatively fixed, with interconnected battle positions stretching from one coast of Korea to the other. On both sides the MLR was fortified with bunkers, dugouts, barbed wire and minefields, and the battlefield came to resemble the trench warfare of World War I. Also as in World War I, terrible casualties resulted when attempts were made to pierce these virtually impregnable lines.

See also OPLR (OUTPOST LINE OF RESISTANCE).

MOBILIZATION

Without mobilization of its reserve military forces, the United States would have lost the Korean War. Its standing (i.e., active) military forces had been so deeply cut by President Harry S Truman and Defense Secretary Louis Johnson that they were no longer combat ready. The three Army divisions committed to initial combat—the First Cavalry Division and 24th and 25th Infantry divisions—had two rather than three maneuver battalions in their infantry regiments, two rather than three firing batteries in their supporting field artillery battalions, only one battery active in their anti-aircraft artillery battalions and only one light tank company per division rather than the three-company medium tank battalions they were authorized. By early August 1950, the Army's General Reserve (i.e., active forces in the United States available for reinforcement) had been stripped to the bone when the Second and Third Infantry divisions, the Fifth, 29th and 187th Regimental Combat teams and a number of individual tank and artillery battalions were committed to combat in Korea.

On July 27, 1950, Congress did authorize President Truman to extend for one year (the infamous "Year for Harry") those enlistments in the armed forces due to expire before July 9,

1951. However, the manpower pool would soon have run dry. In July 1950 the Selective Service system (which had been in a standby registration-only status) issued a call for 50,000 draftees to be inducted in September 1950; it was the end of the year before they finished basic training and were available as overseas replacement.

The Marine Corps was in even more desperate straits. When the war broke out, there were only 74,279 officers and men on active duty in the Marine Corps worldwide. The First Marine Division at Camp Pendleton had been cut so deeply that only its Fifth Marine Regiment was on active duty. When that regiment was shipped to Korea in July 1950 as the nucleus of the First Provisional Marine Brigade, other Marine units throughout the world were stripped to rebuild the First Marine Division, which had been earmarked for the Inchon invasion less than two months away. But active forces alone were insufficient to do the job.

While the manpower-intensive Army and Marine Corps were in the worst shape, the Air Force and Navy likewise would have found it impossible to meet the demands of combat with active forces alone. Fortunately, on June 30, 1950, the Congress (which alone has the Constitutional authority to raise military forces) passed the Selective Service Extension Act of 1950 (Public Law 599, 81st Congress). This act gave the president the authority to order units and individual members of the Organized Reserve Corps (ORC) and units of the National Guard of the United States (NGUS) into active federal service for a period of 21 months.

This call-up was especially dramatic for the Marine Corps, whose reserves were twice the size of its active force. On July 19, 1950, the decision was made to call the Organized Marine Corps Reserve to active duty immedi-ately and the Volunteer Marine Corps Reserve to active duty on August 15, 1950. By September 11, 1950, the ground force elements of the Organized Marine Corps Reserve had ceased to exist because 33,528 of its officers and men had reported for active service. Likewise, by March 31, 1951, the 90,044-man Volunteer Reserve had called 51,942 officers and enlisted personnel to active duty.

Ninety-nine percent of the reserve officers and 77.5% of the enlisted personnel were veterans of World War II. As the first reservists arriving at Camp Pendleton on July 31, 1950, 2,891 were immediately incorporated into the First Marine Division (most into its First Marine Regiment), which sailed for Korea on August 10 to 22, 1950, and made the amphibious assault at Inchon on September 15, 1950. Of the Marines that made the Inchon invasion, 17% were reservists. Another 1,972 reservists were incorporated into the division's Seventh Marine Regiment, which was activated on August 17, 1950, representing more than 50% of that regiment's strength. On September 1, 1950, it too sailed for Korea, landing at Inchon on September 21, 1950.

In addition to ground force elements, 6,341 men of the aviation units of the Organized Marine Corps Reserve were also mobilized, although on a somewhat slower schedule. By January 1951, 30 of its units had been activated, and by October 1951 all were on active duty, including their 30 Marine fighter squadrons. Although not as dramatic, the Navy too made extensive use of its reserve forces. On July 25, 1950, for example, the chief of naval operations ordered the call to active duty of the aircraft carrier USS *Princeton*, then in mothballs at Bremerton, Washington. Recommissioned on August 28, 1950, with a largely reservist crew, it sailed for Korean waters on November 27, 1950. The carriers *Bon Homme Richard, Essex* and *Antietam* followed in 1951. During the war some 22 Naval Reserve fighter squadrons were embarked with the Seventh Fleet Striking Force and flew combat missions over Korea.

Described by Air Force Chief of Staff General Hoyt S. Vandenberg as a "shoestring Air Force" at the beginning of the war, the active Air Force had also suffered from Truman's ill-conceived budget cuts. Unable to meet Far East Air Force's (FEAF) urgent calls for more F-80 Shooting Star jet fighters and F-82 Twin Mustang all-weather fighters, the immediate response was to recall 145 F-51 Mustangs from the Air National Guard and rush them to Korea.

Soon thereafter the Air Force Reserve's 437th Troop Carrier Wing and 452d Bombardment Wing (Light), and later the 403d Troop Carrier Wing, were called to active service and sent to the Far East. In 1951 the Air National Guard's 116th and 136th Fighter-Bomber Wings were also sent to the Far East and remained there until July 1952, when their active service commitment expired. During the Korean War the Air Force mobilized 22 wings of the Air National Guard and 10 wings of the Air Force Reserve and more than 100,000 individual Air Force reservists.

In the Army, the call-up of the National Guard and Army Reserve was also a lifesaver. When the war began, the Army had 591,487 men and women on active duty with an additional 324,761 personnel organized into 4,883 units in the Army National Guard. Also organized into 934 units were the 184,015 personnel of the Active Reserve. Two Army Reserve manpower pools also existed, the inactive 324,602-man Volunteer Reserve and the 91,800-man Inactive Reserve.

Beginning August 14, 1950, 1,457 Army National Guard (ARNG) units were mobilized, including eight of the 27 ARNG divisions—the 28th, 31st, 37th, 40th, 43d, 44th, 45th and 47th Infantry divisions—as well as three of the ARNG's 20 Regimental Combat teams and 43 Antiaircraft Artillery battalions. In all, 138,600 officers and men of the ARNG were federalized: i.e., called from state to federal service.

Two of the federalized ARNG divisions (the 40th and 45th Infantry divisions) were sent to Korea, two (the 28th and 43d Infantry divisions) were sent to bolster NATO defenses in Europe, and the remaining four became U.S.-based training divisions and sources of individual replacements for units in Korea.

In the initial 1950 mobilization, the Army Reserve called 934 of its 6,687 units to active service as well as 46,920 officers and 150,807 enlisted personnel (of which 41,424 officers and 121,500 enlisted personnel were recalled as individual fillers and replacement). During the entire course of the war the Army Reserve contributed a total of 244,300 officers and men, not including 43,000 Reserve officers who were on active duty at the war's beginning.

The most controversial aspect of the reserve call-ups was that the majority were from the unpaid and untrained inactive and volunteer reserves (most of whom were World War II veterans) rather than from the active reserve, which had been participating in paid drill periods. Because the most pressing need was for individual replacements to flesh out existing skeletonized units and to replace combat losses, the inactive reserve manpower pools were the first to be mobilized. Most active reserve units were left intact, to be called only if the war intensified or spread to Europe.

For example, on August 10, 1950, the Army recalled 7,862 male Reserve company-grade (that is, captains and lieutenants) of the Volunteer and Inactive reserves to serve involuntarily as platoon leaders and company commanders in Korea and several months later recalled an additional 10,000 company-grade officers. Also in August 1950, 1,063 Army Medical Service officers were recalled to serve involuntarily as were 109,000 trained enlisted specialists. But while many of these recalled reservists may have been disgruntled, the inequity of the call-up did not affect their combat performance. During the first year of the war Army reservists won six of the 27 Medals of Honor awarded to that time, as well as one-fourth of all other top combat decorations.

See DRAFT; 40TH INFANTRY DIVISION; 45TH INFANTRY DIVISION.

Suggestions for further reading: For Army reserve mobilization see James F. Schnabel, *U.S. Army in the Korean War: Policy and Direction: The First Year* (Washington, D.C.: GPO, 1972) and especially Colonels John D. Stuckey and Joseph H. Pistorious, *Mobilization of the Army National Guard and Army Reserve: Historical Perspective and the Vietnam War* (Carlisle Barracks, PA: Strategic Studies Institute, U.S. Army War College, November 15, 1984). For Navy mobilization see James A. Field, *History of United States Naval Operations: Korea* (Washington, D.C.: GPO, 1962). See also Commanders Malcolm W. Cagle and Frank A. Manson, USN, *The Sea War in Korea* (Annapolis, Md: United States Naval Institute, 1957). For Air Force mobilization see Robert F. Futrell, *The United States Air Force in Korea: 1950–1953*, revised edition (Washington, D.C.: GPO, 1983). For Marine Corps mobilization see Lynn Montross and Captain Nicholas A. Canzona, USMC, *U.S. Marine Operations in Korea 1950-1953:* volume 2, *The Inchon-Seoul Operation*, 1955; and Lieutenant Colonel Pat Meid, USMCR, and Major James M. Yingling, USMC, *U.S. Marine Operations in Korea*: volume 5, *Operations in West Korea*, 1972 (Washington, D.C.: GPO).

MORTARS

Mortars are high-angle fire weapons, making them particularly suitable for Korea's mountainous terrain. Every U.S. rifle company was authorized three 60-mm mortars, every in-fantry battalion three 81-mm mortars and every infantry regiment a six-tube section of 4.2-inch (107-mm) heavy mortars. In addition there were the three 4.2-inch heavy mortar companies of the U.S. Second Chemical Mortar Battalion as well as the mortars of the other United Nations ground forces, such as the 3-inch mortars organic to units of the British Commonwealth Forces.

The North Korean People's Army (NKPA) and Chinese Communist Forces (CCF) were equally well equipped, with 61-mm mortars at the company level, 8-mm mortars at the battalion level and 120-mm mortars at the regimental level. Note that in the case of the 61-mm and 82-mm weapons the tubes were slightly larger than the U.S. equivalents, which meant that the NKPA and CCF could fire captured U.S. ammunition; their ammunition, however, was too large to be fired by U.S. mortars.

See also CHEMICAL MORTARS; FIELD ARTILLERY.

MSR (MAIN SUPPLY ROUTE)

MSR was the military abbreviation for "main supply route," that is, the main road leading from the supply depots in the rear to the front-line positions. Because the road network in Korea was so limited, MSRs became critically important. The major portion of the Eight U.S. Army withdrawal from North Korea in the winter of 1950, for example, was over a single road.

See also ENGINEERS; MILITARY POLICE; RED BALL EXPRESS.

MSTS (MILITARY SEA TRANSPORT SERVICE)

Established as a unified logistic organization by the National Security Act of 1947, the Military Sea Transport Service (MSTS) was ac-

KMAG Advisor and, right, his interpreter instruct a ROK Army 60-mm mortar crew.
(Courtesy U.S. Army Military History Institute.)

tually created in October 1949. At that time it absorbed the old Naval Transportation Service and the shops and seagoing functions of the Army Transportation Corps, which previously had operated most of the troops ships used to transport soldiers overseas.

MSTS consisted of commercially chartered vessels, Navy-manned (USS) and civil-service manned (USNS) transport and cargo ships, and the oil tankers of the Defense Department's Military Petroleum Supply Agency. In addition it controlled the SCAJAP (Shipping Control Administration Japan) fleet of 12 freighters and 39 LSTs (Landing Ship Tanks), which proved to be an especially valuable shipping asset.

Time-distance factors were critical in the Korean War. The ocean distance between San Francisco and Pusan is 4,914 nautical miles, and from Panama to Pusan 8,086 nautical miles. The transcontinental air age was still decades away, and most troops and supplies moved to Korea by sea. Even the 187th Airborne Regimental Combat Team moved to Korea by troop ship. They sailed from Camp Stoneman, California (the military port of embarkation for San Francisco), on September 6, 1950, and did not arrive in Japan until September 20, 1950.

From June 1950 to June 1953, MSTS moved 52,111,299 measurement tons of cargo; 21,828,879 long tons of petroleum; and

4,918,919 passengers to, from and within the Far East.

See MATS (MILITARY AIR TRANSPORT SERVICE).

Suggestions for further reading: James A. Field, *History of United States Naval Operations: Korea* (Washington, D.C.: GPO, 1962). See also Commanders Malcolm W. Cagle and Frank A. Manson, USN, *The Sea War in Korea* (Annapolis, Md: United States Naval Institute, 1957).

MUCCIO, JOHN J(OSEPH) (1900–)

A naturalized American whose parents emigrated from Italy when he was a child, John J. Muccio was appointed a State Department Foreign Service officer in November 1923. From 1926 to 1935 he held a variety of consular posts in Hong Kong, Foochow and Shanghai. After service in Latin America during World War II, Muccio became assistant to Robert Murphy, U.S. political adviser to Germany, in 1945. In July 1947 he was named Foreign Service inspector and in August 1948 was sent to Korea as the personal representative of the president.

In April 1949, Muccio became the first American ambassador to the Republic of Korea (ROK); he served in that post until November 1952. Before the war Muccio's major concerns were the allegations of corruption, mismanagement and misrule on the part of the ROK government and ROK President Syngman Rhee. Replaced by Ellis O. Briggs in November 1952 after the U.S. presidential elections, Muccio was reassigned to the United Nations Trusteeship Council. After later service as ambassador to Iceland and as ambassador to Guatemala, he retired from the Foreign Service in 1961.

See AMBASSADOR TO THE REPUBLIC OF KOREA, U.S.

Suggestions for further reading: See biographic entry in *Political Profiles: The Truman Years*, Eleanora W. Schoenebaum, editor (New York: Facts On File, 1978).

MULE TRAIN

See KOREAN SERVICE CORPS (KSC).

MUSTANG

Navy term for an officer raised from the enlisted ranks. Also the name of the F-51 Mustang fighter plane.

See FIGHTER AND FIGHTER-BOMBER AIRCRAFT.

N

NAKTONG PERIMETER, BATTLE OF

Also known as the "Pusan Perimeter," the Naktong Perimeter battle was the name given to Eighth U.S. Army's (EUSA) initial defense of the Republic of Korea. Beginning on July 5, 1950, when Task Force Smith attempted to slow the North Korean People's Army (NKPA) blitzkrieg at Osan, the battle continued through the fighting withdrawal from Chonan to Taejon to the Kum River, and the withdrawal into the Naktong Perimeter itself on August 1 to 4, 1950. The battle ended on September 16, 1950, when EUSA broke out of the perimeter and went on the offensive following the Inchon invasion farther to the north.

Named for the Naktong River, which formed a major portion of its western boundary, the perimeter stretched some 100 miles from north to south and about 50 miles from east to west. Encompassing the major port city of Pusan, which was in its southeast corner, the perimeter was bounded by the Straits of Korea to the south, the Sea of Japan to the east, the Naktong River to its west (except for the southernmost 15 miles when the river turns eastward) and an irregular line to the north through the mountains above Waegwan to the Sea of Japan at Yongdok. Major battlegrounds along the perimeter included the "Naktong Bulge" in the Masan area in the southwest corner of the perimeter; the Waegwan area and the "bowling alley" in front of Taegu in the center of the line; and Pohang on the northern front.

Units involved in the Naktong Perimeter battles included the U.S. Army's First Cavalry Division, Second Infantry Division, 24th Infantry Division and 25th Infantry Division; the U.S. Marine Corps' First Provisional Marine Brigade; the 27th British Brigade; and the eight divisions of the Republic of Korea (ROK) Army. Air support was provided by Fifth Air Force fighters flying primarily from air bases in Japan, which were less than 200 air miles away, and by Navy and Marine fighters flying from aircraft carriers offshore. On the enemy side, the NKPA mustered some 13 divisions, with the NKPA I Corps' six divisions opposite the Masan front on the southwest of the Naktong River Line tying in with the NKPA II Corps' seven divisions which stretched farther to the northwest opposite Waegwan and to the north.

Initially EUSA was hard pressed because the NKPA seemed to be attacking everywhere at once. On July 29, 1950, the EUSA commander, Lieutenant General Walton H. Walker, made his controversial "stand or die" statement to stiffen U.S. resolve, and for a while the situation was desperate. But a month and a half later the culminating point of the NKPA blitzkrieg had been reached and the tide had turned in favor of EUSA. On the eve of the Inchon invasion, September 15, 1950, enemy forces besieging the

Superior U.S. firepower helped hold the Naktong Perimeter. Here a 155-mm howitzer from the 11th Field Artillery fires at attacking North Korean forces, August 1950.
(Courtesy U.S. Army Military History Institute.)

perimeter stood at about 70,000 men, while within the perimeter EUSA had gathered some 84,478 soldiers and the ROK Army had 72,730 men under arms. Between September 16 and 22, 1950, EUSA attacked outward from the Naktong Perimeter and linked up with X Corps forces at Osan on September 26, 1950. The NKPA collapsed in disarray, and only some 20,000 to 30,000 disorganized NKPA troops reached North Korea after the UN breakout.

From the first U.S. ground force engagement of the war by Task Force Smith at Osan on July 5, 1950, to the breakout from the Naktong Perimeter on September 16, 1950, EUSA suffered 19,165 casualties, of whom 4,280 were killed in action, 12,377 were wounded, 401

were reported captured and 2,107 were missing in action. The price was high, but EUSA's delaying actions and its stubborn defense of the Naktong Perimeter saved the Republic of Korea from certain conquest by the advancing NKPA forces after the June 28, 1950, fall of Seoul and the collapse of the ROK Army.

See Individual listings for units involved; TAEJON, BATTLE OF; TASK FORCE SMITH; YECHON, BATTLE OF.

Suggestions for further reading: See See *U.S. Army in the Korean War* series: Roy A. Appleman, *South to the Naktong, North to the Yalu,* 1961; and Lynn Montross and Captain Nicholas A. Canzona, USMC, *U.S. Marine Operations in Korea 1950–1953: The Pusan Perimeter,* 1954 (Washington,

D.C.: GPO). One of the most detailed accounts of Naktong Perimeter battles is Dr. William Glenn Robertson's *Leavenworth Paper Number 13: Counterattack on the Naktong, 1950* (Washington, D.C.: GPO, December 1985). See also Clay Blair, *The Forgotten War: America in Korea 1950–1953* (New York Times Books, 1987).

NAPALM

An acronym derived from *na*phthenic and *pal*mitic acids, whose salts are used in its manufacture, napalm is a jellied gasoline used in flame throwers, fougasses and aerial bombs. According to the Eighth U.S. Army chemical officer at the time, the aerial bombs were plastic, made in Japan, cost $40.00 each and held 90 to 100 gallons, depending on the type. The normal bomb load was two tanks of gasoline and two tanks of napalm. On an average day the Air Force used 45,000 gallons, the Navy 10,000 and the Marines 4,000 to 5,000 gallons.

Napalm proved very effective against tanks and against enemy trench lines, bunkers and other dug-in enemy personnel. During the course of the war Far East Air Force alone expended 32,357 *tons* of napalm.

Suggestions for further reading: Robert F. Futrell, *The United States Air Force in Korea: 1950–1953*, revised edition (Washington, D.C.: GPO, 1983). "Napalm Bombs in Korea" in Captain John G. Westover, *Combat Support in Korea* (Washington, D.C.: Combat Forces Press, 1955).

NATIONAL DEFENSE SERVICE MEDAL

The National Defense Service Medal was authorized by Presidential Executive Order 10448 to recognize one or more days honorable service in the Armed Forces of the United States during the period June 27, 1950, through July 27, 1954. Although one had to actually serve in Korea to be eligible for the Korean Service Medal or the United Nations Service Medal, one only had to serve on active duty to be eligible for the National Defense Service Medal. The National Defense Service Medal was later authorized for similar service during the Vietnam War era.

See also SERVICE MEDALS, U.S.

NATIONAL GUARD

See MOBILIZATION; 40TH INFANTRY DIVISION; 45TH INFANTRY DIVISION.

NATIONAL SECURITY COUNCIL

Created by the National Security Act of 1947, the Korean War National Security Council (NSC) consisted of the president, the vice president, the secretary of state, the secretary of defense and, as advisers only, the director of the Central Intelligence Agency and the chairman of the Joint Chiefs of Staff.

In those days the NSC staff was just that—a staff that served the administrative and clerical needs of the principals. Not until after the Korean War did President Dwight Eisenhower create the post of national security advisor to coordinate staff activities, a position that evolved into the present-day assistant to the president for national security affairs.

NAVAL FORCES FAR EAST (NAVFE)

When the Korean War began on June 25, 1950, Naval Forces Far East (NAVFE), the naval component of General Headquarters, Far East Command (FECOM), was largely a housekeeping command. Its Task Force 90, Amphibious Force Far East, was the nucleus of an amphibious force; its Task Force 96, Naval Forces Japan, had a small number of warships assigned. In the Philippines, 1,700 miles to the south, was the Seventh Fleet under the opera-

The battleship USS *Missouri* fires a 16-inch salvo at the enemy to cut lines of communication along North Korea's east coast.
(Courtesy U.S. Army Military History Institute.)

tional command of the commander in chief, U.S. Pacific Fleet, in Honolulu, Hawaii. In addition, there were British and Australian Royal Navy warships in Far East waters.

In organizing for combat, NAVFE was given operational control of the Seventh Fleet on June 27, 1950, and on June 29, 1950, British Commonwealth naval forces were also placed under its control. On July 10, 1950, FECOM was designated as the United Nations Command (UNC), and NAVFE became its naval component. Then, on July 14, 1950, the Republic of Korea (ROK) placed its armed forces under UNC control, and NAVFE assumed operational control of ROK Navy forces.

For most of the war, NAVFE had four major combat commands. First was Task Force 77, the Seventh Fleet Striking Force, whose fast carriers operated chiefly in the Sea of Japan off Korea's eastern coast. Next was Task Force 95, the Blockading and Escort Force, which included an Allied navy task group operating

primarily in the Yellow Sea off Korea's western coast, an east coast task group, a minesweeping group and a ROK navy task group. Then there was Task Force 90, the Amphibious Force Far East, which conducted the Inchon invasion and the Hungnam evacuation. Finally, there was Task Force 96, Naval Forces Japan, which provided antisubmarine protection and security for U.S. bases in Japan. The NAVFE commander not only served as the principal naval adviser to the commander in chief, Far East Command/United Nations Command, he also coordinated the Military Sea Transport Service (MSTS) intertheater sea lift between the Zone of Interior (i.e., the United States mainland) and the Far East, and the intratheater sea lift between Japan and Korea.

NAVFE was initially commanded by Vice Admiral C. Turner Joy from August 26, 1949, to June 4, 1952. When he was named as the United States delegate to the armistice talks at Kaesong and then Panmunjom, he was replaced by Vice Admiral Robert P. Briscoe, who served for the remainder of the war in the position.

During the course of the war, U.S. naval air (including land-based Marine air) flew some 275,912 sorties and dropped 178,390 tons of bombs, fired 274,189 air-to-ground rockets and over 71 million rounds of ammunition. These air strikes killed 86,262 enemy troops, destroyed 44,828 buildings, 391 locomotives, 5,896 rail cars, 7,437 vehicles, 2,005 bridges, 249 tanks, 33 power plants, 1,900 supply dumps and 2,464 enemy vessels.

Adding to this total, U.S. warships fired over four million rounds of ammunition (from 16-inch to small arms) at the enemy, destroying 3,334 buildings, 824 vessels and small craft, 14 locomotives, 214 trucks, 15 tanks, 108 bridges and 93 supply dumps, and inflicting 28,566 enemy casualties.

See ACES; AIRCRAFT CARRIERS; AMPHIBIOUS FORCES FAR; BLOCKADE AND

A shore party examines the crater from one of the USS *Missouri*'s 16-inch shells.
(Courtesy U.S. Army Military History Institute.)

ESCORT FORCE; BRISCOE, ROBERT P.; JOY, C. TURNER; NAVY, U.S.; SEVENTH FLEET STRIKING FORCE; UNITED NATIONS NAVAL FORCES.

Suggestions for further reading: James A. Field, *History of United States Naval Operations: Korea* (Washington, D.C.: GPO, 1962). See also Commanders Malcolm W. Cagle and Frank A. Manson, USN, *The Sea War in Korea* (Annapolis, Md: United States Naval Institute, 1957); Richard P. Hallion, *The Naval Air War in Korea* (Baltimore: The Nautical & Aviation Publishing Company of America, 1986).

NAVAL GUNFIRE SUPPORT

See BLOCKADE AND ESCORT FORCE.

NAVY CROSS

First authorized in World War I, the Navy Cross, along with the Distinguished Service Cross (and Air Force Cross after 1960), is America's second highest award for bravery. During the Korean War it was awarded in the name of the president of the United States by the U.S. Navy and Marine Corps for extraordinary heroism, not justifying the award of the Medal of Honor, while engaged in an action against the enemy. The act or acts of heroism had to have been so notable and have involved risk of life so extraordinary as to set the individual apart from his comrades. Subsequent awards were denoted by a gold star worn on the ribbon.

See also DISTINGUISHED SERVICE CROSS.

NAVY, NORTH KOREA/COMMUNIST CHINA

Neither North Korean nor Communist Chinese naval forces posed a significant threat to United Nations forces during the Korean War. North Korea began the war with some 45 small craft, including a few aluminum-hulled Russian torpedo boats. On July 2, 1950, just south of the 38th parallel off Korea's east coast, there occurred the first and last surface naval engagement of the war. Two cruisers—HMS *Jamaica* and the USS *Juneau*—and the frigate HMS *Black Swan* engaged North Korean naval forces and sunk three torpedo boats and two motor gunboats, and took two prisoners.

While North Korean/Chinese ships did not pose a threat, their use of naval mines was another matter. During the course of the war five U.S. warships—four minesweepers and one ocean-going tug—were sunk by mines, and another five destroyers were damaged (*see* BLOCKADE AND ESCORT FORCE, TASK FORCE 95).

See also NAVY, U.S.; UNITED NATIONS NAVAL FORCES.

Suggestions for further reading: James A. Field, *History of United States Naval Operations: Korea* (Washington, D.C.: GPO, 1962). See also Commanders Malcolm W. Cagle and Frank A. Manson, USN, *The Sea War in Korea* (Annapolis, Md: United States Naval Institute, 1957); Richard P. Hallion, *The Naval Air War in Korea* (Baltimore: The Nautical & Aviation Publishing Company of America, 1986).

NAVY, UNITED NATIONS

See UNITED NATIONS NAVAL FORCES.

NAVY, U.S.

Geography alone dictated that the U.S. Navy play a major role in the war in Korea. Korea, a peninsula surrounded on three sides by water, was vulnerable to naval operations. Because Korea is located 4,914 nautical miles away from the United States on the far side of the Pacific Ocean, sea control for the movement of personnel, arms, equipment and supplies was placed at a premium.

During the war the Navy deployed a large number of aircraft carriers, battleships, cruisers, destroyers, minesweepers and other warships to Korean waters. Major operations included the Inchon invasion, the Hungnam evacuation, the interdiction of enemy lines of communication and supply, and the close support of ground operations with both air power and naval gunfire support. In addition, the Military Sea Transport Service (MSTS) moved 52,111,209 measurement tons of cargo, 21,828,879 long tons of petroleum and 4,918,919 passengers to, from and within the Far East.

Among other decorations and awards, seven Medals of Honor were awarded to Navy personnel for conspicuous bravery in action in Korea. During the course of the war, 73 Navy ships were damaged by fire from enemy shore batteries or were struck by mines, and four minesweepers and one ocean-going tug were sunk by enemy mines. Of the more than 5,720,000 Americans who served in the armed forces between June 25, 1950 and July 27, 1953, 1,842,000 were Navy personnel. Of these sailors, 458 were killed in action; 4,043 died of illness, injury or disease; and 1,576 were wounded in action.

See ACES; AIRCRAFT CARRIERS; AMPHIBIOUS FORCES FAR EAST; BLOCKADE AND ESCORT FORCE; HUNGNAM EVACUATION; INCHON INVASION; MOBILIZATION; NAVAL FORCES FAR EAST; SEVENTH FLEET STRIKING FORCE.

Korea's more than 5,000-mile coastline made it vulnerable to American sea power. Here the heavy cruiser USS *Helena* fires her 8-inch guns at enemy installations ashore.
(Courtesy U.S. Army Military History Institute.)

Suggestions for further reading: James A. Field, *History of United States Naval Operations: Korea* (Washington, D.C.: GPO, 1962). See also Commanders Malcolm W. Cagle and Frank A. Manson, USN, *The Sea War in Korea* (Annapolis, Md: United States Naval Institute, 1957); Richard P. Hallion, *The Naval Air War in Korea* (Baltimore: The Nautical & Aviation Publishing Company of America, 1986).

NETHERLANDS

The Netherlands furnished both naval and ground forces to the war in Korea. At sea was the destroyer HMNS *Evertsen*, which served with the Blockading and Escort Force of the U.S. Naval Forces Far East. On land was the Netherlands Battalion (better known as the "Dutch Battalion"), which arrived in Korea in the fall of 1950. Attached to the Second U.S. Infantry Division, it first saw action at Wonju on February 12 to 13, 1951, where it helped repulse a major Chinese attack. The battalion commander, Marinus P.A. den Ouden, who was killed in action, was among the 100 casualties suffered by the unit in that battle. For its bravery at Wonju the Netherlands Battalion was awarded the U.S. Presidential Unit Citation. In a later battle in May 1951 its new battalion commander, W.D.H. Eekhout, was also killed in action. At its peak strength in 1953, there were 819 Dutch soldiers serving with the Netherlands Battalion in Korea.

Casualty figures for Netherlands forces alone are not available, but during the course of the war the United Nations ground forces of

Belgium, Colombia, Ethiopia, France, Greece, the Netherlands, the Philippines, Thailand and Turkey combined lost 1,800 soldiers killed in action and another 7,000 wounded in action. Three Dutch soldiers were repatriated during the prisoner of war exchanges at the end of the war. *See* UNITED NATIONS GROUND FORCES; UNITED NATIONS NAVAL FORCES.

NEW ZEALAND

New Zealand furnished both naval and ground forces to the war in Korea. At sea were the frigates RNZS *Pukaki* and *Tutira*, which operated with the U.S. Naval Command Far East's Blockading and Escort Force, chiefly in the Yellow Sea. On land was the 16th New Zealand Field Artillery, which fought as part of the British Commonwealth Brigade (later the First British Commonwealth Division). At their peak strength in 1953, there were 1,389 New Zealanders serving with the ground forces in Korea. While exact casualty figures for New Zealand alone are not available, during the course of the war 1,263 British Commonwealth soldiers, sailor, airmen and marines were killed in action, and another 4,817 wounded in action. One New Zealander was among those repatriated during the during the prisoner of war exchange following the end of the war. *See also* BRITISH COMMONWEALTH DIVISION; UNITED NATIONS GROUND FORCES; UNITED NATIONS NAVAL FORCES.

Suggestions for further reading: C.N. Barclay, *The First Commonwealth Division: The Story of British Commonwealth Land Forces in Korea, 1950–1953* (Aldershot, UK: Gale & Polden, 1954); Tim Carew, *Korea: The Commonwealth at War* (London: Cassell, 1967); James L. Stokesbury, *A Short History of the Korean War* (New York: Morrow, 1988); Max Hastings, *The Korean War* (New York: Simon & Schuster, 1987).

IX (NINTH) CORPS

IX Corps had seen service in the Asiatic-Pacific theater during World War II. Until it was disbanded on March 28, 1950, as an "economy measure," the corps had controlled the First Cavalry Division and Seventh Infantry Division from its headquarters in Sendai as part of the American occupation of Japan.

Reactivated in response to an urgent request from the U.S. Far East Command (FECOM), on August 10, 1950, IX Corps was formed at Fort Sheridan, Illinois, from cadres provided by the Fifth U.S. Army headquarters there; the corps headquarters, along with the 101st Signal Battalion (only recently called to active duty from the Army Reserve), was ordered to Korea. The corps commander and his staff arrived by air on September 5, 1950, and the rest of the corps arrived by sea in late September and early October 1950. At 1400 hours, September 23, 1950, at the village of Miryang in the Naktong Perimeter, the IX Corps officially became operational. IX Corps would hence serve as one of the Eighth U.S. Army's (EUSA) major battlefield control headquarters throughout the remainder of the war. Like all corps organizations, it had no fixed combat structure. Depending on the tactical situation, IX Corps might command a number of corps artillery battalions as well as several U.S. and Republic of Korea Army (ROKA) infantry division.

Initially commanded by Lieutenant General Frank W. "Shrimp" Milburn, who brought it to Korea, on September 11, 1950, command of IX Corps passed to Lieutenant General John R. Coulter, who had just brought I Corps to Korea. General Coulter led the corps in the breakout from the Naktong Perimeter, the advance into North Korea and the subsequent retreat. In January 1951 he was replaced by Major General Bryant E. Moore. When Moore died of a heart attack on February 24, 1951, Lieutenant General William M. Hoge took command of IX

Corps. General Hoge was succeeded in turn by Lieutenant General Willard G. Wyman. On August 9, 1952, he too was replaced. Major General Reugen E. Jenkins commanded IX Corps for the remainder of the war.

For its services in Korea IX Corps was awarded two Republic of Korea Presidential Unit Citations. Since the end of the Korean War it has remained on active duty as a standby headquarters and is now stationed at Camp Zama in Japan.
See CORPS; X CORPS; ORGANIZATION FOR COMBAT.

Suggestions for further reading: See *U.S. Army in the Korean War* series: Roy A. Appleman, *South to the Naktong, North to the Yalu*, 1961; Walter G. Hermes, *Truce Tent and Fighting Front*, 1966; James F. Schnabel, *Policy and Direction: The First Year*, 1972; and Billy C. Mossman, *Ebb and Flow*, anticipated in 1990 (Washington, D.C.: GPO). For order of battle see Shelby Stanton, *Korean War Order of Battle* (Washington, D.C.: GPO, anticipated 1990). See also Clay Blair, *The Forgotten War: America in Korea 1950–1953* (New York Times Books, 1987).

NORTH KOREA (DEMOCRATIC PEOPLE'S REPUBLIC OF KOREA [DPRK])

See PART I: THE SETTING; KIM IL-SUNG; NORTH KOREAN PEOPLE'S ARMY.

NORTH KOREAN AIR FORCES (NKAF)

When the Korean War began the North Koreans had about 180 Russian-built planes, including 40 Soviet World War II vintage propeller-driven Yakovlev (YAK) fighters, 60 YAK trainers, 70 Ilyushin Shturmovik IL-10 and Lavochkin LA-9 fighter-bombers, and 10 reconnaissance aircraft, including 25-year-old Polikarpov PO-2 biplanes.

Commanded by Major General Wang Yong, a Soviet Air Academy graduate and World War II bomber pilot, this propeller-driven air force was far superior to that of the Republic of Korea. In the first month of the war North Korean YAK-9 fighters strafed Kimpo airfield and elements of the U.S. 19th Infantry Regiment at Chongju on July 10, 1950. The YAK fighters attacked three U.S. F-80s on July 11 and shot down a U.S. B-29 bomber and an L-4 liaison plane on July 12. On July 15 they attacked a formation of four B-26 bombers and damaged one so extensively it had to make an emergency landing.

Counterattacks on North Korean airfields by planes of the Fifth Air Force and the Navy's Task Force 77, and better coordination of U.S. fighter-interceptors, led to the almost complete destruction of the North Korean Air Force; after July 20, 1950, the United States had virtual air supremacy over all of Korea. Except for sporadic attacks—on August 23, 1950, for example, two YAK fighters attacked and damaged a British destroyer off the west coast of Korea—and harassing attacks by PO-2 "Bedcheck Charlies," the main air threat for the remainder of the war came from the Chinese rather than from the North Koreans.
See also BEDCHECK CHARLIES; CHINESE COMMUNIST AIR FORCE.

Suggestions for further reading: See Robert F. Futrell, *The United States Air Force in Korea: 1950–1953*, revised edition (Washington, D.C.: GPO, 1983); Richard P. Hallion, *The Naval Air War in Korea* (Baltimore: The Nautical & Aviation Publishing Company of America, 1986).

NORTH KOREAN PEOPLE'S ARMY (NKPA)

In June 1950, when they launched their cross-border invasion of South Korea, the so-called North Korean People's Army (NKPA), or *In*

Min Gun, consisted of some 135,000 men (including 18,6700 in the Border Constabulary) organized into an Army headquarters, I and II corps headquarters, seven assault infantry divisions, three reserve divisions, a tank brigade, an independent infantry regiment and a motorcycle regiment.

About one-third of these personnel had served in combat with Chinese Communist Forces (CCF) during World War II against the Japanese or during the Chinese civil war against the Chinese Nationalists. After the CCF victory in 1949, they had been repatriated to Korea and formed substantial portions of the NKPA's Fifth, Sixth and Seventh divisions.

Like U.S. divisions of that period, the NKPA divisions were triangular. Each division had three rifle regiments, which in turn had three rifle battalions. Division artillery included twelve 122-mm howitzers, twenty-four 76-mm guns, 12 SU-76 self-propelled guns, twelve 45-mm antitank guns and thirty-six 14.5-mm antitank rifles. In addition to antitank weapons, each regiment had six 120-mm mortars, each battalion had nine 82-mm mortars and rifle companies had their own 61-mm mortars.

At full strength in both men and equipment when they began the war, the NKPA had a series of initial battlefield successes. But they soon tore themselves to pieces in their head-on assaults on the Pusan Perimeter during July and August 1950. When the Inchon invasion in September 1950 cut their lines of communication and supply, they began to disintegrate. It appears no more than 25,000 to 30,000 disorganized North Korea soldiers reached North Korea from the Pusan Perimeter. For all practical purposes, the NKPA had been destroyed.

But when the CCF entered the war in November 1950, they gave the NKPA a new lease on life. Behind the shield provided by the CCF armies, the NKPA was eventually reconstituted. By July 1951 their strength had increased to some 211,100 troops organized into seven corps and 23 divisions, however, they were still deficient in artillery and armor. By 1952, under cover of the truce talks, these deficiencies had been corrected. When the truce agreement was reached in July 1953, the 260,000 strong NKPA was once again a formidable force.

Throughout the war the NKPA was under the personal command of Marshal (and North Korean Premier) Kim Il-sung. He exercised that command through a Soviet-style "front" headquarters, which was roughly equivalent to an American field army or a Chinese Communist Forces (CCF) army group headquarters. Although he was ostensibly in command of the CCF "volunteers" in Korea, it is more likely that Chinese Marshal Peng Teh-huai received his orders from Peking rather than Pyongyang.

See also ARMOR; CORPS; DIVISIONS; FIELD ARTILLERY; INFANTRY; KIM IL-SUNG; MORTARS; NORTH KOREA; NORTH KOREAN AIR FORCE; PENG TEH-HUAI.

Suggestions for further reading: See *U.S. Army in the Korean War* series: Roy A. Appleman, *South to the Naktong, North to the Yalu*, 1961; Walter G. Hermes, *Truce Tent and Fighting Front*, 1966; and Billy C. Mossman, *Ebb and Flow*, anticipated in 1990 (Washington, D.C.: GPO). See also Clay Blair, *The Forgotten War: America in Korea 1950–1953* (New York Times Books, 1987).

NUCLEAR WEAPONS

See ATOMIC WEAPONS.

OAK LEAF CLUSTER

In the U.S. Army and Air Force a metallic oak leaf cluster is worn on the ribbon of a medal to denote subsequent awards of the same decoration. Subsequent awards for U.S. Navy and Marine Corps personnel are denoted by a metallic gold star.

OKINAWA

A 451-square-mile island in the Western Pacific Ryukyus Island chain, which lies southeast of the home Japanese islands and northeast of Taiwan, Okinawa was occupied by the United States after World War II and administered by the U.S. Ryukyus Command. It did not revert to Japanese control until May 15, 1972.

When the Korean War began, the U.S. Army's 29th Infantry Regimental Combat Team was stationed on Okinawa. Its job was to protect the Strategic Air Command (SAC) base at Kadena Air Base as well as the Far East Air Force (FEAF's) 20th U.S. Air Force at Naha Air Base. The 20th Air Force was responsible for the air defense of Okinawa and the Marianas, as well as the air defense of Andersen Air Base on Guam.

In addition to serving as a staging area for B-29 Superfortress raids on Korea (as it would almost two decades later serve as a staging area for B-52 Stratofortress strikes on Vietnam), the harbor at Buckner Bay (Nakagusuku Wan) was used periodically by elements of the U.S. Seventh Fleet.

See also BOMBERS AIRCRAFT; FAR EAST AIR FORCE; 29TH REGIMENTAL COMBAT TEAM.

187TH AIRBORNE REGIMENTAL COMBAT TEAM

Constituted in February 1942 and organized in February 1943 as part of the 11th Airborne Division, the "Rakkasans" of the 187th Glider Infantry Regiment took part in the New Guinea and Leyte campaigns and made an assault landing on Luzon during World War II. Part of the occupation force in Japan until 1949, the regiment returned with the 11th Airborne Division to Fort Campbell, Kentucky, and was stationed there when the Korean War began in June 1950.

By now a parachute rather than a glider unit, the 187th Airborne Infantry Regiment, together with the 674th (105-mm) Field Artillery Battalion and other supporting units, formed the 4,000-man 187th Airborne Regimental Combat Team (RCT). Moving by ship from Camp Stoneman, California, on September 6, 1950, the 187th Airborne RCT arrived in Japan on September 20, 1950. It was then airlifted to Kimpo Airfield near Seoul on September 24

Troopers of the 187th Airborne RCT load up for the Sunchon/Sukchon parachute assault in October 1950.
(Courtesy U.S. Army Military History Institute.)

and 25, 1950. The RCTs Third Battalion took part in the battle for the recapture of Seoul.

Staging out of Kimpo, on October 20, 1950, the RCT made an airborne assault at Sunchon-Sukchon, 30 air miles north of the North Korean capital of Pyongyang, in order to cut off an estimated 30,000 fleeing North Korean People's Army (NKPA) soldiers and rescue U.S. prisoners of war believed to be with those forces. The RCT suffered 46 jump casualties and 65 battle casualties, but although 3,818 NKPA prisoners were taken, the assault missed the main body and no U.S. POWs were recovered.

Remaining in reserve at Pyongyang during the Eighth U.S. Army's (EUSA) drive into North Korea, the 187th Airborne RCT and the British Brigade served as EUSA's rear guard during its subsequent retreat after the Chinese Communist Forces (CCF) intervention. On January 4, 1951, the RCT was committed as conventional infantry to hold part of the central sector of EUSA's defensive line and saw hard fighting at Wonju on February 14, 1951, when attacked by the CCF 197th and 198th divisions.

Returning to EUSA reserve, the RCT made another airborne assault at Munsan-ni north of Seoul on March 23, 1951, again to trap fleeing CCF and NKPA soldiers. Code-named Operation TOMAHAWK, the 18th Airborne RCT (with the Second and Fourth Ranger companies attached) parachuted some 3,447 soldiers into the objective area, but again the main body of the enemy was missed. There were 84 jump injuries, 18 paratroopers were wounded and one was killed in action.

In May 1951 the RCT, again acting as conventional infantry, spearheaded the Second Infantry Division's drive in the Soyang River area until it reverted to EUSA reserve in June 1951. In 1952 the 187th Airborne RCT was withdrawn to Japan as part of the U.S. Far East Command reserve. Elements helped subdue the Koje-do POW camp riots in June 1952, and the RCT returned to Korea in July 1953 as a show of force, but saw no further combat.

Officially still part of the 11th Airborne Division until February 1, 1951, the 187th Airborne RCT then became an independent RCT. Among its commanders in Korea was Brigadier General William C. Westmoreland, who rose to four-star rank as the commander of all U.S. forces in Vietnam from 1964 to 1968 and served as Army chief of staff from 1968 to 1972. The 187th Airborne RCT won two Republic of Korea Presidential Unit Citations for its service in Korea, and its Third Battalion won a Navy Presidential Unit Citation for bravery during the recapture of Seoul and an Army Presidential Unit Citation for bravery at Sukchon.

In addition to other awards won by members of the RCT, three "Rakkasans" won the Medal of Honor for conspicuous bravery on the battlefield. The 187th Airborne RCT suffered 2,115 casualties in Korea, including 442 killed in action or died of wounds, 1,656 wounded in action, 7 missing in action and 10 POWs.

The 187th Airborne Regimental Combat Team Association publishes a periodic newsletter, the *Rakkasan Shimbun*, and hosts reunions for former members of the RCT. Further information can be obtained from Mr. Frank C. Schoch, 1125 Hanover Street, Piscataway, New Jersey 088654. Telephone (201) 752-1342.

Suggestions for further reading: See *U.S. Army in the Korean War* series: Roy A. Appleman, *South to the Naktong, North to the Yalu*, 1961; Walter G. Hermes, *Truce Tent and Fighting Front*, 1966; Billy C. Mossman, *Ebb and Flow*, anticipated in 1990 (Washington, D.C.: GPO). For order of battle see Shelby Stanton, *Korean War Order of Battle* (Washington, D.C.: GPO, anticipated in 1990). See also Clay Blair, *The Forgotten War: America in Korea 1950–1953* (New York Times Books, 1987).

OPLR (OUTPOST LINE OF RESISTANCE)

During the Korean War an OPLR (outpost line of resistance) was a series of strong points in advance of the MLR (main line of resistance). Like a picket line in earlier wars, the purpose of the OPLR was to give early warning of an enemy attack and to confuse and delay such an attack as long as possible while falling back to the MLR.

See MLR (MAIN LINE OF RESISTANCE); OUTPOST BATTLES.

ORGANIZATION FOR COMBAT

In most military organizations the principal infantry combat organization is the *squad*. A U.S. Army rifle squad during the Korean War had nine soldiers, including an SFC (sergeant first class) as squad leader, a sergeant as assistant squad leader, a corporal armed with a Browning automatic rifle (BAR) and six riflemen with M-1 rifles. A U.S. Marine Corps squad had a squad leader and two five-man fire teams, each with a team leader, a BAR man and three riflemen. The primary artillery combat organization was the howitzer or gun crew, and the primary armor combat organization was the tank crew. The tank crew included a tank commander, who also operated the .50-caliber turret-mounted machine-gun; a gunner, who operated the main gun and the coaxial .30-caliber machine-gun; an ammunition loader; a driver; and an assistant driver, who operated the bow-gun, a .30-caliber machine-gun.

These squads or crews were subordinate to a *platoon* (*section* in the artillery). Commanded by a lieutenant as platoon leader and a master sergeant as platoon sergeant, a Korean War era infantry platoon had three rifle squads and a weapons squad with a machine-gun section armed with an M-1919A6 .30-caliber light machine-gun and a 3.5-inch rocket-launcher section.

Commanded by a captain, a *company* (*battery* in the artillery) had several platoons or sections. A rifle company in the Korean War had three rifle platoons and a weapons platoon with a 60-mm mortar section and a 57-mm recoilless rifle section with three five-man squads each. These squads had a squad leader, a gunner, an assistant gunner and two ammunition bearers. A U.S. Army rifle company was authorized six officers and 195 enlisted personnel.

The next combat organization was the *battalion*, commanded by a lieutenant colonel. An Army infantry battalion had 40 officers and 935 enlisted men (a U.S. Marine Corps battalion was slightly larger) and was organized into a headquarters company, three rifle companies and a weapons company with a machine-gun section armed with .30-caliber M-1919A4 light machine-guns and M-1917A1 water-cooled heavy machine-guns, a mortar section with 81-mm mortars and a 75-mm recoilless rifle section. A 105-mm artillery battalion had a headquarters and service battery and three firing batteries, each with six 105—mm howitzers; and a tank battalion had a headquarters company and three tank companies, each with 17 tanks.

Three infantry battalions comprised a *regiment*, commanded by a colonel. The regiment also had a headquarters company, which included an I&R (intelligence and reconnaissance) platoon, a pioneer (engineer) platoon and signal communications units; a heavy mortar company, with 4.2-inch mortars; a medical company; and in some cases a heavy tank company, which actually had some 22 medium M-4A3E8 Sheridan or M-26 Pershing tanks. Regimental Combat Teams (RCTs) included an infantry regiment plus an artillery battalion and other attached elements tailored for a specific combat mission.

Commanded by major generals, the eight U.S. Army *divisions* in Korea each had three infantry regiments, a division artillery with three 105-mm howitzer battalions and one 155-mm howitzer battalion, an antiaircraft artillery battalion, a tank battalion, a reconnaissance company, an engineer battalion, a medical battalion, an ordnance company (battalion after February 1953), a quartermaster company and a signal company. The U.S. First Marine Division, although somewhat larger than an Army division, was similarly structured.

Unlike a division, the size of a *corps* was not fixed. Commanded by a lieutenant general, the I, IX and X corps in Korea had a varying number of infantry divisions attached during the course of the war in order to accomplish their assigned missions. In addition to the divisions they had corps artillery units attached—usually "heavy" field artillery units with 155-mm "Long Tom" guns and 8-inch howitzers—to influence the action.

On the Allied side the highest level tactical headquarters in Korea was the *field army*. The Eighth U.S. Army (EUSA), with its headquarters on the battlefield, not only commanded all U.S. ground forces in Korea, it commanded the ground forces of the other UN nations and those of the Republic of Korea Army (ROKA) as well.

In overall strategic command was the General Headquarters, Far East Command (GHQ FECOM), in Tokyo, which was at the same time the General Headquarters, United Nations Command (GHQ UNC). Commanded by a four-star U.S. Army general (five-star in the case of General MacArthur), the General

Headquarters exercised its authority chiefly through its subordinate FECOM/UNC commands. Although EUSA had operational control over all ground combat force units in the war, the Far East Air Force (FEAF) headquarters in Tokyo, operating through its subordinate Fifth U.S. Air Force headquarters on the battlefield in Korea, controlled all UN air forces. Likewise the commander U.S. Naval Forces Far East (COMNAVFE), operating through the commander, Seventh Fleet, and his Task Force commanders afloat, controlled all UN naval forces engaged in the war.

See EIGHTH U.S. ARMY; FAR EAST AIR FORCE; FAR EAST COMMAND; NAVAL FORCES FAR EAST; UNITED NATIONS COMMAND. For enemy organization for combat *see* CHINESE COMMUNIST FORCES; CORPS; DIVISION; LIN PIAO; KIM IL-SUNG; NORTH KOREAN PEOPLE'S ARMY; PENG TEH-HUAI.

OUTPOST BATTLES

After the front line stabilized in November 1951 along what eventually proved to be the demarcation line between North and South Korea, the fighting over the next 20 months degenerated into a battle for outposts, whose possession served more political and propaganda purposes than military. In some respects it was a replay of the trench warfare of World War I, for both sides were deeply entrenched and both sides made extensive use of artillery. For example, in July 1953, immediately before the armistice, the enemy fired a Korean War record 375,565 rounds of artillery. The month before, UN forces had fired a record 2,710,248 rounds.

Among the better known outposts were such hills as the Nevadas (Carson, Elko, Reno and Vegas), Boulder City, Berlin, East Berlin, Bunker Hill, Old Baldy, Heartbreak Ridge, Pork Chop Hill, Jane Russell, White Horse and Pike's Peak. In battles to gain or retain these outposts, U.S. forces suffered some 63,200 casualties, including 12,300 killed in action.

These losses represented a substantial portion of all U.S. losses in Korea. For example, as the official U.S. Marine Corps history states, "Astonishingly, 1,586 Marines or 39.6 percent of the infantry Marines killed in the entire war were victims of the 'static' outpost warfare in the west. Another 11,244 were listed WIA [wounded in action] during this period—representing 43.9 percent of the total of ground Marines wounded during the three years of conflict."

See HEARTBREAK RIDGE, BATTLE OF; PORT CHOP HILL, BATTLE OF.

Suggestions for further reading: See *U.S. Army in the Korean War* series: Walter G. Hermes, *Truce Tent and Fighting Front* (Washington, D.C.: GPO, 1966). *U.S. Marine Operations in Korea*, volume 5, Lieutenant Colonel Pat Meid and Major James M. Yingling, *Operations in West Korea: 1950–1953* (Washington, D.C.: GPO, 1972). See also Clay Blair, *The Forgotten War: America in Korea 1950–1953* (New York Times Books, 1987).

P

PANMUNJOM

See ARMISTICE AGREEMENT.

PARTISANS

See SPECIAL OPERATIONS.

PARTRIDGE, EARLE E(VERARD) (1900–)

Born July 7, 1900, at Winchendon, Massachusetts, Partridge enlisted in the Army on June 10, 1918, and was sent to France in August 1918, where he served with Company E, 304th Engineer Battalion, 79th Infantry Division, in the St. Mihiel and Argonne campaigns. Discharged from active duty in June 1919, he enrolled at Norwich University but then reenlisted for appointment to the United States Military Academy. Graduating in 1924, Partridge was appointed a second lieutenant in the Air Service.

During the interwar period he served in a variety of aviation assignments, as a flying instructor, as an instructor of mathematics at the Military Academy, as a test pilot and took part in the Army Air Corps' airmail operations. When the United States entered World War II, he was serving on the Air Staff in Washington, D.C. In the spring of 1943 he joined the Northwest African Air Force and served as operations officer and chief of staff of the 12th Bomber Command and as deputy commander of the 15th Air Force. In January 1944 he moved to England and became deputy commander of the Eighth Air Force and later commander of the Third Air Division.

In August 1948, General Partridge was assigned to the Fifth Air Force in Nagoya, Japan, and became its commander that October. When the Korean War began in June 1950, Partridge took the Fifth Air Force to Korea and commanded it in combat there until June 1951. After service with the Air Research and Development Command and as the Air Force's deputy chief of staff for operations, he returned to Japan in February 1954 to command the U.S. Far East Air Force. In July 1955 he was named commander in chief of the North American Air Defense Command (NORAD) and served there until he retired from active duty on July 31, 1959.

See also AIR FORCE, U.S.; FAR EAST AIR FORCE; FIFTH AIR FORCE.

Suggestions for further reading: See Robert F. Futrell, *The United States Air Force in Korea: 1950–1953*, revised edition (Washington, D.C.: GPO, 1983).

PATTON TANK (M-46)

See ARMOR.

PENG TEH-HUAI (PENG DEHUAI) (1898–1974)

Born about 1898 in China's Hunan Province, Peng ran away from home and joined the Army in 1916. By the time of the split between the KMT (Kuomintang or Chinese Nationalists) and the Chinese Communists in 1926, he was commanding the First Regiment of the Fifth Division of Ho Chien's 35th Army. Maintaining his position with the KMT, he had risen to brigade command by 1928. That July he defected and led his troops in the P'ingchiang Uprising. Peng then joined Mao Tse-tung's guerrilla forces n the Chingkangshan mountains.

A veteran of the guerrilla fighting in South China as well as the famous Long March in 1934 to 1935 from South China to new bases in Yenan in northern China and the Chinese civil war, by the time of the Korean War Peng had risen to become deputy commander of the Chinese People's Liberation Army (PLA) under Marshal Chu Teh.

At the time of the Korean War it was thought that Marshal Lin Piao was the initial Chinese Communist Forces (CCF) commander. The Chinese now dispute that fact and claim that from the very beginning overall command of the CCF was held by Marshal Peng Teh-huai from Chinese People's Volunteer's headquarters in Mukden. In any event, by June 1951 Peng was openly acknowledged as Commander Chinese People's Volunteers. Two years later he signed the July 1953 Korean armistice agreement in that capacity.

By 1959 Peng had risen to the post of minister of defense of the People's Republic of China (PRC). At that time he was purged in a power struggle with Mao Tse-tung. He was sent to a labor camp and during the subsequent Cultural Revolution was tortured to death by the Red Guards. After his death on November 29, 1974, he was "rehabilitated" in 1980 and now is once again honored for his role in the Korean War.

See CHINA, PEOPLE'S REPUBLIC OF; CHINESE COMMUNIST FORCES; LIN PIAO.

Suggestions for further reading: Juergen Domes, *Peng Teh-huai: the Man and the Image* (Stanford, CA: Stanford University Press, 1985); Russell Spurr, *Enter the Dragon: China's Undeclared War Against the U.S. in Korea, 1950–1951* (New York: Newmarket Press, 1988); Peng Dehuai, *Memoirs of a Chinese Marshal* (Beijing: Foreign Language Publishing House, 1984); and Eliot A. Cohen, "Only Half the Battle: American Intelligence and the Chinese Intervention in Korea, 1950," in Eliot A. Cohen and John Gooch, *Military Misfortunes* (New York: The Free Press, 1989). See also Samuel B. Griffith, *The Chinese People's Liberation Army* (New York: McGraw-Hill, 1967); Alexander George, *The Chinese Communist Army in Action* (New York: Columbia University Press, 1967); Allan S. Whiting, *China Crosses the Yalu* (Stanford, CA: Stanford University Press, 1960); Colonel William W. Whitson, *The Chinese High Command* (New York: Praeger, 1973); and Robert B. Riggs, *Red China's Fighting Hordes* (Harrisburg, PA: Telegraph Press, 1951).

PERSHING TANK (M-26)

See ARMOR.

PHILIPPINES

In his war message on June 27, 1950, President Harry S Truman not only ordered U.S. troops into Korea, he also ordered increased military assistance to the Philippines, which was then combating an insurrection by Huk guerrillas. In spite of the on-going war at home, the Philippines sent the 1,496-man 10th Infantry Battalion Combat Team with its own tank company, equipped with M-4A3E8 Sherman tanks, and a battery of 105-mm howitzers. For much of the war they were attached to the Third Infantry Division's 65th (Puerto Rican) Infantry Regiment in the mistaken belief they spoke Spanish (in fact they spoke Tagalog).

The Philippine Battalion saw hard fighting while repulsing the Chinese spring offensive in April 1951. Although casualty figures for Philippine forces alone are not available, during the course of the war the United Nations ground forces of Belgium, Colombia, Ethiopia, France, Greece, the Netherlands, the Philippines, Thailand and Turkey combined lost 1,800 soldiers killed in action and another 7,000 wounded in action. Forty-one Filipinos were among those repatriated during the prisoner of war exchanges at the end of the war.

See UNITED NATIONS GROUND FORCES.

PHONETIC ALPHABET

A phonetic alphabet is used in the military to ensure clarity, especially in radio-telephone communications. Other titles were often derived from that alphabet. During the Korean War, for example, a unit's A Company was known as "Able" Company, L Company as "Love" Company, and so on. Following this custom, a white phosphorous (WP) artillery round was known as "Willie Peter" (from the phonetic alphabet's "William" and "Peter").

The same phonetic alphabet was used in World War II and Korea, but after the Korean War a new NATO standard phonetic alphabet was adopted, using different code words (see below). Today (and during the Vietnam War) A Company is "Alpha" Company rather than "Able" Company and so forth.

WORLD WAR II/KOREA	NATO STANDARD
ABLE	ALPHA
BAKER	BRAVO
CHARLIE	CHARLIE
DOG	DELTA
EASY	ECHO
FOX	FOXTROT
GEORGE	GEORGE
HOW	HOTEL
ITEM	INDIA
JIG	JULIETTE
KING	KILO
LOVE	LIMA
MIKE	MIKE
NAN	NOVEMBER
OBOE	OSCAR
PETER	PAPA
QUEEN	QUEEN
ROGER	ROMEO
SUGAR	SIERRA
TARE	TANGO
UNCLE	UNIFORM
VICTOR	VICTOR
WILLIAM	WHISKEY
X-RAY	X-RAY
YOKE	YANKEE
ZEBRA	ZULU

POLICE ACTION

President Harry S Truman used this phrase in a crude attempt to disguise the fact that the United States was at war in Korea. "Police action" was a term bitterly resented by those who served there.

See also DECLARATION OF WAR.

PORK CHOP HILL, BATTLE OF

Site of one of the last U.S. battles of the Korean War on July 6 to 10, 1953, "Pork Chop Hill" (so nicknamed for its shape) was officially named Hill 255 (from its elevation in yards). It was one of a series of outposted hills—White Horse, Arrowhead, T-Bone, Spud, Alligator Jaws, Old Baldy, Arsenal, Erie—located on the eastern side of the Iron Triangle along the Yokkokchon River. Since they formed the line of contact when the war ended, all ultimately became part of the demilitarized zone between the Republic of Korea (ROK) and North Korea.

Earlier, in November 1952, Pork Chop Hill, then held by the Thailand Battalion, attached to the U.S. Second Infantry Division, had been taken under heavy Chinese Communist Forces (CCF) attack, but their assaults had been beaten back. On March 1, 1953, Pork Chop Hill-Old Baldy complex (by then held by the 31st Infantry Regiment) came under an 8,000-round CCF artillery barrage, but no ground attack followed. On March 23, 1953, under cover of an intense artillery and mortar barrage, the CCF 67th Division, 23d Army, launched an attack against Pork Chop Hill, while other CCF units hit Old Baldy to the southwest. Although the enemy made some initial gains at Pork Chop Hill, they were soon repulsed, and the U.N. defenses held. On Old Baldy, however, the Colombian Battalion was caught while relieving company outposts in the area, and the position was overrun. Plans to counterattack and thus regain the position on March 27 and 28 were canceled by General Maxwell D. Taylor, the new Eighth U.S. Army (EUSA) commander. Always the politician and sensitive to the American public and political reaction to U.S. battlefield casualties, he decided that Old Baldy was not essential to EUSA defenses.

Again on April 16, 1953, the CCF made another attempt to seize Pork Chop Hill. After some initial successes, they were repulsed once more on April 18, 1951, by the counterattacks of the 31st Infantry defenders, reinforced by a battalion from the Seventh Infantry Division's 17th Infantry Regiment. But it was the artillery that really did the job. The Seventh Infantry Division's division artillery commander, Brigadier General Andrew P. O'Meara, massed the fires of some nine artillery battalions, which fired 77,349 rounds in the two-day battle.

On July 6, 1953, less than three weeks before the end of the war, the CCF yet again attacked

U.S. Seventh Infantry Division positions on Pork Chop Hill. They again succeeded in gaining a foothold on part of the crest. This time, however, counterattacks failed to dislodge them. After unsuccessful attempts on 7, 8 and 9 July, General Taylor, as he had done earlier with Old Baldy, made the decision on July 10, 1953, that the casualties suffered were not worth Pork Chop Hill's tactical value, and ordered the Seventh Infantry Division to withdraw. Using armored personnel carriers that normally brought food and ammunition to the front, the withdrawal was completed on July 11, 1953, and Pork Chop Hill was abandoned to the enemy. Two weeks later it became part of the demilitarized zone between the ROK and North Korea.
See OUTPOST BATTLES.

Suggestions for further reading: *U.S. Army in the Korean War* series: Walter G. Hermes, *Truce Tent and Fighting Front* (Washington, D.C.: GPO, 1966). See also S.L.A. Marshall, *Pork Chop Hill: The American Fighting Man in Action, Korea, Spring 1953* (New York: Morrow, 1956), which covers the April 1953 action and which was the basis of a movie, *Pork Chop Hill*, starring Gregory Peck.

POW (PRISONER OF WAR) CAMPS

The main United Nations Command (UNC) prisoner of war (POW) camps in the Korean War were on Koje-do and Cheju-do islands off the southern coast of the Republic of Korea. Large numbers of enemy prisoners had been taken following the collapse of the North Korean People's Army (NKPA) after the Inchon invasion in September 1950. From less than a thousand enemy POWs in August 1950, the UNC found themselves with over 130,000 in November. In January 1951 the decision was made to transport the POWs originally housed near Pusan to the island of Koje-do. UNC POW Camp Number 1 was constructed on Koje-do, and 50,000 POWs were transported there at the end of January 1951. Four enclosures, each subdivided into eight compounds, were built, but they were soon swamped with incoming prisoners; UNC control began to break down. Hard-core POW groups began to develop and they seized internal control of the compounds from the guards.

Riots and disturbances began, and in September 1951 15 prisoners were murdered by "people's courts" within the compounds. In October 1951, the 8137th Military Police Group was activated, with three assigned battalions and four escort guard companies, and in November 1951 a battalion of the Second Infantry Division's 23rd Infantry Regiment was sent to bolster security. In February 1952, the 25th Infantry Division's Third Battalion, 27th Infantry Regiment, attempted to regain control of one of the compounds but was attacked by the prisoners and forced to withdraw. Fifty-five POWs were killed, 22 died of wounds and another 140 were injured. The incident caused headlines around the world.

Adding insult to injury, on May 7, 1952, the POWs captured the camp commandant, Brigadier General Francis T. Dodd, and issued a list of demands. After his successor, Brigadier General Charles F. Colson, agreed to some of these demands, Dodd was finally released on May 11, 1952.

In the wake of the Dodd affair the Second Infantry Division's assistant division commander, Brigadier General Hydon L. Boatner, was appointed camp commandant, with orders to get the camp under control. In addition to the Netherlands Battalion already on the island, a British, a Canadian and a Greek rifle company were dispatched, as was the 187th Airborne Regimental Combat Team (RCT) from Japan. Together with the Second Infantry Division's 38th Infantry Regiment and supported by platoons of medium tanks, the task force took control of the POW compounds by force. Thirty-one POWs died and 139 were injured, while one U.S. soldier was speared to death and 14 injured. Enemy POWs were transferred to smaller, more manageable compounds on Koje-do, on Cheju-do Island 50 miles off the South Korean coast and to camps on the mainland. Except for an attempted mass breakout of civilian internees at Pongam-do (a small island near Koje-do) in December 1952, in which 85 POWs were killed and more than a hundred wounded, the UNC Prisoner of War Command generally retained effective control of its POW camps.

On the enemy side, treatment of POWs by the NKPA and by the CCF greatly differed. The NKPA were particularly brutal and made it a practice to mistreat and massacre those who fell into their hands. They had no POW camps per se, merely collection points where POWs were gathered. POWs were moved to the rear on foot, many times a death march. In one such 120-mile march in November 1950, 130 of 700 POWs died. In December 1950 only 75 of a group of 400 prisoners captured at Kunu-ri survived.

The CCF, on the other hand, saw propaganda value in treating prisoners well. When they entered the war in October 1950, they established a POW camp system. The largest was the United States–British Prisoner of War Camp Number 5, located near the city of Pyoktong on the banks of the Yalu River in North Korea. The guards were mostly Chinese, and Camp Number 5 was maintained as a model installation. There were other camps, however, for POWs who refused to cooperate with their jailers, and treatment there was much more severe.

One feature of the CCF camps was a systemic indoctrination program in Communist ideology. Several prisoners made propaganda broadcasts for the enemy, especially in support of the spurious germ warfare campaign, and 21

Americans, one British soldier and 315 ROK soldiers defected to the enemy. This led to a brainwashing scare that upon investigation proved groundless.

See ATROCITIES; BRAINWASHING; MIA (MISSING IN ACTION); POWs (PRISONERS OF WAR).

Suggestions for further reading: For UN POW camps see Walter G. Hermes, *U.S. Army in the Korean War: Truce Tent and Fighting Front* (Washington, D.C.: GPO, 1966). For NKPA/CCF treatment of POWs see Department of the Army Pamphlet 30-101, *Communist Interrogation Indoctrination, and Exploitation of Prisoners of War* (Washington, D.C.: Department of the Army, May 1956).

POWS (PRISONERS OF WAR)

When the war ended in 1953, the United Nations Command (UNC) repatriated some 82,493 enemy prisoners of war (POWs). These included 75,823 prisoners from the North Korean People's Army (NKPA) and 6,670 from the Chinese Communist Forces (CCF). Among their number were 492 female POWs and 9,345 civilian internees. Some 6,670 sick and wounded enemy POWs were exchanged on April 20 to 26, 1953, during Operation LITTLE SWITCH; the remainder were exchanged during Operation BIG SWITCH between August 15 and September 6, 1953.

Likewise, the CCF/NKPA repatriated some 13,444 UN prisoners of war. These included 3,746 Americans, 8,321 ROK (Republic of Korea), 977 from the United Kingdom, 243 Turks, 41 Filipinos, 32 Canadians, 28 Colombians, 26 Australians, 12 Frenchmen, 9 South Africans, 3 Greeks, 3 Netherlanders, 1 Belgian, 1 New Zealander and 1 Japanese. Six hundred eighty-four were repatriated in LITTLE SWITCH and the remainder in BIG SWITCH.

An enemy soldier surrenders on the battlefield.
(Courtesy Lyndon Baines Johnson Library & Museum.)

A major issue during the Korean War was voluntary repatriation: whether POWs should have the option of refusing repatriation or whether they should be forcibly returned. Among NKPA prisoners of war were ROK soldiers who had been captured and forced to join the NKPA ranks, and among the CCF prisoners were Chinese Nationalist soldiers who had been captured in the Chinese civil war and forced into CCF ranks. After some dithering, in January 1952 the UNC came down firmly on the side of voluntary repatriation, and this became a major point of contention in the armistice negotiations. Not until June 1953 did the CCF/NKPA agreed to a Neutral Nation Repatriations Commission (NNRC) for taking custody of POWs refusing repatriation and determining whether that choice was genuine. ROK President Syngman Rhee was adamantly

Five former POWs—three Americans and two Australians—warm themselves after being returned unharmed to the Allied lines by Chinese soldiers, February 1951.
(Courtesy Lyndon Baines Johnson Library & Museum.)

opposed to this agreement and on June 18, 1953, gave orders to ROK Army security guards to release some 25,131 NKPA prisoners who had previously made known their desire not to be repatriated into the South Korean countryside. Disassociating themselves from this action, the UNC went ahead to conclude the armistice on July 27, 1953.

On September 23, 1953, the UNC turned over more than 22,000 nonrepatriates to the NNRC in the demilitarized zone and the CCF/NKPA delivered over 350 UNC nonrepatriates the next day. The NNRC retained custody for the 120 days specified in the armistice agreement then released the POWs in accordance with their wishes. Of the 359 UNC nonrepatriates, 23 were Americans, one was British and 335 were ROK. Two ROK prisoners opted to go to India, and one U.S. and eight ROK prisoners opted to return to UNC control and were repatriated to their respective countries. The rest stayed with the Communists. Of the 22,604 CCF/NKPA nonrepatriates, 628 returned to Communist control, 13 escaped, 38 died while in NNRC custody, 86 went to India and 21,839 were released to UNC control, including 14,235 Chinese, most of whom were repatriated to Taiwan.

One lasting legacy of the Korean War is the fact that 2,233 Allied servicemen, including 389 Americans, who were positively known to be held as prisoners by the NKPA/CCF, were not repatriated in 1953 following the armistice, and no accounting has ever been made of their whereabouts.

See also ATROCITIES; BIG SWITCH; BRAIN-WASHING; LITTLE SWITCH; MIA (MISSING IN ACTION); POW (PRISONER OF WAR) CAMPS.

Suggestions for further reading: Walter G. Hermes, *U.S. Army in the Korean War: Truce Tent and Fighting Front* (Washington, D.C.: GPO, 1966) has an excellent account of POW negotiations as well as an appendix detailing their disposition.

PPCLI (PRINCESS PATRICIA'S CANADIAN LIGHT INFANTRY)

See BRITISH COMMONWEALTH DIVISION; CANADA.

PRESIDENTIAL UNIT CITATIONS, U.S.

The Presidential Unit Citation (Navy), the Presidential Unit Citation (Air Force) and the Presidential Unit Citation (Army) were first authorized in World War II. The latter two were known at the time as "Distinguished Unit Citations"; their titles were changed on November 3, 1966. They were awarded in the name of the president of the United States to units—including units of foreign nations—that displayed gallantry, determination and esprit de corps in accomplishing their mission that under extremely difficult or hazardous circumstances set them apart and above other units participating in the same campaign. The degree of heroism required was the same as that warranting award of a Distinguished Service Cross or Navy Cross to an individual.

The U.S. Army, Navy and Air Force Presidential Unit Citations all share the same requirements but are distinct awards. The Army and Air Force share the same award emblem (a dark blue ribbon encased in a gold frame), which is different from the Navy/Marine Corps version (a horizontally striped blue/yellow/red ribbon). These emblems can be worn permanently by personnel assigned to the unit at the time of the award.

See UNIT AWARDS.

PRESIDENT OF THE UNITED STATES

Article II, Section 2, of the Constitution of the United States provides that "the President shall be Commander-in-Chief of the Army and Navy of the United States ..." When the war began in June 1950, the president of the United States was Harry S Truman, who had been in that office since the death of President Franklin D. Roosevelt on April 12, 1945. In 1952 President Truman declined to run for reelection. In January 1953 he was succeeded by Dwight D. Eisenhower, who served as commander in chief during the remaining seven months of the war.

See EISENHOWER, DWIGHT D.; TRUMAN, HARRY S.

PSYCHOLOGICAL WARFARE

During the Korean War both sides made extensive use of psychological warfare operations at the tactical, operational and strategic levels. At the tactical (i.e., battlefield) level, for example, United Nations tanks and aircraft were painted to resemble tigers in an attempt to spread panic among enemy troops. On the other side, attacking Chinese Communist Forces (CCF) used bugles, whistles and loudspeakers to scare the Allied defenders.

A "Safe Conduct Pass" airdropped by the millions behind enemy lines.
(Courtesy U.S. Army Military History Institute.)

At the operational (i.e., theater of war) level both UN forces and the CCF made extensive use of leaflets to undermine their opponent's morale and encourage them to desert. Here the Allied side had a major advantage. Because they had almost total control of the air, they were able to use bomber aircraft to make "paper runs." Psychological warfare leaflets by the millions were dropped deep behind enemy lines. Extensive use was also made of radio to undermine morale. Allied radio stations targeted Chinese and North Korean audiences, and the enemy responded in kind. For example, broadcasting in English from Seoul when it was in enemy hands, and later from Radio Pyongyang, "Seoul City Sue" had a wide audience among U.S. military personnel, who enjoyed the music she played but found her propaganda messages to be more comedic than compelling.

Strategically (i.e., at the national level), a technique pioneered in the Korean War was the Communist use of what was then called "brainwashing." The enemy extorted "confessions" from Allied prisoners of war, which were then used as part of a world-wide psychological warfare campaign. Such campaigns—germ warfare was the most blatant example—combined Nazi-style big-lie techniques and the Communist worldwide propaganda apparatus to spread wild and inflammatory allegations. Aimed at the Allied home front, their goal was to stir up antiwar sentiments and subvert public support for the war.

See also BRAINWASHING; GERM WARFARE; PUBLIC OPINION.

Suggestions for further reading: For Air Force psychological warfare leaflet operations see Robert F. Futrell, *The United States Air Force in Korea: 1950–1953*, revised edition (Washington, D.C.: GPO, 1983).

PUBLIC OPINION

American public opinion during the Korean War followed almost exactly the same pattern it would follow in the Vietnam War, except that the loss of public support was far quicker in the Korean War than it was in the Vietnam War. President Harry S Truman's disapproval ratings were much higher than President Lyndon Johnson's ever were.

When the United States entered the war in June 1950, over 75% agreed that the U.S. was right in sending troops to Korea. By the time of the Chinese intervention in November 1950 this percentage had dropped to just over 50%. After the intervention it made a short recovery (the "rally 'round the flag syndrome" that emerges when a nation is in trouble), then leveled off at about 50% for the remainder of the war.

When considering the issue of whether America had made a mistake in getting involved, about 65% said it was not a mistake in June 1950. But after the Chinese intervention opinion reversed, and 65% believed it was a mistake. With some temporary ups and downs, that percentage stayed negative until President-elect Eisenhower's visit to Korea after the 1952 elections. At that time 50% thought it was a mistake and 50% did not. When asked, on the eve of the 1952 election, if they thought the war was worth fighting, only about 33% thought it was. This percentage rose slightly when Eisenhower went to Korea but dropped to about 25% by the time the truce talks were signed in July 1953.

The reason for the high initial approval was that most Americans believed the United States was right in countering aggression. They thought we were in for a short and conclusive war. The Chinese intervention destroyed those illusions, and President Truman's dismissal of General MacArthur in April 1951 signaled that our strategies were in disarray. As in the Vietnam War 20 years later, most Americans wanted the United States to win the war and come home. When they found that that was not in the offing, and that the best we could achieve with the strategy that had been adopted was a tie, they lost their patience with the war and with the presidency of Harry S Truman. With one of the lowest public approval ratings of any president in our history, Truman chose not to run for reelection in 1952.

Suggestions for further reading: John E. Mueller's *War, Presidents and Public Opinion* (New York: Wiley, 1973) has several excellent comparisons of trends in popular support for the Korean War and the Vietnam War.

PULLER, LEWIS B. "CHESTY" (1898–1971)

Born June 26, 1898, at West Point, Virginia, Puller attended the Virginia Military Institute before enlisting in the Marine Corps in August 1918. After serving five years as a Marine enlisted man fighting the Caco rebels in Haiti, Puller was commissioned as a Marine second lieutenant in March 1924. He won his first Navy Cross while serving with the Nicaraguan National Guard from 1928 to 1931 and won a second Navy Cross when he again served in Nicaragua from 1932 to 1933. In February 1933, Puller was assigned to the Marine Legation in Peking, China, where he commanded the famed "Horse Marines." When the United States entered World War II, Puller was commanding the First Battalion, Seventh Marine Regiment, First Marine Division.

In October 1942, while still in command of the First Battalion, Seventh Marines, Puller won his third Navy Cross while defending Henderson Airfield on Guadalcanal. Fifteen months later he won his fourth Navy Cross at Cape Gloucester while serving as the Seventh Marine Regiment's executive officer. Puller ended the war as commander of the First Marine Regiment.

In August 1950 Puller was once again assigned as the commander of the First Marine Regiment and led them ashore at Inchon the following month. He was awarded the Army's Distinguished Service Cross and an unprecedented fifth Navy Cross for heroism during the bitter fight to break out of the Chinese encirclement at the Chosin Reservoir in December 1950.

After his promotion to brigadier general in January 1951, Puller served as the assistant division commander of the First Marine Division until his return to the United States in May 1951. He later commanded the Second Marine Division at Camp Lejeune, North Carolina, until his medical retirement from active duty in August 1955. Promoted to lieutenant general upon retirement, General Puller died on October 11, 1971.

See also CHOSIN RESERVOIR, BATTLE OF; FIRST MARINE DIVISION; INCHON INVASION.

Suggestions for further reading: Burke Davis, *Marine! The Life of Lt Gen Lewis B (Chesty) Puller, USMC (Ret)* (Boston: Little, Brown, 1962). See also the five-volume official history, *U.S. Marine Operations in Korea 1950–1953*: Lynn Montross and Captain Nicholas A. Canzona, USMC; *The Pusan Perimeter*, 1954; *The Inchon-Seoul Operation*, 1955; *The Chosin Reservoir Campaign*, 1957; Lynn Montross and Majors Hubard D. Kuokka and Norman W. Hicks, USMC, *The East-Central Front*, 1962; and Lieutenant Colonel Pat Meid, USMCR, and Major James M. Yingling, USMC, *Operations in West Korea*, 1972 (Washington, D.C.: GPO).

PUNCHBOWL, BATTLES OF

A peculiar terrain feature in eastern Korea along what would become the demarcation line when the armistice was signed, the "punchbowl" was an ancient volcanic crater some four to five miles in diameter rimmed by hills ranging from one to two thousand feet. In July 1951 it was held by elements of the North Korean's People's Army (NKPA) II Corps. From its rim they could make observations and bring artillery fire on Allied positions and road networks to the south.

In late July the U.S. Second Infantry Division had seized a foothold on the western edge of the Punchbowl but were bogged down by especially heavy rains. When the weather cleared the Second Infantry Division became embroiled in the Bloody Ridge and Heartbreak Ridge battles to the west of the Punchbowl; on August 18, 1950, the Republic of Korea (ROK) I Corps and the ROK Eighth Division from the U.S. X Corps attacked northeast of the Punchbowl but were held up by the entrenched NKPA 45th, 13th and Second divisions until August 27, 1951, when they finally seized their objectives.

On August 31, the First Marine Division, with its attached First ROK Marine Regiment, attacked to seize the northeast rim of the Punchbowl. By a stroke of good luck they caught the NKPA III Corps in the process of relieving the NKPA II Corps on position. Taking advantage of the resulting confusion, the Marines pressed home their attack and captured the Punchbowl's entire northern lip on September 3, 1951. It remained in Allied hands for the remainder of the war.

Marine casualties (including ROK Marine casualties) in the battle for the Punchbowl included 109 killed in action and 494 wounded in action. NKPA casualties included 656 counted killed in action and 40 prisoners.

Suggestions for further reading: Lynn Montross and Captain Nicholas A. Canzona, USMC, *U.S. Marine Operations in Korea: The East-Central Front* (Washington, D.C.: GPO, 1962). See also *U.S. Army in the Korean War* series:

Walter G. Hermes, *Truce Tent and Fighting Front* (Washington, D.C.: GPO, 1966).

PURPLE HEART MEDAL

The oldest U.S. military decoration, the Purple Heart Medal was first authorized by General George Washington during the Revolutionary War. It was revived in 1932 for award in the name of the president of the United States to any member of the armed forces or to any civilian national of the United States who, while serving under competent authority in any capacity with one of the U.S. Armed Services, was wounded in action against the enemy or as a result of an act of any such enemy or as the result of an act of any hostile foreign force.

Only one award is made for more than one wound or injury received at the same instant or from the same missile, force, explosion or agent. A "wound" is defined as an injury to any part of the body from an outside force or agent sustained under one or more of the circumstances described above. A wound for which the award is made must have required treatment by a medical officer, and records of medical treatment for wounds or injuries received in action as described above must be a matter of official record. Subsequent awards are denoted by an oak leaf cluster (a gold star for Navy and Marine Corps personnel) worn on the medal ribbon.
See DECORATIONS, U.S.

PUSAN

Located in southeastern Korea near the delta of the Naktong River, Pusan was and is South Korea's second largest city. Because of its excellent natural harbor on the Korea/Tsushima Straits between Korea and Japan, it became Korea's chief seaport. Most of the cargo that arrived in Korea during the war went through the port of Pusan. Its deep-water dock facilities could handle up to 30 ocean-going vessels at one time, and 12 to 15 LSTs (landing ships tank) could be unloaded simultaneously. It had a daily discharge potential of 40,000 to 45,000 measurement tons, but constraints of personnel and inland transportation limited the actual capacity to about 28,000 tons daily.
See KOREAN COMMUNICATIONS ZONE; NAKTONG PERIMETER, BATTLE OF.

PUSAN LOGISTICAL COMMAND

See KOREAN COMMUNICATIONS ZONE (KCOMZ).

PUSAN PERIMETER

See NAKTONG PERIMETER, BATTLE OF.

PYONGYANG

Today the capital of North Korea, officially the Democratic People's Republic of Korea (DPRK), Pyongyang served as the country's northern capital during the Koryo Dynasty (935–1392); at the same time Seoul served as the nation's southern capital.

Pyongyang was and is North Korea's largest city, an industrial center and the hub of North Korea's railroads. Located in north-central Korea on the banks of the Taedong River about 50 miles from the DPRK port city of Nampo (also known as Chinnampo) at the mouth of the river on the Yellow Sea, it is about 100 air miles across Korea's narrow waist from the town of Wonsan on the Sea of Japan. Pyongyang was a chief United Nations Command objective following the recapture of Seoul in September 1950.

The plan called for the Eighth U.S. Army (EUSA) to drive on Pyongyang from the south

ROK troops and North Korean civilians celebrate the liberation of Pyongyang, October 1950.
(Courtesy U.S. Army Military History Institute.)

while X Corps made an amphibious landing at Wonsan and attacked the city from the east. These plans were obviated when the Republic of Korea (ROK) First and Seventh divisions captured Pyongyang on October 19, 1950. Less than two weeks later, some 125 air miles to the north, EUSA elements were locked in battle with Chinese Communist Forces (CCF), who had intervened in the Korean War. On Decem-

ber 5, 1950, a month and a half after it had been captured, Pyongyang was abandoned by the retreating EUSA and soon thereafter was reoccupied by the North Korean government. Flattened by continual aerial bombardment throughout the war, Pyongyang has since been rebuilt as the "showcase" of the DPRK.
See PART I: THE SETTING.

RAIDS

See SPECIAL OPERATIONS.

RANGER COMPANIES

On August 25, 1950, the Eighth U.S. Army activated the Eighth Army Ranger Company in Japan. On October 14, 1950, it was attached to the 25th Infantry Division and saw heavy fighting in November 1950 north of Kunu-ri when it came under Chinese Communist Forces (CCF) attack. One of its subsequent commanders was Captain John Paul Vann, who would later go on to fame in the Vietnam War.

Meanwhile, six ranger companies were organized and trained at the Infantry School's Ranger Training Center at Fort Benning, Georgia, and dispatched to Korea. The First Ranger Company arrived in Korea on December 17, 1950, and was assigned to the Second Infantry Division. The Second Ranger Company arrived December 30, 1950, and was assigned to the Seventh Infantry Division. The Third Ranger Company arrived March 24, 1951, and was assigned to the Third Infantry Division. The Fourth Ranger Company arrived December 30, 1950, and was assigned to the First Cavalry Division. The Fifth Ranger Company arrived March 24, 1951, and replaced the Eighth Army Ranger Battalion with the 25th Infantry Division, which was then deactivated. The

Eighth Ranger Company also arrived on March 24, 1951, and was assigned to the 24th Infantry Division.

Successors to the Ranger battalions of World War II, which had all been deactivated after the war, each of these 117-man Ranger companies was trained in both Ranger (commando) and parachute (airborne) operations (the Second and Fourth Ranger companies were attached to the 187th Airborne Regimental Combat Team for the Munsan-ni jump on March 23, 1951). Their training to infiltrate enemy lines was not widely used in Korea. Division commanders were reluctant to send Rangers behind the enemy lines where they might have to be reinforced or rescued.

Instead, Ranger companies most often secured and held key terrain features, provided infantry support for tanks and performed other routine infantry tasks. Even though they performed their assigned missions in a superior manner, they were seen by many division commanders as an uneconomical "luxury." As a result the Ranger companies were all deactivated effective August 1, 1951, and most of their personnel were reassigned to the 187th Airborne Regimental Combat Team.

The Ranger units were not formed again in the U.S. Army until 18 years later, this time on the battlefield in Vietnam in 1969 as Long Range Reconnaissance Patrol (LRRP) units.

While these companies were later deactivated as they withdrew from Vietnam, in 1974 two Ranger battalions were organized as special operating force units and took part in the 1983 assault on Grenada. Later a third battalion and a regimental headquarters were added, and today the Ranger Regiment is stationed at Fort Benning, Georgia.

Suggestions for further reading: For the Eighth Army Ranger Company see Neil Sheehan, *A Bright Shining Lie: John Paul Vann and America Experience in Vietnam* (New York: Random House, 1988). For an overview of Ranger companies in Korea see First Lieutenant Martin Blumenson et al., *Monograph: Special Problems in the Korean Conflict* (Headquarters, Eighth U.S. Army Korea, February 5, 1952). See also Clay Blair, *The Forgotten War: America in Korea 1950–1953* (New York Times Books, 1987).

RASHIN

A port city 17 miles from the Soviet frontier on Korea's eastern coast, the town of Rashin (now known as Najin) is connected to the Soviet port of Vladivostok, which is less than 110 miles away by both rail and road. Although Rashin was bombed by Air Force B-29s in August 1950, the fear of violating Soviet air space led to its being declared off-limits to further bombing the following month. Because of Rashin's sanctuary status, it became the most important supply point in northeast Korea. It had become a major arsenal as well as a rail hub for the transshipment of arms and equipment. After repeated refusals, in August 1951 the State and Defense departments finally agreed to a bombing raid to destroy this vital target.

Political restrictions on the flight paths of the Air Force's B-29 Superfortress bombers made them especially vulnerable to MiG attacks from enemy bases in both Manchuria and the Soviet Union; therefore fighter-escorts were con-

sidered critical. Because Air Force F-86 Sabrejets were out of range, the decision was made to use Navy F9F Panther and F2H2 Banshee jet-fighters from the carrier USS *Essex*. This joint Navy–Air Force raid on August 25, 1951, crippled the rail network in Rashin, an attack repeated on December 10, 1952, when Rashin's munitions factories and rail marshaling yards and locomotives and rail cars were struck again by an all-Navy attack by aircraft from the carriers *Bon Homme Richard* and *Oriskany*.

The raid on Rashin was the first time in the Korean War that Navy carrier fighters escorted Air Force bombers. This procedure was repeated on October 8, 1952, when fighters from the USS *Kearsarge* escorted Air Force B-29 Superfortresses attacking the Korean rail center just north of Wonsan.

Suggestions for further reading: James A. Field, *History of United States Naval Operations: Korea* (Washington, D.C.: GPO, 1962). See also Commanders Malcolm W. Cagle and Frank A. Manson, USN, *The Sea War in Korea* (Annapolis, Md: United States Naval Institute, 1957); Richard P. Hallion, *The Naval Air War in Korea* (Baltimore: The Nautical & Aviation Publishing Company of America, 1986).

RECOILLESS RIFLES

Developed in the closing days of World War II by the U.S. military as infantry antitank weapons, three 57-mm recoilless rifles were authorized in the weapons platoon of each rifle company, and a 75-mm recoilless rifle platoon was authorized in the weapons company of the infantry battalion. When the Korean War began, however, there were practically none on hand. Within the Eighth U.S. Army, for example, 226 recoilless rifles had been authorized but only 21 were received.

In any event, it was soon found that they were worthless as antitank weapons. On July 5,

A 57-mm recoilless rifle team from K Company, 19th Infantry, fires on the enemy in February 1951, while a Signal Corps photographer records the moment on film.
(Courtesy U.S. Army Military History Institute.)

1950, when the 24th Infantry Division's Task Force Smith made the first enemy contact of the war, two 75-mm recoilless rifles took advancing Soviet-supplied T-34 tanks under fire at a range of 700 yards. Although they scored direct hits, the ammunition did not penetrate the enemy armor.

But even though they were not effective against tanks, they proved to be excellent anti-personnel weapons. Portable enough and light enough to be carried up the mountains and into the attack, the 57-mm recoilless rifles in particular gave the infantry company commander his own direct fire artillery to be used against enemy machine-gun emplacements and other field fortifications.

See also INFANTRY; ROCKET LAUNCHERS; SMALL ARMS.

RECONNAISSANCE

Reconnaissance—that is, the seeking out of information about enemy positions and dispositions—is an essential battlefield task. On both sides in the Korean War, front-line rifle companies routinely sent out reconnaissance patrols to keep track of what the enemy was doing. In addition, there were also specialized reconnaissance units. In the U.S. Army, for example, each infantry regiment had an organic I&R (Intelligence and Reconnaissance) platoon; each infantry division had an organic reconnaissance company (only recently increased from a mechanized cavalry reconnaissance platoon), which had a tank section—usually M-24 Chafee light tanks—and several scout sections. Corporal Gordon M. Craig, 16th Reconnaissance Company, First

Cavalry Division, and Sergeant First Class Charles W. Turner of the Second Reconnaissance Company, Second Infantry Division, won the Medal of Honor for their actions in Korea.

The Air Force had specialized aerial reconnaissance units as well, but after World War II they had been sadly neglected. In the spring of 1949 all their tactical reconnaissance organizations, except two squadrons in the United States and one in the Far East, had been deactivated. When the fighting began, the Far East Air Force Bomber Command's 31st (later 91st) Strategic Reconnaissance Squadron had only a handful of RB-17 Flying Fortresses and RB-29 Superfortresses (in the Air Force, the addition of the prefix *R* to an aircraft's identification indicates that it has been modified to serve as a reconnaissance aircraft).

At the tactical level it was equally grim. It was not until January 1951 that the 67th Tactical Reconnaissance Wing, an ad hoc organization put together to fill the gap, was assigned to Fifth Air Force. Working with the First Marine Aircraft Wing's Marine Photographic Squadron 1 (VMJ-1), which flew F2H2P Banshee photo-jet aircraft, the Air Force's RF-51 Mustangs, RF-80 Shooting Stars and RB-26 Invaders were able to cover most of Korea, and with their handful of RF-86 Sabrejets were able to photo "MiG-Alley" (The area in northwest Korea within range of China-based MiGs) as well. During a 12-month period from April 1952 to March 1953 the 67th Wing averaged 1,792 photo-reconnaissance sorties per month and produced 736,684 negatives.

In addition to aerial reconnaissance, maritime reconnaissance by flying boats (amphibious aircraft) such as the Navy's Martin PMB-5S Mariner and the British Royal Air Force's Sunderland proved to be particularly useful in locating enemy minefields along the Korean coast.

See also MILITARY INTELLIGENCE.

Suggestions for further reading: For aerial reconnaissance see Robert F. Futrell, *The United States Air Force in Korea: 1950–1953*, revised edition (Washington, D.C.: GPO, 1983). For maritime reconnaissance see James A. Field, *History of United States Naval Operations: Korea* (Washington, D.C.: GPO, 1962).

RECONNAISSANCE COMPANIES

See CAVALRY; RECONNAISSANCE.

RED BALL EXPRESS

As Eighth U.S. Army forces advanced into North Korea after the Inchon invasion in September 1950—and farther away from the supply depots and ports at Pusan and Inchon—they began to strain their lines of supply. Although the Navy was working to clear the mines blocking Pyongyang's port of Chinnampo so that supplies could be brought in by sea and the Far East Air Force's Combat Cargo Command had begun an airlift of supplies into Pyongyang, truck transportation became critical.

According to the Army's official history, "during September, October and on into November [1950], 76% of Eighth Army's trucks operated on a 24-hour basis. In order to supply I Corps north of the 38th parallel, Eighth Army had to take away from the Second and 25th divisions large numbers of their trucks, thereby virtually immobilizing these divisions. The Second Division at one time furnished 320 trucks that were organized into a *Red Ball Express* (the name derived from similar truck convoys in World War II) to supply I Corps from the Han River.

Other units created similar organizations. During the Chinese spring offensive in 1951, X Corps created a 50 to 60 vehicle "truck bank" to

A U.S. truck convoy crossing the Naktong River passes a knocked-out T-34 tank and a Korean with a heavily loaded A-frame.
(Courtesy U.S. Army Military History Institute.)

meet unexpected requirements by raiding the hospitals and service units in its area and confiscating all vehicles that were not absolutely essential. On one occasion X Corps needed 300 trucks to make an emergency troops movement. Its 52d Transportation Truck Battalion, which included elements of 17 truck companies, could only provide 200, so military policemen were directed to go out on the road and commandeer the remainder.

Drivers worked 12 to 18 hours straight, ordnance companies kept maintenance patrols on the road 24 hours a day and aircraft were used to spot disabled vehicles, which were repaired on the spot or evacuated to the rear for depot repair. Transportation units approached 100% utilization of their truck capacities.

Once Eighth U.S. Army's front lines stabilized in the summer of 1951, the situation be-

came less critical. For one thing, the retreat had shortened the lines of supply and units were now closer to the supply depots and the ports. For another, South Korea's rebuilt rail network took some pressure off the road net. Finally, aerial movement and resupply by the transport aircraft of Far East Air Force's Combat Cargo Command also helped ease the situation.

Suggestions for further reading: See "Transportation Corps" in Captain John G. Westover's *Combat Support in Korea* (Washington, D.C.: Combat Forces Press, 1955)

REFUGEES

See INFILTRATION; MILITARY POLICE; SCORCHED EARTH POLICY; WITHDRAWAL FROM NORTH KOREA.

REGIMENT

During the Korean War the *regiment* was one of the basic combat organizations. In the British Commonwealth Division the regimental designation was only honorific (i.e., the title of regimental commander was an honorary position and the actual fighting unit was the battalion—a system the U.S. Army would adopt prior to the Vietnam War). All other divisions in the Korean War—were organized on what was known as the *triangular division* model: three infantry regiments per division, each with three infantry battalions, which in turn each had three rifle companies.

Commanded by a colonel, a typical U.S. Army infantry regiment had three infantry battalions, each with 40 officers and 935 enlisted men; a heavy mortar company with 4.2-inch mortars; an intelligence and reconnaissance platoon; and in some cases a heavy tank company. It also had a medical company, which provided combat aidmen to the rifle companies, and a headquarters company, with a limited transport and signal capability.

Three U.S. Marine Corps infantry regiments—the First, Fifth and Seventh Marines—served in Korea, as did the 11th Marines, an artillery regiment. Three U.S. Army cavalry regiments (actually infantry regiments in everything but name) served there—the Fifth, Seventh and Eighth Cavalry regiments of the First Cavalry Division—as did 25 U.S. Army infantry regiments—the Ninth, 23d and 38th Infantry regiments of the Second Infantry Division; the Seventh, 15th and 65th Infantry regiments of the Third Infantry Division; the 17th, 31st and 32d Infantry regiments of the Seventh Infantry Division; the 19th, 21st and 34th Infantry regiments of the 24th Infantry Division; the 14th, 24th, 27th and 35th Infantry regiments of the 25th Infantry Division; the 160th, 223d and 224th Infantry regiments of the 40th Infantry Division; and the 179th, 180th and 279th Infantry regiments of the 45th Infantry Division; as well as the Fifth Infantry Regiment, which served much of the war with the 24th Infantry Division, elements of the 29th Infantry Regiment, which was disbanded early in the war, and the separate 187th Airborne Infantry Regiment.

The map symbol for a regiment is a rectangular box superimposed by three vertical lines. Crossed rifles within the box denote an infantry regiment; thus the symbol for the 21st Infantry Regiment would be ⊠ 21.

See also BATTALION; Listings for specific divisions; ORGANIZATION FOR COMBAT.

Suggestions for further reading: Shelby L. Stanton, *Korean War Order of Battle* (Washington, D.C.: GPO, anticipated 1990).

REGIMENTAL COMBAT TEAM

An organizational structure often used during the Korean War, a regimental combat team (RCT) was essentially an infantry regiment with a battalion of artillery and in some cases armor and engineer elements attached. Most were temporary ad hoc organizations put together for a particular operation, but there were two separate RCTs dispatched to Korea. First was the Fifth RCT from Hawaii (Fifth Infantry Regiment plus the 555th Artillery Battalion and a Heavy Tank Company), which arrived in Korea on July 31, 1950. Attached to the 24th Infantry Division to replace the 34th Infantry Regiment, which had been decimated earlier that month, it served with that division for most of the war. Then there was the 187th Airborne RCT (187th Airborne Infantry Regiment plus the 674th Airborne Field Artillery Battalion) from the 11th Airborne Division in Fort Campbell, Kentucky, which remained a separate unit under the control of the U.S. Far East Command.

See FIFTH REGIMENTAL COMBAT TEAM; 29th REGIMENTAL COMBAT TEAM; 187th AIRBORNE REGIMENTAL COMBAT TEAM.

Suggestions for further reading: Shelby L. Stanton, *Korean War Order of Battle* (Washington, D.C.: GPO, anticipated 1990)

REPLACEMENT DEPOTS

Replacement depots, both in the United States (the "ZI" or Zone of Interior in Korean War terminology) and in the Far East, played a major role in the Korean War. Two factors were involved: First, the United States military relied upon an individual rather than a unit replacement system during the Korean War. Instead of a unit being responsible for the processing and shipment of its own troops, replacement depots provided those essential services. Second, most of these replacements were transported by sea. During the war the Navy's Military Sea Transportation Service (MSTS) moved 4,918,919 military passengers to, from and within the U.S. Far East Command. Housing had to be provided while shiploads were gathered together.

The two principal ports of embarkation (POE) were San Francisco, California, and Seattle, Washington. The replacement depot at Camp Stoneman at Pittsburg, California, served the San Francisco POE, and the replacement depot at Fort Lawton in Seattle served that POE. At the other end, replacement depots at Camp Drake and Camp Zama near the Japanese port of Yokohama and at the southern port of Sasebo processed troops for shipment through the replacement depots at Pusan and Inchon to their units in the field.

This system was enormously wasteful, for by either accident or design troops could spend months lost in the replacement depot system.

By the time of the Vietnam War almost all individual replacements were assigned directly to units before they left their home station then transported to the war zone either by commercial air charters or through California's Travis Air Force Base. Camp Stoneman and Fort Lawton had long since been deactivated and turned over to civilian control.

REPUBLIC OF KOREA (SOUTH KOREA)

See PART I: THE SETTING. *See also* REPUBLIC OF KOREA ARMY; RHEE, SYNGMAN; UNITED NATIONS AIR FORCES; UNITED NATIONS NAVAL FORCES.

REPUBLIC OF KOREA AIR FORCE (ROKAF)

See UNITED NATIONS AIR FORCES. *See also* KOREA MILITARY ADVISORY GROUP.

REPUBLIC OF KOREA ARMY (ROKA)

Tracing its origins to the eight Constabulary Regiments formed in 1946 to back up the National Police in maintaining public order, the Republic of Korea Army (ROKA) officially came into being on December 15, 1948, four months after the Republic of Korea had proclaimed its independence.

By June 1950 the ROKA included 115,000 men organized into eight poorly equipped divisions—the Capital Division and the First, Second, Third, Fifth, Sixth, Seventh and Eighth divisions—with half along the border with North Korea and the remainder in reserve. Battlefield reverses in the opening days of the war required that most of these divisions be retrained and reconstituted, and a similar reconstruction took place after Chinese Communist Forces (CCF) intervention. But each time ROKA bounced back stronger than ever, and when the war ended in July 1953 the ROK military had 590,911 men under arms and three corps with some 16 well-trained, well equipped and battle-hardened divisions in the field, with four more in the planning stages.

In 1965 the ROKA would send two divisions to Vietnam to assist the Allied effort there. The ROK Capital (Tiger) Division and the ROK Ninth (White Horse) Division (as well as a ROK Marine Brigade) would be among the last Allied units to leave, departing Vietnam in March 1973.

See KOREA MILITARY ADVISORY GROUP.

Suggestions for further reading: There is no history of ROKA actions in the Korean War in the English language. In the absence of such a work see Major Robert K. Sawyer, USA, *Military Advisors in Korea: KMAG in Peace and War* (Washington, D.C.: GPO, 1962). See also See *U.S. Army in the Korean War* series: Roy A. Appleman, *South to the Naktong, North to the Yalu* (Washington, D.C. GPO, 1961.); Walter G. Hermes, *Truce Tent and Fighting Front*, 1966; and Billy C. Mossman, *Ebb and Flow*, anticipated in 1990 (Washington, D.C.: GPO). For order of battle see Shelby L. Stanton, *Korean War Order of Battle* (Washington, D.C.: GPO, anticipated 1990). See also Clay Blair, *The Forgotten War: America in Korea 1950–1953* (New York Times Books, 1987).

REPUBLIC OF KOREA NAVY (ROKN)

See UNITED NATIONS NAVAL FORCES.

REPUBLIC OF KOREA PRESIDENTIAL UNIT CITATION

The Republic of Korea Presidential Unit Citation was awarded in the name of the president of the Republic of Korea to those units—including U.S. units—that distinguished themselves on the battlefield during the Korean War. The award criteria was much the same as that re-quired for award of the similar U.S. decoration (*see* PRESIDENTIAL UNIT CITATIONS, U.S.).

A streamer was authorized for the unit's colors and the individual award emblem (the blue and red yin-yang symbol from the ROK flag superimposed on a green, red and white striped ribbon, all encased in a gold frame) can be worn permanently by those assigned to the unit at the time of award.

See AWARDS.

RESERVE FORCES

See MOBILIZATION.

REST AND RECUPERATION (R&R)

Although the military had had rest areas in earlier wars, they were on an ad hoc basis. Studies in World War II, however had indicated sharp increases in casualty rates when troops had been engaged in combat in excess of 180 days without relief. Because of these findings, on December 31, 1950, a formal rest and recuperation (R&R) program was established by the Eighth U.S. Army (EUSA) and Japan Logistical Command (JLC).

Selected by their units in Korea, participants were flown to Japan on Air Force transports for five days temporary duty in Japan. On arrival they were paid, issued uniforms, fed and provided with a billet in a Special Services hotel or on one of the many military bases in Japan. Then they were left alone to "rest and recuperate."

Initially, two processing centers were established in Japan: one at Camp Kokura near Ashiya Air Base on Kyushu for soldiers previously stationed with the 24th and 25th Infantry divisions in southern Japan and the other at Camp McNeely near Haneda Air Base (later changed to Camp Drake near Tachikawa Air Base) in the Tokyo-Yokohama area. A third processing center was established in February 1951 at Osaka using Itami Air Base as the point of entry for personnel desiring to spend their R&R in the Kobe-Osaka-Kyoto area.

From the beginning of the program in December 1950 until August 1951, 91,000 UN officers and enlisted men had spent five days R&R in Japan. These included more than 82,000 U.S. personnel, 5,100 British and British Commonwealth personnel, and 3,500 other UN troops. In September 1951, U.S. Far East Air Force (FEAF) standardized the system. "Packets" of 46 persons with an officer or noncommissioned officer in charge were airlifted to and from Korea. By the end of June 1953, FEAF's 315th Air Division (Combat Cargo) had airlifted 800,000 R&R passengers between Korea and Japan.

Suggestions for further reading: Robert F. Futrell, *The United States Air Force in Korea: 1950–1953*, revised edition (Washington, D.C.: GPO, 1983). A more detailed account of the R&R program from its inception until August 1951 is in Captain Billy G. Mossman et al, *Monograph: Logistical Problems and Their Solutions: 25 August 1950–31 August 1951* (Headquarters Japan Logistical Command, February 15, 1952).

RHEE, SYNGMAN (1875–1965)

Born April 26, 1875, in Hwanghae Province (now the provinces of Hwanghae-namdo and Hwanghae-pukto in North Korea), Rhee was sent to Seoul to receive a classical Chinese education in preparation for government service. There he became an active member of the Korean student movement and in 1897 was jailed and tortured. Rhee converted to Christianity while in jail, and after his release in 1904, he came to the United States. He received a B.A. from George Washington University, an M.A. from Harvard and a Ph.D. in theology from Princeton in 1910.

Rhee returned to Korea in 1910, just as the Japanese were seizing control of the country. Again participating in revolutionary activity, he was forced to flee the country. Living in exile in Hawaii, he directed the Korean Christian Institute there. In 1919, he was elected president of the Korean Provisional Government, and from 1920 until 1941 he traveled yearly to Shanghai, China, to attend the annual conventions of that government-in-exile.

In 1945, after the defeat of Japan, Rhee openly criticized the United States for sanctioning the de facto division of Korea at the 38th parallel and was a particular critic of the "occupation" commander at the time, Lieutenant General John R. Hodge. A virulent anti-Communist, Rhee was elected president of the newly formed Republic of Korea (ROK), which was formally proclaimed on August 15, 1948.

Newly elected chairman of the National Assembly Syngman Rhee delivers the opening address at its first meeting on May 31, 1948.
(Courtesy U.S. Army Military History Institute.)

Meanwhile, except for the small Korea Military Advisory Group, all U.S. military forces were being withdrawn from Korea. By the end of 1948, the U.S. Sixth Infantry Division, with headquarters in Pusan, had been withdrawn and deactivated. On January 25, 1949, the U.S. XXIV Corps headquarters in Seoul was also deactivated, and shortly thereafter the U.S. Seventh Infantry Division that had been garrisoning the 38th parallel was transferred to Japan. The Fifth Regimental Combat Team, the last U.S. force in Korea, departed for Hawaii on June 29, 1949.

When North Korea launched its surprise attack on June 25, 1950, Rhee's poorly equipped ROK forces fell back in panic and confusion. Forced to evacuate Seoul, Rhee called upon the United Nations and the United States in particular for aid and assistance. When the UN's call for an immediate cessation of hostilities was ignored, the UN Security Council called on June 27, 1950, for member states to furnish military aid to the ROK and designated the United States as the UN's executive agent.

On July 14, 1950, President Rhee placed the armed forces of the Republic of Korea under the operational control of the United Nations Command (UNC)—in effect, General Douglas MacArthur's General Headquarters, Far East Command, in Tokyo—which further delegated that control to its field commanders. Thus, like the other UN military and naval forces, all ROK ground forces operated under the command of the Eighth U.S. Army, all ROK air forces under Fifth Air Force, and all ROK navy units under Naval Forces Far East.

In the pursuit of the war, Rhee was by and large a most cooperative ally. In 1951, however, he mounted a public campaign to force the United States to arm 10 additional ROK divisions. When General Matthew Ridgway, the new UNC commander, reminded him that, because of corrupt and incompetent ROK

Army senior officers, the ROK Army had already abandoned enough equipment in their headlong flights from the battlefield to equip 10 divisions, Rhee backed down and instead began a program to strengthen ROK Army leadership.

But the pursuit of peace was another matter. Rhee was adamant that the war should not end until Korea had been reunified. When the truce talks began in July 1951, there was fear in Washington that Rhee might sabotage the talks or refuse to abide by the terms of a negotiated settlement. After two years of sniping, Rhee struck in June 1953.

On June 18, 1953, Rhee released some 25,000 North Korea People's Army prisoners of war into the South Korean countryside, thereby hoping to sabotage the truce talks that were on the verge of ending the war. He forbade all ROK personnel from working with the UNC and alerted all ROK Army personnel to be prepared to fight on alone, armistice or no armistice.

President Dwight D. Eisenhower sent Assistant Secretary of State Walter S. Robertson and Army Chief of Staff General J. Lawton Collins to meet with Rhee. First, he was to be offered long-term U.S. military and economic aid if he would cooperate. Second, if he did not cooperate, he was to be warned that all U.S. forces would be withdrawn forthwith, leaving the ROK to fight on alone. Third, if this bluff failed, the task force had a highly-secret plan to stage a coup d'etat (Operation EVERREADY) to replace him with a more amenable leader. In the midst of these talks, the CCF launched a 15-division attack aimed directly at ROK divisions manning the center of the UN line at Kumsong, shattering the ROK Capital Division and forcing the other ROK divisions back some six miles with terrible losses.

Rhee got the message. On July 9, 1953, while the fighting at Kumsong was still raging, he agreed to cease his efforts to obstruct the armistice. When Robertson and Collins left Korea on July 12, 1953, they had Rhee's assurances that his government would "endeavor to cooperate fully and earnestly." But despite these assurances, Rhee never formally accepted the July 27, 1953, agreement. On August 15, 1953, he publicly expressed his government's "wish and determination to march north at the earliest possible time to save our North Korean brethren." Among other reasons, it was fear that he might indeed try to "march north" that led the United States to maintain a large military garrison in Korea long after the end of the war.

Syngman Rhee continued to serve as president of the ROK until April 27, 1960, when his increasingly autocratic government was overthrown in a student-led coup. Once again he fled to Hawaii, where he died on July 19, 1965. *See* PART I: THE SETTING.

Suggestions for further reading: Robert T. Oliver, *Syngman Rhee: The Man Behind the Myth* (New York: Dodd, Mead, 19550; Richard C. Allen, *Korea's Syngman Rhee: An Unauthorized Portrait* (Rutland, VT: Tuttle, 1960). Clay Blair's *The Forgotten War: America in Korea 1950–1953* (New York Times Books, 1987) chronicles Syngman Rhee during the 1950 to 1953 war years. Max Hastings' *The Korean War* (New York: Simon & Schuster, 1987) is much more critical of Rhee and his governmental repression.

RIDGWAY, MATTHEW B(UNKER) (1895–)

Ridgway was born March 3, 1895, at Fortress Monroe, Virginia, where his father a colonel of artillery, was stationed. He graduated from the United States Military Academy in 1917. Posted to the Third Infantry Regiment, he spent World War I on the Mexican border, and in the fall of 1918, he returned to the Military Academy as an instructor of French and Spanish and director of athletics. After six years on the faculty (where he served under General Douglas MacArthur, then West Point superintendent), Ridgway attended the Infantry School, the Command and Staff School and the Army War College and served in a variety of infantry assignments, including service under Colonel George C. Marshall with the 15th Infantry Regiment in China. When World War II began, he was serving in the War Plans Division of the Army general staff in Washington.

Early in 1942, Major General Ridgway replaced General Omar Bradley as commander of the 82d Infantry Division and shortly after assuming command, turned the division into one of the Army's first airborne units. Ordered to North Africa in 1943, he jumped with his division in the invasion of Sicily. In June 1944, he again jumped with the 82d Airborne Division in the Normandy invasion. Named to head the XVIII Airborne Corps, his command fought in the Ardennes, crossed the Rhine at Wesel, fought through the Ruhr pocket, crossed the Elbe and made contact with advancing Soviet forces on May 2, 1945.

After commanding the Mediterranean Theater of Operations, Ridgway served with the Military Staff Committee of the United Nations (where, ironically, he prepared a report on UN Security Council use of military force), chaired the Inter-American Defense Board and was commander of the Caribbean Command. Ridgway then returned to the Army staff in Washington and was serving as the Army's deputy chief of staff for administration when the Korean War broke out.

Used by then Army Chief of Staff General J. Lawton Collins as his "manager" for the conflict, Ridgway was directly involved in the Army's mobilization for the Korean War. Familiar not only with what was going on in Washington, Ridgway had also met personally with General Douglas MacArthur, the Far East Command (FEC) commander during an August 1950 visit to the Far East when he had also taken a first-hand look at the fighting to hold the Naktong Perimeter. Thus, he was no stranger to the war when in December 1950 he was named to command the Eighth U.S. Army (EUSA), replacing Lieutenant General Walton H. Walker, who had been killed in a vehicle accident on December 23, 1950.

Few commanders in military history have faced a more discouraging prospect. EUSA was on the verge of total collapse. The month before, the First Cavalry Division had been badly mauled at Unsan by Chinese Communist Forces (CCF) and the Second Infantry Division virtually annihilated at Kunu-ri. From positions near the Yalu River and the border with China, EUSA had fallen back south of the 38th parallel, and doomsayers were skeptical of their ability to maintain even a toehold on the Korean peninsula in the face of the advancing CCF field armies. There was worry that the Republic of Korea (ROK) Army, also badly mauled by the CCF, might surrender en masse. Meanwhile, X (Tenth) Corps, which had also taken a beating in their withdrawal from the Chosin Reservoir, was in the process of evacuating their forces from Hungnam and moving by sea to join EUSA in South Korea. Morale was at rock bottom, and defeatism was in the air.

Although EUSA may have been defeated, its new commander was not. "If I find the situation to my liking," he asked General Mac-Arthur upon assuming command, "would you have any objection to my attacking?" Mac-Arthur grinned at the audacity of the question. "The Eighth Army is yours, Matt," he replied. "Do what you think best."

In one of the most remarkable achievements in the history of warfare, Ridgway turned the Eighth U.S. Army from dejection and defeat

Left, General Ridgway, newly appointed Eighth U.S. Army commander, confers with General MacArthur on the battlefield in Korea.
(Courtesy Lyndon Baines Johnson Library & Museum.)

into a tough, battle-ready force within a matter of weeks. Although initially forced to fall back to consolidate his lines, on February 21, 1951, Ridgway launched Operation Killer and seized the battlefield initiative from the Chinese. From that time on, the survival of South Korea was never again in doubt.

The secret of Ridgway's transformation of the Eighth U.S. Army was twofold. First was the remarkable strength of his character. His steadfastness, confidence and courage soon permeated the entire Eighth U.S. Army.

Second was his understanding that EUSA's problems were not physical but moral. On January 21, 1951, immediately after assuming command, he had a message read to every unit in Korea. To the question, "Why are we here?," his answer was simple. "We are here because of the decisions of the properly constituted authority of our respective governments ... the loyalty we give, and expect, precludes any slightest questioning of these orders."

To the question, "What are we fighting for?," Ridgway said the question was not confined to Korea or to the defense of our Korean allies, it was a defense of our own freedoms. "In the final analysis," he said, "the issue now joined right here in Korea is whether Communism or individual freedom shall prevail; whether the flight of fear-driven people we have witnessed here shall be checked, or shall at some future time, however distant, engulf our own loved ones in all its misery and despair ... These are the things for which we fight ... ."

On April 11, 1951, President Harry S Truman relieved General MacArthur from command, and General Ridgway was named to serve simultaneously as commander in chief, Far East Command; commander in chief, United Nations Command; commander in chief, Army Forces Far East; and as supreme commander Allied powers in charge of the occupation of Japan. Succeeded as EUSA commander by General James Van Fleet, Ridgway continued to oversee the war in Korea from his headquarters in Tokyo, including the defeat of the CCF spring offensive in 1951 and the beginning of the Korean armistice talks later that same year.

In May 1952 General Ridgway was named to replace General Eisenhower as the supreme commander, Allied powers Europe, and head of the North Atlantic Treaty Organization. He departed that post in October 1953 to become Army chief of staff in Washington. One of his significant accomplishments there was his successful argument that the United States not intervene in Indochina in 1954 to shore up the French in their battles with the Vietminh. After a series of disagreements with the Eisenhower administration over its "massive retaliation" strategies, which relied almost entirely on nuclear weapons for our nation's defenses,

Ridgway retired from active duty in June 1955. Along with John "Blackjack" Pershing, George Marshall, Dwight Eisenhower and Douglas MacArthur, Ridgway was one of the greatest American soldiers of the twentieth century. *See* EIGHTH U.S. ARMY; FAR EAST COMMAND.

Suggestions for further reading: See Matthew B. Ridgway, *Soldier: The Memoirs of Matthew B. Ridgway* (New York: Harper & Row, 1956) and *The Korean War* (Garden City, NY: Doubleday, 1967); See also: biographic entries in *Political Profiles: The Truman Years*, Eleanora W. Schoenebaum, editor (New York: Facts On File, 1978) and Richard F. Haynes' biographical sketch in Roger J. Spiller, editor, *Dictionary of American Military Biography*, (Westport, Conn.: Greenwood Press, 1984) as well as Clay Blair, *Ridgway's Paratroopers* (Garden City, NY: Dial Press, 1985) and *The Forgotten War: America in Korea 1950–1953* (New York Times Books, 1987).

ROCKET ARTILLERY

In addition to the Navy battleship, cruiser and destroyer guns and the Army and Marine field artillery guns and howitzers, rocket artillery (ship-to-shore, air-to-ground and ground-to-ground) was also used during the Korean War.

Navy rocket ships such as LSMR (Landing Ship Medium Rocket) 401, 403, 404, 409, 412 and 525 armed with 5-inch spin-stabilized rockets operated with the Navy's Task Force 90 (Amphibious Force Far East) and Task Force 95 (Blockade and Escort Force). LSMRs supported the landing at Inchon and the evacuation of Hungnam and took part in other shore bombardment operations as well. On May 23 and 25, 1951, for example, LSMR 409 and 412 fired 7,700 rockets at enemy gun emplacements in the Wonsan area.

Air Force and Navy fighters were armed with 5-inch HVARs (high-velocity aircraft rockets) for use against ground targets. The F-80 Shooting Star jet fighter, for example, carried a load of four such rockets.

The U.S. Army had some multiple rocket launcher batteries in Korea, which fired volleys of 4.5-inch ground-to-ground rockets, and the enemy had a limited number of Soviet-supplied Katushka truck-mounted rocket launchers, each of which fired a set of four 82-mm rockets.

Although their lack of accuracy made rocket artillery useless against pinpoint targets, they were very effective against area targets.

See also BLOCKADE AND ESCORT FORCE; FIELD ARTILLERY.

Suggestions for further reading: For Navy rocket ships see James A. Field, *History of United States Naval Operations: Korea* (Washington, D.C.: GPO, 1962). See also Commanders Malcolm W. Cagle and Frank A. Manson, USN, *The Sea War in Korea* (Annapolis, Md: United States Naval Institute, 1957). For Air Force and Navy aerial rockets, see Robert F. Futrell, *The United States Air Force in Korea: 1950–1953*, revised edition (Washington, D.C.: GPO, 1983) and Richard P. Hallion, *The Naval Air War in Korea* (Baltimore: The Nautical & Aviation Publishing Company of America, 1986). For ground-to-ground rockets, see *U.S. Army in the Korean War* series: Roy A. Appleman, *South to the Naktong, North to the Yalu*, 1961; Walter G. Hermes, *Truce Tent and Fighting Front*, 1966; and Billy C. Mossman, *Ebb and Flow*, anticipated in 1990 (Washington, D.C.: GPO).

ROCKET LAUNCHERS

When the United States entered the Korean War, the standard antitank rocket launcher (or "bazooka" as it was then known) was the 2.36-inch model named for the diameter of the launching tube. Proven ineffective in World War II, it was worthless in Korea as well. Used by the infantrymen of Task Force Smith in the opening days of the war against advancing North Korean armor, it was unable to stop the T-34 tanks.

A 3.5-inch model had been in development since the end of World War II but had not been fielded because of difficulties with its ammunition. Only 15 days before the war started, this difficulty had been overcome, and the ammunition ordered into production. On July 3, 1950, the commander in chief, Far East Command, requested that this new rocket launcher be airlifted to Korea, and the first weapons arrived on July 10, 1950. Put into action by soldiers of the 24th Infantry Division's 24th Reconnaissance Company and Third Engineer Battalion during the battle for Taejon on July 20, 1950, these new rocket launchers destroyed three enemy tanks during their first battlefield engagements.

The 3.5-inch rocket launcher became the standard antitank weapon during the Korean War. Not only used against enemy armor, it was also used against enemy fortifications as well. Made of aluminum, it looked like a five-foot length of stovepipe. It was electrically operated and fired a 23-inch long, eight-and-one-half-pound shaped-charge rocket capable of burning through the armor of any tank then known.

See also SMALL ARMS; TAEJON, BATTLE OF.

Suggestions for further reading: See *U.S. Army in the Korean War* series: Roy A. Appleman, *South to the Naktong, North to the Yalu*, 1961; Walter G. Hermes, *Truce Tent and Fighting Front*, 1966 (Washington, D.C.: GPO).

ROYAL AUSTRALIAN REGIMENT (RAR)

See AUSTRALIA; BRITISH COMMONWEALTH DIVISION.

Two First Cavalry Division soldiers compare the new 3.5-inch antitank rocket launcher (foreground) with its ineffective 2.36-inch predecessor.
(Courtesy U.S. Army Military History Institute.)

RUSK, (DAVID) DEAN (1909–)

Born February 9, 1909, in Cherokee County, Georgia, Rusk graduated from Davidson College in 1931 and later studied at Oxford University as a Rhodes Scholar. After receiving his Master of Arts degree in 1934, he returned to the United States and accepted a position as assistant professor of government at Mills College in California.

Rusk entered the Army in World War II and served on the staff of General "Vinegar Joe" Stilwell in the China-Burma-India Theater and later on the Army general staff in the Strategy and Planning Group, Operations Division. It was there in August 1945 that Colonel Rusk helped select the 38th parallel as the dividing line for U.S. and Soviet disarmament of Japanese forces in Korea.

At the request of Secretary of State George C. Marshall, Rusk became director of the State Department's Office of Special Political Affairs in 1947. He rose to become assistant secretary of state for United Nations (UN) affairs, then deputy undersecretary of state.

In March 1950, Rusk took the post of assistant secretary of state for Far East affairs and played a leading role in formulating policy for Korea. Seeing the attack on Korea as another Munich, he recommended strong U.S. action, albeit through the UN wherever possible. He was as strong supporter of Chinese Nationalist leader Chiang Kai-shek and argued against the legitimacy of the Chinese Communist government. Nevertheless, during the Congressional "Great Debate" on U.S. Korean War policy, Rusk testified against widening the war in Korea. Rusk also took part in the Japanese peace treaty and the U.S.–Japan mutual security treaty in 1952.

Rusk left office in January 1953 to work for the Rockefeller Foundation, but would later serve as secretary of state in the Kennedy and Johnson administrations. He again left public office in 1969, and became a professor of law at the University of Georgia.

See ACHESON, DEAN; GREAT DEBATE; STATE DEPARTMENT; 38TH PARALLEL.

Suggestions for further reading: Thomas J. Schoenbaum, *Waging Peace and War: Dean Rusk in the Truman, Kennedy and Johnson Years* (New York: Simon & Schuster, 1988). See also the biographic entry in *Political Profiles: The Truman Years*, Eleanora W. Schoenebaum, editor (New York: Facts On File, 1978).

SANCTUARIES

A sanctuary by definition is a place of refuge or protection, where those sheltered within are immune from attack. In November 1950, setting a precedent that would hobble U.S. military operations for the remainder of the Korean War (and would be carried forward into the subsequent Vietnam War as well), the United States (and thereby the United Nations Command) allowed the Chinese Communist Forces (CCF) and the Chinese Communist Air Forces (CCAF) to treat the area north of the Yalu River that separates Korea from the China territory of Manchuria as a sanctuary.

Although knowing the claim was patently false, the United States played along with the Chinese subterfuge that their forces were Chinese People's Volunteers and that China itself was not involved in the war. To avoid bringing China formally into the war which, it was then supposed, would bring China's "master," the Soviet Union, into the war and to appease our increasingly fearful West European allies, the United States granted China a kind of neutrality.

It was a neutrality to which it was not legally entitled. According to the Hague Convention of 1907, "A neutral country has the obligation not to allow its territory to be used by a belligerent. If the neutral country is unwilling or unable to prevent this, the other belligerent has the right to take appropriate counteraction."

Yet even though MiG-15 fighters flying from Manchurian bases routinely attacked and shot down Allied aircraft over North Korea, the Allied fighters were forbidden even the right of hot pursuit.

A kind of "gentleman's agreement" ensued where the United States would not strike the Manchurian bases so long as Chinese air power was not used against Allied ground troops in Korea, was not used to attack Allied bases outside of Korea (particularly in Japan) and was not used to attack Allied forces in transit to or from Korea. This agreement proved to be cold comfort, however, for the Allied airmen flying missions in northwestern Korea's "MiG Alley," who continued to be attacked by Chinese aircraft flying from Manchurian sanctuaries.
See also RASHIN; MANCHURIA.

Suggestions for further reading: In addition to the military and naval histories of the war, see Rosemary Foot's *The Wrong War: American Policy and the Dimensions of the Korean Conflict, 1950–1953* (Ithaca, NY: Cornell University Press, 1985).

SASEBO

A former Imperial Japanese naval base, the port city of Sasebo is located on the western coast of the Japanese island of Kyushu. When the war began, it was the headquarters of the U.S. Army's 34th Infantry Regiment, 24th Infantry

Division, and was a secondary naval facility for U.S. Fleet Activities Yokuska.

Because of Sasebo's location and its excellent harbor—the Korean port city of Pusan lay only 156 sea miles away across the Tsushima and Korean Straits—Fleet Activities Sasebo soon eclipsed Yokuska (located near Tokyo 500 miles further away from the battle area) as the major anchorage and replenishment area for Naval Forces Far East. In addition to the naval facilities at Sasebo, there was also a large U.S. Army replacement depot located there. Most U.S. military personnel who served in Korea passed through Sasebo either enroute to Korea, enroute back to the United States or both.
See NAVAL FORCES FAR EAST; REPLACEMENT DEPOTS.

SCAP (SUPREME COMMANDER ALLIED POWERS)

See FAR EAST COMMAND.

SCORCHED EARTH POLICY

On November 29, 1950, after his forces were severely mauled by elements of the Chinese Communist Forces (CCF) XIII Field Army, Lieutenant General Walton H. Walker the Eighth U.S. Army (EUSA) commander, issued formal orders for a general withdrawal to new defensive positions near the North Korean capital of Pyongyang. When EUSA reached those positions, however, Walker decided he had insufficient forces to mount a successful defense, and he decided to abandon Pyongyang and all of North Korea. He ordered a further withdrawal south of the 38th parallel to defensive positions along the Imjin River.

To impede the advancing CCF divisions, which General Walker believed lacked sufficient logistic support and were living off the land, he ordered a "scorched earth" policy.

Such a policy was not new in warfare. It had been used by the Soviet Red Army in World War II against the Nazi invaders and, in conjunction with the terrible Russian winter, had proven to be quite successful. With the subzero temperatures of the Korean winter now at hand, Walker hoped his policy would be equally effective.

The enormous U.S. supply depot at Pyongyang was put to the torch, and to further implement the scorched earth policy, all highway and railroad bridges were destroyed. Nothing of value was left behind, and during the December 6 to 13, 1950, withdrawal, the troops were given orders to burn all houses, kill all the livestock and destroy all the rice supplies. For whatever reason, the CCF did not initially pursue. Whether the scorched earth policy worked against them is uncertain, but it did have an effect on the civilian population. Although many North Koreans were already fleeing southward to escape the advancing Chinese, this policy encouraged many others to take flight, and more than one million Korean refugees moved south through the depths of a particularly harsh winter.

On the eastern coast refugees were also on the move. Tenth (X) Corps was withdrawing from the Chosin Reservoir area to the port of Hungnam. During the period December 10 to 24, 1950, 105,000 U.S. and Republic of Korea (ROK) troops were withdrawn by sea, together with 350,000 tons of supplies and 91,000 refugees. Again, everything that could not be evacuated was destroyed by engineer demolition teams or by naval gunfire. Meanwhile, on December 23, 1950, General Walker had been killed in a jeep accident and was replaced as EUSA commander by Lieutenant General Matthew B. Ridgway. On January 4, 1951, after destroying the supply dumps at Inchon and Kimpo, General Ridgway rescinded the "scorched earth" order.

See WITHDRAWAL FROM NORTH KOREA.

Suggestions for further reading: Clay Blair, *The Forgotten War: America in Korea 1950–1953* (New York Times Books, 1987). A new book, Russell Spurr's *Enter the Dragon: China's Undeclared War Against the U.S. in Korea, 1950–1951* (New York: Newmarket Press, 1988), has an account of the suffering of the CCF during the winter of 1950 to 1951.

SEABEES

Officially "amphibious construction battalions," the Navy's Seabees were part of Task Force 90 (Amphibious Force Far East). Among their other projects was the 1952 construction under enemy fire of a 2,400-foot runway on Yo-Do Island in Wonsan harbor for the recovery of aircraft damaged in the Navy's siege of that port city. Scheduled to be completed in 45 days, it was actually finished in 16. In July 1952 alone, eight Corsairs, which otherwise would have been lost, landed safely on this strip.

See also ENGINEERS; NAVY, U.S.; WONSAN.

Suggestions for further reading: James A. Field, *History of United States Naval Operations: Korea* (Washington, D.C.: GPO, 1962). See also Commanders Malcolm W. Cagle and Frank A. Manson, USN, *The Sea War in Korea* (Annapolis, Md: United States Naval Institute, 1957); Richard P. Hallion, *The Naval Air War in Korea* (Baltimore: The Nautical & Aviation Publishing Company of America, 1986).

SEA OF JAPAN

With the Yellow Sea on the west and the Sea of Japan on the east, the Korean peninsula has a 5,400-mile coastline. While the Yellow Sea is relatively shallow, the line along which the Sea of Japan's depth reached 100 fathoms generally runs close to Korea's eastern coastline. This, combined with a tidal range that runs only one to two feet, means that coastal shipping is exposed, and warships can get within gun range of the roads and railroads that run along eastern Korea's narrow coastal strip. These hydrographic factors influenced Naval Forces Far East's task force organization for the conduct of naval operations during the Korean War.

In the North, the main ports are Rashin (also known as Najin), seventeen miles south of the Russo-Korean border, and Hungnam and Wonsan on the Gulf of Korea. The latter two ports would be the sites of naval amphibious operations early in the war and naval blockades in the later years. In the south, there is a minor port at Pohang.

See HUNGNAM, EVACUATION OF; RASHIN; WONSAN; YELLOW SEA.

SEARCH AND RESCUE OPERATIONS (SAR)

Both the Air Force and the Navy conducted extensive search and rescue (SAR) operations in the Korean War to recover downed pilots both on land and on sea. While the Navy and Marine Corps conducted SAR operations on a decentralized basis, the Air Force had a formal organization for air rescue.

When the war began, the U.S. Air Force's Third Air Rescue Squadron was stationed in Japan. Part of the MATS (Military Air Transportation Service) worldwide Air Rescue Service, it was under the operational control of the Far East Air Force (FEAF) and was scattered among various bases where it could best perform emergency air rescue service.

The standard SAR aircraft was the SB-17, a modified version of the World War II bomber, but the squadron also had a few small two-seat H-5A Sikorsky helicopters. Shortly after the war began, a detachment of Grumman SA-16

Albatross amphibian "flying boats" joined the squadron.

The Third Air Rescue Squadron pioneered the employment of new SAR techniques, including the rescue of stranded personnel behind enemy lines. At first, L-5 observation aircraft were tried, but they could not land in the Korean rice paddies. Then on July 22, 1950, a detachment of H-5 helicopters arrived from Japan. These aircraft could land not only on rice paddies but in mountainous terrain as well.

On August 27, 1950, the Fifth Air Force established a Rescue Liaison Office in the Joint Operations Center, and on August 30, the Third Air Rescue Squadron formally organized Detachment F in Korea. On September 4, 1950, the first rescue of a downed pilot behind enemy lines was made. Covered by a rescue combat air patrol of friendly fighters, an H-5 flew in and picked up the pilot, then returned safely to friendly lines.

In March 1951, H-19 helicopters arrived in Korea. Much larger than the H-5, it could carry ten passengers in addition to its crew. As the nature of the war changed after the front lines stabilized in 1951 and more pilots began to be downed by enemy antiaircraft fire ("flak"), Detachment F was redesignated Detachment One, Third Air Rescue Squadron, and a full-scale SAR coordination center was established in the Fifth Air Force Tactical Control Center in Seoul.

As more airstrikes began to be mounted deep within northwest Korea, a new procedure was established. A pilot in trouble would broadcast a "Mayday" and head for a predetermined orbit off Korea's western coast. When his plane went down, initial air cover would be provided by his squadron mates until the SA-16 amphibian arrived. While this worked well in summer months, it was found that when winter arrived, the flying boats were unable to land in the icy waters. To remedy this situation,

it was decided to station H-5 helicopters on Cho-do Island off the North Korean coast. After the island was cleared of enemy personnel, H-5s began operating from there in January 1952 and later from Paengnyong-do Island as well.

In February 1952, the H-5s at Cho-do and Paengnyong-do were replaced by H-19s which had a longer range and a greater lift capability. Originally equipped with floats for water landings, it was found that lowering ropes from its hydraulic-powered hoists was a more practical method.

On March 1, 1953, Detachment One, Third Air Rescue Squadron was redesignated as the 2157th Air Rescue Squadron and concentrated its efforts on SAR operations in North Korea. To help in South Korea, Detachment Two, Third Air Rescue Group, was established at Pohang Air Base with two SA-16s, two H-19s and a paramedic team. In addition, other Third Air Rescue Squadron units in Japan also assisted in SAR operations in the Sea of Japan, and SB-29s from the Second Air Rescue Squadron on Okinawa (later the 33d and 34th Air Rescue Squadrons) accompanied B-29 bombers on their air missions over North Korea to render SAR service as needed.

During the Korean War, 1,670 U.S. Air Force airmen went down in enemy territory. Most did not survive the crash, but air rescue teams saved 170 downed personnel—10% of the total. They also retrieved 84 airmen of other United Nations units from behind enemy lines and within friendly lines picked up and evacuated 86 airmen. In addition to SAR operations, the Air Rescue Service evacuated a total of 8,598 front-line casualties to hospitals in the rear. Another mission was the landing and recovery of intelligence agents along the mud flats of Korea's northwestern coast.

Suggestions for further reading: Robert F. Futrell, *The United States Air Force in Korea:*

1950–1953, revised edition (Washington, D.C.: GPO, 1983).

SEARCHLIGHTS

Both sides used searchlights during the Korean War. Originally developed for antiaircraft units to spotlight enemy planes, they were used for that purpose by the North Koreans and Chinese, who deployed more than 500 searchlights as part of their air defense system. Many were radar controlled, with beams that could reach to 30,000 feet. These mobile searchlights were used extensively against Allied night-fighters and bombers.

On the Allied side, searchlights were used primarily for battlefield illumination. Antiaircraft artillery (AAA) searchlight batteries behind friendly lines would bounce searchlight beams off lowflying clouds, and the light would be reflected onto enemy positions.

In 1951, the Air Force obtained a number of 80 million-candlepower searchlights that had been mounted on World War II Navy antisubmarine airships and mounted them on B-26 bombers for use in night bombing raids. One B-26 pilot, Air Force Captain John S. Walmsley, was awarded the Medal of Honor posthumously for his actions while flying an illumination mission.

Suggestions for further reading: For Army searchlight operations, see *U.S. Army in the Korean War* series: Roy A. Appleman, *South to the Naktong, North to the Yalu*, 1961; Walter G. Hermes, *Truce Tent and Fighting Front*, 1966; and Billy C. Mossman, *Ebb and Flow*, anticipated in 1990 (Washington, D.C.: GPO). For Air Force and enemy use of searchlights, see Robert F. Futrell, *The United States Air Force in Korea: 1950–1953*, revised edition (Washington, D.C.: GPO, 1983).

SECOND INFANTRY DIVISION

Organized in October 1917 on the battlefield in France, the Second "Indianhead" Infantry Division took part in six campaigns on the Western Front in the First World War. In World War II, it went ashore at Normandy and fought in six campaigns across Europe. When the Korean War started in June 1950, it was stationed at Fort Lewis, Washington.

The Second Infantry Division comprised the Ninth, 23d and 38th Infantry Regiments; the black 503d (155-mm) Field Artillery Battalion (deactivated in November 1951 as part of Eighth U.S. Army's [EUSA] desegregation program and replaced by the 12th Field Artillery Battalion); the 15th, 37th and 38th (105-mm) Field Artillery Battalions; the 72d Medium Tank Battalion; the 82d Antiaircraft Artillery Battalion (Automatic Weapons); the Second Combat Engineer Battalion; and the Second Reconnaissance Company.

Alerted on July 8, 1950, the first elements of the Second Infantry Division sailed for Korea nine days later, and the main body sailed on July 20, 1950. By August 19, 1950, the entire division had arrived and was committed to the defense of the Naktong Perimeter. Following the Inchon invasion, the division conducted mop-up operations in southwestern Korea, then joined the rest of EUSA in North Korea. When the Chinese Communist Forces (CCF) intervened in force in November 1950, the Second Infantry Division was holding EUSA's right flank in the Kunu-ri area. Attempting to extricate itself as EUSA withdrew to the south, the Second Infantry Division was overwhelmed and virtually destroyed.

After a brief respite for rebuilding in EUSA reserve, the Second Infantry Division (with the French Battalion attached) again took part in heavy fighting in January and February 1951 in the Hongchon area, including the battle of Chipyong-ni. In April 1951, it defended the

Hwachon Reservoir area and later fought in the Punchbowl, Heartbreak Ridge and the Iron Triangle and at outposts such as Pork Chop Hill. Lt. Col. Bernard W. Rogers, who would later serve as Army chief of staff, was a battalion commander in the Division.

For its actions in Korea, the Second Infantry Division won the U.S. Presidential Unit Citation for its bravery at Hongchon and was awarded two Republic of Korea Presidential Unit Citations. Its Ninth Infantry Regiment won a Navy Presidential Unit Citation for bravery at the Hwachon Reservoir and a Navy Unit Commendation for its actions at Panmunjom, and its 23d Infantry Regiment won Presidential Unit Citations for bravery at the Twin Tunnels and at Chipyong-ni.

In addition to other awards won by members of the division, eighteen "Indianhead" soldiers won the Medal of Honor for conspicuous bravery on the battlefield. During the course of the war the division suffered 25,093 casualties, including 7,094 soldiers killed in action or died of wounds, 16,237 wounded in action, 186 missing in action and 1,516 prisoners of war.

After the armistice, the Second Infantry Division returned to the United States, but in 1965 it again returned to Korea where it is presently stationed, with headquarters at Tongduchon north of Seoul. The Second (Indianhead) Division Association publishes a periodic newsletter, "The Indianhead," and hosts reunions of those who served with the division. Further information can be obtained from Mr. William T. Belvin, P.O. Box 2499, Fort Benning, Georgia 31905. Telephone (404) 563-5005.

See also CHIPYONG-NI; KUNU-RI; NAKTONG PERIMETER.

Suggestions for further reading: See *U.S. Army in the Korean War* series: Roy A. Appleman, *South to the Naktong, North to the Yalu*, 1961; Walter G. Hermes, *Truce Tent and Fighting Front*, 1966; and Billy C. Mossman, *Ebb and Flow*, anticipated in 1990 (Washington, D.C.: GPO). For order of battle see Shelby Stanton, *Korean War Order of Battle* (Washington, D.C.: GPO, anticipated 1990). See also Clay Blair, *The Forgotten War: America in Korea 1950–1953* (New York Times Books, 1987).

SECOND LOGISTICAL COMMAND

See KOREAN COMMUNICATIONS ZONE.

SECRETARY OF DEFENSE

The secretary of defense is a member of the president's cabinet and a member of the National Security Council. Under the president of the United States, who is also the commander in chief, the secretary of defense exercises direction, authority and control over the Department of Defense, which includes the Army, Navy, Air Force and Marine Corps.

Within the Pentagon, it is this civilian secretary, not the uniformed heads of the Joint Chiefs of Staff, who is the "general-in-chief" and actually has operational command over America's armed services. During the Korean War, the chain of command ran from the president to the secretary of defense through the Joint Chiefs of Staff to the commander in chief, Far East Command, in Tokyo.

When the war began, Louis A. Johnson, who had been appointed on March 28, 1949, was serving as Secretary of Defense. Former general of the Army, George C. Marshall, replaced Johnson on September 21, 1950, and served until September 12, 1951. Marshall's successor was Robert A. Lovett, who served from September 17, 1951, until the end of the Truman administration in January 1953. Charles E. Wilson served as secretary of defense during the remaining seven months of the war.

See DEFENSE DEPARTMENT; JOHNSON, LOUIS A.; JOINT CHIEFS OF STAFF; LOVETT, ROBERT A.; MARSHALL, GEORGE C.

Suggestions for further reading: Douglas Kinnard, *The Secretary of Defense* (Lexington, Ky.: University of Kentucky Press, 1980).

SECRETARY OF STATE

The secretary of state is a member of the president's cabinet and a member of the National Security Council. He advises the president of the United States on the formulation and execution of foreign policy with the primary objective of promoting the long-range security and well-being of the United States.

When the Korean War began in June 1950, the secretary of state was Dean G. Acheson, who served in that capacity until the end of the Truman administration in January 1953. He was succeeded by John Foster Dulles who

General MacArthur confers with, left, John Foster Dulles, who was to become secretary of state in the Eisenhower administration in January 1953 and help bring the war to an end.
(Courtesy Lyndon Baines Johnson Library & Museum.)

served as secretary of state during the last seven months of the war.

See ACHESON, DEAN G.; DULLES, JOHN FOSTER; STATE DEPARTMENT.

SENATE HEARINGS, MILITARY SITUATION IN THE FAR EAST

See GREAT DEBATE.

SEOUL

In 1392, shortly after he ascended the throne to found the Yi Dynasty, General Yi Song-gye moved the capital of Korea from Songdo (modern Kaesong) to Seoul (then called Hanyang). Almost 600 years later it remains the capital of the Republic of Korea (ROK).

Seoul (the word literally means "capital" in Korean) lies on the north bank of the Han River on Korea's western coastal plain some twenty miles inland from its port city of Inchon and less than fifty air miles south of the 38th parallel. When the Korean War began on June 25, 1950, the prime North Korean People's Army (NKPA) axis of advance was down the western coastal plain toward Seoul, which fell to the invaders on June 27, 1950.

It remained under enemy occupation until three months later, when on September 25, 1950, it was recaptured by the U.S. First Marine Division following the Inchon invasion. In a ceremony on September 29, 1950, General Douglas MacArthur, the commander in chief, Far East Command, turned the city back to ROK President Syngman Rhee, but Seoul received only temporary respite from the war. On January 3, 1951, it once again fell to the advancing Chinese Communist Forces (CCF), which had pushed the Eighth U.S. Army (EUSA) out of North Korea.

On March 15, 1951, it was the CCF's turn to abandon Seoul, as the EUSA counterattack to

Seoul would change hands four times in the course of the war. Here in September 1950 U.S. Marines fight house-to-house to rid the city of its North Korean occupiers.
(Courtesy U.S. Army Military History Institute.)

drive the CCF out of South Korea, Operation KILLER/RIPPER, flanked the city to the west. The city, now reduced to not much more than a pile of rubble, changed hands for the fourth and final time during the Korean War. From its prewar population of a million and a half, only about 200,000 remained. As *Time* magazine described it at the time, with disease rampant and no water, electricity or food, "The fourth fall of Seoul was a sad business, something like the capture of a tomb."

But Seoul, like a phoenix, was to rise from its ashes. Today, with a population in excess of ten million people, Seoul (site of the 1988 Summer Olympics) is one of the world's largest and most modern cities.

Suggestions for further reading: John W. Riley, Jr., and Wilbur Schramm, *The Reds Take a City* (New Brunswick, NJ: Rutgers University Press, 1951).

SERVICE MEDALS, U.S.

As the name implies, service medals are awarded to members of the Armed Forces to recognize their serving during a particular time period or in a particular place. For the American armed forces, three service medals were awarded for service during the Korean War. All personnel who served honorably on active duty during the period June 27, 1950, through July 27, 1954, were awarded the National Defense Service Medal. Those who actually served in Korea or in waters adjacent to Korea during that time frame were also awarded the Korean Service Medal and the United Nations Service Medal.

See also DECORATIONS, U.S.; KOREAN SERVICE MEDAL; NATIONAL DEFENSE SERVICE MEDAL; UNIT AWARDS; UNITED NATIONS SERVICE MEDAL.

SEVENTH FLEET STRIKING FORCE (TASK FORCE 77)

The Seventh Fleet Striking Force (Task Force 77) was one of the major subordinate commands of U.S. Naval Forces, Far East (NAVFE). As with all naval task forces, its composition varied as ships were attached or detached as required to meet the demands of the assigned mission.

It consisted of the cruisers of the Support Group, Task Group 77.1; the destroyers of the Screening Group, Task Group 77.2; and the fast aircraft carriers of the Carrier Group, Task Group 77.4, which were the heart of the striking force. Eleven attack carriers (CVAs in Navy terminology), many on repetitive tours, served with Task Force 77, which operated primarily off the east coast of Korea in the Sea of Japan. These included the USS *Antietam* (CVA36), *Boxer* (CVA21), *Bon Homme Richard* (CVA31), *Essex* (CVA9), *Kearsarge* (CVA33), *Lake Champlain* (CVA 39), *Leyte* (CVA32), *Oriskany* (CVA34), *Philippine Sea* (CVA47), *Princeton* (CVA37) and *Valley Forge* (CVA45).

While in Korean waters these CVAs had 24 CAG's (Carrier Air Groups) embarked, with a total of one hundred squadrons including twenty-two reserve squadrons. These included 38 F4U Corsair squadrons, 23 AD Skyraider squadrons and 4 F2H Banshee squadrons.
See AIRCRAFT CARRIERS; NAVAL FORCES FAR EAST.

Suggestions for further reading: James A. Field, *History of United States Naval Operations: Korea* (Washington, D.C.: GPO, 1962). See also

Commanders Malcolm W. Cagle and Frank A. Manson, USN, *The Sea War in Korea* (Annapolis, Md: United States Naval Institute, 1957); Richard P. Hallion, *The Naval Air War in Korea* (Baltimore: The Nautical & Aviation Publishing Company of America, 1986).

SEVENTH INFANTRY DIVISION

Organized in December 1917, the Seventh Infantry Division fought in the Lorraine campaign on the Western Front in the First World War. In World War II, it went ashore at Attu in the Aleutians and fought in the Eastern Mandates, Leyte and the Ryukyus campaigns. In September 1945, the Seventh Infantry Division moved to Korea to disarm the Japanese military south of the 38th parallel and remained there until 1949 when it moved to Hokkaido as part of the Japan occupation force. It was located in Hokkaido when the Korean War began in June 1950.

The Seventh Infantry Division comprised the 17th, 31st and 32d Infantry regiments; the 31st (155-mm) Field Artillery Battalion; the 48th, 49th and 57th (105-mm) Field Artillery battalions; the 73d Medium Tank Battalion; the 15th Antiaircraft Artillery Battalion (Automatic Weapons); the 13th Combat Engineer Battalion; and the Seventh Reconnaissance Company.

The Seventh Infantry Division remained behind as the Far East Command reserve when the other infantry divisions in Japan were rushed to Korea in July 1950 and was initially drained of many of its personnel as replacements for those divisions. In August 1950, however, it was designated as part of the Inchon invasion force and brought up to full strength, primarily by the influx of 8,652 untrained KATUSAs (Korean Augmentation to the U.S. Army—Korean soldiers detailed to serve with U.S. units).

A B Company, 17th Infantry, rifle squad takes cover behind a stone wall during action northeast of Kumma-ri in February 1951.
(Courtesy Lyndon Baines Johnson Library & Museum.)

On September 17, 1950, the Seventh Infantry Division followed the First Marine Division across the beach at Inchon, took part in the liberation of Seoul and linked up with advancing Eighth U.S. Army (EUSA) units advancing northward from the Naktong Perimeters. Reembarking at Pusan in October 1950, the division moved up Korea's eastern coast and made an unopposed landing at Iwon 75 miles northeast of Hungnam.

The 17th Infantry Regiment moved northward and reached the Yalu River at Hysenjinon November 21, 1950, but Task Force Maclean, the 31st Infantry Regiment and the First Battalion, 32d Infantry Regiment, were sent east of the Chosin Reservoir to support the First Marine Division and were virtually annihilated when the Chinese Communist Forces (CCF) attacked there in force.

Fighting its way back to Hungnam, the division was evacuated by sea by December 19, 1950, and became part of the EUSA defensive line. It fought on the central front in 1951 in the Yangu-Inje-Hwachon area and in 1952 to 1953 fought in the Iron Triangle area and in the outpost battles at Jane Russell and Pork Chop hills. It was fighting at Pork Chop Hill when the armistice was declared in July 1953.

For its actions in Korea the Seventh Infantry Division won three Republic of Korea Presidential Unit Citations. Its 31st Infantry Regiment won two navy Presidential Unit Citations for bravery at the Chosin and Hwachon reservoirs, and its 32d Infantry Regiment won two Army Presidential Unit Citations for bravery at Kumhwa and Central Korea, two Navy Presidential Unit Citations for bravery at Inchon and the Hwachon Reservoir and a Navy

Unit Commendation for its actions at Panmunjom.

In addition to other awards won by members of the division, twelve "Bayonet Division" soldiers won the Medal of Honor for conspicuous bravery on the battlefield. During the course of the war, the division suffered 15,126 casualties, including 3,905 soldiers killed in action or died of wounds, 10,858 wounded in action, 22 missing in action and 341 prisoners of war.

The Seventh Infantry Division remained in Korea for many years after the end of the war but is now stationed at Fort Ord, California. The Seventh Infantry Division Association publishes a newsletter and hosts periodic reunions of those who served with the division. Further information can be obtained from Mr. Louis S. Wise, Jr., 3001 Richmond Avenue, Matoon, Illinois 61938. Telephone (217) 234-6534.

See also INCHON INVASION; PORK CHOP HILL, BATTLE OF; TASK FORCE MACLEAN/TASK FORCE FAITH.

Suggestions for further reading: *U.S. Army in the Korean War* series: Roy A. Appleman, *South to the Naktong, North to the Yalu*, 1961; Walter G. Hermes, *Truce Tent and Fighting Front*, 1966; and Billy C. Mossman, *Ebb and Flow*, anticipated in 1990 (Washington, D.C.: GPO). For order of battle, see Shelby Stanton, *Korean War Order of Battle* (Washington, D.C.: GPO, anticipated 1990). See also Clay Blair, *The Forgotten War: America in Korea 1950–1953* (New York Times Books, 1987).

SHEPHERD, LEMANUEL C., JR. (1896–)

Born February 10, 1896, at Norfolk, Virginia, Shepherd graduated from the Virginia Military Institute in 1917. Commissioned as a second lieutenant in the Marine Corps on April 11, 1917, he sailed for France two months later. Serving with the Fifth Marine Regiment (part of the Army's Second Infantry Division) on the Western Front, Shepherd was twice wounded in action at Belleau Wood and later saw action in the St. Mihiel and Meuse-Argonne campaigns where he was wounded a third time. For his bravery under fire, Shepherd won the Navy Cross, the Army's Distinguished Service Cross and the French Croix de Guerre.

During the interwar years, Shepherd served as a White House aide, as commander of the Marine detachment on the USS *Idaho*, with the Third Marine Regiment in Tientsin and Shanghai in China and with the Garde d'Haiti. After graduation from the Naval War College in 1937, he commanded the Second Battalion, Fifth Marines. When the United States entered World War II, he was serving with the Marine Corps School at Quantico, Virginia.

Shepherd assumed command of the Ninth Marine Regiment in March 1942 and took that unit into combat in the South Pacific. Promoted to Brigadier General in July 1943, he served as assistant division commander of the First Marine Division in the Cape Gloucester operation and as commander of the First Provisional Marine Brigade in the recapture of Guam. Promoted to Major General, Shepherd assumed command of the Sixth Marine Division and led it through the Okinawa campaign.

When the Korean War broke out in June 1950, General Shepherd was serving as commanding general, Fleet Marine Force, Pacific with headquarters in Honolulu. In this capacity, he participated in the landing at Inchon and the withdrawal from the Chosin Reservoir in December 1950.

On January 1, 1952, he was appointed commandant of the Marine Corps and served in that position during the remainder of the Korean War. He was the first commandant to become a member of the Joint Chiefs of Staff. Retiring from active duty on January 1, 1956, he was recalled later that year to serve as chairman of the Inter-American Defense Board. General

Shepherd again retired from active duty on September 15, 1959.

See COMMANDANT, U.S. MARINE CORPS; MARINE CORPS, U.S.

Suggestions for further reading: See the five-volume official history, *U.S. Marine Operations in Korea 1950–1953*: Lynn Montross and Captain Nicholas A. Canzona, USMC, *The Pusan Perimeter*, 1954; *The Inchon-Seoul Operation*, 1955; *The Chosin Reservoir Campaign*, 1957; Lynn Montross and Majors Hubard D. Kuokka and Norman W. Hicks, USMC, *The East-Central Front*, 1962; and Lieutenant Colonel Pat Meid, USMCR, and Major James M. Yingling, USMC, *Operations in West Korea*, 1972 (Washington, D.C.: GPO). See also Allan R. Millett, *Semper Fidelis: The History of the United States Marine Corps* (New York: Macmillan, 1980).

SHERMAN, FORREST P(ERCIVAL) (1896–1951)

Born October 30, 1896, in Merrimack, New Hampshire, Sherman graduated with the class of 1918 from the United States Naval Academy, which, because of World War I, actually graduated early in June 1917. During the war, he served on convoy duty and on antisubmarine patrols on board the gunboat *Nashville* and the destroyer *Murray*.

During the interwar years, he became interested in naval aviation and won his wings in December 1922. After attendance at the Naval War College in 1926–1927, Sherman served on board the carriers *Lexington* and *Saratoga*. When World War II broke out, he was serving in the Navy's War Plans Division in Washington.

Promoted to captain in May 1942, Sherman commanded the carrier *Wasp*, which supported the landings at Guadalcanal, and was in command when the *Wasp* was sunk by a Japanese submarine on September 15, 1942. Awarded the Navy Cross and later promoted to Rear Admiral, Sherman served for the remainder of the war on Admiral Chester Nimitz's Pacific Fleet staff.

Serving as commander, U.S. Naval Forces, Mediterranean during the "revolt of the admirals" in 1949 when the navy leadership publicly challenged the decision to cancel the supercarrier *United States*, Sherman (who had kept out of the fight) became the surprise candidate to replace Admiral Louis E. Denfield as chief of naval operations (CNO), and he was named to that post by President Harry S Truman on November 2, 1949.

Then the youngest CNO ever appointed, and the first whose career had been devoted to aviation, Admiral Sherman was serving as chief of naval operations when the Korean War began in June 1950. He presided over the dispatch of naval forces to Korean waters and the naval build-up for the war. A strong supporter of General Douglas MacArthur, the commander in chief, Far East Command, Admiral Sherman was the guiding force within the Joint Chiefs of Staff for approval of MacArthur's plans to invade Inchon in September 1950. Nevertheless, he concurred with the other Joint Chiefs in General MacArthur's relief from command in April 1951.

Later that year, Admiral Sherman suffered a heart attack while visiting NATO facilities in Naples, Italy, and died on July 22, 1951. He was succeeded as chief of naval operations by Admiral William M. Fechteler.

See CHIEF OF NAVAL OPERATIONS; JOINT CHIEFS OF STAFF; NAVY, U.S.

Suggestions for further reading: For biographical information, see Clark G. Reynolds' essay in *The Chiefs of Naval Operations*, edited by Robert William Love, Jr. (Annapolis, Md.: Naval Institute Press, 1980). See also James A. Field, *History of United States Naval Operations: Korea* (Washington, D.C.: GPO, 1962); Commanders Malcolm W. Cagle and Frank A. Manson, USN, *The*

Sea War in Korea (Annapolis, Md: United States Naval Institute, 1957); and Richard P. Hallion, *The Naval Air War in Korea* (Baltimore: The Nautical & Aviation Publishing Company of America, 1986).

SHERMAN TANK (M-4A3E8)

See ARMOR.

SILVER STAR MEDAL

First authorized in World War I, the Silver Star Medal is America's third highest award for battlefield bravery. Awarded in the name of the president of the United States for gallantry in action against the enemy, the Silver Star Medal recognizes heroic action of marked distinction of a lesser degree than that required for award of the Medal of Honor or the Distinguished Service Cross/Navy Cross. Subsequent awards are denoted by an oak leaf cluster (gold star for Navy and Marine Corps personnel) worn on the medal ribbon.
See DECORATIONS, U.S.

SMALL ARMS

The small arms of the Korean War—the individual and crew-served weapons with which the war was fought—were enormously varied. On both sides, by and large, they were leftovers from World War II. Among American and Republic of Korea (ROK) troops, the weapons were mainly standard U.S. issue, but many of the other United Nations forces were equipped with their own weapons, which were incompatible with American arms.

These American arms included such World War I weapons as the M-1911A1 .45-caliber automatic pistol (which would continue in service until after the Vietnam War), the M-1918A2 Browning Automatic Rifle (BAR), as well as the Browning M-1917A1 water-cooled .30-caliber machine-gun. There were also the interwar weapons such as the M-1919A4 and A6 .30-caliber air-cooled light machine-guns and the M-1921M2 .50-caliber air-cooled heavy machine-gun as well as the standard small arms from World War II—the Garand M-1 rifle, "Carbine Williams'" M-1A1 semiautomatic carbine and M-2 automatic carbine and the .45-caliber M-3 "Grease Gun" submachine-gun.

British Commonwealth forces were armed with the World War I-vintage .455-caliber Webley and .380-caliber Enfield revolvers, the bolt-action Mark 4 Lee-Enfield .303 rifle (whose first model was produced in 1895), the 1912 model Mark I Vicker water-cooled .303 machine-gun and an excellent light machine-gun, the 1938 model air-cooled .303-caliber Mark 1 Bren gun.

On the enemy side, the North Koreans started out with all Soviet-supplied World War II-vintage weapons, the most notorious of which was the 7.62-mm PPSh41 submachine-gun, better known as the "Burp Gun." Also common was the Soviet Mosin-Nagant Model 1944 7.62-mm carbine with folding bayonet and the Tula-Tokarev TT33 7.62-mm automatic pistol. Machine-guns included the 7.62-mm water-cooled PM1910 Maxim gun on a wheeled mount and the 7.62-mm air-cooled DP1928 light machine-gun. The air-cooled 12.7-mm DShKM1938/46 was their heavy machine-gun.

For their part, the Chinese forces had a mixture of captured Japanese weapons from World War II, American weapons captured from the Nationalists during the Chinese Civil War, Soviet-supplied small arms, and Chinese copies of Soviet-supplied weapons such as the Type 53 (the Chinese version of the Tokarev pistol). In the early days of the war, many Chinese soldiers went into action armed only with grenades and would then arm themselves with the weapons of their fallen comrades.

Captured North Korean small arms, August 1950. Top to bottom: Soviet D5hKM 1938/46 12.7-mm heavy machine-gun with antiaircraft tripod mount; Soviet PM 1910 Maxim water-cooled 7.62-mm machine-gun on a "Sokolov" wheeled mount; Soviet PTRD 14.5-mm antitank gun; Soviet DP 7.62-mm light machine-gun with bipod; Japanese Arisaka Type 99 7.7-mm rifle; Soviet Mosin-Nagant 7.62-mm carbine and a Soviet PPPSh41 7.62-mm "burp gun" submachine-gun.
(Courtesy U.S. Army Military History Institute.)

See also BAYONET; BURP GUN; BROWNING AUTOMATIC RIFLE; M-1 RIFLE; MACHINE-GUN; RECOILLESS RIFLE; ROCKET LAUNCHER.

Suggestions for further reading: Ian V. Hogg and John Weeks, *Military Small Arms of the 20th Century* (Northfield, Ill.: DBI Books, 1985).

SMITH, OLIVER P. (1893–1977)

Born October 26, 1893, in Menard, Texas, Smith graduated from the University of California at Berkeley in 1916. Called to active duty as a Marine Corps second lieutenant on May 14, 1917, he spent World War I on Guam. During the interwar years, Smith commanded the Marine detachment on the USS *Texas*, served on the Marine Corps staff in Washington, spent a tour with the Gendarmerie d'Haiti, and attended both the U.S. Army's Infantry School and the French Ecole Superieure de Guerre. When the United States entered World War II, he was commanding a battalion of the Sixth Marines in Iceland.

Smith joined the First Marine Division in New Britain in January 1944 and commanded the Fifth Marine Regiment at Talasea and in the Peleliu operation. He served as deputy chief of staff for the 10th U.S. Army for the invasion of Okinawa. Named commanding general of the First Marine Division in June 1950, General Smith led the men ashore at Inchon in September 1950. During the breakout from the Chosin Reservoir in November to December 1950, he won the Army's second highest award for bravery, the Distinguished Service Cross, for his heroism in breaking the enemy's stranglehold and leading his division in a fighting 70-mile march to the seaport of Hungnam.

General Smith returned to the United States in May 1951, where he commanded the Marine Corps Base at Camp Pendleton, California, and served as commanding general of the Fleet Marine Force, Atlantic. Advanced in rank to full (four-star) general upon his retirement from active duty on September 1, 1955, General Smith died on December 25, 1977.

See CHOSIN RESERVOIR, BATTLE OF; FIRST MARINE DIVISION; INCHON INVASION.

Suggestions for further reading: See the five-volume official history, *U.S. Marine Operations in Korea 1950–1953*: Lynn Montross and Captain Nicholas A. Canzona, USMC; *The Pusan Perimeter*, 1954; *The Inchon-Seoul Operation*, 1955; *The Chosin Reservoir Campaign*, 1957; Lynn Montross and Majors Hubard D. Kuokka and Norman W. Hicks, USMC, *The East-Central Front*, 1962; and Lieutenant Colonel Pat Meid, USMCR, and Major James M. Yingling, USMC, *Operations in West Korea*, 1972 (Washington, D.C.: GPO). See also Allan R. Millett, *Semper Fidelis: The History of the United States Marine Corps* (New York: Macmillan, 1980).

SMITH, WALTER B(EDELL) (1895–1961)

A professional military officer, Walter Bedell Smith was a veteran of both the First and Second World Wars. During World War II, he served as General Eisenhower's chief of staff in the European Theater of Operations and rose to the rank of Lieutenant General. In 1946, he was appointed the United States' ambassador to the Soviet Union and served in Moscow until March 1949.

In October 1950, Smith was appointed to head the Central Intelligence Agency (CIA) and later was promoted to full (four-star) general. As the director of central intelligence, he is credited with reorganizing the CIA's internal bureaucracy and creating the basic structure that would govern the CIA for the next twenty years. Under his tenure, the office of policy coordination, responsible for covert operations, grew from 322 people in 1949 to 2,812 in 1952, not including 3,142 overseas contract personnel. By then, clandestine collection and covert action accounted for 74% of the CIA's budget and 60% of its personnel strength.

In January 1953, General Smith left the CIA to become an undersecretary of state in the Eisenhower administration. He left government service in 1954 and died on August 9, 1961.

See also CENTRAL INTELLIGENCE AGENCY; DIRECTOR, CENTRAL INTELLIGENCE.

Suggestions for further reading: See biographical sketch in Roger J. Spiller, editor, *Dictionary of American Military Biography* (Westport, Conn.: Greenwood Press, 1984). See also the biographic sketch in Eleanora W. Schoenebaum, editor, *Political Profiles: The Truman Years* (New York: Facts On File, 1978).

SORTIES

A sorty is one trip by one plane. Ten sorties could be 10 aircraft making one trip, one aircraft shuttling back and forth from its base 10 times or any such combination of trips and planes that totals 10 trips. From June 27, 1950, to July 27, 1953, United Nations aircraft flew more than 1,040,708 close support, counter-air, interdiction, cargo and miscellaneous sorties in support of United Nations military operations in Korea.

Suggestions for further reading: For statistics on sorties flown, see Robert F. Futrell, *The United States Air Force in Korea: 1950–1953*, revised edition (Washington, D.C.: GPO, 1983).

SOUTH AFRICA, UNION OF

Ethiopia and the Union of South Africa were the only two African nations to send combat forces to Korea. While Ethiopia sent an infantry battalion, South Africa sent a squadron of F-51 Mustang fighter aircraft. Nicknamed the "Flying Cheetahs," the Second South African Air Force (SAAF) Squadron arrived in Korea in the fall of 1950, and their first base was K-23 in Pyongyang, the capital of North Korea. Flying as part of the Fifth U.S. Air Force's 18th Fighter-Bomber Wing, the SAAF participated in close air support of friendly forces and interdiction strikes on enemy lines of communication.

While specific figures for the South African Air Force Squadron are not available, it is known that at a cost of 152 aircraft lost, land-based friendly foreign aircraft (i.e., Australia's 77th Squadron, South Africa's Second Squadron and the aircraft of the Republic of Korea Air Force) flew some 44,873 sorties, including 6,063 close air support and 15,359 interdiction missions where they expended some 20,000 tons of bombs, rockets, ammunition and napalm. They also participated in some 3,025 counter-air sorties where they destroyed three enemy aircraft and flew 6,578 cargo missions and 13,848 miscellaneous flights.

Statistics are not available for South African casualties in the war, but it is known that nine South Africans were among those repatriated during the prisoner of war exchange following the end of the war.

See also UNITED NATIONS AIR FORCES.

Suggestions for further reading: Robert F. Futrell, *The United States Air Force in Korea: 1950–1953*, revised edition (Washington, D.C.: GPO, 1983).

SOUTH KOREA

See PART I: THE SETTING.

SOVIET UNION (UNION OF SOVIET SOCIALIST REPUBLICS)

One factor that makes the Korean War difficult to understand today is the different way in which we view the Soviet Union and the international Communist movement. In 1950, the accepted wisdom (an idea that the Soviet Union was only too happy to perpetuate) was that there was an international Communist monolith, controlled and directed by the Soviet Union. Since all Communist states were thought to be totally subservient to Moscow, there could be no such thing as an "independent" Communist state that made decisions on its own. Therefore, the war in Korea had to be the work of the Soviet Union. This misperception led President Truman to see the attack on South Korea as a diversion and prompted him to send most of America's military strength to Europe rather than to Korea. Bedeviled by those who put Europe first in World War II, General MacArthur saw the same thing happening in Korea, a factor that increased the tensions between Washington and MacArthur's headquarters in Tokyo and hampered the conduct of the war.

The sad truth is that the U.S. government had totally misread the situation. There was no Communist "monolith," and the Soviet Union's ability to control its allies was limited. As the late Soviet Premier Nikita Khrushchev revealed in 1970, it was North Korean Premier

Kim Il-sung who was the driving force behind the invasion. He had discussed it with Soviet Premier Joseph Stalin (who in turn consulted Chinese Premier Mao Tse-tung before agreeing to give his support), but the initiative was Kim Il-sung's, who was convinced that the United States would not intervene. That version is supported by the fact that at the time of the invasion, the Soviet delegate to the United Nations, Jacob Malik, was boycotting the Security Council, thereby allowing the UN to pass resolutions condemning the attack and setting up the United Nations Command to resist it (all of which Malik could have vetoed if he had been present).

It is not that the Soviet Union was without influence in the war. The threat of intervention from its bases in the Soviet Far East was always present, and the U.S.S.R. provided large quantities of arms and equipment both to the North Koreans and to the Chinese (whom they later billed). And it is significant that agreement on the Korean armistice came only after the 1953 death of Stalin. But contrary to the perceptions at the time, the Korean War was not, as President Truman saw it, an attempt by the Soviet Union to spread communist ideology by force of arms.

By misjudging our enemy, we had diluted our strength. As Henry Kissinger later observed, "We had entered the Korean War because we were afraid that to fail to do so would produce a much graver danger to Europe in the near future. But then the very reluctance to face an all-out onslaught in Europe severely circumscribed the risks we were prepared to run to prevail in Korea."

See PART I: THE SETTING.

Suggestions for further reading: *Khruschev Remembers*, translated and edited by Strobe Talbott (Boston: Little, Brown, 1970). See also Henry Kis-singer, *White House Years* (Boston: Little, Brown & Company, 1979).

SPECIAL OPERATIONS

Although the term "special operations" came into being long after the Korean War was over, there were several instances during the war where such operations were actually conducted. Among them were the sea-launched raids along the Korean coast conducted by U.S. Navy landing parties and the commandos of the 41st Independent Royal Marines. These raids cut enemy lines of supply and communication and tied down large numbers of enemy personnel in coastline defenses.

Partisan operations in North Korea sponsored primarily by U.S. Army units were especially organized for similar purposes. After the withdrawal of the Eighth U.S. Army (EUSA) from North Korea in November 1950, thousands of North Korean partisans took up arms against the Chinese Communist Forces (CCF) then occupying their country and against the Communist government of North Korea and the North Korean People's Army (NKPA). In early January 1951, they held portions of Hwanghae Peninsula south of the North Korean capital of Pyongyang and had established themselves on several islands of North Korea's western coast.

Organized at first on an ad hoc basis under EUSA's G-3 operations section and commanded by Colonel John McGee, a guerrilla leader in the Philippines in World War II, a fledgling U.S. Army special operations unit (later designated Army Unit 8086) furnished food, clothing, communications equipment, arms and ammunition to these partisans and sent American controllers to join in their operations.

By July 1951, the partisan force had grown to about 7,000 men. They had 700 captured weapons and an additional 3,200 provided by the United States as well as a number of junks, which they were using to conduct hit-and-run raids on the mainland. Some 65 Americans were assigned to work with this force. Most of the Americans were guerrilla-war amateurs since the U.S. Army then had no training programs in special warfare. The partisans claimed at that time to have killed 2,112 Chinese and North Korean soldiers and to have taken 169 prisoners.

Although the partisans had been reassured that the long-term United Nations Command (UNC) goal was the liberation of North Korea, these assurances were cast into doubt with the beginning of the armistice negotiations in the summer of 1951. Nevertheless, their numbers continued to grow. Colonel McGee had been replaced by another Philippine-guerrilla veteran, Lieutenant Colonel Jay Vanderpool, who organized the partisan force into regiments and battalions, with U.S. advisers down to the company level. Vanderpool modernized the junk fleet (which could transport some 5,000 armed partisans in a single lift) and installed 106-mm recoilless rifles on board. He also began parachuting partisans behind enemy lines. Several parachute raids in March 1951 and June 1951 led by a British officer who had served in the Special Air Service were particularly successful. By December 1951, the partisans claimed to have inflicted 9,095 enemy deaths, captured 385 prisoners and captured or destroyed over 800 enemy weapons, including six artillery pieces. Unfortunately, 81% of these operations had been away from the enemy's main lines of communication and supply, and only 2.8% had been targeted on the east coast.

That month control of partisan operations was transferred from EUSA in Seoul to the Far East Command (FEC) in Tokyo. Earlier FEC had established a Far East Command Liaison Group, Army Unit 8240, to coordinate all behind-the-lines activities, and this unit absorbed Army Unit 8086. In addition, a new unit, the Combined Command for Reconnaissance Activities, Korea (CCRAK), also known as Army Unit 8242, was formed under the FEC G-2. One benefit of this transfer was better access to aircraft for parachute drops, and 77 partisans were parachuted behind the enemy lines in 1952. Partisan strength reached 16,000 by December 1952. The partisans claimed to have inflicted 25,726 enemy casualties and captured 526 prisoners.

In December 1952, responsibility for partisan operations was once again shifted, this time to the newly established Army Forces Far East (AFFE), the Army component of a reorganized Far East Command, which was designated the executive agent for conduct of covert, clandestine and related activities. In the spring of 1953, AFFE received its first contingent of Army Special Forces personnel who were assigned throughout the command.

As the end of the war neared, concern focused on the status of the partisans, which were then some 22,227 strong and were organized into seven regiments that occupied eighteen island bases and nine sites within North Korea. Under the control of Colonel Glenn Muggleburg, who had been assigned in May 1953, the partisans were withdrawn from North Korea after the July 1953 armistice agreement went into effect and were incorporated into the Republic of Korea Army.

Suggestions for further reading: For Army special operations, the most detailed work is Colonel Rod Paschall, *A Study in Command and Control: Special Operations in Korea, 1951–1953* (Carlisle Barracks, Pa.: U.S. Army Military History Institute, June 1988). For U.S. Navy special operations, see

James A. Field, *History of United States Naval Operations: Korea* (Washington, D.C.: GPO, 1962). See also Commanders Malcolm W. Cagle and Frank A. Manson, USN, *The Sea War in Korea* (Annapolis, Md: United States Naval Institute, 1957).

SPRING OFFENSIVE, 1951

At 1000 hours, April 22, 1951, the Chinese Communist Forces (CCF) struck Eighth U.S. Army (EUSA) across a forty-mile front with twenty-seven infantry divisions—some 250,000 troops—to begin the biggest battle of the Korean War. Eighteen CCF divisions attacked along the Munsan-Uijongbu highway to strike I Corps positions north of Seoul while the other nine CCF infantry divisions struck IX Corps positions along the edge of the Iron Triangle in central Korea. Meanwhile, three NKPA (North Korean People's Army) divisions struck X Corps positions in western Korea.

I Corps was hard pressed, and the British Brigade's Gloucester Battalion was virtually annihilated, but they held the line north of Seoul, and the Republic of Korea (ROK) capital did not fall into enemy hands. In the IX Corps area, the Sixth ROK Division collapsed in a panic and abandoned its positions, creating a ten-mile gap between IX Corps' 24th U.S. Infantry Division and the X Corps' First Marine Division further to the west, which the CCF were quick to exploit. With the Australian and Canadian battalions of the British Commonwealth Brigade at Kapyong containing the nose of the penetration (an action that would earn them a U.S. Presidential Unit Citation for bravery), IX Corps was able to withdraw in good order and reestablish new defense positions some 35 miles to the rear. All across the Allied front, field artillery battalions put out a wall of steel to stop the CCF "human wave" attacks. *Time* magazine quoted one officer as saying, "They're spending people the way we spend ammunition."

By April 30, 1951, the battle was over. United Nations forces had suffered some 7,000 casualties and had temporarily lost some territory in central Korea. But the CCF had been denied its objective of the capture of Seoul and had lost some 70,000 casualties in the process. It was clearly a major victory for EUSA's new commander, Lieutenant General James A. Van Fleet, who had taken command on April 11, 1951, less than two weeks before the battle began.

See also FIELD ARTILLERY; GLOUCESTER HILL, BATTLE OF; VAN FLEET, JAMES A.

Suggestions for further reading: T.R. Fehrenbach's *This Kind of War: A Study in Unpreparedness* (New York: Macmillan, 1963) has a vivid account of the experiences of the Third Battalion, 21st Infantry Regiment, 24th Infantry Division, during this battle, and Clay Blair's *The Forgotten War: America in Korea 1950–1953* (New York Times Books, 1987) contains a particularly lucid overview from which the above account was condensed.

SQUADRON

See WING.

STAFF ORGANIZATION

During the Korean War, military staffs in the United States Army, Air Force and Marine Corps shared a similar organizational structure. At the battalion and regimental level was an executive officer, what the British call a "second in command," who oversaw the functioning of the staff. This staff included an S-1 or adjutant who was responsible for the unit's administration, an S-2 or intelligence officer who was charged with intelligence collection, evaluation and dissemination, an S-3 or operations officer

CCF SPRING OFFENSIVE, 1951

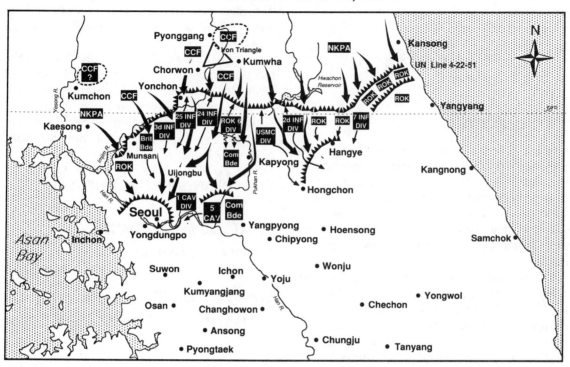

who was responsible for plans and training and an S-4 or supply officer who provided for the unit's supplies and logistics.

At the division, corps and field army level, this basic staff structure was repeated, except that the staff coordinator was no longer also the second in command. Called a chief of staff, the staff he presided over were higher in rank than those at lower levels and the designations were preceded by a "G" for general staff (G-1, G-2, G-3 and G-4). In the Army, those officers serving in such positions were designated in writing as serving on the "general staff with troops" and wore a distinctive general staff insignia (a miniature five-pointed silver star superimposed by the Great Seal of the United States) while serving in that capacity rather than their basic branch insignia.

In the Pentagon, at the Department of the Army and Department of the Air Force level, the structure was much the same, but the titles were more formal—the major general serving as G-2, for example, was officially the assistant chief of staff for intelligence (ACSI) and the lieutenant general serving as the G-3 was called the deputy chief of staff for operations and plans (DCSOPS). Again, Army officers serving there were appointed in writing as members of the "Army general staff" (which were forbidden by law from commanding troops) and wore the general staff insignia.

At the Joint Chiefs of Staff level (and later at the unified command level as well), the staff designations were preceded by a J for joint staff (J-1, J-2, J-3, etc.). The Navy staff at all levels performed similar functions as the other service staffs but used their own distinct naval terminology.

STALIN, JOSEPH (1879–1953)

See SOVIET UNION.

STATE DEPARTMENT

The State Department is responsible to the President for the conduct and formulation of U.S. relations with other nations. During the Korean War, the post of National Security Advisor had not been created, and there was no question that the secretary of state was the president's senior adviser on foreign policy matters.

For example, during the 1951 congressional "Great Debate" on the conduct of the Korean War, General of the Army Omar Bradley, the chairman of the Joint Chiefs of Staff, was asked what were America's objectives in Korea. He explained that war aims were always political, not military, and deferred to the secretary of state. Upon questioning, Secretary of State Dean Acheson stated clearly: Our original aim was restoration of the prewar status quo; after the September 1950 Inchon invasion and the collapse of the North Korean Army, the goal was changed to the liberation of the entire Korean peninsula; and after the November 1950 Chinese intervention, the goal was changed yet again, this time back to the original objective of restoration of the prewar boundaries.

Among the State Department's major problems in the Korean War was maintaining cordial relations with South Korean President Syngman Rhee, a task that fell mainly on the shoulders of U.S. Ambassador John Muccio. Another problem was stiffening the backbone of our European allies, who were constantly wringing their hands, especially after the

Chinese intervention in November 1950. The difference between the bravery of their soldiers and the cowardliness of their politicians was especially stark.

One great irony of the Korean War was the fact that Secretary of State Dean Acheson, and Dean Rusk, his assistant secretary of state for Far East affairs, were constantly accused by critics of being "soft on Communism" when in fact they were both among the most ferocious of the hawks.

See ACHESON, DEAN; MUCCIO, JOHN; RUSK, DEAN; SECRETARY OF STATE.

STRATEGIC AIR COMMAND

See BOMBER COMMAND.

STRATEGIC AIRLIFT

See MATS (MILITARY AIR TRANSPORT SERVICE).

STRATEGY

"Strategy" in its simplest sense is the use of means to accomplish ends. In its broadest sense it has to do with the use of power—political, economic, and psychological as well as military—to achieve the political goals, aims and objectives of a nation. This broad definition recognizes that war is a political act waged in pursuit of political objectives. Military forces are only one of several means available to attain those objectives. Other means include diplomatic efforts, economic pressures and such psychological efforts as the influencing of public opinion.

There can be, as in World War II, a political resolution arrived at primarily through military means (but note that battlefield "victories" only have meaning to the degree that they assist in attaining political ends). Politics, however, always remains the ultimate determinate.

The above formulation of strategy is now part of official U.S. Army doctrine, but at the time of the Korean War the notion held by most top political and military leaders was that politics and the military were diametrically and fundamentally things apart and that when war starts, politics stops. These differing views were at the heart of the Truman-MacArthur controversy (see MACARTHUR). General MacArthur's relief from command by President Truman reestablished politics as war's guiding force.

War itself has three dimensions. The highest is *strategic*, which has to do with attainment of the political goals for which the war is being waged. Next is *operational* (better known as campaign or theater warfare), which has to do with the use of a series of battles to realize the strategic aim. The lowest level is *tactical*, which involves how battles are fought.

At all levels the choices of action are the same—to attack (i.e., take offensive action), to defend (i.e., to await the enemy's attack) or to withdraw. But each level is distinct, and differing courses of action can be waged simultaneously. For example, at the strategic level one may choose to defend, while at the same time launching an attack at the operational and tactical levels to repel the enemy and gain more defensible terrain. As discussed below, this was often the case with U.S. and UN forces during the course of the Korean War.

See MACARTHUR, DOUGLAS; STRATEGY, COMMUNIST FORCES; STRATEGY, ALLIED; STRATEGY, U.S.

Suggestions for further reading: *On War* by Carl von Clausewitz, edited and translated by Michael Howard and Peter Paret (Princeton University Press, 1976); *War & Politics*, by Bernard Brodie (New York: MacMillan, 1973); *Selected Military Writings of Mao Tse-tung* (Peking: Foreign Language Press, 1966). For official Korean War U.S. Army doctrine see *Field Manual 100-5: Field Service Regulations: Operations* (Washington, D.C.: U.S. Government Printing Office, August 1949).

STRATEGY, ALLIED

Although influenced to some degree by its Republic of Korea (ROK) and United Nations (UN) allies, the United States dictated allied strategy during the Korean War. At the political level its diplomatic efforts at the United Nations and elsewhere in the world were successful in isolating North Korea and Communist China (as it was then known) as international pariahs. At the economic level the United States, then the richest and most powerful nation in the world, was able to enforce economic sanctions against countries that traded with the enemy. Ironically, given the influence of Madison Avenue advertising on American life, the weakest element of U.S. power was psychological, a vulnerability the enemy was able to exploit from time to time in its propaganda campaigns to influence and undermine public opinion (see GERM WARFARE).

The primary element of American power during the Korean War, however, was military. As discussed earlier (see STRATEGY), there are three levels of warfare—strategic, operational and tactical. At each level there are three broad courses of action available—the offensive (that is, attack and carry the war to the enemy), the defensive (i.e., await the enemy's attack) and the withdrawal (i.e., break contact with the enemy and retreat). At various times during the Korean War, allied forces would use all three of these courses of action.

Allied forces began the war on a temporary strategic and operational defensive, with the initial objective of containing the enemy invasion. At the tactical level, the course of action initially pursued was withdrawal, but once the Naktong Perimeter line was established, tactics varied between defense and limited counterattacks to regain ground lost to enemy assaults.

All this changed with the Inchon invasion in September 1950. Allied forces went on the strategic, operational and tactical offensive with the objective of rolling back communism and liberating North Korea. But with the intervention of Chinese Communist Forces (CCF) in November 1950, allied forces were forced back into the strategic defensive and to an operational and tactical withdrawal from North Korea (*see* WITHDRAWAL). By June 1951, after hard fighting along what was to become the demilitarized zone (DMZ) between North and South Korea, the enemy attack was contained. Requests by General James Van Fleet, the Eighth U.S. Army commander, to resume the strategic offensive were denied for political reasons, and allied forces went on the strategic, operational and, for the most part, tactical defensive for the remainder of the war.
See STRATEGY, COMMUNIST FORCES; STRATEGY, U.S.; VAN FLEET, JAMES.

STRATEGY, COMMUNIST FORCES

Starting with the cross-border invasion of South Korea in June 1950, North Korean military strategy (as well as the strategy of the Chinese Communist Forces [CCF] that later came to North Korea's support) remained constant. The political objective of the communist forces was the conquest of South Korea, and to that end they remained on the strategic offensive throughout the entire war (see discussion at STRATEGY on battlefield courses of action). Although strategy involves the use of political, economic, and psychological as well as military power, the communist forces relied almost exclusively on military power for the attainment of their political aims.

Their political clout was negligible since neither North Korea nor Communist China was then a member of the United Nations, and both nations lacked widespread diplomatic recognition. Economic power was also feeble, for North Korea and China were still struggling to recover from Japanese occupation, the ravages of World War II and (most importantly) the effects of state socialism on their nationalist economies. Enemy psychological power, however, did play a role in the war.

Although not nearly so sophisticated (nor so successful) as it would become during the later Vietnam War, communist psychological warfare had some success in attacking and undermining allied public support for the war. The old worldwide Comintern (Communist International) network of communist party members and sympathizers was mobilized and such propaganda tracts as then hard-line Stalinist I.F. Stone's "The Hidden History of the Korean War" sought to blame South Korea and the United States for starting the war. Propaganda campaigns (*see* GERM WARFARE) were also launched, and allied prisoners of war were also used to manipulate public sentiment.

From their cross-border invasion in June 1950 through their final assaults on the Naktong Perimeter in September 1950 North Korean forces were on the strategic, operational and tactical offensive. After the allied invasion of Inchon in September 1950 the invaders were forced into a withdrawal at the operational and tactical levels to the farthest reaches of North Korea, but their strategic posture remained constant. From November 1950 through May 1951 the North Korean forces reinforced by the CCF, resumed the operational and tactical attack until their offensive was contained by allied counterattacks along what was to become the demilitarized zone (DMZ) between North and South Korea. While they did launch attacks at the tactical level from time to time, communist forces went on the operational and, for the most part, tactical defensive until the end of the war.

At the strategic level, however, they remained on the offensive until the very end, that is, they never wavered in their goal to destroy the allied armed forces, seize Seoul and occupy the territory of South Korea. It was only allied military action that frustrated that ambition.

See STRATEGY; STRATEGY, ALLIED; STRATEGY, U.S.

STRATEGY, U.S.

As discussed earlier (*see* STRATEGY, ALLIED), U.S. military strategy in Korea was not only synonymous with allied strategy, it in fact shaped and determined allied strategy. But that military strategy had an effect on the United States and its ability to wage war that went far beyond the Korean battlefield.

From the beginning of the war in June 1950 until China's intervention in November 1950 the United States had followed the same military strategies it had pursued throughout its existence. As in earlier wars, it had initially assumed the strategic defensive to buy time until it could build up sufficient strength to attack the enemy and destroy his armed forces. That moment came with the Inchon invasion in September 1950, and the United States assumed the strategic offensive to roll back communism and liberate North Korea. When the Chinese intervened in November 1950, the United States was forced into a strategic withdrawal from North Korea and then back on the strategic defensive along what was to become the demilitarized zone between North and South Korea.

When the communist offensive was finally contained in June 1951, the United States, if it had followed its traditional method of waging

No matter how good tactics and operations, "victory" in Korea was not possible with a Washington-imposed strategy of the strategic defensive. The best result possible was a stalemate. Here General Ridgway, then the operational commander in Korea, confers with his tactical battlefield leaders.
(Courtesy U.S. Army Military History Institute.)

war, would have resumed the strategic offensive to destroy the enemy armies and drive them from the Korean peninsula. In fact, the then Eighth U.S. Army commander, General James Van Fleet, proposed just such an operation. Instead the United States remained on the strategic defensive and sought to end the war not by military means but through truce talks and diplomatic negotiations.

That course of action was prompted by a change in U.S. political policy. Although not well understood either then or now, the policy decision forced a profound change in U.S. military strategy, a change that has had a major impact on the American way of waging war.

In November 1950, in response to China's intervention in the war, the United States abandoned its strategic policy of rolling back communism and liberating North Korea and opted for a strategic policy of containing communist expansion (a policy that remains in effect as of this writing). Driven by the desire to limit the spread of the war and to avoid a nuclear confrontation with the Soviet Union, this policy rested on the assumption, first articulated by the State Department's George F. Kennan several years earlier, that the best way to deal with communist states was not to attack them directly but instead to contain their expansion and allow the contradictions inherent in communist ideology to cripple them from within.

While in the long run this proved to be a valid assumption, as in the late 1980s one communist state after another has had to face the fact that Marxism-Leninism was bankrupt, there was insufficient appreciation of the effect this policy change would have on military strategies, which of necessity must be in consonance with national policies. "Rollback of communism" and "liberation" translated into the military strategy of the *strategic offensive*, America's traditional way of war, in which the battle was carried to the enemy and battlefield victory was achieved by destroying his armed forces, seizing his capital, occupying his territory and destroying his will to resist.

The national policy of containment, on the other hand, translated (unwittingly, it must be emphasized) into the military strategy of the *strategic defensive*. Instead of an active strategy of carrying the war to the enemy, the strategic defensive was passive. Its purpose was to frustrate enemy offensive operations and protect the status quo.

This change in strategy posed three unforeseen problems. First, it was out of consonance with the enemy, which was still pursuing the strategic offensive. As General MacArthur testified during the 1951 congressional "Great Debate" on the conduct of the Korean War, "It seems to me the worst possible concept, militarily, that we would simply stay there, resisting aggression so-called ... it seems to me that [the way you 'resist aggression' is to] destroy the potentialities of the aggressor to continue to hit you ... When you say, merely, 'we are going to continue to fight aggression,' that is not what the enemy is fighting for. The enemy is fighting for a very definite purpose—to destroy our forces."

The second problem was that the strategic defensive could not, in and of itself, ever be conclusive. The best battlefield result possible was stalemate. Some other means, such as diplomatic negotiations, would be necessary to resolve the conflict. That's exactly what happened in Korea. The battlefield was stalemated in 1951, and two years of diplomatic negotiations ensued before the Korean armistice agreement in 1953.

In the meantime the American people (who wanted a quick resolution to the conflict, a resolution not possible given the national policy of containment) lost patience with the war and withdrew their support for both the war and its commander in chief, President Harry S Truman.

The same pattern would recur in Vietnam when once again the American people would lose their patience for a stalemated war and would once again force its Commander-in-Chief, President Lyndon B. Johnson, out of office.

It is important to understand that what was really at fault was not the national policy of containment or its supporting defensive military strategy. Both have served the nation well and make a great deal of political and military sense, especially in the nuclear age when forcing an enemy to the wall risks nuclear war. The problem was that these changes in the

American way of war were never adequately explained to the American people. They saw (and still see) war in World War II terms, where total victory is national policy and the military takes the strategic offensive to destroy the enemy's armed forces, occupy his territory, seize his capital and break his will to resist. Like General MacArthur (who also saw war in traditional terms) they believed there was no substitute for victory.

It was never explained to them that historically almost all wars have been limited. For example, the United States never invaded Spain nor occupied Madrid in the Spanish-American War. It was never explained to them that "victory" in war need not be total victory as in World War II but simply the realization of the political goals for which war is being waged—in Korea (after the Chinese intervention) the restoration of the status quo ante bellum. And it was never explained to them that it would be limited wars like Korea, not total wars like World War II, that would be the paradigm of conflict in the nuclear age.

Frustrating as the Korean War was for the American people and for those who fought there, U.S. military strategy in Korea proved successful. By any reasonable measurement, the United States "won" the Korean war. The status quo ante bellum was restored and the Republic of Korea survives to this day as a free and independent nation. "Unfortunately," as General Maxwell D. Taylor later wrote, "there was no thorough-going analysis ever made of the lessons to be learned from Korea," and that success was never fully appreciated. As a consequence Americans specifically rejected the Korean war paradigm—the only paradigm that offered any hope for success—when the United States later became involved in the war in Vietnam.

See STRATEGY; STRATEGY, COMMUNIST FORCES; VAN FLEET, JAMES A.

Suggestions for further reading: For a comparison of Korean War and Vietnam War strategies see Colonel Harry G. Summers, Jr., *On Strategy: A Critical Analysis of the Vietnam War* (Novato, Calif.: Presidio Press, 1982; New York: Dell, 1984). See also Colonel Harry G. Summers, Jr., *Sound Military Decisions* (New York: Random House, 1990).

STRATEMEYER, GEORGE E(DWARD) (1890–1969)

Born November 24, 1890, in Cincinnati, Ohio, Stratemeyer graduated from the United States Military Academy in 1915. After initial service with the infantry on the Texas border, he underwent flying instruction and officially transferred to the Army Air Corps in 1920. Stratemeyer taught at the Military Academy and at the Army Command and General Staff College at Fort Leavenworth, Kansas, and was then assigned to command the Seventh Bomb Group at Hamilton Field, California. He then attended the Army War College and served on the Air Staff. He was in command of the Southeast Air Corps Training Center at Maxwell Field, Alabama, when the United States entered World War II.

General Stratemeyer went to the China-Burma-India (CBI) Theater in 1943. In April 1944, he became the commander of the Army Air Force in the China Theater with headquarters at Chungking and remained there until March 1946. After the war, he commanded the Air Defense Command and organized the Continental Air Command at Mitchell Field, New York.

In April 1949, General Stratemeyer became the commanding general, Far East Air Force (FEAF) and was in command there when the Korean War began. He was instrumental in organizing and directing the air support during the critical early days of the war. Stratemeyer suffered a serious heart attack in May 1951, and in June 1951, he relinquished his command to General Otto P. Weyland. General Stratemeyer retired from active duty on January 31, 1952, and died on August 9, 1969.

See also FAR EAST AIR FORCE; FAR EAST COMMAND; AIR FORCE, U.S.

Suggestions for further reading: See Robert F. Futrell, *The United States Air Force in Korea: 1950–1953*, revised edition (Washington, D.C.: GPO, 1983).

TACTICAL AIRLIFT

See COMBAT CARGO COMMAND; TRANSPORT AIRCRAFT.

TACTICS

The best known tactical innovation of the Korean War was the "human wave" attacks used by the Chinese Communist Forces (CCF). At first, this tactic was unnerving because the perception was that the "Chinese hordes" had such an inexhaustible supply of infantry that they could overcome any defensive position by sheer force of numbers alone with no concern for the casualties involved.

When General Matthew B. Ridgway assumed command of the Eighth U.S. Army in late December 1951, one of his first acts was to debunk such notions. Previously road-bound United Nations (UN) forces were sent up into the mountains to take on the CCF on their own turf, and the "human wave" attacks were seen for what they really were—frontal assaults that were particularly vulnerable to the enormous UN advantage in firepower.

In order to avoid the slaughter that ensued, the CCF resorted to night warfare when U.S. artillery and airstrikes were more difficult. If the CCF could not seize their objectives before dawn, more often than not they would break off their attack and fall back to the safety of their own lines.

Although not new, another enemy tactic that enjoyed some early success was the infiltration of Allied lines to ambush lines of supply and communication and to attack Allied positions from the flanks or rear. Easy to do because the extensive frontages assigned to UN units created gaps in the defensive line, these enemy infiltration tactics at first caused panic among troops who believed they had been cut off and surrounded. Soon Allied units learned to establish all-around perimeter defenses and use these strong points as bases from which to cut off and destroy these enemy infiltrators behind the lines.

The major U.S. tactical innovation of the Korean War, one pioneered by the Marine Corps, was the use of helicopters for battlefield resupply and for battlefield movement of forces.

Suggestions for further reading: For Army tactics, see *U.S. Army in the Korean War* series: Roy A. Appleman, *South to the Naktong, North to the Yalu,* 1961; Walter G. Hermes, *Truce Tent and Fighting Front,* 1966; and Billy C. Mossman, *Ebb and Flow,* anticipated in 1990 (Washington, D.C.: GPO). For Marine Corps tactics, see the five-volume official history, *U.S. Marine Operations in Korea 1950–1953*: Lynn Montross and Captain Nicholas A. Canzona, USMC, *The Pusan*

Night attack became a favorite CCF tactic to avoid U.S. firepower, but as this blast from a tank cannon illustrates, darkness was no shield from the American fire.
(Courtesy Lyndon Baines Johnson Library & Museum.)

Perimeter, 1954; *The Inchon-Seoul Operation*, 1955; *The Chosin Reservoir Campaign*, 1957; Lynn Montross and Majors Hubard D. Kuokka and Norman W. Hicks, USMC, *The East-Central Front*, 1962; and Lieutenant Colonel Pat Meid, USMCR, and Major James M. Yingling, USMC, *Operations in West Korea*, 1972 (Washington, D.C.: GPO). See also Allan R. Millett, *Semper Fidelis: The History of the United States Marine Corps* (New York: Macmillan, 1980) and Clay Blair, *The Forgotten War: America in Korea 1950–1953* (New York Times Books, 1987).

TAEJON, BATTLE OF

Located 100 miles south of Seoul and 130 miles northwest of Pusan, Taejon, with a population of about 130,000, was the sixth largest city in South Korea. Because of its location, in early July 1950 Taejon became the nerve center for the war. On July 3, 1950, Major General William F. Dean, commanding general of the 24th Infantry Division, landed at the Taejon airstrip and the next morning assumed the additional duty of commander of United States Army Forces in Korea (USAFIK). Replacing the Far East Command's advance party, the General Headquarters, Advance Command and Liaison Group, which had been in Taejon since July 1, 1950, USAFIK was the senior U.S. headquarters in Korea until July 13, 1950, when the Eighth U.S. Army (EUSA) established its headquarters in Taegu farther to the south and assumed operational command of the war.

But Taejon remained the command center for the 24th Infantry Division, whose division

THE FALL OF TAEJON

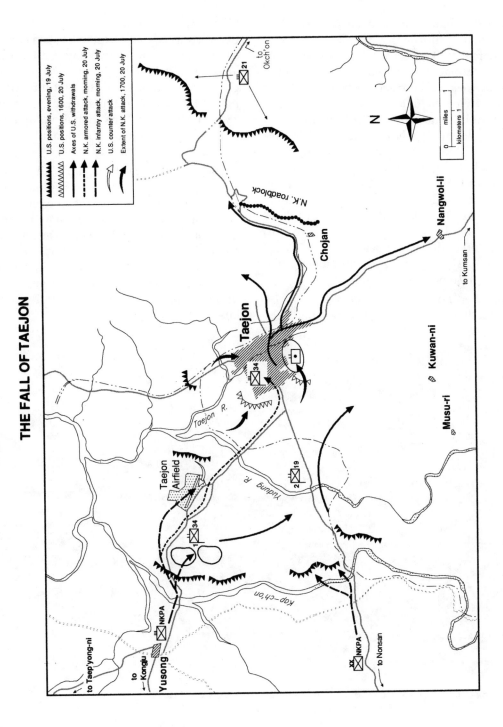

headquarters had been established there when the division's units deployed to Korea. It was from there that Dean commanded the series of delaying actions that were to culminate in the battle for Taejon. These actions began with the division's First Battalion, 21st Infantry (Task Force Smith), engagement at Osan on July 5 with the advancing North Korean People's Army (NKPA) and included the fights at Pyongtaek and Chonan by the 34th Infantry Regiment on July 6 to 8 at Chochiwon by the 21st Infantry Regiment on July 8 to 12 and at the Kum River by the 19th and 34th Infantry Regiment on July 13 to 16. Originally, Taejon was to be just another delaying position, and General Dean had no intention of fighting a last-ditch battle for the city.

Plans were to evacuate Taejon on July 19, 1950, but the day before, at a meeting with Lieutenant General Walton H. Walker, the EUSA commander, Dean was asked to hold the city for an additional two days until the newly arrived First Cavalry Division could get into position. Dean ordered the 21st Infantry, with light M-24 Chaffee tanks from A Company, 78th Heavy (sic) Tank Battalion, attached to Okchon six miles to the division into defensive positions around the city.

On July 19 the battle began. While the NKPA Third Division and the Fifth Regiment, NKPA Fourth Division made a wide envelopment of Taejon and isolated the division with a decisive mile-long roadblock between Taejon and Okchon. This roadblock cut the division off from its 21st Infantry Regiment, which, because of communications failures, was unaware of the disaster impending at Taejon until it was too late.

A T-34 tank knocked out by General Dean in the battle for Taejon, July 1950.
(Courtesy U>S> Army Military History Institute.)

On July 20, 1950, attacking from north and northeast, the NKPA Third Division, supported by T-34 medium tanks from the 107th and 203d Tank regiments, 105th Armored Brigade, fought its way into the city itself. Slowed somewhat by fire from the newly arrived 3.5-inch antitank rocket launchers (one team manned by General Dean himself), enemy pressure by this time was so great that the city was ordered evacuated. But withdrawing units soon ran into the enemy roadblock on the Taejon-Okchon road and other roadblocks on the Kumsan road to the south. General Dean himself became separated from his troops, and after wandering the hills for 36 days in an unsuccessful attempt to reach friendly lines, was taken prisoner on August 25, 1950, and spent the rest of the war in a POW camp. The 24th Infantry Division had bought EUSA the two days it needed, but the price had been grim. In addition to its commander, the division took 1,150 casualties among the 3,933 soldiers involved in the battle. Of these, 48 were known dead, 228 wounded and 874 missing in action, most of whom were later confirmed as killed in action. In addition to the personnel casualties, most of the division artillery's howitzers were lost, and the 24th Quartermaster Company lost 30 of its 34 trucks. By the time it was relieved by elements of the First Cavalry Division at Yongdong on July 22, 1950, and withdrew into the Naktong Perimeter, the division had taken heavy casualties. Going into action with some 16,000 soldiers less than three weeks earlier, the division left Yongdong with a total strength of 8,660 soldiers.

For its delaying actions against superior enemy forces during the first weeks of the war, the 24th Infantry Division was awarded both the United States Presidential Unit Citation and the Republic of Korea Presidential Unit Citation. General Dean was awarded the Medal of Honor.

See DEAN, WILLIAM F.; TASK FORCE SMITH; 24TH INFANTRY DIVISION.

Suggestions for further reading: The most detailed account of the battle of Taejon is contained in Roy A. Appleman's *South to the Naktong, North to the Yalu* (Washington, D.C.: GPO, 1961).

TAFT, ROBERT A(LPHONSO) (1889–1953)

Born September 9, 1889, in Cincinnati, Ohio, the son of former President and Chief Justice William Howard Taft, Robert Taft graduated from Yale University in 1910 and from Harvard Law School in 1913. Twice rejected in his attempts to enlist in the Army in World War I because of poor eyesight, he joined the staff of Herbert Hoover's Food Administration and helped organize relief efforts in Europe in 1918.

Upon his return to the United States, Taft entered Ohio politics as a Republican candidate in 1920 and served in the state assembly off and on until 1938 when he was elected to the United States Senate. In 1944, he became the de facto leader of the Republican minority in the Senate (refusing the formal position of Senate minority leader because of its administrative duties).

Taft refused to support the ratification of the North Atlantic Treaty in 1949, not only because he believed it smacked of imperialism but also because it expanded the president's power to commit the United States to action without congressional approval. But although he opposed U.S. intervention in Europe, he supported President Harry S Truman's commitment of ground troops in Korea. A member of the China Lobby, he agreed with General Douglas MacArthur, the commander in chief, Far East Command, that Chinese Nationalist troops be used in the war. While supporting MacArthur on that issue, however, he opposed using either American troops or nuclear weapons against mainland China.

Like many Americans, Taft was torn between his desire to resist the spread of Communism and his opposition to overseas involvement. Known as "Mr. Republican," he tried but failed to get his party's nomination for the presidency in 1948 and again in 1952. Taft became Senate majority leader when Republicans captured the Congress during the 1952 Eisenhower landslide, but he only held the position a few short months. Suffering from inoperable cancer, he retired as majority leader in June 1953 and died on July 31, 1953.
See CHINA LOBBY; CONGRESS, U.S.

Suggestions for further reading: See biographic entry in *Political Profiles: The Truman Years*, Eleanora W. Schoenebaum, editor (New York: Facts On File, 1978).

TANK BATTALIONS

See ARMOR.

TASK FORCE

"Task Force" was a term widely used during the Korean War. For the Army, it was used to identify an ad hoc organization composed of a variety of units temporarily assembled under a single designated commander to accomplish a specific mission. The organization usually carried the name of that commander (i.e., Task Force MacLean, Task Force Smith) and was disbanded when the mission was completed.

For the Navy, "task force" and "task group" were (and are) routine subdivisions of the fleet. They too have no fixed structure, being tailored for the mission at hand; but unlike the Army task forces, they tend to be semipermanent in nature and, like Task Force 77, Naval Forces Far

East's fast carrier striking force, endure for the duration of the war.

TASK FORCE MACLEAN/TASK FORCE FAITH

On November 27, 1950, X Corps, in what has been called "the most ill-advised and unfortunate operation of the Korean War," ordered the First Marine Division and the Army's Task Force MacLean to attack north from their positions west and east of the Chosin Reservoir. The operation was designed to take pressure off Eighth U.S. Army units fifty air-miles to the west which were under heavy attack from the Chinese Communist Forces (CCF) 130,000-man Thirteenth Army Group, which had just entered the war. Unbeknownst to those ordering the attack, the 120,000-man CCF Ninth Army Group was lying in wait.

Task Force MacLean, named for the commander of the U.S. Seventh Infantry Division's 31st Infantry Regiment, Colonel Allan D. "Mac" MacLean, had been formed in mid-November 1950 to relieve First Marine Division elements east of the Chosin Reservoir. It consisted of the Second and Third Battalions, 31st Infantry Regiment (2/31 and 3/31), and the M-26 Pershing tanks of the regiment's Heavy Tank Company; the First Battalion, 32d Infantry Regiment (1/32), under the command of Lieutenant Colonel Don C. Faith; the 105-mm howitzers of the 57th Field Artillery Battalion; and a platoon of eight quad-50's and 40-mm dusters from D Battery, 15th Antiaircraft Artillery (Automatic Weapons) Battalion.

By November 27, 1950, the task force had relieved the Fifth Marine Regiment, which joined the rest of the First Marine Division farther north to the west of the reservoir. The force had taken up positions east of the reservoir with Faith's 1/32 to the north, the 3/31 and two

105-mm batteries farther south and still further south at the village of Hudong, the rear command post and the tank company. The 2/31 and one battery of 105-mm howitzers was lagging far behind and had yet to arrive. Counting 700 attached Republic of Korea (ROK) troops, Task Force MacClean was some 3,200-men strong.

Soon after arriving at Hudong, MacLean had sent his I&R (Intelligence and Reconnaissance) platoon out to scout enemy locations. It disappeared without a trace. That night three CCF divisions struck the Marines west of the reservoir, and the CCF 80th Division struck Task Force MacClean. The battle of Chosin Reservoir had begun. Usually portrayed as a Marine epic, the travail of the Army's Task Force MacClean has been largely ignored.

With his task force strung out north to south along the east bank of the reservoir and vulnerable to defeat in detail (having his battalions picked off one at a time), MacLean was hard pressed from the start. The 1/32 had suffered 100 casualties, and the 3/31 had also taken severe losses. The next day, when his tanks attempted to move up in support, they were attacked by Chinese gunners using American 3.5-inch antitank rocket launchers and were forced to retreat. When the CCF resumed the attack on the night of November 28–29, MacLean withdrew 1/32 south into the 3/31 perimeter. In the process MacLean was gunned down and captured (he later died in captivity); and with the 3/31 commander, Lieutenant Colonel William R. Reilly severely wounded, Faith assumed command. Task Force MacLean had become Task Force Faith.

Again the regiment's tank company at Hudong four miles to the south tried to break through, and again they were repulsed. On November 30, 1950, Faith was ordered to fight his way south to the perimeter at Hagaru at the southern tip of the Chosin Reservoir, then under the command of the First Marine Regiment's Colonel Lewis B. "Chesty" Puller. Hampered by some 500 wounded and by temperatures that a times reached 35 degrees below zero, Faith found his task force surrounded and abandoned. Transferred from Seventh Division to First Marine Division control, they were told by the hard-pressed Marines that they would have to fend for themselves. Under heavy CCF attack again on the night of November 30, to December 1, Task Force Faith suffered another 100 casualties. Knowing he could not survive another such attack, Faith put his 600 wounded on trucks and began to move south. Attacked not only by CCF mortars and small arms fire but also by U.S. aircraft that mistakenly dropped napalm on his lead elements, Faith's column was stopped by a series of CCF roadblocks and Faith himself severely wounded by a Chinese grenade. Finally reaching Hudong, they found that the regimental tank company, which they believed would prove to be their salvation, had already been withdrawn to Hagaru. It was the end of Task Force Faith. In the CCF final assault on the column, Colonel Faith (who was subsequently awarded the Medal of Honor posthumously for his actions during the withdrawal) was killed, as were most of the other wounded. Only 385 of the task force's 3,200-man force survived.

"The fate that overtook Task Force Faith," wrote Army historian Roy E. Appleman, "was one of the worst disasters for American soldiers in the Korean War."

See also CHOSIN RESERVOIR, BATTLE OF.

Suggestions for further reading: The definitive work on Task Force MacLean/Task Force Faith is Roy A. Appleman's *East of Chosin: Entrapment and Breakout in Korea 1950* (College Station, Tex.: Texas A&M Press, 1987). For the battle in larger perspective, see Clay Blair, *The Forgotten War: America in Korea 1950–1953* (New York Times Books, 1987).

TASK FORCE 90

See AMPHIBIOUS FORCE FAR EAST.

TASK FORCE 95

See BLOCKADE AND ESCORT FORCE.

TASK FORCE 77

See SEVENTH FLEET STRIKING FORCE.

TASK FORCE SMITH

Task Force Smith—named after its commander, Lieutenant Colonel Charles B. ("Brad") Smith—was the first U.S. unit to fight in the Korean War. Some 440 men strong, its infantry units consisted of the 24th Infantry Division's First Battalion, 21st Infantry Regiment (less A and D company) plus a two-gun 75-mm recoilless rifle platoon from M Company, Third Battalion, 21st Infantry (and several Third Battalion officers). The task force also had two 4.2-inch mortars from the regiment's Heavy Mortar Company. In Korea, it would be joined by Battery A, 52d Field Artillery Battalion, and the artillery battalion commander, Lieutenant Colonel Miller O. Perry.

Stationed with the regiment at Camp Wood in the city of Kumamoto on the Japanese islands of Kyushu, Smith (with no prior warning) was alerted at 2245 hours, June 30, 1950, to put together a task force for movement to Korea. Four hours later, this force was enroute by truck for Itazuki air base 75 miles away. Shuttled from Itazuki to Pusan airfield in Korea in six C-54 Skymasters, the task force arrived in Korea on July 1, 1950. There it boarded trains and headed north to Taejon, where it arrived the next day.

Ordered to take up blocking positions to the northeast by Brigadier General John Church, the Far East Command's senior representative in Korea, Smith made a forward reconnaissance on July 2 and selected an initial position about three miles north of Osan. He moved his task force north to Pyongtaek on July 4, 1950, where it joined its attached artillery unit which had moved from its home station at Camp Hakata in Fukuoka, Japan. During the early morning hours of July 5, Smith moved his task force into position north of Osan.

At 0700 hours, July 5, 1950, elements of the North Korean People's Army (NKPA) Fourth Division, supported by the 107th Tank Battalion, 105th Armored Brigade, approached the task force's positions and were taken under artillery fire. This fire did not stop the thirty enemy T-34 medium tanks nor did direct hits from the task force's 75-mm recoilless rifles or 2.36-inch anti-tank rocket launchers. As the tanks approached the artillery positions, the two lead tanks were knocked out by direct fire from a 105-mm howitzer firing AT (antitank) rounds. This gun was soon knocked out of action, and the tanks continued unimpeded.

After a lull, at 1000 hours, Smith's position came under another tank-supported enemy attack. Although the NKPA infantry took a terrible beating from the U.S. fire, their tanks again advanced unimpeded. Smith became so heavily engaged that when he attempted to pull back, as planned, to a delaying position farther south, he found it almost impossible to extricate his forces. As a result, the task force fell back in some disarray. When it reassembled at Taejon several days later, five officers and 148 enlisted men were missing in action. Today a monument marks the spot where it made its stand.

See also NAKTONG PERIMETER, BATTLE OF; TAEJON, BATTLE OF.

Suggestions for further reading: The best account of Task Force Smith's operation is Brigadier General Roy K. Flint's "Task Force Smith and the 24th Infantry Division: Delay and Withdrawal 5–19 July 1950" in *America's First Battles*, edited by Charles E. Heller and William A. Stofft (Lawrence, Kansas: University Press of Kansas, 1986). See also *U.S. Army in the Korean War* series: Roy A. Appleman, *South to the Naktong, North to the Yalu* (Washington, D.C. GPO, 1961.); Clay Blair, *The Forgotten War: America in Korea 1950–1953* (New York Times Books, 1987).

TAYLOR, MAXWELL D(AVENPORT) (1901–1987)

Born August 26, 1901, at Keytesville, Missouri, Taylor graduated from the United States Military Academy in 1922. After routine troop assignments, he taught French and Spanish at the Military Academy and, after graduating from the Army Command and General Staff College in 1935, was assigned to the U.S. Embassy in Tokyo, Japan, to learn Japanese. Taylor graduated from the Army War College in 1940 and was sent on a special assignment to Latin America before commanding the 12th Artillery Battalion at San Antonio, Texas. He was serving in the office of the chief of staff U.S. Army when the United States entered World War II.

In the spring of 1942, Taylor was assigned as chief of staff and division artillery commander of the 82d Infantry Division and remained with that division when it was converted to the 82d Airborne Division. After commanding the 82d Airborne Division artillery in combat during the Sicily campaign, he was sent on a secret mission behind enemy lines to make contact with the Italian government. In February 1944, Taylor was named to command the 101st Airborne Division and jumped with that division into Normandy on D-day and later at the Market-Garden operation in Holland. After World War II, Taylor served as superintendent of the United States Military Academy, served a tour of duty in Europe, and returned to Washington to serve as the Army's G-3 (chief of operations).

On February 11, 1953, General Taylor replaced General Van Fleet as commander of the Eighth U.S. Army (EUSA) in Korea. Always the consummate politician and sensitive to the desires of Dwight D. Eisenhower, the new commander in chief, Taylor avoided combat—and casualties—as best he could, ordering the abandonment of both Old Baldy and Pork Chop Hill.

In November 1954, Taylor was named commander in chief, Far East Command, and in May 1955, he succeeded General Matthew B. Ridgway as Army chief of staff. Retiring due to a policy dispute with President Eisenhower, he became a crony of Senator John F. Kennedy and, when Kennedy was elected to the presidency, became his civilian military adviser. Kennedy subsequently recalled him to active duty and appointed him chairman of the Joint Chiefs of Staff. President Lyndon B. Johnson later appointed him as ambassador to the Republic of Vietnam. During the 1960's, Taylor played a large part in politicizing the military and setting it on the wrong course in Vietnam. General Taylor died in April 1987.

See EIGHTH U.S. ARMY.

Suggestions for further reading: Maxwell D. Taylor, *The Uncertain Trumpet* (New York: Harper, 1960), *Swords and Plowshares* (New York: Norton, 1972). See biographical sketch in Roger J. Spiller, editor, *Dictionary of American Military Biography*, (Westport, Conn.: Greenwood Press, 1984).

X (TENTH) CORPS

The X Corps had fought at New Guinea, made an assault landing at Leyte and fought in the southern Philippines during World War II. Deactivated in Japan in January 1946, it was called back to active duty there on August 26, 1950. Formed around a General Headquarters, Far East Command (GHQ FECOM), special planning staff already in existence, it was commanded by the FECOM chief of staff, Major General Edward M. Almond, who also retained his staff position.

The initial justification for keeping X Corps directly under GHQ FECOM instead of (as with the I and IX Corps) placing it under Eighth U.S. Army (EUSA) control was that X Corps would serve as the headquarters for the GHQ Reserve then building in Japan—the Army's Seventh Infantry Division, with the First Marine Division enroute—and then would be the control headquarters for the Inchon invasion. General of the Army Douglas Mac-Arthur, the FECOM commander, believed the invasion would end the war in a matter of weeks, allowing X Corps to be disbanded and Almond and his staff to return to their old duties in Tokyo.

But when the Inchon invasion on September 15, 1950, succeeded, MacArthur kept X Corps under his direct command for another amphibious invasion at Wonsan on Korea's eastern coast. When Wonsan was captured by advancing Republic of Korea Army (ROKA) forces, X Corps (after some considerable delay caused by mines in the harbor) landed its First Marine Division there on October 25, 1950, to join the ROK I Corps which was also under X Corps operational command. Meanwhile, the Army's Seventh Infantry Division landed at Iwon further up the coast. The Army's Third Infantry Division was brought ashore to guard the port of Hungnam even farther to the north while the First Marine Division and the Seventh Infantry Division struck inland toward the Chosin Reservoir and the Manchurian border. FECOM drew the boundary between EUSA and the still independent X Corps from the 39th parallel up the watershed of the mountains that formed Korea's central spine to the banks of the Yalu RIver on the Korean–Manchurian border.

Although elements of the 17th Infantry Regiment, Seventh Infantry Division, reached the Yalu River, a disaster was in the making. Between EUSA and X Corps, in the mountains just south of the border, were some 300,000 soldiers of the Chinese Communist Forces (CCF). When the CCF launched their attack in November 1950, X Corps' entire flank was exposed, and on November 30, 1950, X Corps was ordered to withdraw into the Hamhung-Hungnam area. On December 7, 1950, X Corps was further ordered to evacuate North Korea by sea and join forces with EUSA, which was withdrawing from North Korea by land along the western coast.

Their withdrawal complete on December 24, 1950, X Corps' independent existence came to an end. EUSA's new commander, General Matthew B. Ridgway, insisted that General Almond relinquish his dual position as FECOM chief of staff, and X Corps, like the I and IX Corps, became one of EUSA's tactical control headquarters. In July 1951, Lieutenant General Edward M. Almond, one of the most controversial commanders of the war, was replaced by Major General Clovis Ethelbert Byers. At the war's end, X Corps was under the command of Lieutenant General Isaac D. White.

For its services in Korea, X Corps was awarded two Republic of Korea Presidential Unit Citations, one for the Inchon and Hungnam operations and one for its overall battlefield performance. After the Korean War, X Corps was again deactivated and is no longer on the active rolls of the Army.

See ALMOND, EDWARD M.; CORPS; CHOSIN RESERVOIR, BATTLE OF; HUNGNAM EVACUATION; I CORPS; INCHON INVASION; IX CORPS; ORGANIZATION FOR COMBAT; WITHDRAWAL FROM NORTH KOREA; WONSAN.

Suggestions for further reading: See especially Shelby Stanton's *America's Tenth Legion: X Corps in Korea 1950* (Novato, CA: Presidio Press, 1989) and Clay Blair's *The Forgotten War: America in Korea 1950–1953* (New York Times Books, 1987). See also *U.S. Army in the Korean War* series: Roy A. Appleman, *South to the Naktong, North to the Yalu*, 1961; Walter G. Hermes, *Truce Tent and Fighting Front*, 1966; and Billy C. Mossman, *Ebb and Flow*, anticipated in 1990 (Washington, D.C.: GPO). For a Marine Corps perspective, see the five-volume official history, *U.S. Marine Operations in Korea 1950–1953*: Lynn Montross and Captain Nicholas A. Canzona, USMC, *The Pusan Perimeter*, 1954; *The Inchon-Seoul Operation*, 1955; *The Chosin Reservoir Campaign*, 1957; Lynn Montross and Majors Hubard D. Kuokka and Norman W. Hicks, USMC, *The East-Central Front*, 1962; and Lieutenant Colonel Pat Meid, USMCR, and Major James M. Yingling, USMC, *Operations in West Korea*, 1972 (Washington, D.C.: GPO). For order of battle, see Shelby Stanton, *Korean War Order of Battle* (Washington, D.C.: GPO, anticipated 1990).

THAILAND

Thailand contributed air, naval and ground forces to the war in Korea. A Royal Thai Air Force air transport detachment was sent to aid in the war, and when it arrived on June 24, 1951, its C-47 Skytrain aircraft were initially attached to the U.S. Air Force's 21st Troop Carrier Squadron. Two Royal Thai Navy frigates, the HMRTN *Bangpakon* and *Prasae*, also served with the U.S. Naval Command Far East's Blockade and Escort Force.

On October 3, 1950, the advance elements of the Thai infantry battalion arrived in Korea. At their peak in 1952, 2,174 Thai soldiers were serving in Korea. Among other combat operations, the Thai battalion, then attached to the Second U.S. Infantry Division, took part in the defense of Pork Chop Hill.

Casualty figures for Thai forces alone are not available, during the course of the war the United Nations ground forces of Belgium, Colombia, Ethiopia, France, Greece, the Netherlands, the Philippines, Thailand and Turkey combined lost 1,800 soldiers killed in action. Another 7,000 were wounded in action.

See COMBAT CARGO COMMAND; PORK CHOP HILL, BATTLE OF; UNITED NATIONS AIR FORCES; UNITED NATIONS GROUND FORCES; UNITED NATIONS NAVAL FORCES.

THIRD INFANTRY DIVISION

Organized in 1917, the Third "Marne" Infantry Division took part in heavy fighting in the Champagne-Marne and Aisne-Marne battles in World War I (from which it derived its nickname) as well as four other campaigns on the Western Front. During World War II, it participated in 10 campaigns, including the amphibious assaults on North Africa, Sicily, Anzio and southern France.

When the Korean War began in June 1950, the Third Infantry Division, by then reduced to only two regiments of infantry, was scattered, with its Seventh Infantry Regiment at Fort Devens, Massachusetts, and its 15th Infantry Regiment at Fort Benning, Georgia. Already at reduced two-battalion strength, these regiments were further decimated when a battalion from Fort Devens (commanded by Lieutenant Colonel Harold K. Johnson, who would rise to become Army chief of staff from 1964 to 1968) was redesignated as the Third Battalion, Eighth Cavalry Regiment, and a battalion from Fort Benning was redesignated as Third Battalion, Seventh Cavalry Regiment. Both were sent to Korea to join their new parent units in the First Cavalry Division.

To bring the division to wartime strength, the 65th Infantry Regiment from Puerto Rico was assigned to the division but was sent ahead independently to bolster the Naktong Perimeter defenses, as was the division's Ninth (155-mm howitzer) Field Artillery Battalion. The 64th Medium Tank Battalion from the Second Armored Division at Ford Hood Texas, was also assigned to the division. Other divisional units included the 10th, 39th and 58th (105-mm howitzer) Field Artillery Battalions; the Third Antiaircraft Artillery Battalion (Automatic Weapons); the 10th Combat Engineer Battalion; and the Third Reconnaissance Company.

The division sailed from San Francisco, California, on August 20, 1950, and landed in Japan on September 16, 1950. There its strength was augmented by thousands of KATUSAs (Korean Augmentation to the U.S. Army—Korean soldiers detailed to serve with U.S. units). Two months later the division embarked again and landed at Wonsan on Korea's eastern coast on November 21, 1950. Joined with its 65th Infantry Regiment, the division moved to the Hungnam area where it covered the withdrawal of X Corps from the Chosin Reservoir and the evacuation of Hungnam.

The Third Infantry Division withdrew by sea on December 24, 1950, and went into position north of Seoul as part of the Eighth U.S. Army's defensive line. The division linked up with the 187th Airborne Regimental Combat Team after its March 1951 parachute assault at Munsan-ni and defended the Imjin River line during the Chinese Communist Forces (CCF) April 1951 spring offensive. During the next two years, the division conducted combat operation in the Chorwon-Kumwha area, fought at the Jackson Heights and Arrowhead outposts, and blocked a CCF push in the Kumsong area in July 1953. The Greek Battalion was attached to the division during many of its combat operations.

During eight campaigns on the Korean battlefield, the Third Infantry Division was awarded two Republic of Korea Presidential Unit Citations and the Chryssoun Aristion Andrias (Bravery Gold Medal of Greece). In addition, the First Battalion, Seventh Infantry Regiment (then commanded by Lieutenant Colonel Frederick C. Weyand, who would rise to become Army chief of staff from 1974 to 1976), won a Presidential Unit Citation for its bravery at Choksong, the Second Battalion for its bravery at Kowang-ni and the Third Battalion for bravery at Segok. The First Battalion, 15th Infantry Regiment, won two Presidential Unit Citations for its bravery at Panmunjom and the Hwachon Reservoir, and the Second Battalion, 15th Infantry, won a Presidential Unit Citation for bravery at Kowang-ni.

In addition to other awards won by members of the division, eleven of its soldiers won the Medal of Honor for conspicuous bravery on the battlefield. During the course of the war, the division suffered 10,078 casualties, including 2,160 soldiers killed in action or died of wounds, 7,753 wounded in action, 5 missing in action and 160 prisoners of war.

Now a mechanized division, the Third Infantry Division is presently stationed in West Germany. The Society of the Third Infantry Division publishes a newsletter and hosts periodic reunions of those who served with the division. Further information can be obtained from Mr. Harry P. Smith, 6095 Wilson Boulevard, Arlington, Virginia 22055.

See BLACK SOLDIERS IN KOREA; HUNGNAM EVACUATION.

Suggestions for further reading: See *U.S. Army in the Korean War* series: Roy A. Appleman, *South to the Naktong, North to the Yalu*, 1961; Walter G. Hermes, *Truce Tent and Fighting Front*, 1966; and Billy C. Mossman, *Ebb and Flow*, anticipated in 1990 (Washington, D.C.: GPO). For order of battle, see Shelby Stanton, *Korean War Order of Battle* (Washington, D.C.: GPO, anticipated 1990). See also Clay Blair, *The Forgotten War: America in Korea 1950–1953* (New York Times Books, 1987).

THIRD LOGISTICAL COMMAND

See KOREAN COMMUNICATIONS ZONE.

38TH PARALLEL

The 38th parallel—the 38th degree of north latitude as it bisects the Korean peninsula—became the arbitrary demarcation line between North and South Korea from 1945 to 1948 and the border between the Republic of Korea (ROK) and the Democratic People's Republic of Korea (DPRK) from 1948 to 1950. According to former Secretary of the Army Robert T. Stevens, he and former Secretary of State Dean Rusk were Army colonels serving as staff officers in the Army General Staff's Policy Section, Strategy and planning Group, Operations Division in August 1945, and they were the ones responsible for selecting the 38th parallel as the dividing line in Korea.

In any event, their boss and chief of the Policy Section, Colonel (later General) Charles H. Bonesteel, had been given the responsibility to come up with a draft of the surrender procedures to be given to the Japanese government, including designation of the nations and commands that were to accept the surrender of Japanese forces throughout the Far East. When it came to Korea, the prime consideration was to establish a surrender line as far north as it was thought the Russians would accept. If the

Russians did not agree, their troops (already in the Soviet Far East just across Korea's northern border) could reach the southern tip of Korea before the nearest American troops—600 miles away on Okinawa—could arrive. Noting from the map that the 38th parallel cut Korea almost exactly in half, that line was proposed by the Army staff and, after some discussion, was approved by President Harry S Truman and accepted by Soviet Premier Joseph Stalin as the hypothetical line dividing the zones within which the Japanese forces in Korea would surrender to appointed American and Russian authorities.

Not intended by the United States as a north-south barrier, the 190-mile length of this demarcation line was militarily indefensible. It cut across more than 75 streams and 12 rivers, intersected the mountain ridges at variant angles

The 23d Infantry marks the spot where it crossed the 38th parallel.
Courtesy U.S. Army Military History Institute.)

and severed several hundred lesser roads, eight major highways and six north-south rail lines. But regardless of U.S. intentions, the Soviets had other ideas. By October 1945, they had turned the border into a fortified zone and stopped all interzonal travel. Rejecting the 1947 call for countrywide elections under United Nations supervision, the Democratic People's Republic of Korea, with headquarters in Pyongyang, was proclaimed in September 1948. The 38th parallel had become the border between North and South Korea.
See DEMILITARIZED ZONE.

Suggestions for further reading: James F. Schnabel, *U.S. Army in the Korean War: Policy and Direction: The First Year* (Washington, D.C.: GPO, 1972).

TRANSPORT AIRCRAFT

Transport aircraft during the Korean War were all propeller-driven. They fell into two broad categories—the tactical (intratheater) airlift of the Far East Air Force (FEAF) Combat Cargo Command (later designated the 315th Air Division) and the strategic (intercontinental) airlift of the Military Air Transport Service (MATS).

In the first category were the ancient but still serviceable C-46 Commando and the C-47 Skytrains which were flown by United States Air Force (USAF) personnel as well as by members of the Royal Hellenic (Greek) and Royal Thai Air Forces. More common were C-54 Skymasters, C-119 Flying Boxcars and, toward the end of the war, the giant C-124 Globemasters. MATS also used C-54s, C-119s and C-124s, but in addition they used C-97 Stratofreighters, C-118 Liftmasters, C-121 Super Constellations, as well as a variety of civilian chartered aircraft.

See also AIR FORCE, U.S.; COMBAT CARGO COMMAND; FAR EAST AIR FORCE; MATS (MILITARY AIR TRANSPORT SERVICE).

Suggestions for further reading: See Robert F. Futrell, *The United States Air Force in Korea: 1950–1953*, revised edition (Washington, D.C.: GPO, 1983).

TROOP SHIPS

See MSTS (MILITARY SEA TRANSPORT SERVICE)

TRUCE TALKS

See ARMISTICE AGREEMENT.

TRUMAN, HARRY S (1884–1972)

Born May 8, 1884, in Lamar, Kansas, Truman joined the Missouri National Guard after graduation from high school and in May 1917 was elected first lieutenant of Battery F, Second Missouri Field Artillery. Called to federal service on August 5, 1917, the unit was redesignated the 129th Field Artillery, 35th Infantry Division. After training at the Artillery School at Fort Sill, Oklahoma, Truman was shipped to France in March 1918, where he assumed command of Battery D, 129th Artillery, and saw action in the Vosges, at St. Mihiel, and in the Meuse-Argonne campaign. Promoted to captain in October 1918, Truman returned to the United States in April 1919 and was released from active duty on May 6, 1919.

Backed by the Pendergast machine that then controlled Kansas City, Missouri, Truman became active in local politics in 1922 and with Tom Pendergast's help was elected to the United States Senate in 1934. A strong supporter of President Franklin D. Roosevelt's programs, Truman came to national prominence during World War II when he was chairman of a watchdog committee investigating the nation's defense industries.

In 1944, he was elected as Roosevelt's vice president and assumed the presidency when Roosevelt died on April 12, 1945. It was Truman who brought World War II to a successful conclusion, making the difficult decision to use atomic weapons against Japan. Truman authorized aid to Greece and Turkey when the Cold War with the Soviet Union began. In 1947 he announced the "Truman Doctrine," which declared, "It must be the policy of the United States to support free peoples who are resisting attempted subjugation by armed minorities or by outside pressures."

Truman won reelection in his own right in November 1948 and worked for the ratification of the North Atlantic Treaty in 1949, which for the first time in history committed the United States to a mutual defense pact in Europe. In January 1950 he ordered a reassessment of U.S. defense policy known as NSC-68 (National Security Council Document number 68), which recommended that the United States unilaterally accept responsibility for the defense of the world. After the North Korean invasion of South Korea in June 1950, Truman ordered the commitment of U.S. troops to Korea and gained congressional approval to mobilize America's reserve forces in support of the war.

Given all this, Truman proved to be a weak wartime commander in chief. His ill-conceived budget cuts prior to the war had reduced the military to the point where they could not begin to meet the missions Truman assigned to them. When war did come, the precedent Truman set by failing to seek a declaration of war from Congress would have long-term ramifications, as would his change in national policy from roll-back and liberation to containment after the Chinese intervention in the war in Novem-

Right, President Truman presents General MacArthur the Distinguished Service Medal in October 1950 at Wake Island while U.S. Ambassador to Korea John Muccio looks on.
Courtesy Lyndon Baines Johnson Library & Museum.)

ber 1950. It was not the decision that was in error. The error was the failure to appreciate the effect this change would have on military strategy. As a result, a major divergence developed between Truman and his field commander, General Douglas MacArthur. This divergence was exacerbated both by Truman's long-time contempt for the military in general and for MacArthur in particular as well as by MacArthur's failure to see that he could not influence Truman the way he had influenced his predecessor. When he wanted a change in policy, MacArthur had habitually leaned on President Roosevelt, whom he had served as Army chief of staff and as a World War II theater commander. Roosevelt, a master at the game, would lean right back. But when Mac-Arthur tried to pressure Truman to change his mind on how the war should be fought, Truman lost his composure and ordered Mac-Arthur fired.

In so doing, he in effect ordered himself fired as well, for the loss of public support that ensued, coupled with domestic scandals among his cronies, was so severe that in March 1952, Truman announced he would not run for reelection. Truman left office in January 1953 and retired to his home in Independence, Missouri, where he died on December 26, 1972.
See STRATEGY.

Suggestions for further reading: See Harry S Truman, *Memoirs by Harry S Truman: Years of Decision* and *Years of Trial and Hope* (Garden City, NY: Doubleday, 1955, 1956). See also Richard F. Haynes, *The Awesome Power: Harry S Truman as Commander-in-Chief* (Baton Rouge, LA: Louisiana State University Press, 1963); Roy Jenkins, *Truman* (New York: Harper & Row, 1986); and the biographic entry in *Political Profiles: The Truman Years*, Eleanora W. Schoenebaum, editor (New York: Facts On File, 1978).

TUMEN RIVER

The 324-mile Tumen River flows easterly from the mountains of central Korea and empties into the Sea of Japan. Its course forms the borders between eastern Manchuria and North Korea and between North Korea and the Soviet Union. Like the Yalu River to its west, it was an important landmark during the Korean War.
See also YALU RIVER.

Suggestions for further reading: Rinn-sup Shinn, et al, editors, *Area Handbook for North Korea* (Washington, D.C.: GPO, 1969).

TURKEY

Next to the United States, the United Kingdom and Canada, Turkey was one of the major contributors of combat forces for the Korean War. At a peak strength of 5,455 men, the Turkish Brigade (officially the Turkish Army Command Force), which included its own artillery regiment, took part in some of the hardest fighting of the war.

It was originally commanded by Brigadier General Tahsin Yazici, who battled against the British and Australians in World War I as a division commander at Gallipoli in 1916 and took a reduction in rank to brigadier to take the brigade to Korea, and later by Brigadier General Sirri Acar. The Brigade joined the Eighth U.S. Army (EUSA) in November 1950, just in time to meet the onslaught of the Chinese intervention. Part of the U.S. Second Infantry Division's blocking force at Kunu-ri, the Turkish Brigade lost one-fifth of its personnel during the withdrawal from North Korea. But it was quick to recover. The brigade's bayonet charge against Chinese positions in January 1951 led then EUSA Commander General Matthew B. Ridgway to order all infantry units on the line to fix bayonets on their rifles.

Casualty figures for Turkish forces alone are not available, during the course of the war the United Nations ground forces of Belgium, Colombia, Ethiopia, France, Greece, the Netherlands, the Philippines, Thailand and Turkey combined lost 1,800 soldiers killed in action. Another 7,000 were wounded in action, over half of whom were from the Turkish Brigade. Two-hundred-forty-three Turks were among those repatriated during the prisoner of war exchanges at the end of the war.
See KUNU-RI, BATTLE OF; UNITED NATIONS GROUND FORCES.

Suggestions for further reading: Clay Blair, *The Forgotten War: America in Korea 1950–1953* (New York Times Books, 1987).

An infantry scout dog and his handler look out across a frozen rice paddy south of Kumson, November 1951.
Courtesy U.S. Army Military History Institute.)

24TH INFANTRY DIVISION

Organized in February 1921 as the "Hawaiian Division," the division split in October 1941. One part formed the 25th Infantry Division and the remainder was redesignated the 24th "Victory" Infantry Division in October 1941. It received its baptism of fire at Pearl Harbor during the Japanese attack there on December 7, 1941, and took part in five campaigns in World War II, including amphibious assaults on New Guinea, Leyte and the southern Philippines. When the Korean War broke out in June 1950, the 24th Infantry Division was stationed on Kyushu and the southern part of Honshu in Japan as part of the occupation force there.

The division initially comprised the 19th, 21st and 34th Infantry Regiments (each with only two rather than three active battalions); the 11th (155-mm) Field Artillery Battalion; the 13th, 52d and 63d (105-mm) Field Artillery Bat-

talions; Company A, 78th Heavy (sic) Tank Battalion with M-24 Chaffee light tanks; the 26th Antiaircraft Artillery Battalion (Automatic Weapons); the Third Engineer Battalion; and the 24th Reconnaissance Company.

The first American unit to fight in Korea, the 24th Infantry Division dispatched the First Battalion, 21st Infantry (Task Force Smith after its commander, Lieutenant Colonel Charles B. Smith), to Korea on July 1, 1950, and the remainder of the division soon followed. From July 2 until July 23 the division was decimated in a series of delaying actions at Osan, Cho'nan, Choch'iwon, the Kum River and Taejon, and its commander, Major General William F. Dean, was taken prisoner.

Committed to the defense of the Naktong Perimeter, the division was reinforced when the Sixth Medium Tank Battalion from the Second Armored Division at Fort Hood, Texas, arrived in Korea on August 8, 1950, and their 90-mm-gun M-46 Patton medium tanks replaced the ineffectual 75-mm-gun Chaffee light tanks of the 78th Tank Battalion. On August 31, 1950, the Fifth Infantry Regiment and its 555th (105-mm) Field Artillery Battalion replaced the hard-hit 34th Infantry Regiment and the 63d Field Artillery Battalion which were reduced to paper strength. The troops of the First Battalion, 34th Infantry, formed the newly activated Third Battalion, 19th Infantry, and the troops of the Third Battalion, 34th Infantry, formed the Second Battalion, 21st Infantry.

As part of the breakout force after the September 1950 Inchon invasion, the 24th Infantry Division mopped up the Taejon area and then crossed the 38th parallel into North Korea in October 1950. On November 1, 1950, the 21st Infantry Regiment reached Chong-go-dong, eighteen air miles from Sinuiju and the Yalu River, the geographic highwater mark of Eighth U.S. Army's (EUSA) effort to reach the Manchurian border. Forced to withdraw when First Cavalry Division units further to the east came under attack from the newly committed Chinese Communist Forces (CCF), the division withdrew to the Ch'ongch'on River line and then to positions south of Seoul.

Counterattacking to seize the southern portion of the Iron Triangle in March 1951, the division helped slow and then turn back the CCF spring offensive in April 1951. Taking up positions in the central sector of the EUSA defensive line, in January 1952, the 24th Infantry Division (less the Fifth Infantry Regiment and the 555th Field Artillery Battalion, which remained behind to form the again independent Fifth Regimental Combat Team), was replaced on the line by the 40th Infantry Division and moved to Japan to become part of the Far East Command reserve. Although the division returned to Korea in July 1953 to

bolster EUSA's rear area security, it saw no further action then.

For its delaying actions in July 1950, the 24th Infantry Division was awarded the U.S. Presidential Unit Citation for bravery. The division also won two Republic of Korea Presidential Unit Citations, while elements of its 21st Infantry Regiment won a U.S. Presidential Unit Citation for bravery at Sanghong Jongni. In addition to other awards won by members of the division, seven "Victory Division" soldiers won the Medal of Honor for conspicuous bravery on the battlefield. During the course of the war, the division (less the Fifth Regimental Combat Team, whose 4,222 losses are tabulated separately) suffered 11,889 casualties, including 3,735 soldiers killed in action or died of wounds, 7,395 wounded in action, 152 missing in action and 607 prisoners of war.

Now a mechanized division, the 24th Infantry Division is presently stationed at Fort Stewart, Georgia, where it maintains a museum that includes exhibits on its Korean War experiences. The 24th Infantry Division Association publishes a newsletter, "Taro Leaf," and hosts periodic reunions of those who served with the division. Further information can be obtained from Mr. Kenwood Ross, 120 Maple Street, Springfield, Massachusetts 01103-2278. Telephone (413) 713-3194.

See also DEAN, WILLIAM F.; FIFTH REGIMENTAL COMBAT TEAM; NAKTONG PERIMETER, BATTLE OF; TAEJON, BATTLE OF; TASK FORCE SMITH.

Suggestions for further reading: See *U.S. Army in the Korean War* series: Roy A. Appleman, *South to the Naktong, North to the Yalu*, 1961; Walter G. Hermes, *Truce Tent and Fighting Front*, 1966; and Billy C. Mossman, *Ebb and Flow*, anticipated in 1990 (Washington, D.C.: GPO). For order of battle, see Shelby Stanton, *Korean War Order of Battle* (Washington, D.C.: GPO, anticipated 1990). See also Clay Blair, *The Forgotten War: America in Korea 1950–1953* (New York Times Books, 1987).

25TH INFANTRY DIVISION

Organized in August 1941 from the old four-regiment "Hawaiian Division," the 25th "Tropic Lightning" Infantry Division took part in the defense of Pearl Harbor during the Japanese attack there on December 7, 1941, and fought in the Central Pacific, Guadalcanal, North Solomons and Luzon campaigns in World War II. When the Korean War broke out in June 1950, the 25th Infantry Division was stationed on the main Japanese island of Honshu as part of the Occupation force there.

The division was initially composed of the 27th, and 35th Infantry regiments (each with only two rather than three active battalions); the full-strength 24th Infantry Regiment (a black unit officered primarily by white officers); the 90th (155-mm) Field Artillery Battalion; the 8th, 64th and 159th (105-mm) Field Artillery Battalions; Company A, 79th Heavy (sic) Tank Battalion with M-24 Chaffee light tanks; the 21st Antiaircraft Artillery Battalion (Automatic Weapons); the 65th Engineer Battalion; and the 25th Reconnaissance Company.

In August 1950, the newly organized 89th Medium Tank Battalion with M-4A3E8 Sherman tanks replaced the 79th Tank Battalion, and the remnants of the 29th Regimental Combat Team from Okinawa became the third battalions of the 27th and 35th Infantry Regiments. Later, on October 1, 1951, as part of the desegregation of Eighth U.S. Army (EUSA), the black 24th Infantry Regiment and its 159th Field Artillery Battalion were disbanded and replaced by the 14th Infantry Regiment from Fort Carson, Colorado, and the 69th (105-mm) Field Artillery Battalion.

The second U.S. Army division to be committed to the Korean War, the 25th Infantry Division landed in Korea during the period July 10 to 18, 1950. It launched the first successful counterattack of the war at Yechon and saw particularly heavy fighting in the defense of the Naktong Perimeter, especially in the Masan area. Its 27th Infantry Regiment became EUSA's "fire brigade" and was used to counter threatened breaches of the defensive line. After the breakout following the September 1950 Inchon landing, the 25th Infantry Division attacked westward to Chonju, mopping up bypassed enemy units in South Korea.

Moving north, it took part in the battles along the Chongchon River line with the Chinese Communist Forces (CCF). Returning south, it manned part of EUSA's defensive line, took part in combat operations in the Iron Triangle area and engaged in battles at Korean outposts Elko, Reno, Vegas, Berlin and East Berlin.

For its actions in Korea, the 25th Infantry Division won two Republic of Korea Presidential Unit Citations, while its 27th Infantry Regiment was honored with three U.S. Presidential Unit Citations and its 35th Infantry Regiment with one for their bravery in combat actions at Taegu, Sanggnyong-ni, the Han River and the Nam River respectively. In addition to other awards won by members of the division, thirteen "Tropic Lightning" soldier won the Medal of Honor for conspicuous bravery on the battlefield. During the course of the war, the division suffered 13,685 casualties, including 3,048 soldiers killed in action or died of wounds, 10,186 wounded in action, 67 missing in action and 384 prisoners of war.

After the Korean War, the 25th Infantry Division returned to its birthplace in Hawaii, but in 1966 was once more in battle, this time in Vietnam. After four years of hard fighting on the western approaches to Saigon in the guerrilla-infested Cu Chi area, the division returned to Schofield Barracks in Hawaii where it is presently stationed.

The division maintains a museum at Schofield Barracks that has exhibits on its Korean War experience. The 25th Infantry Division Association publishes a periodic newsletter, "Tropic Lightning," and hosts reunions of those who served with the division. Further information can be obtained from Mr. Joseph S. Grasso, 25th Infantry Division, 31 Beach Ave., Great Neck, New York, NY 11023. Telephone (516) 482-3477.

See also BLACK SOLDIERS IN KOREA; 29TH REGIMENTAL COMBAT TEAM; YECHON, BATTLE OF.

Suggestions for further reading: See *U.S. Army in the Korean War* series: Roy A. Appleman, *South to the Naktong, North to the Yalu*, 1961; Walter G. Hermes, *Truce Tent and Fighting Front*, 1966; and Billy C. Mossman, *Ebb and Flow*, anticipated in 1990 (Washington, D.C.: GPO). For order of battle, see Shelby Stanton, *Korean War Order of Battle* (Washington, D.C.: GPO, anticipated 1990). See also Clay Blair, *The Forgotten War: America in Korea 1950–1953* (New York Times Books, 1987).

29TH REGIMENTAL COMBAT TEAM

At the outbreak of the war, the 29th Regimental Combat Team (RCT) was stationed on Okinawa in the Ryukyu islands to guard the Strategic Air Command (SAC) bases there. Like most Army regiments then, the RCT had only two of its authorized three infantry battalions.

On July 15, 1950, the First and Third Battalions, 29th Infantry Regiment, were ordered to Korea, with the regimental headquarters remaining on Okinawa to train a new SAC defense force. On July 25, 1950, they were committed to combat in the Chinju area on the Nakton River line, and both battalions suffered particularly heavy casualties. For bravery in these actions, the First Battalion, 29th Infantry, won a Presidential Unit Citation.

Subsequently, both battalions were integrated into the 25th Infantry Division, with the First Battalion, 29th Infantry, becoming the Third Battalion, 35th Infantry, and the Third Battalion, 29th Infantry, becoming the Third Battalion, 27th Infantry.

Suggestions for further reading: See *U.S. Army in the Korean War* series: Roy A. Appleman, *South to the Naktong, North to the Yalu*, 1961; Walter G. Hermes, *Truce Tent and Fighting Front*, 1966; and Billy C. Mossman, *Ebb and Flow*, anticipated in 1990 (Washington, D.C.: GPO). For order of battle, see Shelby Stanton, *Korean War Order of Battle* (Washington, D.C.: GPO, anticipated 1990). See also Clay Blair, *The Forgotten War: America in Korea 1950–1953* (New York Times Books, 1987).

U

UNIT AWARDS

See PRESIDENTIAL UNIT CITATIONS; MERITORIOUS UNIT COMMENDATIONS; REPUBLIC OF KOREA PRESIDENTIAL UNIT CITATION. *See also* DECORATIONS, U.S.; SERVICE MEDALS, U.S.

UNITED KINGDOM (UK)

The United Kingdom (UK) was the first nation after the United States to provide land, sea and air forces for the defense of the Republic of Korea. First on the scene was a British Royal Navy contingent under the command of Rear Admiral Sir W.G. Andrews. It included the aircraft carrier HMS *Triumph*, the cruisers HMS *Belfast* and *Jamaica*, the destroyers HMS *Cossack* and *Consort* and the frigates HMS *Black Swan*, *Alacrity* and *Heart*. As the war progressed the British Royal Navy would later provide the aircraft carriers HMS *Glory*, *Ocean* and *Theseus*, the cruisers HMS *Birmingham*, *Kenya* and *New Castle*, the destroyers HMS *Cockade*, *Comus* and *Charity*, the frigates HMAS *Morecombe Bay*, *Mounts Bay* and *Whitesand Bay* and the hospital ship HMS *Maine* as well as a number of other warships. In addition, some Royal Marine Commando units also served in Korea.

On August 29, 1950, the first of the land forces, the British 27th Brigade from Hong Kong, disembarked at Pusan. Composed of the First Battalion of the Middlesex Regiment and the First Battalion of the Argyll and Sutherland Highlanders Regiment, it initially formed part of the Naktong Perimeter defense line. It was followed by the *Cromwell* and *Centurion* tanks of the King's Royal Irish Hussars and then on October 24, 1950, by the 29th British Brigade, which consisted of three infantry Battalions— the Fifth Northumberland Fusiliers, the First Battalion of the Gloucestershire Regiment and a battalion of the Royal Ulster Rifles—plus the gunners of the 45th Royal Artillery. In July 1951, the 27th and 29th brigades were combined to form the First British Commonwealth Division. With the division were flights of artillery spotter aircraft from the Royal Air Force, which also conducted maritime reconnaissance with its three squadrons of Sunderland flying boats.

Unlike the American Army, which adopted an individual rotation system in Korea, the British rotated entire units. Thus, a battalion from the King's Own Scottish Borderers replaced the Argyll and Sutherland Light Infantry, a battalion from the Royal Norfolk Regiment replaced the Royal Ulster Rifles and so on. During the course of the war, battalions of nine British regiments served in Korea. These included the Gloucestershire Regiment, the Northumberland Rusiliers, the Royal Ulster Rifles, the Argyll and Sutherland Highland Light In-

A sergeant from the Argylls supervises the disembarking of his men from the HMS *Ceylon* in August 1950 as the British 27th Brigade arrives from Hong Kong.
(Courtesy U.S. Army Military History Institute.)

fantry, the Kings Own Scottish Borderers, the Middlesex Regiment, the Black Watch, the King's Liverpool Regiment and the Royal Norfolk Regiment.

At their peak strength in 1953, British ground forces totaled 14,198 soldiers. While casualty figures for UK ground forces alone are not available, during the course of the war 1,263 British Commonwealth soldiers, sailors airmen and marines were killed in action and another 4,817 wounded in action. During the prisoner of war exchanges following the end of the war, 977 British servicemen were repatriated, and one chose to stay under Communist control.

See also AIRCRAFT CARRIERS; BRITISH COMMONWEALTH DIVISION; GLOUCESTER HILL, BATTLE OF; UNITED NATIONS AIR FORCES; UNITED NATIONS NAVAL FORCES.

Suggestions for further reading: Clay Blair, *The Forgotten War: America in Korea 1950–1953* (New York Times Books, 1987). See also listing at British Commonwealth Division.

UNITED NATIONS

When the Korean War broke out in June 1950, the United Nations (UN) was a relatively new organization. It had been formed at San Francisco, California, in 1945 and was headquartered at Lake Success, New York, in 1946. Nevertheless, it had been involved with Korea almost since its beginning (see PART I: THE SETTING).

In November 1947, the UN General Assembly voted to establish a nine nation UN Temporary Commission on Korea (UNCOK) to supervise elections to a Korean National Assembly, which would establish a national government. But the Soviet Union denied UNCOK permission to enter North Korea, thus preventing that part of the country from participating in the election. South Korea held an election under UN auspices in May 1948, and on August 15, 1948, the government of the Republic of Korea (ROK) was formally inaugurated.

The UN General Assembly recognized the lawful nature of the ROK government on December 12, 1948, and on March 4, 1950, UN Secretary General Trygve Lie announced that eight military observers would be sent to Korea to observe incidents along the 38th parallel.

On June 25, 1950, when the North Korean People's Army (NKPA) launched its cross-border invasion of the ROK, the UN secretary general saw it as an attack on the UN and called a meeting of the Security Council for the next day. When the Security Council met on June 25 (June 26 Korean time), it adopted a resolution labeling the invasion "a breach of the peace" and calling for an immediate end to the hostilities and a withdrawal of the NKPA to North Korea. All UN members were asked to render every assistance to the UN in the execution of the resolution.

The vote was nine to zero with one abstention (Yugoslavia) and one absence (the Soviet Union, which had been boycotting Security Council meetings since January 10, 1950, over the issue of seating the People's Republic of China instead of the Republic of China as

China's official representative). Voting for the resolution were the Republic of China, Cuba, Ecuador, Egypt, France, India, Norway, the United Kingdom and the United States.

On June 27, 1950, the UN Security Council passed another resolution calling upon member nations to give military aid to the ROK in repelling the North Korean attack and on July 7, 1950, adopted a resolution appointing President Truman the executive agent for the Security Council in carrying out the fight against aggression in Korea. It asked member nations to furnish military forces to a unified command under the United States.

On July 10, 1950, President Truman appointed General Douglas MacArthur, the commander in chief, Far East Command, to serve in the additional capacity of commander in chief of the United Nations Command (UNC), which was formed on July 24, 1950, with headquarters in Tokyo. MacArthur was directed to send a biweekly report of his actions through the Joint Chiefs of Staff (JCS) to the UN Security Council.

On August 1, 1950, Yakov Malik, the Soviet delegate to the UN, ended the Soviet boycott and took over the presidency of the Security Council. Since the Soviet Union had veto powers in the Security Council, this put an end to further Security Council directives on the war. But the deed had already been done, and Malik could not undo the previous resolutions since the United States, the United Kingdom, France and China also had the power to veto any such attempt. Thus the Korean War was fought under the auspices and under the flag of the UN.

Directives continued to be issued but now by the General Assembly rather than the Security Council. In December 1950, for example, a United Nations Service Medal was authorized by the UN General Assembly to honor those Allied servicemen who served in Korea. As of this writing the UN Command is still in existence in Korea, and periodic reports of its activities are still provided to the UN Security Council.

See UNITED NATIONS COMMAND; UNITED NATIONS SERVICE MEDAL.

Suggestions for further reading: Trygve Lie, *In the Cause of Peace Seven Years with the United Nations* (New York: Macmillan, 1954). See also James F. Schnabel, *U.S. Army in the Korean War: Policy and Direction: The First Year* (Washington, D.C.: GPO, 1972).

UNITED NATIONS AIR FORCES

While the United States provided the overwhelming majority of air force assets for the UN forces in Korea, other United Nations countries also provided air force units to the war.

These included such combat aircraft as the carrier-based Sea Furies, Seafires and Fairey Fireflies aboard the Royal Australian Navy's HMAS *Sydney* and the British Royal Navy's HMS *Glory, Ocean, Theseus* and *Triumph*; the ground-based F-51 Mustangs (later Meteor-8 jets) of the Royal Australian Air Force's 77th Squadron, which had been based at Iwakuni Air Base in Japan when the war started; and the F-51 Mustangs of the Second South African Air Force Squadron's "Flying Cheetahs." The British Royal Air Force provided artillery spotter aircraft and three squadrons of Sunderland flying boats; Belgium provided several DC-4 air transports; Greece supplied the eight C-47 Skytrain transports of Flight 13 Royal Hellenic Air Force; and the Royal Canadian Air Force and Royal Thai Air Force provided air transports as well.

The Republic of Korea (ROK) Air Force had specifically been denied combat aircraft by the United States just months before the Korean War began. Most of the 16 light planes it did have—At-6 trainers and L-4 and L-5 liaison planes—were destroyed by North Korean Air Force YAK fighters in the opening days of the war. After the war began, however, the ROK Air Force was finally equipped with the F-51 Mustang fighters that had been requested six months earlier and its forces integrated into the UN air effort.

At a cost of 152 aircraft lost, land-based friendly foreign aircraft flew 44,873 sorties, including 6,063 close air support and 15,359 interdiction missions where they expended 20,000 tons of bombs, rockets, ammunition and napalm. During their 3,025 counter-air sorties, including escort of bombers over North Korea, they destroyed three enemy aircraft—two by Meteor-8 jets from the Royal Australian Air Force's 77th Squadron and one by Royal Navy Lieutenant Peter Carmichael from HMS *Ocean* flying a propeller-driven Seafury. They also flew 6,578 cargo missions and 13,848 miscellaneous flights.

See also AIRCRAFT CARRIERS; AUSTRALIA; BELGIUM; CANADA; FIFTH AIR FORCE; FIRST MARINE AIRCRAFT WING; KOREA MILITARY ADVISORY GROUP; THAILAND; UNION OF SOUTH AFRICA; UNITED KINGDOM.

Suggestions for further reading: Robert F. Futrell, *The United States Air Force in Korea: 1950–1953*, revised edition (Washington, D.C.: GPO, 1983); James A. Field, *History of United States Naval Operations: Korea* (Washington, D.C.: GPO, 1962). See also Commanders Malcolm W. Cagle and Frank A. Manson, USN, *The Sea War in Korea* (Annapolis, Md: United States Naval Institute, 1957); Richard P. Hallion, *The Naval Air War in Korea* (Baltimore: The Nautical & Aviation Publishing Company of America, 1986).

UNITED NATIONS COMMAND (UNC)

On July 7, 1950, the Security Council of the United Nations passed a resolution authorizing the use of the United Nations flag in Korea, recommended a unified command there and asked the United States to provide the Security Council with "appropriate" reports on the actions taken under that unified command. The vote was seven to zero with three abstentions (Egypt, India and Yugoslavia) and one absence (the Soviet Union).

On July 8, 1950, President Harry S Truman issued a statement saying he had designated General Douglas MacArthur as the "Commanding General of the Military Forces" under the unified command, and on July 10, 1950, the Joint Chiefs of Staff notified MacArthur of his new command.

This designation as "Commander in Chief United Nations Command" was in fact MacArthur's fourth concurrent command. He was already supreme commander for the Allied powers (SCAP), acting as the agent for the 13-nation Far Eastern Commission directing the occupation of Japan; the commander in chief, Far East in command of all U.S. military forces in the western Pacific; and the commanding general, U.S. Army Forces Far East.

An important development occurred on July 14, 1950, when Republic of Korea (ROK) President Syngman Rhee placed the military forces of the Republic of Korea under the operational control of the United Nations commander. General MacArthur further delegated this authority to the commanding general, Eighth U.S. Army, who directed the ROK Army through his own chief of staff. In order to extend such unity of command throughout the force, on July 24, 1950, General MacArthur established a formal United Nations Command with headquarters in Tokyo. As commanding general, U.S. Army Forces Far East, he was already the UN ground force commander, and on August 27, 1950, MacArthur officially designated the Far East Air Forces and the U.S. Naval Forces Far East as part of the UN command,

making their commanders the chiefs of the UN air and sea forces respectively.

Thus, for all intents and purposes, the General Headquarters United Nations Command (GHQ UNC) and the General Headquarters Far East Command (GHQ FEC) became one and the same. All UN and ROK ground forces were under the operational control of the commanding general, Far East Air Force (FEAF); and all naval forces under the operational command of the commander, Naval Forces Far East (NAVFE) or their subordinate commanders.

Because legally there is only an armistice in the Korean War, as of this writing the United Nations Command still exists. Although Far East Command is no more (having long since been superseded by the U.S. Pacific Command in Honolulu, Hawaii), the commanding general, Eighth U.S. Army with headquarters in Seoul, Korea, has served also as the commander in chief United Nations Command (since July 1, 1957).

See also FAR EAST COMMAND.

Suggestions for further reading: Roy H. Appleman *U.S. Army in the Korean War: South to the Naktong, North to the Yalu* (1961) and James F. Schnabel, *U.S. Army in the Korean War: Policy and Direction: The First Year* (1972) (Washington, D.C. GPO).

UNITED NATIONS GROUND FORCES

The peak strength of United Nations ground forces in Korea stood at 932,539 personnel on July 31, 1953—590,911 from the Republic of Korea (ROK) Army and Marines, 302,483 from the United States Army and Marines and 39,145 from other UN countries. The largest of these other UN forces was that of the British Commonwealth with 24,085 personnel—14,198 from the United Kingdom; 6,146 from Canada; 2,282 from Australia; 1,389 from New Zealand;

and 70 (down from a high of 333) from India's medical detachment.

Next in size was Turkey, whose infantry brigade totaled 5,455 men. Other ground forces (each about 1,000 men strong) included the Belgian infantry battalion (which had a 44-man Luxembourg platoon attached), and the Colombian, Ethiopian, French, Greek, Netherlands, Philippine and Thailand infantry battalions. Also counted were the 77 Italian, 105 Norwegian and 154 Swedish medical personnel.

During the course of the war 1,263 members of the British Commonwealth forces—Britain, Canada, Australia and New Zealand—were killed in action and another 4,817 were wounded. Belgium, Colombia, Ethiopia, France, Greece, the Netherlands, the Philippines, Thailand and Turkey among them lost 1,800 killed. Another 7,000 were wounded, of whom half were Turks. By comparison, the Republic of Korea Army lost 415,000 killed and had 429,000 wounded.

See ARMY, U.S.; AUSTRALIA; BELGIUM; BRITISH COMMONWEALTH DIVISION; CANADA; COLOMBIA; ETHIOPIA; FRANCE; GREECE; MARINE CORPS, ROK; MARINE CORPS, U.S.; NETHERLANDS; NEW ZEALAND; PHILIPPINES; REPUBLIC OF KOREA ARMY; THAILAND; TURKEY; UNITED KINGDOM.

Suggestions for further reading: See Max Hastings, *The Korean War* (New York: Simon & Schuster, 1987). *U.S. Army in the Korean War* series: Roy A. Appleman, *South to the Naktong, North to the Yalu*, 1961; Walter G. Hermes, *Truce Tent and Fighting Front*, 1966; and Billy C. Mossman, *Ebb and Flow*, anticipated in 1990 (Washington, D.C.: GPO). For order of battle, see Shelby Stanton, *Korean War Order of Battle* (Washington, D.C.: GPO, anticipated 1990). See also Clay Blair, *The Forgotten War: America in Korea 1950–1953* (New York Times Books, 1987).

UNITED NATIONS NAVAL FORCES

The United States provided the majority of warships during the Korean War (see NAVY, U.S.), but other countries did provide naval forces to serve under the operational control of the commander, U.S. Naval Forces Far East. The largest such force was the warships provided by the navies of the British Commonwealth. First on the scene was a British Royal Navy contingent under the command of Rear Admiral Sir W.G. Andrews. It included the aircraft carrier HMS *Triumph*, the cruisers HMS *Belfast* and *Jamaica*, the destroyers HMS *Cossack* and *Consort* and the frigates HMS *Black Swan*, *Alacrity* and *Heart*. Also part of this initial task force were the Royal Australian Navy's destroyer HMAS *Bataan* and frigate HMAS *Shoalhaven*.

As the war progressed the British Royal Navy provided the aircraft carriers HMS *Glory*, *Ocean* and *Theseus*, the cruisers HMS *Birmingham*, *Kenya* and *New Castle*, the destroyers HMS *Cockade*, *Comus* and *Charity* and the hospital ship HMS *Maine* as well as a number of other warships. Australia provided the carrier HMAS *Sydney*, the destroyer HMAS *Warramunga*, the frigate HMAS *Murchison* and the frigates HMAS *Morecombe Bay*, *Mounts Bay* and *Whitesand Bay*. From New Zealand came two frigates, HMNZS *Pukaki* and *Tutira* and from Canada came the destroyers HMCS *Athabaskan*, *Cayuga* and *Sioux* as well as the destroyer HMCS *Nootka*, which captured a North Korean minelayer in September 1952, the only enemy ship captured at sea during the war.

Other UN countries sent naval forces as well. Colombia sent the frigate *Almirante Padilla*, from France came the frigate RFS *La Grendiere*, from the Netherlands came the destroyer HMNS *Evertsen*, from Thailand came the frigate HTMS *Bangpakon* and *Prasae* and from Denmark came the hospital ship *Jutlandia*. For the most part, these UN naval forces operated as part of the Naval Task Force operating in the Yellow Sea off Korea's western coast.

Although technically not part of the United Nations, once the war began the Republic of Korea Navy (ROKN) was placed under the operational command of U.S. Naval Forces Far East. Established in 1948 and trained by U.S. Coast Guard personnel, when the war started the 7,000-man ROKN had fifteen motor minesweepers, one LST (Landing Ship Tank) and one frigate, the ROKS *Bak Soo San*, which had been purchased by subscription from ROKN officers and men. During the course of the war it acquired a number of additional frigates, including the ROKS *Apnok, Kum Kang San, Sam Kak San* and *Chi Ri San* as well as several additional LSTs and other craft. Initially operating independently as Task Group 96.7 responsible for blockade operations south of the 37th parallel, the ROKN, along with other UN naval forces, was later incorporated into Task Force 95, the Blockade and Escort Force.

See BLOCKADE AND ESCORT FORCE.

Suggestions for further reading: James A. Field, *History of United States Naval Operations: Korea* (Washington, D.C.: GPO, 1962). See also Commanders Malcolm W. Cagle and Frank A. Manson, USN, *The Sea War in Korea* (Annapolis, Md: United States Naval Institute, 1957); Richard P. Hallion, *The Naval Air War in Korea* (Baltimore: The Nautical & Aviation Publishing Company of America, 1986).

UNITED NATIONS SERVICE MEDAL

Established by United Nations General Assembly Resolution 483 (V), December 12, 1950, the United Nations Service Medal was awarded to members of the armed forces of the United States and other Allied nations who were dispatched to Korea or adjacent waters for service on behalf of the United Nations in the action in Korea during the period June 27, 1950,

through July 27, 1954. Award of the Korean Service Medal automatically establishes eligibility for award of the United Nations Service Medal.

See also KOREAN SERVICE MEDAL; SERVICE MEDALS, U.S.

UNSAN, BATTLE OF

Around dusk on November 1, 1950, near the village of Unsan, a crossroads in west-central North Korea about 50 air miles southeast of the Yalu River, two 10,000-man CCF (Chinese Communist Forces) infantry divisions of the CCF's 39th ARMY, XIII Army Group, launched an attack on two battalions of the Eighth U.S. Army's (EUSA) Eighth Cavalry Regiment, First U.S. Cavalry Division and the 15th Regiment of the First Republic of Korea (ROK) Division. This attack marked the beginning of recognized CCF intervention in the Korean War.

There had been earlier engagements with the Chinese. Only the week before, the First ROK Division had had a sharp engagement with CCF elements just north of Unsan. Backed up by U.S. artillery and armor, they had held their ground. The Sixth ROK Division on their right flank (EUSA's eastern-most unit—there was a fifty-mile gap between it and X Corps elements advancing up Korea's eastern coast) had been routed by the CCF 38th Army. Yet EUSA and Far East Command (FECOM) intelligence experts dismissed these battles as the work of volunteers and militarily insignificant. But Unsan would not be so easily dismissed.

As the Chinese attack drove forward, the 15th ROK Regiment collapsed, and the CCF drove a wedge between the Eighth Cavalry Regiment's First and Second Battalions. Running out of ammunition, the First Battalion was ordered to withdraw through their Third Battalion. But the withdrawal turned into a rout. The Eighth Cavalry's supporting 99th Field Ar-

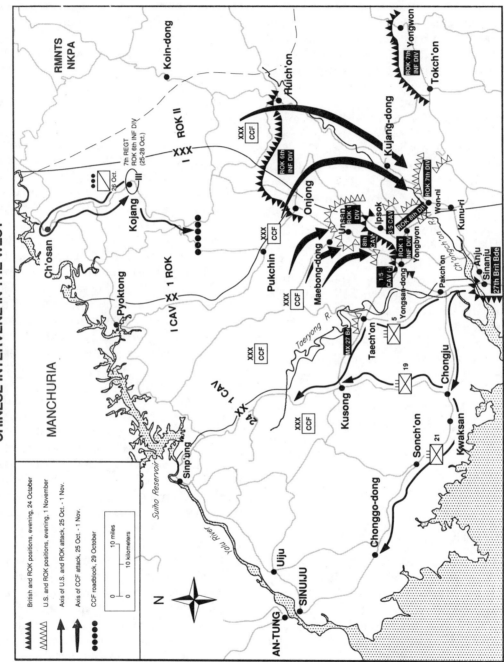

CHINESE INTERVENE IN THE WEST

tillery Battalion abandoned 12 of its 105-mm howitzers and 265 of the First Battalion, Eighth Cavalry's 800 men were killed or captured. An attempted counterattack by the Fifth Cavalry Regiment (whose commander, then Colonel Harold K. Johnson, would serve as Army chief of staff during the Vietnam War) was beaten back with over 350 casualties. In the end, the Third Battalion, Eighth Cavalry was abandoned to its fate, and 600 of its troopers were killed or captured.

The Eighth Cavalry Regiment was so badly mauled it needed a complete reorganization before it could again be committed to combat. Although still not realizing the full significance of the CCF intervention, the EUSA pulled back to the banks of the Chongchon river, anchoring its open right flank on the town of Kunu-ri—within the month to be the site of another EUSA debacle.

See CHINESE COMMUNIST FORCES; EIGHTH U.S. ARMY; WITHDRAWAL FROM NORTH KOREA.

Suggestions for further reading: Clay Blair's *The Forgotten War: America in Korea 1950–1953* (New York Times Books, 1987) has an excellent overview of the battle of Unsan. An account of the battle from the Chinese perspective is in Russell Spurr's *Enter the Dragon: China's Undeclared War Against the U.S. in Korea, 1950–1951* (New York: Newmarket Press, 1988).

VANDENBERG, HOYT S(ANFORD) (1899–1954)

Born January 24, 1899, in Milwaukee, Wisconsin, Vandenberg graduated from the United States Military Academy in 1923 and was commissioned in the Army Air Corps. During the interwar years he served as a flight instructor, as commander of the Sixth Pursuit Squadron in Hawaii, as a student at the Command and General Staff College, as an instructor at the Air Corps Tactical School and as a student at the Army War College. When the United States entered World War II he was serving on the Air Corps Staff in Washington.

In August 1942, he was assigned to England as chief of staff of the 12th Army Air Force. Promoted to brigadier general in December 1942, he returned to the Air Staff and helped plan the Allied invasion of Europe. Vandenberg returned to England in March 1944 and served first as deputy to the commander of the Allied Expeditionary Air Force and then as commander of the Ninth Army Air Force, the largest air force in World War II.

Vandenberg was appointed in June 1946 as director of the Central Intelligence Group, the forerunner of the Central Intelligence Agency. Returning to Army Air Force duty in April 1947, he became the first vice chief of staff in the newly created United States Air Force (USAF) in October 1947 and succeeded General Carl Spaatz as Air Force chief of staff (CSAF) in April 1948.

General Vandenberg was serving as Air Force chief of staff when the Korean War began and continued in that position until the closing days of the war. He presided over the Air Force build-up for the war and took part in the decision to invade Inchon in September 1950 and the decision to remove General Douglas MacArthur from command in the spring of 1951.

General Vandenberg was succeeded by General Nathan F. Twining as CSAF on June 30, 1953, only 27 days before the end of the Korean War. Vandenberg died at Walter Reed Army Hospital in Washington, D.C. on April 2, 1954.

See AIR FORCE, U.S.; JOINT CHIEFS OF STAFF.

Suggestions for further reading: For biographical information see Jon A. Reynolds' essay in *Dictionary of American Military Biography* edited by Roger J. Spiller (Westport, Conn.: Greenwood Press, 1984) and the biographic entry in *Political Profiles: The Truman Years*, Eleanora W. Schoenebaum, editor (New York: Facts On File, 1978). See also Robert F. Futrell, *The United States Air Force in Korea: 1950–1953*, revised edition (Washington, D.C.: GPO, 1983).

VAN FLEET, JAMES A(NDREW) (1892–)

Born March 19, 1892 at Coytesville, New Jersey, Van Fleet graduated from the United States Military Academy in 1915. Sent to France with the Sixth Infantry Division, he commanded the 17th Machine Gun Battalion in the Gerardmer and Meuse-Argonne in the First World War where he was wounded in action and won the Silver Star Medal for gallantry in action.

During the interwar years Van Fleet served as an ROTC instructor, commanded a battalion of the 42d Infantry in Panama, served as an instructor at the Infantry School and commanded a battalion of the 29th Infantry at Fort Benning, Georgia. When the United States entered World War II he was commanding the Eighth Infantry Regiment of the Fourth Infantry Division.

Van Fleet led his regiment ashore in the assault at Utah Beach on D-Day in June 1944. Again wounded in action, he won the Distinguished Service Cross and a second Silver Star Medal. Promoted to brigadier general, he served as assistant division commander of the Second Infantry Division where he was yet again wounded in action and won a third Silver Star Medal. Then, as division commander of the 90th Infantry Division, he won his second and third Distinguished Service Crosses. In March 1945, Van Fleet led III Corps in its breakout from the Remagen bridgehead and its advance into Austria.

Named director of the military advisory group in Greece by President Harry S Truman in early 1948, he directed the supply and training of government forces during the Greek civil war. When the Korean War began he was commanding the Second U.S. Army at Fort George G. Meade, Maryland.

On April 11, 1951, Van Fleet replaced General Matthew Ridgway as commander of the Eighth U.S. Army in Korea who in turn

General James A. Van Fleet, the commander of Eighth U.S. Army through some of the hardest fighting of the war, was himself a highly decorated combat infantry veteran of World Wars I and II.
(Courtesy U.S. Army Military History Institute.)

replaced General Douglas MacArthur in Tokyo. Less than two weeks later the Chinese launched their 1951 spring offensive, and Van Fleet was forced into the difficult task of withdrawing his forces under enemy fire. Stopping the enemy offensive in May 1951, he successfully counterattacked to restore the Eighth U.S. Army lines. One of his major achievements was the expansion and training of South Korea's military forces. After the armistice negotiations began in July 1951, Van Fleet's tactical and operational freedom of action was severely limited by diplomatic and political considerations.

Embittered not only by the lack of political support but also by the loss of his son, Air Force Captain James A. Van Fleet Jr., in a bombing raid over North Korea in April 1952, Van Fleet decided to retire and was replaced as Eighth U.S. Army Commander by General Maxwell D. Taylor on February 11, 1953. On his return to the United States, Van Fleet claimed that he could have achieved total victory in Korea in 1951 but for the pusillanimous military and political decisions. Van Fleet retired from active duty on April 30, 1953 as a four-star general.

See EIGHTH U.S. ARMY.

Suggestions for further reading: For biographical information see Marvin Cain's essay in *Dictionary of American Military Biography*, edited by Roger J. Spiller (Westport, Conn.: Greenwood Press, 1984). The best work on U.S. military leadership in the Korean War is Clay Blair's *The Forgotten War: America in Korea 1950–1953* (New York Times Books, 1987).

V DEVICE

To denote an award for heroism for those U.S. decorations that can be awarded for either bravery or meritorious service—that is, the Legion of Merit, the Bronze Star Medal, the Air Medal—a metallic V device is worn on the medal ribbon.

VETERANS

As with much of the data on the Korean War, information about veterans is hard to gather. One complicating factor is the use of different time frames to define the Korean War era. The most logical time frame is the period June 27, 1950 (when the North Korean invasion began) to July 27, 1953 (when the Koran armistice agreement ended the shooting). Using these dates, 5,764,143 personnel served in the armed forces during the Korean War.

But the Veterans Administration uses the dates June 27, 1950, through January 31, 1955, to define the Korean War era, and using that criterion, there were 6,807,000 American veterans of the Korean War. To further complicate the statistics, 1,476,000 personnel served in both World War II and Korea and 887,000 served in both Korea and Vietnam, and it varies from one source to another as to which war their service is credited. (Many senior personnel served in World War I, World War II and Korea, but the VA does not tabulate those numbers.)

Drawing a statistical portrait from the 1980 census, the Veterans Administration found 5,415,500 living Korean-era veterans. These included 374,200 black veterans, 147,800 hispanic veterans and 120,300 female white, black and hispanic veterans. As of March 31, 1988, the latest date for which figures are available, the number of living Korean War veterans had declined to 4,998,000.

See also BATTLE FATIGUE; BLACK SOLDIERS IN KOREA; DRAFT; MEMORIAL; VETERANS ASSOCIATIONS; WOMEN IN THE MILITARY.

Suggestions for further reading: Stephen J. Dienstfrey and James J. Byrne, *Veterans in the United States: A Statistical Portrait from the 1980 Census* (Washington, D.C.: Veterans Administration, October 1984); Stephen J. Dienstfrey and Robert H. Feitz, *Chart Book on Black and Hispanic Veterans* (Washington, D.C.: Veterans Administration, September 1985); Lynn R. Heltman, *Veteran Population of the United States and Puerto Rico by Age, Sex and Period of Service: 1970 to 1985* (Washington, D.C.: Veterans Administration, January 1986); and *Veteran Population: March 31, 1988* (Washington, D.C.: Veterans Administration, 1988).

VETERANS ASSOCIATIONS

Associations for veterans who served in the Korean War include such traditional organizations as the *Veterans of Foreign Wars*, the *American Legion*, the *Disabled American Veterans*, the *Catholic War Veterans*, the *Jewish War Veterans* and the like. In addition, many units have their own associations and host periodic reunions of those who served together in wartime. These range from the large Army and Marine division associations to smaller Army, Navy, Air Force and Marine Corps veterans groups to informal company-level get togethers. For example, the Korean War veterans of L Company, 21st Infantry Regiment, have had an annual reunion for years.

There are also new organizations such as the *Korean War Veterans Association*, P.O. Box 65330, Washington, D.C., and *The Chosin Few*, whose membership is open to all who took part in the withdrawal from the Chosin Reservoir in 1950. As of this writing many of these organizations, old and new alike, are raising money for the Korean War Veterans Memorial to be built in Washington, D.C.

See MEMORIAL; VETERANS. *See also* CHOSIN RESERVOIR, BATTLE OF; Army and Marine division listings for addresses of their veterans associations.

W

WAKE ISLAND CONFERENCE

On October 15, 1950, President Harry S Truman, at his request, met with General of the Army Douglas MacArthur, the Commander in chief, Far East Command. They met at Wake Island in the Pacific to discuss what they believed to be the final phase of United Nations actions in Korea. President Truman was accompanied by his military advisers—General Omar Bradley (the chairman of the Joint Chiefs of Staff) and Secretary of the Army Frank Pace—and by Ambassadors Philip C. Jessup and Averell Harriman as well as Assistant Secretary of State Dean Rusk.

Most of the one-day meeting was taken up by a discussion of the military situation in Korea and an appreciation of postwar rehabilitation. MacArthur was extremely optimistic, believing that organized enemy resistance would end by Thanksgiving. If things went according to schedule, he said, the Eighth U.S. Army could be withdrawn to Japan by Christmas. When asked by the President of the chances of Chinese intervention, MacArthur replied, "Very little." In his view, China had lost its ability to intervene effectively.

In later years, Truman made some statements to credulous oral historians about MacArthur's supposedly contemptuous attitude toward him at the conference, but newsreel footage and the testimony of those who were there refute these remarks. In fact, the meeting was cordial; the president gave MacArthur yet another Distinguished Service Medal; and both parties left Wake Island believing the Korean War was practically at an end.

Suggestions for further reading: *U.S. Army in the Korean War* series: Roy A. Appleman, *South to the Naktong, North to the Yalu*, 1961; Walter G. Hermes, *Truce Tent and Fighting Front*, 1966; and Billy C. Mossman, *Ebb and Flow*, anticipated in 1990 (Washington, D.C.: GPO). See also Clay Blair, *The Forgotten War: America in Korea 1950–1953* (New York Times Books, 1987).

WALKER, WALTON H(ARRIS) (1889–1950)

Born December 3, 1889, in Belton, Texas, Walker graduated from the United States Military Academy in 1912. After service along the Mexican border in 1916, he saw combat with the 13th Machine Gun Battalion on the Western Front in World War I and took part in the St. Mihiel and Meuse-Argonne campaigns.

During the interwar years, he taught at the Infantry School, the Military Academy and the Coast Artillery School and served a tour with the 15th Infantry in Tientsin, China, and with the Army's War Plans Division in Washington. After commanding the 36th Infantry Division and the Third Armored Brigade, when the United States entered World War II he was commanding the IV Armored Corps at Camp Young, California.

In 1943 his unit was redesignated XX Corps and sent to England to become part of General George S. Patton's Third Army. Walker's "Ghost Corps" was particularly well regarded. It fought its way across Europe and ended the war in Linz, Austria. After the war, Walker commanded Fifth Army in Chicago, then was sent to Japan in 1948 to assume command of the Eighth U.S. Army (EUSA).

When the Korean War began, Walker directed the commitment of EUSA to combat and its subsequent withdrawal into the Naktong Perimeter and is famous for his "stand or die" speech there. Under his leadership the Naktong Perimeter held until the pressure was relieved by the September 1950 Inchon invasion.

After linking up with the X Corps invasion force, Walker led EUSA on a headlong dash into North Korea in pursuit of the disintegrating North Korean People's Army (NKPA). In November 1950, he was poised north of the Chongchon River just south of the Yalu River that divides Korea and Manchuria for the final assault that was anticipated would bring the war to an end. Instead, EUSA was itself assaulted by the surprise attack of the 130,000-man Chinese Communist Force's Thirteenth Army Group which forced EUSA into a 130-mile retreat to new defensive position south of the 38th parallel.

To General Walker's credit, except for the rearguard Second Infantry Division which was practically annihilated, the rest of EUSA withdrew in good order. Just as the withdrawal was completed, however, Walker was killed in a vehicle accident at Uijongbu on December 23, 1950. He was succeeded as EUSA commander by General Matthew B. Ridgway.

See EIGHTH U.S. ARMY; NAKTONG PERIMETER, BATTLE OF; WITHDRAWAL FROM NORTH KOREA.

Suggestions for further reading: See biographical sketch in Roger J. Spiller *Dictionary of American Military Biography* (Westport, Conn.: Greenwood Press, 1984). See also Roy A. Appleman, *U.S. Army in the Korean War: South to the Naktong, North to the Yalu* 1961, and Billy C. Mossman, *U.S. Army in the Korean War: Ebb and Flow* anticipated in 1990 (Washington, D.C. GPO). For an analysis of General Walker's leadership, see especially Clay Blair's *The Forgotten War: America in Korea 1950–1953* (New York Times Books, 1987).

WAR CORRESPONDENTS

See MEDIA.

WEYLAND, OTTO P(AUL) (1902–1979)

Born January 27, 1902, at Riverside, California, Weyland graduated from Texas A&M College in 1923. After completing flight instruction, he served with the 12th Observation Squadron at Fort Sam Houston, Texas, and then as a flight instructor at Kelly Field in Texas. Graduating from both the Air Corps Tactical School and the Army Command and General Staff School, Weyland was commanding the 16th Pursuit Group in the Panama Canal Zone when the United States entered World War II.

After service on the Air Staff, Weyland went to England as commander of the 84th Fighter Wing, and in February 1944, became the commander of the XIX Tactical Air Command which worked closely with General George S. Patton's Third Army in its sweep across Europe.

Serving as deputy commandant of the Army Command and General Staff School, on the Air Staff and as deputy commandant of the National War College, Weyland was named commanding general of the Tactical Air Command in July 1950.

With the outbreak of the war in Korea, however, he was sent to the Far East first on temporary duty and then in June 1951 to replace the ailing General Stratemeyer as commanding general, Far East Air Force (FEAF). General Weyland remained in that assignment for the remainder of the war. While in command of FEAF he won the Silver Star Medal for leading a bomber attack over North Korea and became the first Air Force general to be shot at by MiG jet fighters.

In April 1954, he again became the commanding general of the Tactical Air Command and served there until his retirement from active duty on July 31, 1950. General Weyland died on September 2, 1979.

See also AIR FORCE, U.S.; FAR EAST AIR FORCE; FAR EAST COMMAND.

Suggestions for further reading: Robert F. Futrell, *The United States Air Force in Korea: 1950–1953*, revised edition (Washington, D.C.: GPO, 1983).

WING

A wing is a major organizational element of the Air Force, Navy and Marine Corps. There is a major difference, however, between a Navy/Air Force wing and a Marine Corps wing. An Air Force wing is commanded by a colonel and is usually subordinate to a numbered Air Force (i.e., Eighth Fighter-Bomber Wing, Fifth Air Force). It is made up of several squadrons (a squadron, commanded by a lieutenant colonel, consisted of several flights of approximately five aircraft each). Although strength varied by the type of aircraft involved, during the Korean War an Air Force fighter-bomber wing at full strength would have about 75 aircraft.

A Marine Corps wing was, and is, an entirely different matter. For example, the First Marine Aircraft Wing (MAW) in Korea was commanded by a major general and was divided into two Marine Aircraft Groups—MAG 12 and MAG 33. Each of these MAG's (which were equivalent to Air Force wings) were commanded by a colonel and, like their Air Force counterparts, consisted of several squadrons each.

Today, a Navy carrier air wing is similar to an Air Force wing. During the Korean War, however, the most common naval aviation unit was a Carrier Air Group (CAG). Although it had as many aircraft as an Air Force wing, it was commanded not by a Navy captain (equivalent to an Air Force colonel) but by a Navy commander (equivalent to an Air Force lieutenant colonel).

WITHDRAWAL FROM NORTH KOREA

A military unit in combat has three basic options—attack, defend or withdraw. Of the three, the most difficult is to withdraw, especially to withdraw under enemy pressure. The danger is that such a retreat will turn into a rout where all control is lost and troops end up in a panic, fleeing for their lives.

Bad as it was, the withdrawal of United Nations forces from North Korea in the winter of 1950 under pressure of advancing Chinese Communist Forces (CCF) was not a rout. At the time there were two separate UN military commands in Korea—the Eighth U.S. Army (EUSA) commanded by Lieutenant General Walton H. Walker on the western side of the peninsula and the U.S. X Corps commanded by Lieutenant General Edward M. Almond on the eastern side. Between them were rugged and thought-to-be impassable mountain ranges, with peaks up to 9,000 feet and, as it turned out,

The suffering of the Korean civilian refugees who fled before the advancing Chinese armies was made much worse by the terrible winter weather. Here in January 1951 a refugee column moves south along Korea's eastern coast.
(Courtesy U.S. Army Military History Institute.)

the 300,000-plus men of the Ninth and 13th CCF Army Groups.

During the period November 1, 1950, through January 6, 1951, the EUSA was forced from its forward positions in North Korea and retreated southward to new defensive positions south of Seoul, which was once again abandoned to the enemy. Blocking for this 200-mile retreat down Korea's western coast was the Second U.S. Infantry Division, which took terrible losses in the process. Along with this withdrawing Army came some one million North Korean civilians (out of a population of 9,500,000) fleeing from the advancing Chinese.

Meanwhile, on the eastern coast, X Corps' First Marine Division and the Army's Seventh U.S. Infantry Division, some of whose elements had also reached the Yalu River and some of whom were at the Chosin Reservoir, were forced back into the port of Hungnam. That port was used during December 10–24, 1950, to evacuate 105,000 U.S. and ROK (Republic of Korea) military personnel, 17,500 vehicles; 350,000 tons of cargo; and 91,000 refugees by sea to South Korea.

In the midst of this withdrawal, the EUSA commander, Lieutenant General Walton H. Walker, was killed in a vehicle accident on December 23, 1950. By January 25, 1951, however, under the inspired leadership of its new commander, Lieutenant General Matthew B. Ridgway, EUSA (which now included X Corps) had recovered from the trauma of the withdrawal from North Korea and was once again ready to resume the offensive.

See CHOSIN RESERVOIR, BATTLE OF; HUNGNAM EVACUATION; KUNU-RI, BATTLE OF; SCORCHED EARTH POLICY; RIDGWAY, MATTHEW B.; TASK FORCE MACLEAN/FAITH; UNSAN, BATTLE OF.

Suggestions for further reading: See Billy C. Mossman, *U.S. Army in the Korean War: Ebb and Flow* (Washington, D.C.: GPO, anticipated in 1990); Lynn Montross and Captain Nicholas A. Canzona, USMC, *U.S. Marine Operations in Korea: 1950–1953: The Chosin Reservoir Campaign*, 1957; James A. Field, *History of United States Naval Operations: Korea*, 1962 (Washington, D.C.: GPO). See also Clay Blair, *The Forgotten War: America in Korea 1950–1953* (New York Times Books, 1987). For the Chinese perspective see Russell Spurr's *Enter the Dragon: China's Undeclared War Against the U.S. in Korea, 1950–1951* (New York: Newmarket Press, 1988).

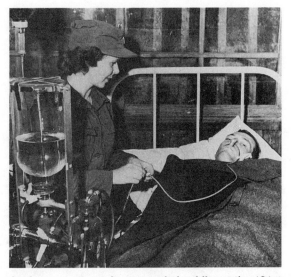

An Army nurse tends a wounded soldier at the 121st Evacuation Hospital in Yongdong-po in October 1950.
(Courtesy U.S. Army Military History Institute.)

WOMEN IN THE MILITARY

Women served in the Korean War from the very beginning. Fifty-seven Army nurses arrived in Pusan in early July 1950 to set up a hospital there, and 12 moved forward to a Mobile Army Surgical Hospital (MASH) at Taejon on the edge of the battle area. As air evacuation of casualties began, flight nurses played an active role. Before the end of the war, some 500 to 600 nurses would served in Korea, and a great many others would serve in hospitals in Japan and elsewhere in the Far East.

WACs and WAFs (i.e., members of the Women's Army Corps [WAC] and Women in the Air Force [WAF]) did serve at a number of bases in the Far East—there was a WAC detachment in support of General Headquarters, Far East Command, in Tokyo, for example—but none were permitted to serve in Korea itself.

When the Korean War began, there were 22,000 women on active duty, with about 7,000 in the health professions and the remainder in "line" assignments in the WACs, WAFs, WAVEs (Women in the Navy) and Women Marines. By the early spring of 1952 there were 46,000 women on active duty—13,000 WAFs, 10,000 WACs, 8,000 WAVEs, 2,400 Women Marines and the remainder in the health professions. While the precise number of women who served on active duty during the Korean War era is unknown, the Veterans Administration found that as of the 1980 census there were 120,300 female white, black and hispanic veterans of the Korean War still living.

One of the lasting legacies of the Korean War as far as women in the armed services is concerned was the formation of the Defense Advisory Committee on Women in the Armed Services (DACOWITS). Recommended by Anna Rosenberg, then assistant secretary of defense of manpower, and approved by Secretary of Defense George Marshall, DACOWITS held its first meeting on September 18, 1951, and to this day continues to serve the interests of women in the military.

See also MEDICAL CARE AND EVACUATION.

Suggestions for further reading: Major General Jeanne Holm, USAF (Retired), *Women in the Military: An Unfinished Revolution* (Novato, CA: Presidio Press, 1982).

WONSAN

A port city and rail center on Korea's eastern coast about 110 air miles north of the 38th parallel at Korea's narrow waist, Wonsan was to be the site of a X Corps post-Inchon invasion, with D-Day set for October 20, 1950. While the Eighth U.S. Army was driving on the North Korean capital of Pyongyang from the south, X Corps would move overland and attack it from the east.

Before the invasion could be mounted, however, Wonsan fell to the advancing Republic of Korea (ROK) Capital Division and the ROK Third Division on October 10, 1950. With the invasion now downgraded to a landing, another snag developed. It was found that the harbor had been mined with some 2,000 to 4,000 Soviet-supplied contact and magnetic mines. A major Navy minesweeping effort ensued that would continue intermittently until the end of the war.

Meanwhile, Pyongyang fell to the First ROK Division on October 19, 1950, obviating the original purpose for the Wonsan landing. Now X Corps, once ashore, would attack not west but north. The First Marine Division finally landed on October 25–27, 1950, and struck out up the coast toward the Hungnam and the Chosin Reservoir beyond. On November 11, 1950, the 15th Infantry Regiment of the U.S. Army's newly arrived Third Infantry Division landed to mop up bypassed North Korean People's Army (NKPA) elements still operating in the area, followed by the Seventh Infantry Regiment on November 17.

After being occupied by Allied forces since October, on December 3, 1950, in the face of the Chinese Communist Forces intervention farther north, Wonsan was ordered evacuated. Screened from enemy pressure by naval gunfire support from the cruiser USS *St. Paul* and the destroyers USS *Charles S. Speery* and USS *Zellars*, the Navy brought out 3,834 military personnel; 1,146 vehicles; 10,013 bulk tons of cargo; and 7,009 civilian refugees. On December 7, 1950, Wonsan was abandoned to the enemy.

But two months later, on February 16, 1951, the Navy returned to begin a siege of the city that would continue for the next 861 days. The siege went on so long that the Navy officer in charge was dubbed the "Mayor of Wonsan" and given a gold key as his badge of office. But it was serious business.

Subjected to constant counterbattery fire from enemy shore batteries, the blockade force occupied seven of the harbor islands—Yo-do (where the Seabees would later build a 1,200-foot emergency airstrip), Mo-do, Sa-do, Sin-do, Tae-do, Ung-do and Hwangto—where the Navy maintained a number of siege ships on station around the clock. These U.S. and Allied warships ranged from destroyers and cruisers to the battleships USS *New Jersey* and *Wisconsin*. It is estimated that the siege tied down some 80,000 NKPA troops in the area plus considerable amounts of enemy artillery. It was lifted on July 27, 1953 when the armistice went into effect.

Suggestions for further reading: For the land campaign, see Clay Blair's *The Forgotten War: America in Korea 1950–1953* (New York Times Books, 1987). Commanders Malcolm W. Cagle and Frank A. Manson, USN, have extensive coverage of the Wonsan siege in their *The Sea War in Korea* (Annapolis, Md: United States Naval Institute, 1957).

X CORPS

See X [TENTH] Corps.

YALU RIVER

The 491-mile Yalu River flows from Mount Paektu in central North Korea westward to the Yellow Sea. Its course forms the western boundary between North Korea and Manchuria. While important for irrigation and inland navigation, its main value lies in its hydroelectric plants. These plants, and the Yalu River bridges over which Chinese soldiers and war materials moved to the front, were frequent bombing targets during the Korean War. *See also* PART I: THE SETTING; TUMEN RIVER.

Suggestions for further reading: Rinn-sup Shinn, et al., editors, *Area Handbook for North Korea* (Washington, D.C.: GPO, 1969).

YECHON, BATTLE OF

On July 20, 1950, at the town of Yechon, the first successful counterattack of the Korean War was launched. Yechon was an important road hub about fifty miles north-north-east of Taegu and ten miles from what would soon be the northern portion of the Naktong River line.

The day before, elements of the advancing North Korean People's Army (NKPA) had captured Yechon. General Walton Walker, the Eighth U.S. Army (EUSA) commander, then ordered the U.S. 25th Infantry Division, newly arrived from Japan, to drive them out. The task

fell to the division's 24th Infantry Regiment, a segregated unit composed of all black soldiers and officered by predominantly white officers, and on July 20, 1950, the Regiment's Third Battalion launched its counterattack. The NKPA was driven out, and the town turned over to troops of the Republic of Korea Army (ROKA) Capital Division.

At the time when victories for American arms were few, the counterattack was widely publicized, and the slogan "Remember Yechon" was used to build morale. But a decade later when the first volume of the Army's official history was published (Roy A. Appleman's *U.S. Army in the Korean War: South to the Naktong, North to the Yalu*), the Yechon battle was dismissed as insignificant.

Believing the record had been deliberately distorted, David K. Carlisle, a 1950 graduate of the United States Military Academy and a platoon leader in the Regiment's 77th Engineer Company, began what was to prove to be almost a 30-year crusade to set the record straight. Finally, in 1988, the secretary of the army agreed to a re-examination of the fighting record of black soldiers in the Korean War. As of this writing, the re-examination is still in progress.

See also BLACK SOLDIERS IN KOREA.

Suggestions for further reading: The best account of the Yechon controversy is in Clay Blair's

The Yellow Sea's shallow depth and 20 to 30 foot tides made it a difficult area for naval operations. Here the outgoing tide at Inchon in September 1950 strands the invasion fleet in the harbor's mud flats.
(Courtesy Lyndon Baines Johnson Library & Museum.)

The Forgotten War: America in Korea 1950–1953 (New York Times Books, 1987).

YELLOW SEA

The Yellow Sea lies between mainland China and the Korean peninsula and forms the western border of Korea. This western coast is highly indented and irregular with a multitude of small offshore islands, which were used by Allied forces during the war as guerrilla bases for raids on the mainland. The Yellow Sea is shallow, with a mean depth of about 140 feet, a fact that facilitated North Korean use of water mines. The tidal difference ranges from 20 to 40 feet.

In the north, the main ports are Nampo (called Chinnampo during the Korean War) at the mouth of the Taedong River, serving the North Korean capital of Pyongyang, and Sinuiju at the mouth of the Yalu River. In the south, the main port is Inchon, serving the South Korean capital of Seoul. In addition, there are smaller ports at Mokpo and Kunsan. *See also* BLOCKADE AND ESCORT FORCE; INCHON INVASION.

Suggestions for further reading: Kenneth G. Clare, et al., editors, *Area Handbook for the Republic of Korea* and Rinn-Sup Chinn, et al., editors, *Area Handbook for North Korea* (Washington, D.C.: 1969).

Z

ZONE OF THE INTERIOR (ZI)

During the Korean War, the military term *Zone of the Interior* or ZI was used in official documents to designate the continental United States.

selected bibliography

SELECTED BIBLIOGRAPHY

The Korean War ranks among our most neglected wars, a fact that becomes obvious when compared with the Vietnam War. As of 1982, less than 10 years after the American withdrawal, the bibliographic guide had some 6,000 entries for Vietnam. But almost forty years after the Korean War began, less than half that number of works have been produced. For example, Keith D. McFarland's *The Korean War: An Annotated Bibliography* (New York: Garland, 1986) lists only some 2,600 titles for Korea.

Caught between World War II, which ended less than five years before the Korean War began, and the Vietnam War, which began less than six years after the Korean War ended (on July 8, 1959, the first two American soldiers were killed by the Viet Cong), the Korean War fell through the crack. This is especially true at the Army's Center of Military History, which has the responsibility for the compilation, writing and publication of the official account of the war. Although the Army carried over 80% of the load on the Korean War battlefield, it has been the most neglectful of all the services in telling the war's story.

Almost thirty years ago, in 1961, the Air Force published its official history of the war. A year later the Navy account was published, along with the fourth volume of the Marine Corps' detailed five-volume work. In 1961, the first volume of the Army's five-volume series was published as well. But while the Marine Corps finished their official history in 1972, the Army still is two volumes short.

Although more than a generation has passed since the end of the war, the Army's volume on theater logistics is still in the preliminary stages, and only this year is *Ebb and Flow*, the volume covering one of the most critical periods of the war—including the withdrawal from North Korea, General Ridgway's magnificent performance as Eighth U.S. Army commander, and the relief of General MacArthur—scheduled to be printed.

Meanwhile the gap has been partially filled by several recent works, some of which even come close to T.R. Fehrenbach's *This Kind of War: A Study in Unpreparedness* (New York: Macmillan, 1963), which many, myself included, believe is the best book written on the

Korean War. Particularly noteworthy is Clay Blair's monumental *The Forgotten War: America in Korea 1950–1953*. Using battlefield leadership as his central theme, Blair presents a detailed and comprehensive account of the first year of the war.

This bibliography cannot hope to provide the last word on the Korean War. As noted above, new works—some 40 books within the last five years—are constantly coming into print. Nor is it meant to be exhaustive. As with McFarland's annotated bibliography cited above, such a work would be a book unto itself. This is intentionally a selective bibliography, and the works listed are primarily those cited as **Suggestions for further reading** in the Almanac itself. A deliberate attempt has been made to include diverse points of view in order to provide as broad a perspective as possible on the war. As a result, some of the books listed present strong and parochial views. It is hoped, however, that readers and researchers will find the bibliography as a whole to be both objective and evenhanded.

Acheson, Dean. *Present at the Creation: My Years at the State Department*. New York: Norton, 1969.

Alexander, Bevin. *Korea: The First War We Lost*. New York: Hippocrene, 1986.

Allen, Richard C. *Korea's Syngman Rhee: An Unauthorized Portrait*. Rutland, VT: Tuttle, 1960.

Appleman, Roy E. *U.S. Army in the Korean War: South to the Naktong, North to the Yalu*. Washington, D.C.: GPO, 1961.

———. *East of Chosin: Entrapment and Breakout in Korea 1950*. College Station, TX: Texas A&M Press, 1987.

———. *Disaster in Korea: The Chinese Confront MacArthur*. College Station, TX: Texas A&M Press, 1989.

Atlee, C.R. *As it Happened*. New York: Viking, 1954.

Barclay, C.N. *The First Commonwealth Division: The Story of British Commonwealth Land Forces in Korea, 1950–1953*. Aldershot, UK: Gale & Polden, 1954.

Bartlett, Norman, ed. *With the Australians in Korea*. Canberra: Australian War Memorial, 1954.

Beech, Keyes. *Tokyo and Points East*. Garden City, NY: Doubleday, 1954.

Beloff, Max. *Soviet Policy in the Far East 1944–1951*. New York: Oxford University Press, 1953.

Berger, Carl. *The Korea Knot: A Military-Political Puzzle*. Philadelphia: University of Pennsylvania Press, 1957.

Biderman, Albert D. *March to Calumny: The Story of American POWs in the Korean War*. New York: Macmillan, 1963.

Blair, Clay. *The Forgotten War: America in Korea 1950–1953*. New York: Times Books, 1987.

———. *Beyond Courage*. New York: McKay, 1955.

Blumenson, Martin. *Mark Clark*. New York: Jonathan Cape, 1985.

Bradbury, William C., Samuel M. Meyers and Albert Biderman. *Mass Behavior in Battle and Captivity: The Communist Soldier in the Korean War*. Chicago: University of Chicago Press, 1968.

Bradley, Omar, and Clay Blair. *A General's Life*. New York: Simon & Schuster, 1983.

Braestrup, Peter. "Outpost Warfare," *Marine Corps Gazette*, November 1953.

———. "Back to the Trenches," *Marine Corps Gazette*, March 1955.

———. *Battle Lines: Report of the Twentieth Century Fund Task Force on the Military and the Media.* New York: Priority Press Publications, 1985.

Buck, Pearl. *The Living Reed.* New York: John Day, 1963.

Bueschel, R.M. *Communist Chinese Air Power.* New York: Praeger, 1968.

Burchett, Wilfred G. *This Monstrous War.* Melbourne: J. Waters, 1953.

Cagle, Malcolm W. and Frank A. Manson, *The Sea War in Korea.* Annapolis, Md: United States Naval Institute, 1957.

Campigno, A.J. *A Marine Division in Nightmare Alley.* New York: Comet Press Books, 1958.

Carew, Tim. *Korea: The Commonwealth at War.* London: Cassell, 1967.

Chung Kyung Cho. *Korea Tomorrow: The Land of the Morning Calm.* New York: Macmillan, 1959.

Clare, Kenneth G., et al. *Area Handbook for the Republic of Korea.* Washington, D.C.: GPO, 1969.

Clark, Mark W. *From the Danube to the Yalu.* New York: Harper & Brothers, 1954.

Clews, John. *The Communists' New Weapon: Germ Warfare.* London: Lincoln Praeger, 1953.

Cohen, Eliot A. and John Gooch. *Military Misfortunes.* New York: The Free Press, 1989.

Collins, J. Lawton. *War in Peacetime: the History and Lessons of Korea.* Boston: Houghton Mifflin, 1969.

———. *Lightning Joe: An Autobiography.* Baton Rouge, LA: Louisiana State University Press, 1979.

Corr, Gerald H. *The Chinese Red Army.* New York: Schocken Books, 1974.

Cowdrey, Albert E. *The Medics' War.* Washington, D.C.: GPO, 1987.

Crossland, Rochard B. and James T. Currie. *Twice the Citizen: A History of the United States Army Reserve, 1908–1983.* Washington, D.C.: Office of the Chief, Army Reserve, 1984.

Cummings, Bruce. *The Origins of the Korean War: Liberation and the Emergence of Separate Regimes 1945–1947.* Princeton: Princeton University Press, 1981.

Cutforth, Rene. *Korean Reporter.* London: Wingate, 1952.

Davis, Burke. *Marine! The Life of Lt. Gen. Lewis B. (Chesty) Puller, USMC (Ret).* Boston: Little, Brown, 1962.

Davis, Larry. *MiG Alley: Air-to-Air Combat over Korea.* Carrollton, TX: Squadron/Signal Publications, 1978.

———. *Air War over Korea: A Pictorial Record.* Carrollton, TX: Squadron/Signal Publications, 1982.

Dean, Philip. *I Was a Captive in Korea.* New York: Norton, 1953.

Dean, William F. and William L. Worden. *General Dean's Story.* New York: Viking, 1954.

Domes, Juergen. *Peng Te-huai: The Man and the Image.* Stanford: Stanford University Press, 1985.

Drysdale, Douglas B. "41 Commando," *Marine Corps Gazette,* August 1951.

Dulles, John Foster. *War or Peace.* New York: Macmillan, 1950.

Farrar-Hockley, Anthony. *The Edge of the Sword.* London: Frederick Muller, 1954.

Fehrenbach, T.R. *This Kind of War: A Study in Unpreparedness.* New York: Macmillan, 1963.

———. *The Fight for Korea, From the War of 1950 to the Pueblo Incident.* New York: Grosset & Dunlap, 1969.

Field, James A. *History of United States Naval Operations: Korea.* Washington, D.C.: GPO, 1962.

Flint, Roy K. "Task Force Smith and the 24th Division," in *America's First Battles 1776–1965,* edited by Charles E. Heller and William A. Stofft. Lawrence, KS: University Press of Kansas, 1986.

Flynn, George Q. *Lewis B. Hershey: Mr. Selective Service.* Chapel Hill: University of North Carolina Press, 1985.

Foot, Rosemary.*The Wrong War: American Policy and the Dimensions of the Korean Conflict, 1950–1953.* Ithaca, NY: Cornell University Press, 1985.

Foreign Relations of the United States. 7th vol. Washington, D.C.: GPO, 1976.

Forty, George, *At War in Korea.* London: Allen, 1982.

Futrell, Robert F. *The United States Air Force in Korea: 1950–1953.* (Rev. ed.) Washington, D.C.: GPO, 1983.

Gallagher, Kenneth S. and Robert L. Pigeon, eds. *Infantry Regiments of the United States Army.* New York: Military Press.

Geer, Andrew. *The New Breed: The Story of the U.S. Marines in Korea.* New York: Harper & Row, 1952.

Geisler, Patricia. *Valour Remembered: Canadians in Korea.* Ottawa: Department of Veterans Affairs, 1982.

George, Alexander L. *The Chinese Communist Army in Action: The Korean War and its Aftermath.* New York: Columbia University Press, 1967.

Gittings, John. *The Role of the Chinese Army.* New York: Oxford University Press, 1967.

Goldberg, Alfred, ed. *A History of the United States Air Force, 1907–1957.* Princeton: D. Van Nostrand Co., 1957.

Goodman, Allan E. *Negotiating While Fighting: The Diary of Admiral C. Turner Joy at the Korean Armistice Conference.* Stanford, CA: Hoover Institution Press, 1978.

Goodrich, Leland M. *Korea: U.S. Policy in the UN.* New York: Council on Foreign Relations, 1956.

Gough, Terrence J. *U.S. Army Mobilization and Logistics in the Korean War: A Research Approach.* Washington, D.C.: GPO, 1987.

Goulden, Joseph. *Korea: The Untold Story of the War.* New York: Times Books, 1982.

Grajdanzev, Andrew J. *Modern Korea.* New York: John Day, 1944.

Griffith, Samuel B. *The Chinese People's Liberation Army.* New York: McGraw-Hill, 1967.

Grimsson, Thor and E.C. Russell. *Canadian Naval Operations in Korean Waters 1950–1953.* Ottawa: Queen's Printers, 1965.

Gugeler, Russell A., ed. *Combat Actions in Korea.* Washington, D.C.: Combat Forces Press, 1954.

Gurney, Gene. *Five Down and Glory.* New York: Putnam, 1958.

Hallion, Richard P. *The Naval Air War in Korea.* Baltimore: The Nautical & Aviation Publishing Company of America, 1986.

Hammel, E.M. *Chosin: Heroic Ordeal of the Korean War.* New York: Vanguard Press, 1981.

Hastings, Max. *The Korean War.* New York: Simon & Schuster, 1987.

Haynes, Richard F. *The Awesome Power: Harry S Truman as Commander-in Chief.* Baton Rouge: Louisiana State University Press, 1963.

Heinl, Robert D. Jr. *Victory at High Tide: The Inchon-Seoul Campaign.* Philadelphia: Lippincott, 1968.

Hermes, Walter G. *U.S. Army in the Korean War: Truce Tent and Fighting Front.* Washington, D.C.: GPO, 1966.

Higgins, Marguerite. *War in Korea: The Report of a Woman Combat Correspondent.* Garden City, NY: Doubleday, 1951.

Higgins, Trumbull. *Korea and the Fall of MacArthur.* New York: Oxford University Press, 1960.

Hill, Jim Dan. *The Minute Man in Peace and War: A History of the National Guard.* Harrisburg, PA: Stackpole, 1964.

Hogg, Ian V. and John Weeks. *Military Small Arms of the 20th Century.* Northfield, Ill.: DBI Books, 1985.

Hopkins, William B. *One Bugle No Drums: The Marines at Chosin Reservoir.* Chapel Hill, NC: Algonquin, 1986.

Hoyt, Edwin P. *The Pusan Perimeter.* New York: Stein & Day, 1984.

———. *On to the Yalu.* New York: Stein & Day, 1984.

———. *The Bloody Road to Panmunjom.* New York: Stein & Day, 1985.

Huston, James A. *The Sinews of War: Army Logistics 1775–1953.* Washington, D.C.: GPO, 1966.

Jackson, Robert. *Air War over Korea.* New York: Scribner, 1973.

Jacobs, Bruce. *Korea's Heroes: The Medal of Honor Story.* New York: Berkley Publishing Co., 1961.

James, D. Clayton. *The Years of MacArthur: Triumph and Disaster 1945–1964.* Boston: Houghton Mifflin, 1985.

Joy, C. Turner. *How Communists Negotiate.* New York: Macmillan, 1953.

Kahn, E.J., Jr. *The Peculiar War: Impressions of a Reporter in Korea.* New York: Random House, 1952.

Kam, Ephraim. *Surprise Attack: The Victim's Perspective.* Cambridge, MA: Harvard University Press, 1988.

Karalekas, Ann. *History of the Central Intelligence Agency.* Laguna Hills, CA: Aegean Park Press, 1977.

Karig, Walter, Malcolm W. Cagle and Frank A. Manson. *Battle Report: The War in Korea.* New York: Holt, Rinehart, 1952.

Kim, Chong Ik, and Han-Kyo. *Korea and the Politics of Imperialism.* Berkeley: University of California Press, 1967.

Kim Chum-Kon. *The Korean War.* Seoul: Kwangmyong Publishing Co., 1973.

Kinkead, Eugene. *In Every War But One.* New York: Norton, 1959.

———. *Why They Collaborated.* New York: Longman, 1960.

Kiyosaki, Wayne S. *North Korea's Foreign Relations: The Politics of Accomodations 1945–1975.* New York: Praeger, 1976.

Knox, Donald. *The Korean War: An Oral History; From Pusan to Chosin.* New York: Harcourt Brace Jovanovich, 1985.

Kohn, Richard H., and Joseph P. Harahan. *Air Superiority in World War II and Korea.* Washington, D.C.: Office of Air Force History, 1983.

Koon Woo Nam. *The North Korean Communist Leadership 1945–1965.* University, AL: University of Alabama Press, 1974.

Korb, Lawrence J. *The Joint Chiefs of Staff: The First Twenty-five Years.* Bloomington, IN: Indiana University Press, 1976.

Korea 1950. Washington, D.C.: GPO, 1952.

Korea 1951–1953. Washington, D.C.: GPO, 1956.

Langley, Michael. *Inchon Landing: MacArthur's Last Triumph.* New York: Times Books, 1979.

Leckie, Robert. *The March to Glory.* Cleveland: World Publishing Co., 1960.

———. *Conflict: The History of the Korean War 1950–1953.* New York: Putnam, 1962.

Lee, Ki-baik. *A New History of Korea.* Cambridge, MA: Harvard University Press, 1984.

Lie, Trygve. *In the Cause of Peace Seven Years with the United Nations.* New York: Macmillan, 1954.

Linkletter, Eric. *Our Men in Korea.* London: Her Majesty's Stationery Office, 1954.

Lott, Arnold S. *Most Dangerous Sea.* Annapolis: Naval Institute Press, 1959.

Lowe, Peter. *The Origins of the Korean War.* New York: Longman, 1986.

Lyons, Eugene M. *Military Policy and Economic Aid: The Korean Case 1950–1953.* Columbus: Ohio State University Press, 1961.

MacArthur, Douglas. *Reminiscences.* New York: McGraw-Hill, 1964.

MacDonald, Callum A. *Korea: The War Before Vietnam.* New York: The Free Press, 1986.

MacGregor, Morris J. *The Integration of the Armed Forces 1940–1965.* Washington, D.C.: GPO, 1985.

Mahon, John K. *History of the Militia and the National Guard.* New York: Macmillan, 1983.

Malcolm, D.I. *The Argylls in Korea.* London: Thomas Nelson, 1952.

Manchester, William. *MacArthur: American Caesar.* New York: Dell, 1979.

Marshall, S.L.A. *Pork Chop Hill: The American Fighting Man in Action, Korea, Spring 1953.* New York: Morrow, 1956.

———. *The River and the Gauntlet: Defeat of the Eighth Army by the Chinese Communist Forces, November 1950, in the Battle of the Chongchon River, Korea.* New York: Morrow, 1953.

———. *The Military History of the Korean War.* New York: Franklin Watts, 1963.

McCune, George M., with Arthur M. Gray, Jr. *Korea Today.* Cambridge, MA: Harvard University Press, 1950.

McFarland, Keith D. *The Korean War: An Annotated Bibliography.* New York: Garland, 1986.

McGovern, James. *To the Yalu: From the Chinese Invasion of Korea to MacArthur's Dismissal.* New York: Morrow, 1972.

McGuire, F.R. *Canada's Army in Korea.* Ottawa: Historical Section, Army General Staff, 1956.

McLellan, David S. *Dean Acheson: The State Department Years.* New York: Dodd, Mead, 1976.

Meade, Edward G. *American Military Government in Korea.* New York: King's Crown, 1951.

Meid, Pat, and James M. Yingling. *U.S. Marine Operations in Korea: Operations in West Korea.* Washington, D.C.: GPO, 1972.

Melady, John *Korea: Canada's Forgotten War.* Toronto: Macmillan, 1983.

Meskos, Jim. *Armor in Korea: A Pictorial History.* Carrollton, TX: Squadron/Signal Publications, 1984.

Michener, James A. *The Bridges at Toko-ri.* New York: Random House, 1953.

Middleton, Harry J. *The Compact History of the Korean War.* New York: Hawthorn, 1965.

Miller, Merle. *Plain Speaking: An Oral History of Harry Truman.* New York: Berkley Publishing Co., 1973.

Millett, Allan R. *Semper Fidelis. The History of the United States Marine Corps.* New York: Macmillan, 1980.

Momyer, William W. *Airpower in Three Wars.* Washington, D.C.: GPO, 1978.

Montross, Lynn. *Cavalry of the Sky: The Story of U.S. Marine Combat Helicopters.* New York: Harper & Brothers, 1954.

Montross, Lynn and Nicholas A. Candoza. *U.S. Marine Operations in Korea 1950–1953: The Pusan Perimeter.* Washington, D.C.: GPO, 1954.

———. *U.S. Marine Operations in Korea 1950–1953: The Inchon-Seoul Operation.* Washington, D.C.: GPO, 1955.

———. *U.S. Marine Operations in Korea 1950–1953: The Chosin Reservoir Campaign.* Washington, D.C.: GPO, 1957.

Montross, Lynn, Hubard D. Kuokka and Norman W. Hicks. *U.S. Marine Operations in Korea 1950–1953: The East-Central Front.* Washington, D.C.: GPO, 1962.

Mosley, Leonard. *Marshall, Hero for Our Times.* New York: Hearst Books, 1982.

Mossman, Billy C. *U.S. Army in the Korean War: Ebb and Flow.* Washington, D.C.: GPO (anticipated in 1990).

Mueller, John E. *War, Presidents and Public Opinion.* New York: Wiley, 1973.

Mulvey, Timothy J. *These Are Your Sons.* New York: McGraw-Hill, 1972.

Nelson, M. Frederick. *Korea and the Old Order in East Asia.* Baton Rouge: Louisiana State University Press, 1945.

Noble, Harold J. *Embassy at War.* Seattle: University of Washington Press, 1975.

O'Ballance, Edgar. *Korea: 1950–1953.* Hamden, CT: Archon Books, 1969.

Oliver, Robert T. *Why War Came to Korea.* New York: Fordham University Press, 1950.

———. *Verdict in Korea.* State College, PA: Bald Eagle Press, 1952.

———. *Syngman Rhee: The Man Behind the Myth.* New York: Dodd, Mead, 1955.

O'Neill, Robert. *Australia in the Korean War 1950–1953.* Canberra: Australian Government Press, 1981.

Paige, Glenn D. *The Korean Decision June 24–30, 1950.* New York: Free Press, 1968.

Pannikkar, Kavalam M. *In Two Chinas: Memoirs of a Diplomat.* London: Allen Unwin, 1955.

Parker, G.W. *A History of Marine Medium Helicopter Squadron 161.* Washington, D.C.: Marine Corps History & Museums Division, 1978.

Parker, G.W., and F.M. Batha, Jr. *A History of Marine Observation Squadron Six.*

Washington, D.C.: Marine Corps History & Museums Division, 1982.

Paschall, Rod. *A Study in Command and Control: Special Operations in Korea 1951–1953.* Carlisle Barracks, PA: US Army Military History Institute, 1988.

Pate, Lloyd W. *Reactionary.* New York: Harper, 1956.

Peng Dehuai. *Memoirs of a Chinese Marshall (1898–1974).* Translated by Zheng Longpu. Beijing: Foreign Languages Publishing House, 1984.

Perry, Mark. *Four Stars.* Boston: Houghton Mifflin, 1989.

Poats, Rutherford M. *Decision in Korea.* New York: McBride Co., 1954.

Pogue, Forrest C. *George C. Marshall: Statesman 1945–1959.* New York: Viking Press, 1987.

Rees, David. *Korea: The Limited War.* New York: St. Martin's Press, 1964.

——, ed. *The Korean War: History and Tactics.* New York: Orbis, 1984.

Ridgway, Matthew B. *Soldier: The Memoirs of Matthew B. Ridgway.* New York: Harper, 1956.

——. *The Korean War.* Garden City, NY: Doubleday, 1967.

Riggs, Robert B. *Red China's Fighting Hordes.* Harrisburg, PA: Telegraph Press, 1951.

Riley, John W. Jr., and Wilbur Schramm. *The Reds Take a City.* New Brunswick, NJ: Rutgers University Press, 1951.

Rovere, Richard, and Arthur M. Schlesinger. *The General and the President and the Future of American Foreign Policy.* New York: Farrar, Straus & Young, 1951.

Russ, Martin. *The Last Parallel: A Marine's War Journal.* New York: Rinehart & Co., 1957.

Sawyer, Robert K. *Military Advisers in Korea: KMAG in Peace and War.* Washington, D.C.: GPO, 1962.

Scalapino, Robert A., and Ching-sik Lee. *Communism in Korea.* Berkeley, CA: University of California Press, 1972.

Schaller, Michael. *The American Occupation of Japan.* New York: Oxford University Press, 1985.

Schnabel, James F. *Policy and Direction: The First Year.* Washington, D.C.: GPO, 1972.

Schnabel, James F., and Robert J. Watson. *The History of the Joint Chiefs of Staff: The Joint Chiefs of Staff and National Policy: The Korean War.* Wilmington, DE: Michael Glazier, 1979.

Schoenbaum, Thomas J. *Waging Peace and War: Dean Rusk in the Truman, Kennedy and Johnson Years.* New York: Simon & Schuster, 1988.

Schoenebaum, Eleanora, ed. *Political Profiles: The Truman Years.* New York: Facts On File, 1978.

Schram, Stuart. *Mao Tse-tung.* New York: Simon & Schuster, 1966.

Scutts, J. *Air War Over Korea.* London: Arms & Armour Press, 1982.

Shinn, Rinn-sup, et al. *Area Handbook for North Korea.* Washington, D.C.: GPO, 1969.

Simmons, Robert R. *The Strained Alliance: Peking, Pyongyang, Moscow and the Politics of the Korean Civil War.* New York: Free Press, 1975.

Smith, Robert. *MacArthur in Korea.* New York: Simon & Schuster, 1982.

Spanier, John W. *The Truman-MacArthur Controversy and the Korean War.* Cambridge, MA:

The Belknap Press of Harvard University, 1959.

Spiller, Roger J., ed. *Dictionary of American Military Biography.* Westport, CT: Greenwood Press, 1984.

Spurr, Russell. *Enter the Dragon: China's Undeclared War Against the U.S. in Korea, 1950–1951.* New York: Newmarket Press, 1988.

Stanton, Shelby. *Korean War Order of Battle.* Washington, D.C.: GPO (anticipated in 1990).

———. *America's Tenth Legion X Corps in Korea.* Novato, CA: Presidio Press, 1989.

Stewart, James T. *Airpower: The Decisive Force in Korea.* Princeton, NJ: D. Van Nostrand Co., 1957.

Stokesbury, James L. *A Short History of the Korean War.* New York: Morrow, 1988.

Stone, Isador F. *The Hidden History of the Korean War.* New York: Monthly Review Press, 1952.

Stueck, William. *The Road to Conflict: U.S. Policy Towards China and Korea.* Chapel Hill: University of North Carolina Press, 1981.

Suk, Lee Hyung, ed. *History of UN Forces in the Korean War.* 5 vol. Seoul: Korean Ministry of National Defense, 1973.

Summers, Harry G., Jr. "An Unofficial History." *Infantry,* December 1963.

———. *On Strategy: A Critical Analysis of the Vietnam War.* Novato, CA: Presidio Press, 1982.

———. *Vietnam War Almanac.* New York: Facts On File, 1985.

———. *Sound Military Decisions.* New York: Random House, 1990.

Talbott, Strobe, ed. and trans. *Khrushchev Remembers.* Boston: Little, Brown, 1970.

Taylor, Maxwell D. *Swords and Plowshares.* New York: Norton, 1972.

Thompson, Reginald. *Cry Korea.* New York: White Lion, 1951.

Truman, Harry S. *Memoirs: Years of Trial and Hope.* Garden City, NY: Doubleday, 1956.

Ulanoff, Stanley M., ed. *Fighter Pilot.* Garden City, NY: Doubleday, 1962.

U.S. Congress. Senate. Joint Committee on Armed Services and Foreign Relations. *Military Situation in the Far East: Hearings to Conduct an Inquiry into the Military Situation in the Far East and the Facts Surrounding the Relief of General of the Army Douglas MacArthur from His Assignments in that Area.* 82d Cong. First Sess. 5 vol.

———. U.S. Congress. Senate. Committee on Veterans Affairs. *Medal of Honor Recipients 1863–1973.* 93d Cong. 1st Sess.

U.S. Department of the Army. Pamphlet 30-101. *Communist Interrogation, Indoctrination and Exploitation of Prisoners of War.* Washington, D.C.: GPO, 1956.

Vatcher, William H., Jr. *Panmunjom: The Story of the Korean Military Negotiations.* New York: Frederick Praeger, 1958.

Voorhees, Melvin B. *Korean Tales.* New York: Simon & Schuster, 1952.

Walker, Richard L. *China Under Communism: The First Five Years.* New Haven, CT: Yale University Press, 1955.

Westover, John G., ed. *Combat Support in Korea.* Washington, D.C.: Combat Forces Press, 1955.

White, William L. *The Captives of Korea: An Unofficial White Paper of the Treatment of War Prisoners.* New York: Scribner, 1955.

Whiting, Allan S. *China Crosses the Yalu.* Stanford: Stanford University Press, 1960.

Whiting, Charles. *Bradley.* New York: Ballentine Books, 1971.

Whitney, Courtney. *MacArthur: His Rendezvous with History.* New York: Knopf, 1956.

Whitson, William W. *The Chinese High Command.* New York: Praeger, 1973.

Willoughby, Charles A., and John Chamberlain. *MacArthur, 1941–1951.* New York: McGraw-Hill, 1954.

Wilson, John B. *Army Lineage Series: Armies, Corps, Divisions and Separate Brigades.* Washington, D.C.: GPO, 1987.

Wood, Herbert F. *Strange Battleground: The Operations in Korea and Their Effect on the Defense Policy of Canada.* Ottawa: Queen's Printers, 1966.

Young, Kenneth. *Negotiating with the Chinese Communists: The United States Experience 1953–1957.* New York: McGraw-Hill, 1968.

Zelman, Walter A. *Chinese Intervention in the Korean War.* Berkeley: University of California Press, 1967.

index